W9-BIQ-438

GOETHE
THE POET

GOETHE THE POET

Karl Viëtor

HARVARD UNIVERSITY PRESS
Cambridge · Massachusetts
1949

•

TRANSLATED FROM THE GERMAN BY MOSES HADAS
LONDON · GEOFFREY CUMBERLEGE
· OXFORD UNIVERSITY PRESS ·

TO *Alice Beatrice*

Preface

It is probable that there is already a sufficiently large number of books, good, bad, or indifferent, in which one can read the story of Goethe's life. At any rate I am not tempted to retell that story. I believe it to be true that the biographical approach (and in lesser degree the psychological) has not always increased our comprehension of works of art. I hope I have not been misled by my own predilections in assuming that lovers of poetry in the English-speaking world may welcome a book of interpretation and of criticism, especially when it is also a book about Goethe.

For however praiseworthy, however dignified the celebration of the two-hundredth anniversary of Goethe's birth may prove to be, I fear the event will also show that neither in England nor in America does Goethe enjoy as thinker and poet that acclaim to which his rank and importance in modern history clearly entitle him. Perhaps, then, the time has come to do something for a better understanding of this great man, a man who must always be included among the few geniuses of the first rank to have appeared in Western civilization. He was the last Titan of the literary world, and historically he is closer to us than is any other.

The theme of my book is, then, neither the development of Goethe's creative power nor the history of his artistic life. Rather it has been my purpose to try to comprehend his productive personality and the expressions of that personality in works of literary art. I have attempted to consider and to interpret individually all that Goethe wrote, from the earliest productions which bear the stamp of his individuality down to, and including, those works, rich in wisdom, which he wrote in his old age. I have employed any sort of material, biographical or historical, which would further this purpose. In selecting from the enormous mass at hand, in eliminating what I did not use, I have been guided by this single principle: does the material contribute to a better comprehension of Goethe's creative existence and of his work?

I must express my gratitude for the help which has been given me in completing my manuscript and in preparing it for the press. For the inspiring interest and tireless industry of my wife I am more grateful than any words can say. I wish also to thank Professor Moses Hadas for undertaking the onerous task of translating the German manuscript. To Professor Bayard Quincy Morgan I must say a special word of thanks for the translations of poetry he made and for the kind interest he was good enough to take in the last chapters. And I am grateful to my Harvard colleagues and friends, Heinrich Schneider, Stuart Atkins, Hans Epstein, Howard Mumford Jones, William Harold McClain, and Gerard Francis Schmidt for valuable assistance.

Karl Viëtor

Cambridge, 1949

The illustration on the title page is used by courtesy of W. C. Hamilton and Sons and Print *magazine*

CONTENTS

NATURE

MIND

WISDOM

NATURE

Rococo

WHEN HE WAS EIGHTEEN, GOETHE HIMSELF HAS SAID, GERMANY TOO HAD JUST TURNED EIGHTEEN, AND THERE WAS MUCH TO BE DONE. KAIROS, DEITY OF THE Opportune Moment, smiled upon his beginnings, just as it frequently showed him favor in later life. Development of modern German culture came late. When it reached the point where brilliant achievement was possible, Goethe, too, had attained sufficient growth to step forward with resolute independence and utter his own pronouncements. The moment of his maturity coincided with a general current. The fresh breeze of spirit which enabled the nation to soar filled to swelling the sails of Goethe's own ship of life. In Europe generally new forces were manifested at this period; the youthful generation was in revolt against the rational ideal of eighteenth-century culture. As a positive counterpoise there was developed the concept of nature. Rousseau was the philosophic guide of this antirationalist movement, and Goethe became its representative poet. Life itself seemed to awaken from the spell which an "age of puny scribblers" had cast over it, and to course in the arteries of the cultural organism with quickened freedom.

> Wide, high, glorious the view
> Gazing round upon Life,
> While from mount unto mount
> Hovers the spirit eterne,
> Life eternal foreboding.[1]

[1] Weit, hoch, herrlich der Blick / Rings ins Leben hinein! / Vom Gebirg zum Gebirg / Schwebet der / ewige Geist, / Ewigen Lebens ahndevoll. (*An Schwager Kronos*, translated by Edgar A. Bowring, *The Poems of Goethe*, p. 226, London: Parker, 1853.)

Truly this was an age for young men; they felt that all that mattered was yet to be done—that the true nature of life was yet to be discovered, and that true creative literature was yet to be written.

Youthful prodigies, familiar in the history of music, are rarely possible in literature. Creative literature is the most spiritual of the arts and demands high intellectual maturity for attainments beyond mere virtuosity of form. It is normal for a young poet, even one as gifted as Goethe, to imitate the style and motifs prevalent in his age. About the middle of the eighteenth century two major tendencies are discernible in German literature. One embraced philosophic or religious poems and ponderous lyrics in the exalted tone of the ancient ode. A significant and original example of this tendency is to be found in the sentimentality and pathos of Klopstock. Among the pious bourgeoisie his Christian epic, *The Messiah,* won him the position which Milton achieved in England. Like other German poets of the age, Goethe was indebted to Klopstock to an almost incalculable extent for training in poetic and rhythmic expression.

But the divergence of Goethe's nature from that of the great master of the age was too sharp for him to feel any inclination to follow Klopstock up the steep path of the exalted style. "Grace and sublime pathos are disparate." Goethe rather favored the agreeable manner of the rococo literature which flourished in the France of Louis XV. This literature reflected the habits of feudal society and of the bourgeoisie influenced by that society; its distinguishing marks were an urbane freedom in manners, brilliance of wit, and elegance of form. It is a *littérature du plaisir.* The superficial resplendence of life conceived as an agreeable pastime radiates forth from the gracefully flowing verses, the gallant images, and the decorative forms of this artificial poetry. In order to enjoy fuller freedom and to revel undisturbed in the bright unruffled pool of sensual refinement, the Anacreontic poets wisely eschewed anything that might lead to profundity of feeling. The genius of this world of pleasure is the coquettish Cupid; not Eros, the god of great passion. Serious philosophic reflection can find no place where provocative point and brilliant wit hold sway.

Germany had no society which could really adopt this gallant Rococo, for it had neither a cultural center comparable to Paris nor a gentry that could vie with the French in wealth and manners. In the castles and courts of German nobles, for whom Versailles was a pattern admired but never emulated, the frivolity of the French and their social forms and language were imitated, their furniture and fashions were borrowed. But the German bourgeoisie, poor, pious, and industrious, found its new cultural rallying-point not in the mansions of the nobility but in the universities. Thus it happened that imitation of French rococo poetry was academic rather than social. Models were found not only in the *poésie legère* of the French but also in the Greek poems circulated under the name of Anacreon, charming pictures celebrating the delights of wine and love. Youthful scholars in love with life pictured erotic yearnings in ornate strophes and posed as experienced roués. From France also was derived the pastoral, a type of verse comedy in which persons of fashion masked as shepherds, nymphs, and fauns engaged in a stylized game of love.

Such were the poetic conventions which Goethe found in full sway when he entered the University of Leipzig in 1765, at the age of sixteen. It was with a tinge of irony that he designated the prosperous city a "petty Paris." But he could only mean that in this city, which possessed a wealthy merchant class and a flourishing university (both rare phenomena in poor and backward Germany), social life displayed a far more liberal and more polished character than it did in his native Frankfort on the Main. There the citizenry was also prosperous, but it was governed by a Lutheran patriciate which was patriarchal in manner and conservative in spirit. The poems written by the Leipzig student attempt to give expression to the first stirrings of love with assumed frivolity and in the guise of a practiced seducer, as current taste dictated:

> E'en sweeter for kissing the breast of the second
> Than ever the breast of the former to kiss.[2]

A pastoral masque, *Die Laune des Verliebten* ("The Lover's Mood"), similarly displays the precocious virtuosity of a poet writing in the Anacreontic fashion. But the poems also reveal a different and a more serious sentiment:

> What good to me is all enjoyment? [3]

[2] Es küsst sich so süsse der Busen der zweiten, / Als kaum sich der Busen der ersten geküsst. (*Unbeständigkeit,* translated by B. Q. Morgan.)

[3] Was hilft es mir, dass ich geniesse . . .

and the first lament of a wounded heart:

Be void of feeling!
A heart too quickly stirred
Is a possession sad
Upon this changing earth.[4]

Shakespeare and the Greeks, whom Goethe now begins to study, he is not yet capable of grasping, nor yet the new interpretation of ancient art presented in the writings of Winckelmann. But the German painter A. F. Oeser brought him to the realization that in art only the simplicity of nature is true and that beauty is one with simplicity and calm. But how was a young man to attain such mastery?

The conflict between conventional taste, to which the young poet subjected himself, and the urge to immediate and natural expression of free impulses led to a crisis whose final outcome was physical collapse. After three years Goethe returned to Frankfort, sick and depressed. In this state he came for a time under the influence of his mother and her friend Susanna Katharina von Klettenberg, who belonged to Pietist conventicles (her picture is preserved in the *Bekenntnisse einer schönen Seele* ["The Confessions of a Beautiful Soul"] in *Wilhelm Meister*). If his religious "awakening" did not endure, at least Goethe retained a deep regard for the figure of Christ and the humanity of his teachings. The undogmatic emotional devotion with which he first became familiar in the earnest practice of the Pietists opened his understanding for a different, but spiritually related, experience, represented by the writings of the unorthodox magical scientists—the works of Paracelsus and his followers, the pansophists and alchemists like Johann Baptist van Helmont and Georg von Welling. He now read the writings of the modern French mystics, Pierre Poiret and Mme Guyon. He began to apprehend that in nature as in the human soul there were hidden secrets of which "the learned mob" and the official science of the enlightened century knew nothing. These experiences led him to the forgotten world of the German Renaissance, the realm of Gottfried von Berlichingen and Doctor Faust.

[4] Sei gefühllos! / Ein leichtbewegtes Herz / Ist ein elend Gut / Auf der wankenden Erde. (*Dritte Ode an Behrisch*, translated by Edgar A. Bowring, *The Poems of Goethe*.)

Strasbourg

GOETHE RESUMED HIS STUDIES IN THE SPRING OF 1770. HE WENT TO STRASBOURG, THE CAPITAL OF ALSACE, WHICH HAD BEEN ATTACHED TO FRANCE POLITICALLY for almost ninety years but whose population had remained German in language and culture. Here he completed his juristic studies. And more important, the butterfly emerged here from the chrysalis, genius spread its wings for its first flight. Finally, "a freer looking about, a freer drawing of breath" had come. All that he had done hitherto was merely preparation; he himself now thought that the verses he had made were frigid and arid. His year in Strasbourg was as decisive for his youth as the later sojourn in Italy was for his maturity.

For the first time the twenty-year-old boy was in love. The girl is like a figure from one of Goethe's favorite books, *The Vicar of Wakefield*. Friederike Brion was the daughter of the pastor of Sesenheim, a village situated in the beautiful Rhine valley near Strasbourg. Quite different from the girls of Frankfort and Leipzig, she was a wild flower, fresh, simple, and genuine. Hers was a heart that knew nothing of convention and made no gesture of defense, that gave itself wholly to its first strong emotion without reckoning profit and loss—such a heart that did not have to be captivated by the wiles of a seducer. Goethe's autobiography describes the idyll of Sesenheim and recounts the story of his love. Reality recalled is doubtless enhanced by purer touches of poetry, but the true character and significance of what happened is not falsified. Nor is the role actually played by the poet spared from moral consideration. For the first time he realized that even an honorable and sincere emotion could not endure; that the impulsive urge of youth to seek new experiences is stronger than the binding power of love. So much the worse for the girl, who had no realization of the aimless restlessness, of the demonic forces, in the breast of her beloved, and who gave herself entirely to him. What was a pleasant adventure for the man on his road to the realities of life took on the grim colors of doom for the girl. But both behaved as their nature and temperament dictated. For their brief bliss the girl paid with her happiness, Goethe with an abiding sense of helpless guilt. The disparity between emotion which is genuine and craves permanence, and the unrestrained impulse to life which is insatiable, and the inevitable guilt which is its consequence, produces the ominous conflict which appears as a fixed motif in Goethe's dramatic works of this period. This fact proves how intense was the shock and how difficult the readjustment afterwards. Reality vouchsafed a solution in reconciliation. Eight years later Goethe again visited the vicarage at Sesenheim, and reported to his lady at Weimar: "The second daughter once loved me, more handsomely than I deserved and more ardently than others upon whom I bestowed much passion and loyalty. I had to leave her at a time when it almost cost her her life. She passed over very lightly what remained of the effects of that illness." [1]

The poems which are the artistic fruit of this episode open a new era in Goethe's creative work, and in the history of German poetry as well. Viewed in the light of the Anacreontic poems of Leipzig, they mark a complete revolution. Convention is utterly banished; social consciousness gives way to personal consciousness. Intimate details of life with his beloved gave rise to these poems; they are truly "occasional poems." There is no longer a trace of technical bravura; simple and strong emotions are given straightforward expression. These are the first verses in the German language in which life itself, the bright and joyous abundance of existence, finds utterance. And nature responds to the human heart in full harmony. Gloriously the landscape reflects the happiness of the soul; man and nature are joined in an exultant paean to life:

> O earth! O sunlight!
> O bliss! O joy! [2]

Only in Mozart's symphonies can we find similar joy of life, expressed with similar intimacy and grace.

The most powerful artistic production of this period is the lyrical ballad *Willkommen und Abschied* ("Welcome and Departure"). It describes the night ride to Sesenheim, the welcome in the arms of

[1] Die zweite Tochter vom Hause hatte mich ehemals geliebt, schöner als ichs verdiente, und mehr als andre, an die ich viel Leidenschaft und Treue verwendet habe, ich musste sie in einem Augenblick verlassen, wo es ihr fast das Leben kostete, sie ging leise drüber weg mir zu sagen, was ihr von einer Krankheit jener Zeit noch überbliebe. (Letter to Charlotte von Stein, September 28, 1779.)

[2] O Erd', o Sonne! / O Glück, o Lust! (*Mailied.*)

the beloved, the happiness of union and the sorrow of parting in the morning—only an instant, but one of the highest poignancy in the new life of passion:

> I went—thou stoodst with eyes cast downward,
> Looked after me with tearful gleam:
> Yet, to be loved, what bliss transcendent!
> To love, ye gods! What bliss supreme! [3]

At that time, too, Goethe wrote *Heidenröslein* ("Heath Rose"), a poem in the manner of the folk song, an original composition reflecting very free treatment of an old symbolic motif of folk poetry: the beloved is like a flower on the open heath, her fate is that of the broken blossom. Here as elsewhere Goethe's models were folk songs, for he now sought and achieved the expression of simple truth and natural beauty in rhythm and language.

Herder

AN ACCIDENT WHOSE PERFECT TIMELINESS MAKES IT SEEM AN ACT OF PROVIDENCE BROUGHT TO STRASBOURG THE MAN WHO WAS BETTER ABLE THAN ANY of his contemporaries to help the young poet find himself. In the course of a journey which took him from the Baltic provinces of Russia to western Germany, Herder had arrived at the Alsatian town, and there an eye infection forced him to remain for seven months. The theologian from East Prussia had already made a name for himself as a literary critic. He was five years older than Goethe, and so far surpassed him in maturity that he could serve for a time as Goethe's spiritual guide. In Herder young Germans found a staunch mentor and a most gifted theorist to support them in their philosophic and literary revolt against the rigid rationalism of the age and the

[3] Ich ging, du standst und sahst zur Erden / Und sahst mir nach mit nassem Blick: / Und doch, welch Glück, geliebt zu werden! / Und lieben, Götter, welch ein Glück! (*Willkommen und Abschied,* based on translation by William Gibson, *Poems of Goethe,* p. 120, London: Simpkin Marshall and Company, 1883.)

tyranny of French culture. He himself was then in a state of intellectual restlessness, actuated by profound resentment against the predominance of scholarly writing, narrow rationalism and pedantry in general. Gigantic plans for reform, visions of new models and new goals, a Rousseauesque enthusiasm for the new man, "the man of nature," clamored for utterance.

Herder made a great impression upon Goethe. For his part, the mordant man found the young poet "somewhat light and sparrow-like," though promising. He rid Goethe completely of his superficial self-satisfaction and intellectual pride. Morally Goethe was affected by significant doctrines such as the one holding that the contrast between nature and culture, which was the basis of Rousseau's criticism of the age, was valid in the aesthetic realm also. Goethe learned to realize that there was a poetry which possessed greater truth and therefore greater beauty than the poetry of cultivated "taste." In the songs which the people sang (Herder was the first to call them folk songs), the old ballads of kings and heroes, of the joys and sorrows of simple hearts, songs despised and forgotten by the educated men of the time—in these and in the sagas and the fairy tales Herder ventured to see the timeless models of true poetry. To the young poets of his day he declared that this was the way poetry ought to be written. The greatest advantage of the folk songs he found in the fact that in them the entire inner life found expression. Sensual experience, the native soil of all art, was in their symbolism still one with thought. Finally, these songs demonstrated that poetry is not the artificial product of bookish education, but flourishes wherever human nature expresses itself with freedom and with truth.

Views of this sort were in the air. They had appeared in England, but they had never been fully developed there. What Thomas Percy's collection of ballads, the *Reliques of Ancient English Poetry* (1765), had done for the English, Herder wished to do for Germany. Consistent with his view of the world-wide character of poetry, he had begun to assemble not German folk songs alone but simple popular poems from many literatures. So prompted, Goethe too began to gather folk songs in the villages of Alsace, "from the lips of the oldest grannies." Goethe's affection for this sort of poetry never ceased, his admiration for its simple perfection was never diminished. When the romanticists followed Herder and made the first great collection of German folk songs, Goethe showed the friendliest interest in their efforts.

Through Herder Goethe became familiar with the intellectual currents which flowed together in Europe from diverse sources and converged to form a mighty stream of antirationalist doctrines and tendencies. In Germany, Herder's friend and compatriot Hamann had made a beginning of rehabilitating the irrational. In the oracular writings of this Protestant mystic, the character and worth of such disdained modes of experience and such disregarded strata of the inner life as are involved in emotion and faith, presentiment and intuition, the depths of the soul, the inward chaos, and the secret of individuality were again recognized and restored to their rights. Reading the Bible from a new point of view, Hamann became convinced that poetic speech was the first language of man; in such speech had God spoken to man through His prophets. But the ancient and genuine language of poetry had nothing in common with the abstract idiom of the modern sophisticates. True poetry was observation and reflection in one; it spoke in images, similes, and symbols of the supersensual and nonsensual, in keeping with the twofold nature of man. Spontaneous feeling, observation, and imagination, Hamann taught, are the eternal wellsprings of artistic creation. It is these principles that Goethe has in mind when he says that Hamann was the author from whom he learned most at this period. Through Hamann he began to grasp the idea of existence as comprising the entirety of human nature, an idea which became the prime foundation of his philosophy of life and of art: "All that man undertakes to do, whether by deed or word or otherwise, must spring from the union of all his forces; all that is isolated is to be rejected." [1] This, however, would apply to exaggerated irrationalism also.

Here the powerful influence of the teachings of Jean Jacques Rousseau must be noticed. These, too, Goethe learned to understand through Herder. In Rousseau's philosophy the notion of nature became an absolute norm by which all things were to be measured. For him this straightway involved everything that modern culture was not, a concept totally at variance with the achievements which were mod-

[1] Alles, was der Mensch zu leisten unternimmt, es werde nun durch Tat oder Wort oder sonst hervorgebracht, muss aus sämtlichen vereinigten Kräften entspringen; alles Vereinzelte ist verwerflich. (*Dichtung und Wahrheit*, Part III, Book XII.)

ern culture's pride. Science and arts, advances in philosophic thought, civilized society and its political organization, the entire hyperintellectualized culture with its fetish of reason and its materialistic tendencies—all of this was rejected by Rousseau and made responsible for the current corruption of Europe. Man was born free, but now he is everywhere in chains. By nature he is good and peaceful, but intellectual culture has made him unhappy and evil. His original simplicity and innocence have been destroyed by urban civilization. In nature there is only harmony, in the life of man nothing but confusion and disorder. "Among the elements unison prevails, among men chaos." If we would be content with what we are by nature we should not have to lament our fate. Rousseau too establishes man's original oneness as a norm against the intellectual one-sidedness of modern man. To avoid distorting truth, reason must preserve its natural connection with our emotions, passions, instincts, and intuitions. The heart and the voice of native conscience are better guides than the opinions of presumptuous philosophy. "We can be men without being scholars." If we cannot return to the forests and live with the animals, we can at least return to our "old and genuine innocence."

With Rousseau's political ideas, as with his pessimistic view of history, his German disciples could do nothing. In France his teachings played a large part in the doctrinal preparation for the Revolution. There was nothing analogous across the Rhine. Yet Rousseau's diagnosis and criticism of contemporary culture, his rehabilitation of emotional and irrational forces, his ideal of a natural humanity, and especially his vague, but for that very reason useful, notion of nature as the supreme value, all laid the foundation for the new doctrines of life and art which arose in Germany under Herder's leadership. "Has anything ever been seen more wonderful than a pulsing heart with its unlimited stimuli? An abyss of mysterious inward forces, the true image of organic omnipotence . . . With all his mysterious powers, stimuli, and impulses, inner man is nevertheless whole . . . Our thought depends upon feeling." Such sentences from Herder's writings give striking evidence of Rousseau's influence. The program of cultural regeneration by forcing the "mysterious" powers, the praise of the heart, the doctrine that life is more than speculation, that feeling and acting are better than reflecting are all suggested by Rousseau. But his radical abhorrence of culture and his antirationalism were not lost upon his German devotees. They began to develop the idea of a new totality, a harmony of nature and spirit, which subsequently received its final form in the theories of idealistic humanism.

To Goethe the ideas of Rousseau were more effective by their general character and tendency than by their specific content. What he could learn as artist from the *Nouvelle Héloïse* is to be seen in the composition of *Werther*. The realm of the cultural critic's thought, as communicated to him by Herder, had more general, less immediate uses; it opened a path to free development for the creative powers within him. By the concept of poetry which would be simply true to nature, Goethe was relieved of the oppressive weight of a literary tradition, which confronted the young German movement in the form of contemporary rationalism and its literary conventions. The sophisticated literature of France need not be the model after all; and if it was for the French, it could no more be mandatory for German poets than could the classical antiquity which it invoked. For every nation, culture, and epoch must achieve greatness and truth according to its own character. It is inherent in individuals and peoples alike to seek individuality. French flowers could not be cultivated in German gardens.

Originality, connoting the capacity to produce something new and unique by virtue of the personal life of the individual, and not by imitation of an alien model, became the watchword of the new aesthetics. But the individual's life was rooted not in thought or opinion but in the depths of the unconscious ego, in personal feeling, and in the mysterious urge of an individual will. The Strasbourg cathedral, a work of German architecture, was before Goethe's eyes, and he now came to understand the grand proportions of its style which violated convention. In it he found a revelation of the truth "that the great spirit is chiefly distinguished from the petty in that its work is independent, that without regard to what others have done it seems to coexist with its purpose from time immemorial, while the petty mind at once manifests its poverty and limitations by badly applied imitation."[2] For Goethe beauty is no longer con-

[2] . . . dass der grosse Geist sich hauptsächlich vom kleinen darin unterscheidet, dass sein Werk selbständig ist, dass es ohne Rücksicht auf das, was andre getan haben, mit seiner Bestimmung von Ewigkeit her zu ko-existieren scheine; da der kleine Kopf durch übelange-

formity to classicist aesthetics and criticism but a demonstration of the true expression of an independent creative individuality.

> And Nature, teaching you, will fill
> Your soul with power.[3]

It is not a matter of representing according to nature, but of creating along with nature. Rousseau's canonization of the natural is brought into connection with Edward Young's glorification of the primal creative power of the "original genius" (*On Original Composition*, 1759), with Hamann's religious worship of genius, and with the powerful impression made by Klopstock's estimate of the independent poet. It was the time, Goethe says in retrospect, when poetic genius became aware of itself.

But to "speculative efforts" Goethe had no inclination: "God save our senses and preserve us from the theory of sensuality." Two essays which bring the new views of "original" works of art to fruition are poetic encomia rather than critical treatises. *Von deutscher Baukunst* ("On German Architecture"; written in 1772) explores the peculiar character of the style of Gothic cathedrals, which at that time were looked down upon. What the ideals of classic regularity regarded as barbaric disorder is revealed to the intuition of the enthusiast as "a sublime, spreading tree of God," soaring to heaven "with a thousand branches, a million twigs." An art which possesses "character," which is the true expression of a strong individuality, is of equal value with art executed according to the general rules of objective beauty.

The other essay is in praise of Shakespeare. The discovery of Shakespeare, for which Lessing had prepared the way, was one of the great contributions of the *Sturm und Drang* movement. In Voltaire, on the other hand, this movement saw an opponent of true poetry, a vain and presumptuous representative of "an aged and respectable literature" (as Herder said); Voltaire was never forgiven for his depreciation of Shakespeare. But Shakespeare, in the view of Herder and his generation, embodied all that constituted the true and masterly poet. In his image, as the German enthusiasts limned it, they developed their ideal of a new drama; in his person

brachte Nachahmung, seine Armut und seine Eingeschränktheit auf einmal manifestiert. (Letter to Johann Gottfried Roederer, September 21, 1771.)

[3] Und wenn Natur dich unterweist, / Dann geht die Seelenkraft dir auf. (*Faust*, v. 423, translated by Alice Raphael, p. 21, New York: Jonathan Cape and Harrison Smith, 1930.)

they came to understand what perfect poetic genius was, and why modern genius must differ from ancient genius. Shakespeare is Sophocles' brother, says Herder, little as his dramas resemble Sophocles'; but he is his brother as "servant of nature," in his own fashion, and in accordance with his culture and his age. So in Goethe's effusive *Zum Schäkespears Tag* ("On Shakespeare's Day": Shakespeare's name day, which was ceremoniously celebrated in Goethe's parental home on October 14, 1771), the world of Shakespeare's dramatic figures is described as a colorful and changing kaleidoscope revealing the eternal spectacle of the individual's will in conflict with "the necessary course of the whole." Shakespeare's people are large and powerful; nothing can be more "natural" than they. The style and form of the northern drama of character, which Goethe seeks to rejuvenate in his own manner, are here given precedence over the French drama of the conflict of ideas. While Goethe later lost his love of the Gothic, and even rejected it as an aberration, his admiration for Shakespeare remained always, though he later gave it a different and more critical basis. When he prepared a version of *Romeo and Juliet* for the Weimar theater in 1812, he was of the opinion that he had gained a fuller "insight" than ever into Shakespeare's talent, but at the same time he found that "like everything ultimate" Shakespeare was unfathomable. A later poem styles him "star of sublimest height" and the ever valid touchstone of Goethe's own aspirations.

Through Herder also Goethe learned to regard contemporary English authors as the models closest to the Germans in national character and artistic style. This kinship was especially true of the novelists. The novels of Richardson and Sterne and the stories of Oliver Goldsmith pleased Goethe for their truth to nature, their realistic characterization, their emotional warmth. But it is significant that the young poet could admire the gay abandon and the humor of the English but could not emulate these qualities. Their attitude and view of life was too alien to a passion which, like his, was bent on exploring the depths of life. For Goethe a humorous writer was always a problematic phenomenon. Only the skeptic, he remarked at a later stage, could succeed in taking the world so lightly that he could maintain humor as a permanent mood.

Enthusiasm for folk epic and folk song led Herder to Ossian. The same mixture of archaic sublimity and melancholy sentimentality which suited contemporary taste and gave Macpherson's "Gaelic" discoveries such sensational success captivated the German critic completely. He regarded the cantos of this "northern Homer" as completely genuine and as examples of the oldest European folk poetry. For a short time Goethe too allowed himself to be borne along on the wave of the Ossian fashion. The landscapes of his Strasbourg compositions and his *Werther* show the impression which the rhapsodies of the Scottish "bard" made upon him. Some of the cantos Goethe translated at that time into a beautiful poetic prose. They are very effectively introduced in a significant passage of *Werther*.

It was more important that Goethe now learned to read the poets of antiquity with new eyes. In the education of the boy Roman literature had played a large part. But now he began to study original Greek antiquity, as discovered by Winckelmann and Herder. He read Homer in the original, and later Pindar's lofty lyrics. The Greek seemed to him the son of nature, a magnificent pattern of primitive naturalness and unity, a synthesis of power and form. Pindar is now his supreme example of spiritual mastery, of controlled strength, of ordered dithyramb. The first poetic fruit of this discovery is *Wanderers Sturmlied* ("Wanderer's Storm Song"), a poem in free verse written shortly after the Strasbourg period. Its boldly compounded diction and powerfully striking rhythms grandly proclaim the youthful genius's triumphant faith in life.

German Drama

THE IMPRESSION WHICH SHAKESPEARE MADE UPON HIM NURTURED IN GOETHE THE VISION OF A NEW DRAMA. IT WAS IN ANY CASE NATURAL FOR HIM, DURING THESE years, to cast into dialogue form and to dramatize historical material which engaged his interest. This new drama could be no other than a presentation of a powerful character, for only the "great man" seemed important in history. The project of a historical drama with some classical hero like Caesar or Socrates gave way to plans for something more germane to the new national sentiment. It was to be a

German pendant to Shakespeare's dramas of English kings—"out of our own age of chivalry, in our own language"—a monument in the tradition of the great "Nordic" poet, begotten of his spirit and fashioned in his style, insofar as a poet of another age and another people could so fashion it.

The *Geschichte Gottfriedens von Berlichingen mit der eisernen Hand, dramatisiert* ("The Story of Gottfried von Berlichingen with the Iron Hand, Dramatized") presents a broad canvas of the deeds of the sixteenth-century German knight and of the era in which he lived. Material was furnished by Götz's own biography, which revealed a spirited and self-willed man in conflict with his anarchic age. And so it is in the drama. The evils of the day compel the upright hero to wage a solitary and desperate struggle on behalf of the right, on behalf of traditional German freedom and independence. The sound-minded individual's natural and sacred right to live his life in accordance with his own will finds itself in conflict with the current of a new age in which dark forces of disintegration and violence threaten to engulf the individual.

> When Germany within herself was 'gainst herself divided,
>
> . . . . .
>
> When on fair earth brute force alone
> And cunning greed and daring bold prevailed.[1]

The tragic motive of the drama, whose final overtone is reconciliation, lies in the conflict between the primal demand for personal freedom, requisite for a life of moral dignity, and the corrupt forces of the age. The peace-loving and reasonable man is forced to break his word, to become a rebel, to "help himself." In the end it is not he who is judged, but his age, which has no place for his honorable and vigorous character. Götz's guilt is that of true tragedy—inevitable and hence guiltless. This was a view which challenged the rational morality of the eighteenth century; what was offered in substitution, however, was not the ideal of political liberty but of superior moral insight. Götz's stature is not truly heroic, he is not really a great man; he is merely a good man according to the gauge of normal human goodness. His

[1] Wo Deutschland, in und mit sich selbst entzweit, / . . . / Wo auf der schönen Erde nur Gewalt, / Verschmitzte Habsucht, kühne Wagnis galt. (*Maskenzüge*, translated by W. H. McClain.)

rebellion is made necessary by circumstances, and has nothing to do with a political program. The political element is simply negative, a disturbing interference with his personal life. If the drama has a message, it is in Goethe's wish to place before his effete age a virile character of German pattern. The revolutionary tendency implicit in the material is entirely subordinate to the ideal of a free individual living according to his own law. Upon the life and works of such an individual rest the welfare of society and the flowering of culture.

If the first German drama following Shakespeare's model is wanting in internal dynamism, it compensates by the abundance and diversity of its life. Weislingen (who is the first of a series of lovers made faithless by restless passion, depicted by Goethe to allay his feeling of guilt), the demonic seductress Adelheid, the other female figures, the political atmosphere of the episcopal court, the Luther-like figure of Father Martin—all are creatures of Goethe's imagination. Herder had felt that the essence of Shakespeare's composition was lyric rather than dramatic; he thought Shakespeare ought to be "sung." In Goethe's drama the effect of the English model is of a different order. Delight in characteristic detail and lifelike portraiture of individuals leads to a form which grows rampantly into epic proportions and transcends the limitations of the stage. Germans read Shakespeare's plays in the translations which Wieland had made, and these were in prose. The variegated texture of their action was therefore even more formless in German dress than in the original. This effect is apparent in Goethe's play. Shakespeare's plays have twenty scenes at most; in *Götz* there are fifty-eight. Even Herder was dismayed by the disordered abundance of scenes large and small and of principal and subordinate actions in which the unrestrained fancy of his friend found expression. Moreover, German drama here made its initial break with the uniform, polished language of literature, and substituted speech truer to life and more appropriate to the various characters. This usage conformed to the new ideal and was hailed as release from a convention grown insipid. "Noble and free like his own hero," a contemporary critic wrote in praise of *Götz's* revolutionary form and language, "the author has trodden the wretched rule-book under foot."

In a more closely knit version, published two years later, and better adapted to the requirements of the theater, *Götz von Berlichingen mit der eisernen Hand* ("Götz von Berlichingen with the Iron Hand," as it was now called) became the favorite play of its time. Its success called forth a new type of drama, the plays of chivalry, whose subject matter and spirit represented the youthful national feeling of the German bourgeoisie more vigorously than did any other product of contemporary German literature. When Frederick II, the Prussian king whose tastes had been formed by French literature and who wrote in French, dismissed *Götz* in his *De la littérature allemande* (1780) as a repulsive imitation of bad English plays, a forthright reply (written by Justus Möser) declared that *Götz* was a folk play, where the taste of courtiers did not count. And in fact, *Götz* was the first modern drama in the German language which addressed itself to all Germans and was intelligible to all. Questionable as the aesthetic merits of this "monster" might be, the young poet had made a lucky strike.

In one respect this first German drama in the Shakespearean manner was inferior to the original: the element of comedy was far weaker. Goethe's attempted synthesis of tragedy and comedy was not successful; it would be more accurate to say that such a synthesis was not in his character, either at this period or later. In the years following he produced a number of short pieces in which the weaknesses of his own epoch, the degeneration of current sentimentality as well as of the cult of nature, were ridiculed in a style more amiable and easygoing than caustic. These dramatic farces and satires imitate the coarse manner of the old German tradition. The verse is the doggerel *Knittelvers*. At that time Goethe was reading the carnival farces of Hans Sachs and the boorish Grobian writings of the age of the Reformation. The most delightful of these jolly pieces is called *Satyros oder der vergötterte Waldteufel* ("Satyrus, or the Deified Forest-Demon"). This "document of the divine impudence of our youth," as Goethe later styled the piece, ventures to mock his friend Herder's foibles, the enthusiasm for a Rousseauesque state of nature (Rousseau had identified the satyrs of antiquity with his "primitive men"), and the magisterial and oracular tone; but the pretentious airs of the modern cult of genius are also made ridiculous.

In all the world nought stands above me,
For God is God, and I am I.[2]

[2] Mir geht in der Welt nichts über mich: / Denn Gott ist Gott, und ich bin ich. (*Satyros*, Act II, translated by W. H. McClain.)

The young poet thrusts out here at his own affectations in order to purge himself of them.

Another figure in the world of the knightly Gottfried von Berlichingen and Hans Sachs, the vigorous and colorful world of the "Gothic" period when the Middle Ages wane and a new epoch begins to take shape, is that half-legendary hero of the German Renaissance, Doctor Faust. There were folk books which recounted his life with admiration or admonition, and there were folk dramas and puppet plays which went back to Christopher Marlowe's *Doctor Faustus*. Even an enlightened century had not forgotten the audacious man who dared scorn God and the devil. Lessing had confirmed the fact that the Germans were still enamored of their Doctor Faust; he had regarded this legend as proper material for a poet who, with Shakespeare as his point of departure, should seek a path to a new drama appropriate to the German national character. He had himself contemplated venturing on the difficult enterprise.

Goethe must have begun to work on his Faust drama during his Strasbourg period. To him the "far-striding practitioner of magic and the black arts," as transmitted by colorful popular tradition, seemed not a wicked sinner but rather a tragic brother of the modern genius. In his restless, searching speculation, in his contempt for professional natural science and his will to wrest its secrets from the cosmos in new and bolder ways—in these attitudes as in his uneasy spiritual state Goethe felt himself akin to the hero of the legend. "I too had busied myself with all knowledge, and had soon come to realize its futility. I too had tried all varieties of life, and always I had returned more dissatisfied and more tormented." [3] Deep longing for genuine wisdom and the wish to approach the divine near enough to glimpse it could strike the child of so philosophic a century only as great and good. And indeed, was not Faust, suspended between God and the devil, an apt mythical symbol of the human soul, which "all the forces of heaven and hell interpenetrate and affect"? Preoccupation with the writings of latter-day Neoplatonists, of theosophists, and of magicians (Goethe speaks of such writings in the eighth book of his

[3] Auch ich hatte mich in allem Wissen umhergetrieben und war früh genug auf die Eitelkeit desselben hingewiesen worden. Ich hatte es auch im Leben auf allerlei Weise versucht und war immer unbefriedigter und gequälter zurückgekommen. (*Dichtung und Wahrheit*, Part II, Book X.)

Dichtung und Wahrheit) had given him a new appreciation of the unorthodox, prerationalist approach to the study of nature. The legends of Faust contain an additional motive. The magus demands that the devil provide higher pleasures for his senses. He wishes to possess the most beautiful of women, Helena herself. This insatiable figure desires not only a superior spiritual existence but also a profounder sensual experience—in keeping with the twofold nature of man.

In Goethe's first sketch, the *Urfaust,* this second motive becomes the principal theme. As in Marlowe the hero introduces himself in a monologue. He sits brooding in his Gothic study, in despair at the sort of knowledge the academic faculties are capable of offering. He has gone through them all, to learn only

> That we in truth can nothing know!
> This in my heart like fire doth burn.[4]

Now he wishes to make trial of other, occult sciences, of magic, to find whether they may disclose to him the innermost organization of the cosmos and the *semina rerum.* He throws open one of the fanciful books, such as the astrologers of the sixteenth century wrote, and studies one of the figures of the universe which represented the macrocosm schematically in "a beautiful concatenation." There spreads before him a vision of the infinite universe, of the vast cosmos in endless motion, with all its forces in harmony. But for Faust's spirit to be satisfied the meaning of the fanciful symbol must be grasped intellectually. But how can a finite being hope to deal with the infinite? Faust essays it through the spirit who holds sway in the earthly sphere. He summons, and the Earth Spirit appears. But when the spirit stands before him, Faust cannot endure the monstrous apparition. The scene ends with the audacious superman thrown back into his old limitations and in deeper despair than ever. No path to the innermost secrets of nature seems open to him now that the way of magic itself has failed.

The scenes which follow—Faust contemplating suicide, the Easter chimes recalling the simple happiness of childhood and filling him with new hope, the Easter promenade, the appearance of Mephisto, the love

[4] Und sehe, dass wir nichts wissen können! / Das will mir schier das Herz verbrennen. (*Faust,* v. 364, translated by Anna Swanwick, p. 19, London: Bell, 1879.)

potion, even the profound scene of the pact with the evil spirit which is indispensable for the progress of the action—all these were written later. The principal content of the oldest form is the almost completely developed love tragedy of Faust and Margarete. It is the immortal story, set forth with profound truth, of how a titanic man forces a simple creature into his erratic life, how by her and with her he experiences for the first time the rapture of primal existence, happiness in mind and heart, how this rapture which yearns for eternity is all too soon exhausted and the "sensual-hypersensual suitor" ends in despair and the girl in disgrace and death without Heaven's absolution.

Would Faust be judged and condemned to hell? But can there be a question of guilt when we are shown how overpowering was the yearning for the moment of supreme feeling and how powerless was the man driven by passion and delivered to forces which grappled and seized him with the primitive might of nature? Only to the extent in which he embraces nature can his spirit hope to fill his phantasms with reality. Neither innocence nor goodwill avails the child of nature; things happen as happen they must. But for deeds committed through the necessity of passion another necessity which governs mankind, that of morality, calls us to account before the seat of judgment. To this necessity Gretchen's being is sacrificed, and to it also Faust's lordly demand for higher life must yield. "You wish to fly," says Mephisto in triumphant mockery, "yet your head grows dizzy." But this cannot be the end of a striving whose direction is worthy and whose goal is ideal. In Goethe's representation Faust is no longer the simple magus. His longing for the extraordinary, for the highest knowledge and the deepest feeling of life, his demand to discover how far the bounds of human experience can be extended, are in themselves noble and good according to the new notion of human greatness. But at the same time we are shown into what tragic conflicts the lofty desires of men lead them when they force human beings "to step out of the bounds of morality."

Thirst for rapturous delight drives Faust down into the dark element which cannot be brought into harmony with his enhanced feeling. That which was to lead him to the foundations of mother nature serves but to add to his intellectual bankruptcy. Yet for this to be the final judgment Goethe would have had to be a moralist; but in fact he knew, young as he was, that human existence and the complicated entirety of life cannot be justly evaluated from the moral point of view. Even at that early period he must have contemplated carrying his hero through other and more ideal experiences and eventually to that highest knowledge which Faust had not been able to find in this early stage of his odyssey through life. At any rate, Goethe later declared that the meeting between Faust and Helena belonged to his earliest concepts. This would confirm the assumption that the unrestrained and titanic genius who is the hero of the first part was thought of only as the first stage in a character development which should lead through an antithesis, as yet dimly realized, to a synthesis which can hardly as yet have been envisaged.

In form *Urfaust* is a variegated structure employing all the lyric and dramatic means which the young poet could master. It presents an opulent ensemble of linguistic, metrical, and scenic modes of expression. We must remember that Goethe had occupied himself with this work, which grew steadily, over a period of several years (until 1775). As the course of his artistic development enlarged his resources, his expression reflects a succession of many modes: prose realistic or pathetic, lyric stanzas, free verse, and rhymed *Knittelvers*, according to the character of the persons and the scenes. One would despair of finding a unity of stylistic principle in this colorful mélange if the diverse modes were not separate paths to a single goal, which was to give expression, as true as life itself, to the ideas, feelings, persons, events, whose interplay constitutes the inner unity of the many-faceted piece.

The Grandeur and Misery of Genius

GOETHE WAS LOOKED UPON AS THE PERFECT EMBODIMENT OF THE IDEAL OF THE INDEPENDENT CREATIVE ARTIST WHICH GERMAN YOUTH GLORIFIED AS "ORIGINal genius." Contemporary descriptions of him are all pitched in this key.

"Goethe was with us, a handsome lad of twenty-five, all genius and strength and energy from crown to toe; a heart filled with emotion, a fiery spirit, soaring with the wings of an eagle" (letter from Heinse to Gleim and Klamer Schmidt, September 13, 1774). "Full of spirit, full of flame" (letter from Christian Stolberg, May 17, 1775). "A true original genius with unbounded freedom of intellect" (J. G. Sulzer, after a visit with Goethe). "All that he says bears the stamp of genius" (letter from Isaak Iselin to Rudolf Frey, July 10, 1775). "A man possessed . . . in whom virtually no act or word can be attributed to personal caprice. One need be with him for only an hour to realize the utter absurdity of expecting him to think or act otherwise than he actually thinks and acts" (letter from Friedrich Jacobi to Wieland, August 27, 1774). "He is the most terrifying and the most lovable of men" (letter from Lavater to Zimmermann, August 27, 1774). "Goethe would have comported himself magnificently as the collaborator of a prince. That is his proper milieu. He might well be a king" (letter from Lavater to Zimmermann, October 20, 1774). "If he ever attains happiness he will make thousands happy; if he does not, he will always remain a meteor, at whom our contemporaries will forever gape and whom our children will admire" (letter from J. G. Schlosser to Lavater, October 17, 1773). "Posterity will marvel that such a man ever lived" (Klinger).

He who produced this enchantment felt that his genius drove him whithersoever it listed, that his life was directed by involuntary compulsion rather than by his own will. When he speaks, it is as if a higher spirit gave utterance through him, as it did through the writers of the religious texts, communicating superhuman truth in human fashion.

> Thus, I myself myself was not,
> And a God through me did speak
> When I to speak did think;
> And when I thought a deity spoke,
> 'Twas I myself.[1]

He calls himself "a restless man" who moves from one state of inner ferment to another, utterly immoderate in life's joys and pain, eagerly yearning to bind himself to reality in conduct and creation, to play some part in the world, to live with his fellow men as "brother, man,

[1] So war ich selbst nicht selbst, / Und eine Gottheit sprach, / Wenn ich zu reden wähnte; / Und wähnt' ich, eine Gottheit spreche, / Sprach ich selbst. (*Prometheus,* Act I, translated by W. H. McClain.)

God, worm, and fool." His motto was "All for Love." As a poet he wished to be sensitive for everyone, to carry everyone along in the strength which streamed from his own heart. Fanatically devoted to feeling, he rejected with impatience all moral rigor, but also all systematic explanations of the world. "Better bad, by feeling, than good, by reason." "If knowledge becomes science, it is no longer of any value." In a visitor's album he wrote a saying of Shaftesbury's: "The most ingenious way of becoming foolish is by a system." In the moral realm, therefore, he despised abstract principles. Ideals of virtue he found fantastic and unreal; only the man who is bold enough to be good and evil, like nature, could like nature be true. But though he turned to all life with love, avid for partnership with mankind, in the end he found himself thrown back upon himself, alone and unredeemed from the abundant fullness of his heart. His experience was like that of the Satyr in his comedy:

> For whom then glows thy life, my heart?
> Thy eagle-eye, what does it see?
> Nature pays thee homage all about,
> And all is thine;
> Yet thou'rt alone,
> And know but misery! [2]

The Deity too, he now discovers, is not always ready to reciprocate respect and love. And so he complains, "I have trodden the winepress alone"; he discovers the truth of "Physician, heal thyself."

In the fragment called *Prometheus* (written in 1773), Goethe attempts to liberate himself from this tormenting conflict by "transforming it into a picture." Like nothing else in the whole body of his work, this significant sketch expresses in a provocative fashion the new self-awareness and self-understanding of the artist. When the eighteenth century sought to comprehend the nature of the creative artist in its highest significance, it likened him to that figure of Greek myth in whom the creation of culture is celebrated as a free and independent contribution of mankind. Shaftesbury had praised the true poet as being "indeed a second maker: a just Prometheus." Goethe himself had said of Shakespeare that he vied with Prometheus.

[2] Dein Leben, Herz, für wen erglüht's? / Dein Adlerauge, was ersieht's? / Dir huldigt ringsum die Natur, / 's ist alles dein; / Und bist allein, / Bist elend nur? (*Satyros*, Act III.)

Goethe represents Prometheus not as the enchained sufferer but as the great creator who, like God, fashioned men after his own image and introduced them to life. Like Aeschylus he gives Prometheus the scornful pride of the demigod who has no need of the gods and refuses to serve them. He also gives him Faust's titanic longing for the fullness of life. Prometheus disclaims indebtedness to the gods for qualities which make the great man. "We are all eternal!" And again, "Therefore I am eternal, for I exist!" [3] Man too participates in the infinity of being by virtue of his metaphysical nucleus, his individuality, which Aristotle called *entelechy* and Leibniz *monad*. There is only one single force to which the great man bows, and that force is destiny. But to the force of destiny even the Olympians are subject. It is an extreme individualism which is here expressed in the image of the myth, an individualism rooted in creative man's urge to independence. Creative capacity is regarded as a "gift of nature," which can neither be promoted nor hampered by external forces. Of his own powers Prometheus says, "They are mine, and mine is their use." In later life Goethe thought this was a thoroughly sans-culotte radicalism. The Christian God upon whose grace men depend and whose favor they seek through prayer is rejected; in his place there appears the notion of the universal-divine, in which man too has a portion by reason of his creative force. The new picture of nature and man appears here in poetic presentiment. But tireless efforts and lifelong search were necessary before this poetic anticipatory picture acquired the assurance and explicitness of an actual and firm perception.

This is the parting of the ways, where Goethe forsook the Christian attitude toward the divine and sought access to the secrets of the universe through the realm of human creativeness. Into this crisis he was thrust by painful experiences in his own life—disappointed love of men and of God. With all his thirst for the abundance of life, all his yearning for the realization, in his works, of his innermost visions, in the end he found himself again banished to the desolation of loneliness. It was such experiences as these that evoked so vigorous a reaction. His attitude has as little to do with atheism as with *Weltschmerz* or with despair of life and mankind. Side by side with his proud faith in the independent strength and greatness of man was his gallant

[3] Wir alle sind ewig! *and* So bin ich ewig; denn ich bin! (*Prometheus,* Act I, translated by W. H. McClain.)

acceptance of life, with its rapture and its pain, and his *amor fati.* When the creatures in the dramatic fragment begin their existence with independent energies and with struggle for pleasure and possessions, Prometheus praises them:

> Ye are not degenerate, O my children,
> You temper diligence with sloth
> And mildness with cruelty;
> You are both covetous and generous,
> . . . . .
> Are like to animals and to gods! [4]

Thus Goethe sees man as a living unity composed of opposites, at once sensual and spiritual, animal and moral. It is precisely from this unification of his twofold nature that his essence results.

The poem, "Hymn to Prometheus," presents the substance of the drama's thought and feeling in purer form.

> Didst thou not accomplish all thyself,
> Holy glowing heart? [5]

Since the poet was thrown back upon himself nothing any longer seemed certain to him except the creative basis of his own being and its expression in his work. But upon such a view his life could not be permanently based. A mode of reconciliation of the creative man with the gods, of the hybrid individual with the universal spirit, had not been set forth in the dramatic fragment and was yet to be achieved. Goethe composed soon after the hymn *An Schwager Kronos* ("To Kronos as Coachman"), to the god of "almighty time," the charioteer of life's journey, which breathes courage for a new sortie and reveals intoxicated readiness to confront fate.

> Up, then, nor idle be,—
> Striving and hoping, up, up! [6]

[4] Ihr seid nicht ausgeartet, meine Kinder, / Seid arbeitsam und faul, / Und grausam mild, / Freigebig geizig / . . . / Gleichet den Tieren und den Göttern. (*Prometheus,* Act II, translated by W. H. McClain.)

[5] Hast du nicht alles selbst vollendet, / Heilig glühend Herz? (*Prometheus,* translated by Friedrich Bruns, *Goethes Gedichte und Sprüche in Prosa,* p. 29, edited by Bruns for the Goethe Society of America, New York: Oxford University Press, 1932.)

[6] Auf denn, nicht träge denn, / Strebend und hoffend hinan! (*An Schwager Kronos,* translated by Edgar A. Bowring, *The Poems of Goethe,* p. 226.)

A third mythical hymn, called *Ganymed*, expresses the yearning of the ego for union with the "all-friendly father," who affects all things and inclines to all beings with loving kindness. This is, as it were, a complementary pendant to *Prometheus*.

The problem of the genius is dealt with in a realistic style and as a phenomenon of the age in the tragedy *Clavigo* (1774). This is the first work which Goethe issued under his own name, but it rates only as an "occasional" piece, for which the material was provided by Beaumarchais' *Voyage d'Espagne*. The hero is one of those "half-great, half-petty" people whose pride and presumption exceed their powers. To their own and their victims' sorrow, they venture on paths they are unable to follow. Psychological understanding of the type as expressed here involves no moral judgment, just as there is no moral judgment in *Werther*. Observed from within, what appears superficially as knavery proves to be the catastrophe of an individuality which is inadequate to its demands for greatness and independence. Claims to the right to live according to one's own moral standard, the tormented man's inability to accommodate himself to social mores, the faithlessness and cruelty of an insatiable urge toward life—all of this is characteristic of the contemporary type of genius, and was familiar enough to Goethe as a danger to which he was himself liable. The doom which the poet prepares for his hero is a judgment upon himself.

La Maladie du Siècle

"I AM WEARY OF BEWAILING THE FATE OF OUR GENERATION OF HUMAN BEINGS, BUT I WILL SO DEPICT THEM THAT THEY MAY UNDERSTAND THEMSELVES, IF that is possible, as I have understood them."[1] It is the state of his generation's soul which Goethe sets forth in *Werther;* the extreme character of the case affords a complete diagnosis. "Look you, the end of this disease is death! The goal of such sentimental enthusiasm is

[1] Ich bin müde, über das Schicksal *unsres Geschlechts* von Menschen zu klagen; aber ich will sie darstellen, sie sollen sich erkennen, wo möglich, wie ich sie erkannt habe.

suicide!"[2] The disease of which Goethe speaks threatened the young intelligentsia everywhere in Europe, but nowhere more than in Germany. It was the softening and the excess of emotion which we call sentimentality. A tense and idealistic youth found itself cut off from the world of great action, worthy achievement, and lofty striving by an antiquated social order. In all cultural matters, in science, art, philosophy, the bourgeoisie had assumed leadership and justly felt that it possessed the highest moral cultivation. But in politics and society the middle class was still under constraint, still subject to the domination of princely absolutism and feudal caste. The storm clouds of revolutionary change had just begun to appear on the horizon. In the sultry calm which preceded the great storm shortly to break in France, there developed a state in which spiritual energies were pent up within and active striving was flung back upon itself. Idealistic feeling and will languished ineffectually. "Here we have to do with men living in the most peaceful of circumstances whose lives have been spoiled for them by want of deeds and by their exaggerated demands upon themselves."[3] Where the inner life was intensified to such a pitch, any accidental passion that arose must lead to a crisis which could only be resolved by the most fatal means. "Look you, the end of this disease is death!"

In the spring of 1772 Goethe went for several months to Wetzlar, a small town not far from Frankfort, where the supreme judiciary of the German realm had its seat. Here he came to know a young girl called Charlotte Buff. She entranced him by her gay kindliness and the healthy naturalness of her character. When Goethe met her, Lotte was the fiancée of a young man who was Goethe's friend, but passion did not inquire what was permissible or possible. Unattainable as she was in her steady loyalty to her fiancé and to her husband later, Goethe loved Lotte with an intensity which was only increased by his tortured vacillation between hope and despair. Finally he summoned strength "himself to desire what was necessary" and to flee before he was enmeshed by inextricable complications.

He had escaped the grimmest fate only by a hair's breadth. When he was again in Frankfort, alone and suffering, he heard from his

[2] Siehe, das Ende dieser Krankheit ist Tod! Solcher Schwärmereien Ziel ist Selbstmord!

[3] Wir haben es hier mit solchen zu tun, denen eigentlich aus Mangel von Taten, in dem friedlichsten Zustande von der Welt, durch übertriebene Forderungen an sich selbst das Leben verleidet. (*Dichtung und Wahrheit,* Part III, Book XIII.)

Wetzlar friends that a young man called Jerusalem had taken his own life. He had been in the same situation as Goethe, but had not been able to bring himself to escape in time. "The poor lad! When I came back from my walk and he met me out in the moonlight, I said to myself the man was in love. Lotte must still remember that I smiled over it. God knows, loneliness undermined his heart . . ."[4] Goethe's own experience was associated with the melancholy history of young Jerusalem. For a year and a half the elements were assembled until the composition crystallized into a whole. Goethe must have written down Werther's story quickly, in the space of a few weeks during the spring of 1774 ("almost unconsciously, like a sleepwalker"), so completely formed was the story in his mind. Only now did he feel himself fully healed, and "as after a general confession, again happy and free and justified for a new life." But the past was still so immediately present to him that his composition exhibits the colors of living reality throughout. Rich as the age was in autobiographical sketches and documents of personal confession, no other writing is capable of communicating reality with such masterly art. Goethe's book went straight to the heart of a generation devoted to the cult of nature. Its success was unprecedented.

Die Leiden des jungen Werthers ("The Sorrows of Young Werther"), as the title of the anonymously published first version of 1774 reads, is a romance in letters. The author poses as an editor of private papers. Such fictions were popular in the eighteenth century. The role assumed by the author, looked at from the point of view of his audience, amounted to a concession to the mass of readers that the truth of reality is superior to the higher truth of poetry; such a concession was no artistic deprivation to the author. At the same time he was able to swathe the autobiographic content in a veil and withdraw it from importunate curiosity. What was highly personal and intimate appeared as something objective and documentary. The epistolary novel was a new species, a creation of the century which had shown great interest in the secrets of the individual and "the immediacy of existence." The most important models were Richardson's novels and Rousseau's *La Nouvelle Héloïse*. Both involve correspondence between

[4] Der arme Junge! Wenn ich zurückkam vom Spaziergang und er mir begegnete hinaus im Mondschein, sagt ich, er ist verliebt. Lotte muss sich noch erinnern, dass ich drüber lächelte. Gott weiss, die Einsamkeit hat sein Herz untergraben . . . (Letter to Kestner, November 1772.)

several persons. Goethe does not dispense with the dialogue form but transforms it to a "conversation in spirit" which the writer conducts with a hidden interlocutor.

In their origin as in their effect these are no true letters but highly intimate confessions which a lone man makes to himself, monologues of a suffering soul. Only Werther's voice is heard; the friend to whom he writes appears only in the reactions which his replies evoke. This new form gave psychological depth to the epistolary novel and at the same time supreme artistic simplicity. Nowhere and at no time has it been surpassed. The models for the descriptive parts, with their objectively faithful portrayal of rural life, idyllic and patriarchal conditions, and simple folk, were the new novels of the English—those of Sterne, and above all the books of Oliver Goldsmith. Goethe gratefully calls them his teachers, and says that they are "as interesting, as affectionate," as their own domestic life. In them Goethe found confirmation for the realistic tendency of his own narrative style: "Proceed from the domestic, and spread yourself, if you can, over the whole world." [5]

Among European novels *Werther* is the first in which an inward life, a spiritual process and nothing else, is represented, and hence it is the first psychological novel—though naturally not the first in which the inner life in general is seriously dealt with. The conflict between an immoderately burgeoning passion and the ordered world of society is here described, as it were, "from within." The scene is the soul of the hero. All events and figures are regarded only in the light of the significance they have for Werther's emotion. All that happens serves but to nourish the absolutism of Werther's emotion—a fatal propensity which swells to a demonic possession and engulfs all other inward forces and possibilities.

The germ of the disease is already present in Werther before he is attacked by his passion; his passion only serves to aggravate it. As Werther describes himself at the beginning of the book, he is already a lonely man who seeks refuge from life in the bosom of nature because nothing will satisfy his insatiable heart. He speaks of nothing as frequently as of this heart, which he spoils like an ailing child. For him it is the epitome of his worth, the source of his personal life. "Ah, what I know, anyone may know. My heart is mine alone." His inner

[5] Geh vom Häuslichen aus, und verbreite dich, so du kannst, über alle Welt.

being appears capable of satisfaction only by an emotional realization of the infinity of the universal. But this is an experience which increasingly alienates him from life. Only idyllic landscapes give him inward peace; only with children and simple folk can he associate on terms of friendship; the patriarchal world of the *Odyssey* is to him a "lullaby." But his soul is filled with dark premonitions and yearning, and he sinks into his twilight dreams. This man could be healed, could be saved only by a transformation which would force him to move among the realities of life, to expend his pent-up inner riches in plans and deeds. But this transition from the sentimental state of youth to the sphere of adult activity does not come about.

The encounter with Lotte gives his searching emotion an object to which it can fasten. Now begins the spiritual event constituting the inner action of this book, which, by the standards of literary composition, is rather a lyrical drama than a novel. Goethe himself has referred to this psychic process as an illness, since every great passion is a sort of disease. As we look on, the passion of love tightens its grip upon the unresisting sufferer; we see how its effect is the more disruptive because it draws to itself all the forces which constitute Werther's greatness: his gifts of unqualified feeling, his demands for the fullness of existence, his readiness to devote himself wholly to the great thing which has seized upon him. The hero is destroyed by what is noble and good in him. Later Goethe once said: "Man's longing for the ideal, when deprived of its objectives, or when these are spoiled, turns back on itself, becomes refined and intensified until it seems to outdo itself." [6] Werther is ruined because of and in spite of his possession of a great heart, an ideal soul. He suffocates by the abundance of his inward life. Qualities which might have raised his being to a pinnacle in friendlier times and under more favorable circumstances become his doom.

Goethe's expressions leave no doubt as to what he considers the cause of Werther's ruin in the outer world. The cause lies in the fatal conditions under which the intellectual young men of the age had to live. Since the age denied them opportunity to act greatly, they were left with no other satisfaction than to dream and to feel greatly. The

[6] Das Ideale im Menschen, wenn diesem die Objekte genommen oder verkümmert werden, zieht sich in sich, feinert und steigert sich, dass es sich gleichsam übertrumpft. (To F. W. Riemer, August 1808.)

fulfillment which they could not find in active life they were forced to seek in inward existence. Mme de Staël has described this situation excellently:

> Since the form of their governments afforded them no possibility to win fame and serve their country, they devoted themselves to every sort of philosophic speculation and sought in heaven a field for the activity which narrow limitations denied them on earth. They found satisfaction in ideals because reality offered them nothing to occupy their imagination.

Because the world had no room for them, they wished to expand their egos to infinity. "I turn back into myself and discover a world" (Ich kehre in mich selbst zurück und finde eine Welt).

To the motive of inward passion grown rank there was added another, which explained why the pent-up dynamism could not unburden itself outwardly. Even the modest activity which was permitted to bourgeois officials was made impossible for Werther by the painful scandal which thrust him out of a society composed of the gentry. Now every path to the sphere of action was barred to him; after a vain attempt at flight he submitted without resistance to his "endless sorrow through which any vital force that was in him must eventually be extinguished." Could a man be more lonely than he now was? Things went so far that he lost even his communion with nature. The pantheistic feeling for the "unmeasured sea," the ever-creating abundance of the universal spirit in which his ego, suffering in its limitations, sought self-forgetfulness, was now displaced by the picture of an "ever-devouring, ever-regurgitating monster," an unfeeling destructive power with no concern for the survival of the individual. In the composition of the book the alternation of seasons corresponds to the transformation of inward mood. The month is May when Werther's love begins; it is December when his end comes. So, too, in the first portion his companion is the vital and energetic Homer; in the second the melancholy, unbelieving Ossian, whose gloomy pathos introduces the fateful moment when Werther locks the unattainable in his arms for a single time and so loses her forever.

Nothing in this book, not even its truth of expression unparalleled at the time, so deeply stirred Goethe's contemporaries as the self-destruction of the hero. Without charity, but also without reproach (as is appropriate to "true representation"), the suicide is here presented as the necessary consequence of a passion whose power transcended the "bounds of humanity." Christians found it immoral; rationalist skeptics and libertines thought it ridiculous to take passion so seriously. But among young men who themselves suffered from Werther's malaise there were many to whom his example gave courage to put a period to their suffering as he had done. The poet found it necessary to admonish such readers, who did not understand that the book was to be read, so to speak, against the grain, in a motto affixed to the second edition in Werther's name: "Be a man, do *not* follow me."

Then and later Goethe was accused of having provoked the "Werther fever" by his "dangerous book." He replied quite justly that he had not originated the disease but had only uncovered the evil which was latent in the young men of his time. The nature of such an epidemic of soul sickness Goethe could report correctly, inasmuch as he had with difficulty succeeded in saving himself from a similar crisis. Outbreaks of world-weariness, he says, recur in the history of civilized nations periodically. Byronism was a somewhat analogous phenomenon. In the life history of the individual something of the same sort occurs. In all ages *taedium vitae* is a problem in the development of high-spirited young people. "Frustrated fortune, hampered activity, unsatisfied wishes are not the lesions of a specific age but of every individual man. It would be too bad if everyone did not go through a period when *Werther* struck him as if it were written for him alone." [7] Otherwise, for all of its artistic excellence, *Werther* would be nothing more than a document in the spiritual history of Europe and not the great work it is—the exemplary representation of a tragic conflict arising out of the situation of the modern individualist. Idealism of feeling, which demands complete realization, founders here on the reef of social usage as it is established by the formal order of civilization and by fate.

The huge success of the book gave a firm foundation to Goethe's poetic fame and made it secure. *Werther* was immediately translated into many languages. In England, France, and Italy the history of Werther was dramatized, painted in pictures, and sung in verses. Scenes from *Werther* were painted on china and fans. Rebuttals and censorial prohibitions only contributed to make the novel even more

[7] Gehindertes Glück, gehemmte Tätigkeit, unbefriedigte Wünsche sind nicht Gebrechen einer besonderen Zeit, sondern jedes einzelnen Menschen, und es müsste schlimm sein, wenn nicht jeder einmal in seinem Leben eine Epoche haben sollte, wo ihm der "Werther" käme, als wäre er bloss für ihn geschrieben. (Eckermann, January 2, 1824.)

popular. When Goethe met Napoleon in 1808 the Emperor proved to know *Werther* intimately. It was one of the few books which Bonaparte took with him on his adventurous expedition to Egypt. He declared that he had read it seven times. When, also in 1808, the great actor Talma invited Goethe to visit him in Paris, he assured the poet that *Werther* was still as popular in France as it had been thirty years before; everyone would envy Talma the privilege of having its author as a guest. Small wonder that the author, who was then ready for a different art and for whom this work was only a snakeskin which he had sloughed off in his process of transformation, now groans:

> How often, alas, have I both cursed and regretted those pages
> Which brought the sorrows of my youth before men.
> Had Werther been my brother, and had I slain him,
> Scarcely could his sad spirit pursue me more vengefully.[8]

In *Werther* Goethe liberated himself from the grave danger which threatened the children of the age of sentimentality; he demonstrated his withdrawal from sentimentality a second time by representing the sentimental type in a drama. The middle-class drama *Stella* (1776; Goethe called it "a play for lovers") has for its hero a man for whom there is no other life than that of emotion. But whereas Werther ruins no one but himself, Fernando, himself an unresisting sufferer, makes miserable the two women between whom he is unable to decide. When he is not in love, he feels he is not living; and when an old emotion begins to be exhausted, he must yield to a new. For this morbid figure love is only a means to self-enjoyment. He belongs to no one wholly, either as husband or as lover or as father. He is one of those problematic characters, like Weislingen and Clavigo, who pay for their selfish love with the tormenting feeling of helpless regret: "Heart, oh my heart! If you are capable of such feeling and such action, why have you not also the power to forgive yourself what has happened!"[9] The women in this play are also characterized by strong and simple emotions; they are resourceful enough to save the tormented man from Werther's fate by a fantastic compromise marriage involving a *ménage à trois*.

[8] Ach, wie hab' ich so oft die törichten Blätter verwünschet, / Die mein jugendlich Leid unter die Menschen gebracht. / Wäre Werther mein Bruder gewesen, ich hätt' ihn erschlagen, / Kaum verfolgte mich so rächend sein trauriger Geist. ("Römische Elegien," No. 2, manuscript version. Translated by W. H. McClain.)

[9] Herz! Unser Herz! o wenn's in dir liegt, so zu fühlen und so zu handeln, warum hast du nicht auch Kraft, dir das Geschehene zu verzeihen! (*Stella*, Act III.)

Later Goethe gave this sentimental play the tragic ending which is more realistic and in better accord with the demands of moral feeling.

New Love

"IT WAS A SINGULAR DECREE OF THE DIVINITY THAT HOLDS SWAY OVER US THAT IN THE STRANGE COURSE OF MY LIFE I SHOULD ALSO EXPERIENCE THE FEELINGS of a fiancé." [1] Goethe adds that for a decent man it is "the pleasantest of all memories." During the last year in Frankfort he met Lili Schönemann. She was sixteen years old, the daughter of a rich middle-class family, pretty, attractive, and capricious. The love which developed between the young genius and the spoiled young lady was legitimized by a sort of discreet betrothal, with some difficulty and against the opposition of Lili's mother and also of Goethe's parents. But soon it appeared that the lovers did not agree well with one another. Relatives and friends intervened with their criticisms and their plots and schemes. The conventional life in the home of Lili's mother and the people whom Goethe met there were heartily distasteful to him. His deeply felt poem *An Belinden* ("To Belinda") expresses his inner conflict. How pure his feeling for her when he dreamt of her in the loneliness of his chamber, yet how strange and ill-assorted he felt when he spent the evening with her in the elegant salon face to face with the "intolerable visages" of fashionable society! But feeling triumphs over all, so that wherever she is present there also are the sweetness and brightness of life.

> Nor is bloom of early spring
> Dearer than thou art.
> Where thou art is love and goodness,
> Nature, where thou art.[2]

[1] Es war ein seltsamer Beschluss des hohen über uns Waltenden, dass ich in dem Verlaufe meines wundersamen Lebensganges doch auch erfahren sollte, wie es einem Bräutigam zu Mute sei.

[2] Reizender ist mir des Frühlings Blüte / Nun nicht auf der Flur; / Wo du, Engel, bist, ist Lieb' und Güte, / Wo du bist, Natur. (*An Belinden*, translated by William Grasset Thomas, *The Minor Poetry of Goethe*, p. 77, Philadelphia: Butler, 1859.)

A journey, a secret flight, offered itself as a desperate escape from his growing tribulations. Recovery of "diligence and serenity" was at stake. Goethe went to Switzerland with friends for a few months. Would he be able to forget Lili? There were moments when the grandeur of Alpine scenery (which Goethe saw for the first time) recalled the feeling of inner freedom and productivity. The exquisite fruit of such a free mood is a poem which is without peer among the lyrical works of Goethe's youth. *Auf dem See* ("On the Lake") no longer exhibits the passionate hypertension of his earlier nature verses. The feeling of the moment is expressed with simple truth. It is a "through-composed" (*durchkomponiertes*) poem, constructed after the manner of a sonata in three movements of varying rhythms. Its phases echo a spiritual movement, and in such a way that what is related is not a completed thing but rather a living process in the act of unfolding. The soul and its reflection in word and rhythm, inner movement and its expression, are here as closely welded as it is possible for them to be. At the spectacle of majestic nature, which is the subject matter of the poem, the soul breathes freely, but only for the moment; yearning for the distant love again thrusts forward powerfully. But it is dismissed by a new determination.

> Off! thou dream; though sweet thy spell,
> Here is life and love as well.[3]

Now movement and countermovement oscillate in the sustained rhythm of the third part. The eye is opened wide to the beautiful present, to the early morning landscape at the lake with its rippling calm. A man who can see these things and set them forth in this manner is serene and healthy in soul. Another poem tells why Goethe did not descend to Italy when he was on the Gotthard. He is like a bird who has escaped from its cage but still carries a portion of the cord which had restrained him.

> The free-born bird of old no more is seen,
> For he another's prey hath been.[4]

[3] Weg, du Traum! so gold du bist: / Hier auch Lieb' und Leben ist. (*Auf dem See*, translated by Paul Drysen, *Goethe's Poems*, p. 65, New York: Christern, 1878.)

[4] Er ist der alte freigeborne Vogel nicht, / Er hat schon jemand angehört. (*An ein goldnes Herz, das er am Halse trug*, translated by Edgar A. Bowring, *The Poems of Goethe*, p. 93.)

When Goethe returned to Frankfort at the end of July he discovered that in his absence an attempt had been made to convince his beloved of the need for a full separation. But Lili had declared that she was herself ready to go to America with him if that were necessary. Again Goethe is with her, and the old torment begins anew. But his inward feeling now inclines to resignation. From the moments of enchantment he awakens to the painful realization that he is a tamed bear, a denizen of the enchantress' colorful menagerie along with other tamed men. He abjures the irresistible woman:

> For if ye know her not, then thank your fates 'tis so.[5]

Even in Weimar Goethe suffered from this passion now grown hopeless. The octogenarian recalled the fiancée of his youth with affectionate gratitude and said that she was the first and also the last whom he had truly loved and that he had never come so close to his "proper fortune" as he then came.

Demon and Destiny

THAT IN THE DEPTHS OF HIS SOUL AND BENEATH ALL THE RESTLESSNESS OF PASSION GOETHE RETAINED AND AFFIRMED A CLEAR AND STRONG SENSE OF THE HAPpiness of existence is demonstrated by the drama which he began during his last months in Frankfort. *Egmont* was planned as a historical drama after the manner of *Götz*. The material belonged to the same epoch and the motive was similar: a solitary, independent man who seeks in vain to assert himself against his anarchic age. But Egmont's stature fascinated the poet to such a degree that his character and fate became the sole theme. Now the historical events constitute only a colorful background before which the hero can enact his sad and beautiful role. The war of liberation of the Dutch Protestants against the Spanish Catholics which constitutes the historical theme is not given sufficient weight in any scene to engage interest for its own

[5] Kennt ihr sie nicht, so danket Gott dafür. (*Lilis Park*, translated by William G. Thomas, *The Minor Poetry of Goethe*, p. 86, Philadelphia: Butler, 1859.)

sake. The figure of the hero itself is employed with little regard for historical tradition. In the end this tradition only affords the poet a means to set forth matter not dependent upon time and place: a human attitude which he realized or strove to realize in himself, a mood which dominated him at the end of his youth.

All that Egmont does and says reveals his frankness and friendliness to men and to life. He seems to be a favorite of the gods and he radiates "free life," nature humanized. "He walks with free stride, as if the world were his." The life which he leads can only be gauged in the scale of the beautiful, of harmonious and self-contained calm. Anxiety for the future and brooding over the past are alien to a man like Egmont, for whom the pure joy of the present is everything. "If you take life too seriously, what is its use? If the morning does not arouse us to new joys, and we can hope for no pleasures in the evening, is it worth while to dress and undress?" [1] He is dominated by a feeling that existence cannot deny its favor to one who loves it with such pure faith. To him life itself is actually life's sole purpose. Egmont's existence is shut off from the divine as well as against the disruptive elements of life. The gallant and spirited man can imagine the end only as a bright conclusion to a well-filled life. When the end proves in fact to be quite different, the strength of his readiness to meet fate is revealed. The high point of the drama is Egmont's reconciliation with death, the departure of this lover of life from the "beautiful, friendly habit of life and work." "Every day I have had pleasure"— a man who can say that of himself can confront the anguish of death with calm disposition. "I cease to live, but I have lived."

Not for a moment does Egmont fall into the pose of sublime pathos. As long as it seems possible he hopes for flight, for deliverance. Between the extremes of stoic resignation and idealism filled with pathos this hero goes his way with a happy equanimity, derived from his faith in the friendly nature of life. He has no other gods. The dream vision of the goddess of liberty which fills his last quiet sleep bears the features of the girl who had made his days beautiful with her love and her loyalty. This unheroic drama closes with a "symphony of victory." The beautiful overture in which Beethoven has trans-

[1] Wenn ihr das Leben gar zu ernsthaft nehmt, was ist denn dran? Wenn uns der Morgen nicht zu neuen Freuden weckt, am Abend uns keine Lust zu hoffen übrig bleibt, ist's wohl des An- und Ausziehens wert?

formed the substance of this poesy into the symbolism of music resounds with the same bright and triumphant tone.

In the figure of Klärchen Goethe again glorified the type of young girl to which his youth owed so much happiness. She is the simple child of nature, true and faithful in her feeling, and utterly obedient to the force that has taken possession of her and will quickly prove to be her doom. But here the simple sweetheart is transformed into a heroine when the tragic peripety threatens the man she admires. She "follows her beloved with a profound conviction of the eternity of love," whereas the crowd looks on, inert and with no real participation, while its hero is destroyed.

Egmont's real antagonist is not the Spaniard Alba, who causes his death, but a mysterious force inherent in life, which occupies the position of destiny in Greek tragedy. Goethe attempts to describe its nature, insofar as it may be described in words, in the last book of *Dichtung und Wahrheit*. In nature, as in the life of man, he says, he had discovered something which could be grasped neither by the power of reasoned analogy nor by the hypothesis of a hostile power. Incalculable as the sway of pure accident, this power seems nevertheless to be the instrument of a higher providence, for in some peculiar manner it links the individual with the necessary course of the whole, in life and in history. Following the usage of Socrates and Plotinus, Goethe called this power the demonic. During his early years at Weimar, while he was working at the completion of his *Egmont*, the feeling grew in him that the will of this power, imperceptible to the senses, was effective above all in the make-up of great individuals, and hence in himself also; in some extraordinary fashion this power was identical with the innermost essence of individuality, yet it far transcended the purposeful will of the ego. "Man may turn whithersoever he will, he may undertake whatever it may be, always he will return to that path which nature had once designated for him." [2] "No man can alter a fiber of his being, however much he may add to his stature." [3] In the first of his Orphic *Urworte* (written at a later period), entitled *Dämon*, we read: "Such *must* thou be, thyself thou canst not

[2] Der Mensch mag sich wenden, wohin er will, er mag unternehmen, was es auch sei, stets wird er auf jenen Weg wieder zurückkehren, den ihm die Natur einmal vorgezeichnet hat.

[3] Kein Mensch kann eine Faser seines Wesens ändern, ob er gleich vieles an sich bilden kann.

fly" (So musst du sein, dir kannst du nicht entfliehen). Inborn individuality thus appears as a sharply defined nucleus which in the course of life shapes a man's destiny. Goethe thought that such inevitability appeared with particular clarity in the lives of great individuals like Napoleon; in their actions such men were instruments, rather than free agents, and they could be overcome only by the world-spirit itself. "A huge force emanates from them, and they exercise incredible power over all creatures."

Egmont, too, Goethe placed under the sway of the demonic. He endowed him with "measureless delight in life, boundless confidence in himself, the gift of drawing all men to himself"—with an unshakable self-assurance which rests upon the conviction that life would not forsake its friend before he attained the culmination of his being, and with intrepid gallantry adequate to any vicissitude. But this very trust in his demon eventually becomes the cause of Egmont's fall. Oranien (Orange), the clever politician, saves himself while there is yet time. He seeks in vain, by reasoning with Egmont, to shake him also from his blind self-assurance which is so like that of the sleepwalker. But Egmont can live only if he surrenders to the power which works in his ego and out of it.

> As if scourged onward by invisible spirits, time's horses of the sun hurtle the light chariot of our fate; and for us nothing remains but to grasp the reins courageously and guide the wheels now to the right and now to the left, avoiding a stone here and a fall there. Whither it all leads, who knows? We can scarcely even remember whence we came.[4]

Goethe placed these sentences from *Egmont* at the end of his autobiography. In his relationship to Lili, in the significant turn which brought him to Weimar, he found evidence of a higher demonic destiny which directed his life according to its will.

Only in Rome does Goethe appear to have grasped these phenomena to such an extent that he could make them the basis of Egmont's character and attitude. In any case it was in Rome, in the summer of 1787, that the drama, which was begun twelve years before, was

[4] Wie von unsichtbaren Geistern gepeitscht, gehen die Sonnenpferde der Zeit mit unsers Schicksals leichtem Wagen durch; und uns bleibt nichts, als mutig gefasst die Zügel festzuhalten und bald rechts bald links, vom Steine hier vom Sturze da, die Räder wegzulenken. Wohin es geht, wer weiss es? Erinnert er sich doch kaum, woher er kam. (*Egmont,* Act II, "Egmonts Wohnung.")

completed. None of his previous works, he confessed to his friends in Weimar, was executed with greater inward freedom and with greater conscientiousness. No other, we may say, gives such powerful and such beautiful expression to Goethe's youthful confidence in life; but already it was amalgamated with a darker element, with the mature perception of the man.

The Harvest of Youth

Ich war dazu gelangt, das mir inwohnende dichterische Talent ganz als Natur zu betrachten . . .[1]

IF WE EXAMINE PASSAGES IN GOETHE'S EARLY WRITINGS IN WHICH HE SPEAKS OF LANGUAGE AND FORM, WE FIND THAT THE RELATION BETWEEN FEELING AND EXpression was for him the prime artistic problem. It was his conviction that true poetry must communicate as immediately and with as little alteration as possible the inward life which clamors for expression, the joys and sorrows of the poet's ego. Hence the form of composition is relatively unimportant compared to the natural truth it communicates. What mattered were the individual traits of present perceptive experience, not the general quality of the beautiful. Personal emotion, expressed with the warmth of the living moment, must not be chilled in impersonal molds. The author must "proceed to his composition with his first enthusiasm," the energy of his heart must be poured forth freely. "This characteristic art is the sole true art," Goethe declared, though emotion might be so strong that it could find only halting expression. A "heart wholly filled with an emotion" is what makes the poet. There is no concern here for art, for technical mastery. "Feeling is everything," and its truth can be shown only by spontaneous utterance. Even of the language of *Werther* Goethe says that it is only "childish babble and noise" when compared with real emotion. An essay written as late as 1775 declares that every form, "even the most

[1] I had reached the point of treating my native poetic talents as if they were part of nature . . . (*Dichtung und Wahrheit,* Part IV, Book XVI.)

keenly felt," has an element of falsity; and, while Goethe considers it proper to talk about the form of the drama, his paramount concern is to feel the inner emotions which are expressed in the form. These are attitudes and thoughts which, it would appear, could lead to no style other than a naturalistic expressionism, a spontaneous utterance of amorphous inner life which no form is capable of encompassing.

In Goethe's critical writing these views are exaggerated. For him, as for his contemporaries of the generation of *Sturm und Drang*, the important thing was to combat the aesthetic views of the enlightenment, which discoursed on the properties of a beautiful work of art as if they were objective qualities which might be itemized and produced at will. In opposition to this attitude Herder and Goethe set forth the view that a work of art is a structure resembling a living organism; it grows as a unit, internally and externally, in content and in form, ever according to the vital process of which it is a symbol. Goethe writes in a letter to Herder that nothing in an essay of his so pleased him as the proposition that poetic expression grows out of thought and feeling, and that the relation of the expression to what is expressed is like that of the body to the soul and not like that of the garment to the body. But in his lyrics Goethe is not an orthodox disciple of his own doctrine. Not even the earliest poems in the new "natural" manner, such as *Willkommen und Abschied*, are without form. Their structure is plain enough: out of the crescendo and the diminuendo of a culminating moment of love, the simple "inner form" takes its growth. *Werther*, much as its style of living immediacy attempts to avoid the impression of intentional arrangement, is nevertheless most definitely articulated internally by the constantly intensified dynamic of the love delusion, whose suspense is artfully accentuated by retarding elements. The dramatic works in the style of Shakespeare, *Götz* and the sketch of the *Faust* drama, go farthest in the direction of loose form. Yet even here it cannot be said that we have a chaos of disconnected scenes.

The general spiritual basis for this style of composition is the ideal of nature. Goethe's relation to the world is that of sensitive contact with the universal-divine presence. He feels it as a formless, ever-present power surging up everywhere about us, its essence filling and permeating the universe. He describes such experience as floating "in the infinitely holy ocean of our Father, who may not be comprehended but who is accessible." What perception is unable to comprehend intellectually, groping feeling can touch sensually. We have come to the essence of pantheism: God is experienced in and through nature; God and existence are one; He is the being "which produces all things in himself and through himself." As early as 1770 Goethe cites in his journal a Latin passage which says that we perceive God only through inspection of nature, that he is the only reality and embraces everything. Reality is the divine made manifest. The paradoxical view, that we can become aware of the infinite only in the finite, of the general only in the particular, constitutes the mystic basis of this experience. But its corollary is the notion that no finite form can wholly comprehend the infinite and hence that the process of formation and transformation continues incessantly. The words in which the Earth Spirit describes his activity in the first scene of *Faust* present the picture of a vital force which operates in a perpetual rhythm of bringing together and separating, of coming into being and perishing.

> In the swirling of life, the storm of action,
> I rise and fall,
> Weave back and forth.
> I am the womb and the tomb,
> An ocean eternal,
> A changing, glowing
> Life in ferment:
> Thus working on the roaring loom of time,
> I weave God's living garment.[2]

Images such as these depict a boundless activity, which is prevented by an immanent principle from losing itself in the infinite. The centrifugal tendency is opposed by a centripetal tendency. What we have then is a rhythmically ordered movement, upward and downward, hither and yonder, not an unordered diffusion in all directions. Life processes are governed by a regulated pulse-beat, induced by polar opposition. The notion of a fundamental polar structure of life, which

[2] In Lebensfluten, im Tatensturm / Wall' ich auf und ab, / Webe hin und her! / Geburt und Grab, / Ein ewiges Meer, / Ein wechselnd Weben, / Ein glühend Leben, / So schaff' ich am sausenden Webstuhl der Zeit, / Und wirke der Gottheit lebendiges Kleid. (*Faust*, v. 501, translated by Carlyle F. MacIntyre, p. 25, Norfolk, Connecticut: New Directions, 1941.)

becomes so important in Goethe's later concept of the world and for his interpretation of nature, makes its appearance even in his earliest independent thinking. In the discourse *Zum Schäkespears Tag* (1771), we read: "What we call evil is only the obverse of the good" (Das, was wir bös nennen, ist nur die andere Seite vom Guten), a portion in the whole of moral life. In this view the negative pole is as indispensable as the positive, for without it there could be no motion and hence no life.

The view that the motions of life proceed from polar opposition appears more definitely in Goethe's early dramas than in his theoretical expositions. In the former the traditional scheme of good hero and evil antagonist is replaced by a different distribution of forces in which opposing viewpoints are personified in characters, but in such fashion that the greater whole of the action develops out of them and encompasses them all. Such are Götz and Weislingen, Faust and Mephisto, Clavigo and Carlos, Egmont and Alba. This mode of dramatic dynamism appears even more clearly in the contrast between Tasso and Antonio. There can be no question of good and evil where the issue is a fundamental condition of life. The devil himself must assist in creation. Later Goethe said that he endeavored from the beginning not to think in dualistic terms but to develop the imperfect out of the perfect, darkness out of light, resistance out of activity, evil out of good. If this was indeed his original mode of regarding the world and life it amounted as yet only to an intuition, a presentiment that it was so and could not be otherwise. There was as yet no differentiated insight into the organization of nature. He does indeed already assume that "all things weave themselves into a whole" (as we read in the *Urfaust*), but he had not yet arrived at the comprehension of the large order, the consistent regularity of creative nature. Its working seemed like oceanic limitlessness, a "wondrous confusion," held together by nothing but the polar rhythm of the vital process. It wanted a more precise examination and a deeper penetration, a more intensive and more methodical effort, to attain an adequate picture of the natural order. The path of pantheism by which the ego sought to approach the universal-divine emotionally could only lead to moments of mystic union and intuitive insight, which could not satisfy the intellectual spirit. So Faust found to his anguish:

A wondrous show! But ah! a show alone!
Where shall I grasp thee, infinite nature, where? [3]

One who experiences world and life as boundless infinity will create, as a poet, forms which seek to give expression to such experience. For him any style which strives for strict precision and clarity must seem out of accord with nature and hence "untrue." How can systematizing reason ever hope to be adequate to this experience?

I tremble, stammer, nothing more,
Yet ne'er my task surrender;
I know thee, Nature, to the core,
Thine essence I must render.[4]

But he can grasp nature only through emotion and through the stammering word, through a form which is not definite and precise but vague and manifold. Each poetic work thus represents in symbolic manner the qualities of the universe and the life in it.

As for humanity, Goethe's preponderant interest at this time was in the secret of individuality. How is it possible that the universe should be comprised wholly of independent individual beings who are nevertheless in intimate connection with the infinite whole? How can the ego participate feelingly in the infinity of the cosmos and still maintain its separate, limited existence? How is it possible that the individual should belong to the great order of nature and yet work independently, according to his own fashion, and thus himself transform himself? "Nature forms man, he transforms himself, and yet this transformation is in turn nature" (Die Natur bildet den Menschen, er bildet sich um, und diese Umbildung ist doch wieder natürlich). Hence there is a possibility for free self-determination, unknown to other beings. The old view that the individual is an image of the universe, that he can therefore be called a microcosm, and hence is, as Faust says, an "image of divinity," was given new currency by the monad theory of Leibniz. When Werther calls his soul a mirror of the infinite deity, the allusion is to the doctrine that each monad is a

[3] Welch Schauspiel! Aber ach! ein Schauspiel nur! / Wo fass' ich dich, unendliche Natur? (*Faust*, v. 454, translated by Anna Swanwick, p. 22, London: Bell, 1879.)

[4] Ich zittre nur, ich stottre nur, / Und kann es doch nicht lassen; / Ich fühl', ich kenne dich, Natur, / Und so muss ich dich fassen. (*Künstlers Abendlied*, translated by B. Q. Morgan.)

living, creative, reflecting mirror which fashions a picture of the world after its own manner. In the artist this creative receptivity reaches its culmination. He creates his forms and figures, as Shaftesbury says, in the same manner as nature does. From such notions of modern metaphysics as reached Goethe through the current of tradition he selected certain ones without adopting the complete philosophic system. He seized upon only such individual ideas and doctrines as could be related to concrete experience. He accepted only those which proved that some predecessor had experienced the same feelings which influenced and enriched him. He lived in a kind of naïve pragmatism. Out of individual experiences he did indeed seek to obtain a whole, a picture, but not a schematic system.

From the beginning Goethe's concept of the world was a confluence of many streams of tradition, which gradually crystallized into a unified whole, from which, in his maturity, there arose one of the greatest syntheses which the history of modern thought has produced. Now, as later, its basis was the pantheistic doctrine which had developed in European philosophy since the time of Giordano Bruno. Nature and spirit, phenomenon and essence, are one; the infinite is distributed in purely finite, independent, individual phenomena which together constitute a great all-embracing unity. Unity in multiplicity is the essence of the world. This Goethe first came to sense and believe at this time, overwhelmed as he was by the immeasurable multiplicity of the individual phenomena of life. The Renaissance's faith in the primal worth of life and of nature is here connected with confidence in the good qualities of the world and admiration for the illuminating beauty of its forms. If this faith and this confidence could be retained and deepened, then the demons of disappointment in life and cosmic pain could never carry off the victory. These things too the young poet knew. Faust, Clavigo, Fernando, Werther—all were crushed in their attempts to realize their infinite striving or their yearning for the abundance of existence. They suffer from the problem peculiar to mankind, involved in the fact that men belong to *two* realms. "Alas, that nothing is whole, nothing pure, in the world."

When he took leave of Frankfort, and at the same time of his youth, Goethe wrote in his journal: "Am I in the world only to be forever implicated in guiltless guilt?" And in a poem of the same period we read:

Could my whole being but once
Be filled, O Eternal, with thee! [5]

The task which confronted him was the perception which resolves this contradiction, namely, that there can be no such "implementation," and that moral perfection is a never-ending practical duty, a restless striving. The definitive answer appears only in the last act of *Faust*, where it is declared that man must find the substance of his life in the eternal feeling of dissatisfaction, in tirelessly striding forward, and that this is at once "torment and happiness." But the young Goethe had not attained to this ultimate wisdom. How could he have? But so much he had achieved that he could say Yes to life as it is, that he could accept the misery whose echoes we hear in *Faust* and *Werther* and still be ready to face life bravely in its relentless reality.

To bear the woe of earth and all its joy,
To tussle, struggle, scuffle with its storms,
And not be fearful in the crash of shipwreck.[6]

[5] Könnt' ich doch ausgefüllt einmal / Von dir, o Ew'ger, werden! (*Sehnsucht*, translated by W. H. McClain.)

[6] Der Erde Weh, der Erde Glück zu tragen, / Mit Stürmen mich herumzuschlagen / Und in des Schiffbruchs Knirschen nicht zu zagen. (*Faust*, v. 465, based on translation by Carlyle F. MacIntyre, p. 21.)

MIND

Weimar

THE CITY AT WHICH GOETHE ARRIVED IN NOVEMBER 1775 WAS THE MINIATURE CAPITAL OF A SMALL INDEPENDENT COUNTRY. IT HAD ABOUT 6,000 INHABITANTS at the time, and the entire duchy of Saxe-Weimar-Eisenach had fewer than 100,000. The officials and the citizens of Weimar all lived in the shadow of the stately castle. As late as 1803 Mme de Staël declares: "Weimar is not a small city, it is a large château." Goethe came to Weimar as the guest of the Duke Karl August, who was then eighteen years old. The young duke had been brought up by his mother, a woman of distinction, who had been widowed at eighteen and had held the regency for seventeen years. As tutor for her growing son, the educated duchess had obtained the services of Wieland, by far the most worldly and liberal among the German authors of the time, who from that time on resided at Weimar.

For Goethe this change of place meant a change of cultural climate also. He had come from the bourgeois mediocrity and the busy activity of a city of capitalists and merchants, where, as the spoiled son of an independent family, he had been able to live according to his own tastes, but where his quick and free nature had always made him a misfit. Now he found himself transported to the attractive atmosphere of a small aristocratic society gathered about a clever and highly cultivated woman, the Duchess Anna Amalia. Previously he had been able to look upon the whole world as an open field where he could exercise his gifts and energies; now he came into a milieu whose demands upon him he was at first unable to satisfy. He had sufficient perception to recognize the advantages of this "narrow-broad situation." In his journal he formulates its positive effect as a "more definite feeling of limitation and hence of truer expansion." Friendly reaction to his presence was not wanting. Wieland expressed the feelings of his new friends when he praised Goethe for trying to make all who approached him happy and for being himself happy for having participated in their existence: "A great, noble, substantial, and misunderstood man." Goethe sums up his first four years at Weimar in a letter to his mother:

> I have everything that a man can desire, a life in which I exercise myself daily and daily grow; and this time I will come to you healthy, without passion, without bewilderment, without dull business, but like a favorite of heaven who has spent half of his life, and out of past sorrow hopes for much good for the future, and has kept his breast prepared for future suffering.[1]

Three years later he wrote: "I could not think of or imagine a better place."

To be sure, the price which Fortune is wont to exact for her gifts had to be paid. Present in the new situation were forces which perceptibly disrupted the quiet process of Goethe's ripening to manhood. The Duke, who soon became Goethe's closest friend, was an absolute lord, but he was eight years younger than Goethe. Karl August's predilection for noisy restlessness, his impatient demands for primitive pleasures, forced the poet, if he wished to maintain and secure his new position, to join in a life which was bound to be repulsive to him because of its disturbing similarity to his own period of *Sturm und Drang* which he had already brought to an end. All over Germany stories were told of the mad goings-on at Weimar, and Goethe was made responsible for the scandalous behavior. Klopstock, the solemn guardian of the new ideal of poetic dignity, felt compelled to say a word of warning and admonition. Goethe's reply was: "Spare us such letters in the future." But to intimate friends Goethe himself remarked that his life was now like a sleigh-ride, "jingling and promenading up and down." "What a life!"

But he felt that even these unwanted experiences benefited him. They hastened his maturity and made him surer and firmer in his calm

[1] Ich habe alles was ein Mensch verlangen kann, ein Leben in dem ich mich täglich übe und täglich wachse, und komme diesmal gesund, ohne Leidenschaft, ohne Verworrenheit, ohne dumpfes Treiben, sondern wie ein von Gott Geliebter, der die Hälfte seines Lebens hingebracht hat, und aus vergangnem Leide manches Gute für die Zukunft hofft, und auch für künftiges Leiden die Brust bewährt hat. (August 9, 1779.)

opposition to the unrestrained vitality of his younger friend. In this school he learned prudence and patience, learned to accept the alien element in others as long as it was genuine and strong. Yet he was able to tolerate all of this only because he understood that his friend's condition was a natural stage in the development of a vigorous personality, a process of fermentation which had to be gone through. Just as the Duke recognized and respected the extraordinary man in Goethe, so the poet saw in the Duke the promise of hidden potentialities which merited respect. This was the foundation of a mutual relationship which survived all trials to the end. Goethe pictures his friend in this boisterous period in the great poem *Ilmenau* (1783):

> A noble heart, from Nature's proper way
> By close-confining destiny diverted.
> . . . . .
> In him, despite deep yearning for the truthful,
> Error is passionately clasped.
> . . . . .
> For him no path too strait, no cliff too steep.[2]

He admonishes the self-willed young ruler:

> But he who strives to govern others well
> Must ever able be much to renounce.[3]

In his old age Goethe called the Duke a man made out of whole cloth, by nature a great man, and acknowledged the presence in him of a demonic power which was too strong to exist within the limited proportions of his life's orbit. But with all of the respect which Goethe showed his prince, according to the custom of the day, he never descended to courtly flattery and servility, and even ventured many an outspoken and bold word when such a word seemed necessary.

In order to secure his position in the duchy and to earn his pay, it was inevitable that Goethe should participate in the business of administration. From the summer of 1776 he was associated with the min-

[2] Ein edles Herz, vom Wege der Natur / Durch enges Schicksal abgeleitet / . . . / Noch ist, bei tiefer Neigung für das Wahre, / Ihm Irrtum eine Leidenschaft / . . . / Kein Fels ist ihm zu schroff, kein Steg zu schmal. (Translated by B. Q. Morgan.)

[3] Allein wer andre wohl zu leiten strebt, / Muss fähig sein, viel zu entbehren. (*Ilmenau*.)

istry as privy councilor. He held, successively or concurrently, the commission of war (no great matter: Weimar had 660 soldiers), the department of road construction, the presidency of the administrative officials, and the commission of mines. His official duties were a burden which he bore with impatience. He groaned that he was not born for details, and furthermore, that he was much better suited for private existence than for an official post. Moreover, anyone who devoted himself to administration without being the sovereign authority was either a Philistine, a rogue, or a fool. But he also felt that precisely these tasks for which he was at first so inadequate had much to teach him, and that he daily grew richer by daily giving so much. Herder, who observed the spectacle with distaste, remarked that, in addition to all his official posts, Goethe was also director of pleasures, court poet, and "everywhere the first actor and dancer, in short, the factotum of Weimar." Goethe accepted it as a matter of expediency when in 1782 the Duke procured him a patent of nobility from the Emperor, because he could then play his role at court and in the country more conveniently. He could take no great satisfaction in the honor, he tells his lady in confidence. "We Frankfort patricians have always considered ourselves on a par with the nobility." As his coat of arms he received his beloved morning star, with six rays. After his return from Italy Goethe did not resume his official positions. But he remained the Duke's confidant even in political matters. He retained only supervision over the museums, the Weimar library, the university at Jena, and (from 1791 to 1817) the direction of the Weimar theater.

Goethe's concept of how practical politics should be managed, and how one should rule and administer, conforms to the views on the subject which prevailed among the enlightened political theorists of the second half of the eighteenth century. The principle of *raison d'état* was still in force. Thus social life was divided into two spheres: that of the ruling power, whose justification was no more questioned than its functions, and that of the ruled. In this system citizens could be thought of only as passive subjects who needed to form no common political will. The activity of the individual never came into contact with the sphere of the state. Policy and administration were solely in the hands of the ruler, the absolute prince, and his ministers. For the free development of the citizen's powers there remained only the sphere of professional activity and cultural improvement. This order

Goethe did not question. But it was obvious to him that neither the prince nor his officials could use and abuse their power capriciously, and that they must rather feel and comport themselves as ministers of the whole. He found that the *Compte rendu au Roi,* which the French minister Necker published in 1781, was an "excellent piece." He studied it diligently, along with the replies made to it. The stand taken in this treatise was Goethe's own: the state must care for all social classes; the prince must show himself "the good shepherd" of his subjects. The welfare of the entire population must be the highest consideration of social policy carried out in the spirit of patriarchal benevolence. Goethe conducted himself as minister accordingly. He sought to promote the welfare of the duchy. But the economic conditions of the small country were too modest, and its means too slight, for anything decisive to be done. "But unfortunately out of nothing nothing can come . . . Nevertheless, one waters a garden since one cannot provide rain for the country." [4]

Clear as was Goethe's insight into the failings of the current regimes in the German states, nothing was further from his mind than the notion that things might be improved by radical changes or even by revolution. The fact that intelligence and energy were so seldom united in a single person seemed to him a shortcoming which had to be accepted. "There are only a few who have intelligence and are at the same time capable of action. Intelligence expands, but cripples; action vitalizes, but limits." [5] On the other hand, Goethe did not believe that the German citizen had any real eagerness to participate in power. Like other German thinkers of his times, whose general philosophic outlook was as liberal and spirited as his, Goethe saw in a social order which embraced masters and subjects, rulers and ruled, an expression of the natural order, of simple necessity. Despotism, to be sure, even he considered as unnatural as it was fatal. All classes must serve the whole. But certain abuses, including the political ones, he considered as little capable of improvement as the shortcomings of human nature itself. A man who wished to alter them by force would squander his time and do more harm than good. Things could be cor-

[4] Nur leider aus nichts wird nichts . . . Indessen begiesst man einen Garten, da man dem Lande keinen Regen verschaffen kann. (Letter to Charlotte von Stein, June 9, 1784.)

[5] Es sind nur wenige, die den Sinn haben und zugleich zur Tat fähig sind. Der Sinn erweitert, aber lähmt; die Tat belebt, aber beschränkt. (*Wilhelm Meisters Lehrjahre,* Book VIII, chapter v.)

rected only by a will to equalize; everything depended on the balance of opposites, not on radical struggle.

These views Goethe developed through his practical experience as official and statesman during his early period at Weimar, and he never altered them basically. If we wish to formulate a single sentence expressing Goethe's political views, we might say that they reflect a personality who revered authority exercised with justice, and whose conservative mode of thought was balanced by the realization that there is rigidity in no sphere of life but everywhere continuous development. Goethe did not believe in planned and purposeful alteration of basic conditions; he trusted rather in the gradual organic growth of all living forms.

"Bliss of Nearest Nearness"

IN THIS PERIOD OF LEARNING AND RELEARNING, WHICH GOETHE HIMSELF CALLS HIS "NOVITIATE," NOTHING AND NO ONE WAS OF AS GREAT SIGNIFIcance as one woman, Charlotte von Stein. When Goethe came to Weimar she was thirty-three years old; for eleven years she had been the wife of a court official, a man of average gifts, to whom she had borne seven children. A woman already past her bloom, brought up with strict views on duty and morality, she obviously had neither need nor inclination for adventures. Her spirit, pitched in a key of idealism, led her to make the highest moral demands upon herself and others. She was not prepared to admit of compromise; human disillusionment she could neither forgive nor forget. Her notion of love centered in a community of intellect and soul: "And wished an angel when I loved a man."

Goethe's vigorous wooing first drove her back upon herself. She did not understand that the poet who possessed such true insight into men and the world did not conform to her strict moral standard. Did he really respect women? She thought that he and she could never become friends. But how could a woman who hungered for intellectual communion resist the enticement of becoming the confidante of such

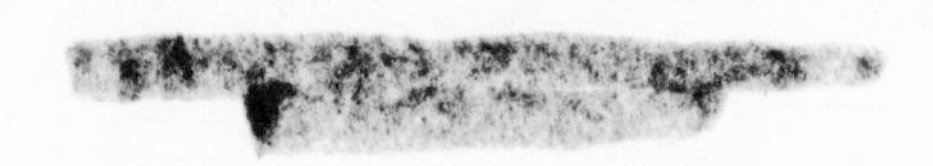

a man? His letters to her and his poems dedicated to her combined wooing and homage, passion and gratitude, yearning for ever-closer communion and readiness to conduct himself according to her wishes—combined them in a manner so delicate and at the same time so irresistible that, step by step, Charlotte could only yield. But it required several years before she surrendered herself entirely to her feelings. And even then she may not have become wholly his. Weimar gossip never dared imagine this relationship as such relationships are ordinarily imagined—and we can readily picture what a small capital can do if it wishes. If she had not destroyed her letters we would have certainty where we are now reduced to surmise. The crisis which eventually drove Goethe to Italy is intelligible only if we assume that Charlotte demanded a renunciation which in the end the man was no longer able to make.

> I cannot help living always for her,
> For whose sake I am not supposed to live.[1]

When, upon his return from Italy, she heard of his relationship to his "little darling," Christiane, and was deeply annoyed, he wrote her: "And what sort of relationship is it? For whom is it a deprivation? Who makes claims to the feelings which I bestow on the poor creature? Who to the hours which I spend with her?"[2] This must surely mean that Charlotte could not and would not be to him what his new beloved was.

In his writings Goethe constantly offered Charlotte new homage. Everywhere we find expression of a feeling of gratitude, of thankfulness for a pure happiness renewed and confirmed by every encounter. It is natural, he said, that one sex should experience sensually in the other the good and the beautiful. When Epimetheus (in the dramatic fragment *Pandora*) praises the overwhelming effect exercised by the beautiful when it is encountered embodied as a perfect phenomenon, he says that it appeared to him "in youthful, female form." Even at the end of *Faust* the supremely divine to which man's upward striving

[1] Leb' ich doch stets um derentwillen, / Um derentwillen ich nicht leben soll. (From the poem beginning: "Hier bildend nach der reinen stillen / Natur . . ." Translated by W. H. McClain.)

[2] Und welch ein Verhältnis ist es? Wer wird dadurch verkürzt? Wer macht Anspruch an die Empfindungen, die ich dem armen Geschöpf gönne? Wer an die Stunden, die ich mit ihr zubringe?

is directed is called the "eternal feminine." The letters and poems to Charlotte von Stein are filled with expressions in which the man's idealizing love creates a picture of human perfection. Before this "angel of a woman" he bows in grateful reverence.

The poem in which Goethe includes everything that he felt for his beloved and all that she meant to him was written at the beginning of his love, in April 1776.

> Why gav'st thou us these penetrating glances . . .[3]

He asks destiny why it is fated for men like himself to experience love not as a transitory illusion but as a deep and binding understanding, a mutual self-recognition in which one individual loses himself in the other. He seeks to explain to himself the importunate earnestness of a love such as he feels, a love which unites souls, by the thought that so intimate a bond is only possible if the present union is a recurrence of an earlier union.

> Ah! Thou wert in ages past
> My sister, or, may be, my wife.[4]

At the same time Goethe wrote to Wieland: "I can explain the importance—the power, which this woman has over me, only in terms of metempsychosis.—Yes, we were once man and wife! Now we have knowledge of one another—veiled, in a spiritual mist.—I have no name for us—the past—the future—the all."[5] Then we have the verses in which he expresses more clearly than in any of his letters what his love for Charlotte and his association with her meant for his inner life.

> On my heated blood shed'st moderation,
> Gav'st a goal to my mad, erring course,
> Thus my breast, when racked with desperation,
> In thy angel arms renewed its force.[6]

[3] Warum gabst du uns die tiefen Blicke . . . (*An Charlotte von Stein.*)

[4] Ach du warst in abgelebten Zeiten / Meine Schwester oder meine Frau. (*An Charlotte von Stein.*)

[5] Ich kann mir die Bedeutsamkeit—die Macht, die diese Frau über mich hat, anders nicht erklären als durch die Seelenwanderung.—Ja, wir waren einst Mann und Weib!—Nun wissen wir von uns—verhüllt, in Geisterduft.—Ich habe keine Namen für uns—die Vergangenheit—die Zukunft—das All. (Undated letter, perhaps April 1776.)

[6] Tropftest Mässigung dem heissen Blute, / Richtetest den wilden irren Lauf, / Und in deinen Engelsarmen ruhte / Die zerstörte Brust sich wieder auf. (*An Charlotte von Stein,* translated by B. Q. Morgan.)

Another time he says that she returned his purest feelings to him even purer.

No woman heretofore had meant so much to him. The greatest profit of this love was that the powers which could constrain his inward demon and satisfy his titanic unrest were strengthened. The man had to attain to clarity, firmness, and balance, so that the poet could achieve works of classical maturity. His beloved possessed what he sought; she could give him what he now needed more than anything else. He presented her character in idealized purity in the figure of Iphigenie. The bitter experiences of subsequent estrangement and the corrosive power of time did not dim Goethe's realization of how decisive for his entire future existence his association with Lida (as he calls her in the poems) had been. When at the age of seventy he attempted to say to whom his heart had most deeply and most unqualifiedly belonged and to whom he owed most as man and poet, he names, along with Shakespeare, only Charlotte.

> To one only belonging wholly,
> To revere one only, solely,
> So are joined the heart and mind!
> Lida! Bliss of nearest nearness!
> Shakespeare! Star of loftiest height!
> For what I am, I thank you twain.
> Days and years have passed with fleetness,
> Still there remains, in rich completeness,
> From those dear hours a priceless gain.[7]

[7] Einer Einzigen angehören, / Einen Einzigen verehren, / Wie vereint es Herz und Sinn! / Lida! Glück der nächsten Nähe, / William! Stern der schönsten Höhe, / Euch verdank' ich, was ich bin. / Tag' und Jahre sind verschwunden, / Und doch ruht auf jenen Stunden / Meines Wertes Vollgewinn. (*Zwischen beiden Welten*, based on translation by William Gibson, *The Poems of Goethe*, p. 328.)

New Lyric

IF GOETHE IS GERMANY'S GREATEST POET AND ONE OF THE GREATEST THAT THE WEST HAS SEEN, HIS FAME RESTS IN LARGE PART UPON HIS LYRIC POEMS. IN THIS genre he soared far above contemporary convention and reached heights hitherto unattained. The tone of natural simplicity for which the folk song had been his model no longer sufficed his richer and maturer personality. He retained the simple strophic form, the melodic flow of verse, the song elements in general; he remained true in expression of feeling, a master in the use of concrete imagery and of symbolic devices. But the naïve naturalism and spontaneous warmth of youth was now replaced by a mastery founded upon conscious control of all means of representation. His shortest lyrics reveal artistic and human maturity no less impressively than his more complex poems.

> Over all the hilltops
> Is rest,
> In all the treetops
> Thou feelest
> Scarce a breeze;
> The birds are stilled in the forest.
> Only wait, soon like these
> Thou too shalt rest.[1]

This is a night song of the "Wanderer," which Goethe composed spontaneously while standing alone upon a mountain, wrapped in the silence of nature at eventide. It is a genuine "occasional" poem, first of all in the sense that it was evoked by a specific, deeply felt experience. We know the place, the day, and the hour: it was written on the evening of September 6, 1780, on the plank wall of a hunting lodge in the Thuringian forest. But the occasion does more: it opens a momentary vista into the whole of existence. Is not life itself a journey

[1] Ueber allen Gipfeln / Ist Ruh, / In allen Wipfeln / Spürest du / Kaum einen Hauch; / Die Vögelein schweigen im Walde. / Warte nur, balde / Ruhest du auch. (*Wanderers Nachtlied,* translated by Emery Neff, *A Revolution in European Poetry,* p. 64, New York: Columbia University Press, 1940.)

at whose end waits the rest which will put a period to all unrest? Out of the silence of night, the dread of transitoriness seizes upon the soul of the wanderer. But at the same time there is another, friendly element, a foretaste of the final rest in which the heart's restless pendulum will come to its pause. Like the quiet of the night death will be good, a heavenly genius of peace.

The most important poem of this period is the song *An den Mond* ("To the Moon"; written after 1777). Again a restless heart engages in a dialogue with nature, who is man's fraternal partner, though man is separated from it by his aspiration for an individual existence. In the quiet light of the full moon, whose magic enchantment Goethe always loved, his soul reveals its hitherto silent depths. Rapture and anguish, yearning for permanence and the melancholy realization of the instability of life, are experienced, in the aftermath of self-contemplation, as natural and unalterable—like the changeful life of the river along whose bank the poet wanders. The steady crescendo of feeling reaches its culmination and is resolved in the solemnly stated conclusion. There is soulful praise for the man who is able to bear the insoluble problems of existence quietly within himself, without despairing of life, content if he have only a comrade with whom to share his inward experience. Other feelings and ideas chime in, overtones of the harmony which has been sounded. Through image, symbol, and rhythm the silent stirrings of the soul are given expression such as music alone can give.

During these years also the songs of *Der Harfner* ("The Harpist") and *Mignon,* which occur in the first version of *Wilhelm Meister,* were written. There are few verses in the modern poetry of any nation which are so purely lyrical, so complete an expression of an absolute emotion and nothing else, as the famous *Nur wer die Sehnsucht kennt* (familiarly but inadequately rendered as "None but the Lonely Heart"). Did anyone know what *Sehnsucht* was before Goethe told it here?

The second principal group of poems of the first Weimar period are the great hymns and rhapsodies. *Harzreise im Winter* ("Harz Journey in Winter"; 1777) was written on the occasion of a solitary excursion on the Brocken, the highest peak of the Harz range. It closes with solemn praise of the deity who is sublimely distant and at the same time "mysteriously manifest," like the mountain's peak above the plain. To him the poet surrenders himself with full trust. "The gods alone know what they want and what they want of us; their will be done." In the hymn *Meine Göttin* ("My Goddess"), phantasy is celebrated as the pleasing companion and liberator of men. *Grenzen der Menschheit* ("Limits of Humanity"), on the other hand, recalls with maturer insight the soaring pride of youth which is expressed in the Prometheus poem. The existence of the individual is represented as a wave in the eternal current of life, a link in the endless chain of humanity. The most beautiful in this group of poems in free verse is the *Gesang der Geister über den Wassern* ("Song of the Spirits over the Waters"). On his second journey to Switzerland Goethe saw the high waterfall at Interlaken, and it made "an endlessly agreeable and deep impression" upon him. The sight of the quiet and gently billowing spray filled his soul with a deep peace which permitted him to see the vicissitudes of life in their natural necessity under the aspect of the waters—permanence even in change, cohesion even in fragmentation. In imagery and idea all of these poems treat of man as he is integrated into the course of nature and subjected to the sway of superior powers.

Another hymn discourses on the special position of man in the whole universe and of the dignity which is peculiar to him and him alone. This poem is called *Das Göttliche* ("The Divine"); it speaks of that which raises man above nature and gives him his peculiar rank among other beings. Goethe here portrays man in the spirit of classic humanism, in words of perfect beauty and grandeur without being rhetorical. Man alone is capable of being selfless, kindly, brotherly, and of behaving according to intelligence and conviction. Capacity to lead his life according to his own law is here celebrated as the peculiarly divine in man. More than anything else it raises him above unfeeling nature and inert destiny. It is his determination to make himself fully human, which for man is tantamount to making himself moral. Thus, while he is fulfilling himself more completely as man, he approaches nearer to the gods, whom he envisages in accordance with the purest idea which he can conceive of himself. The poem closes with an injunction, as it had begun. It challenges the will, the noblest conceivable, to soar, to attain perfection.

The Voice of Humanity

Es hört sie jeder,
Geboren unter jedem Himmel . . .[1]

IPHIGENIE AUF TAURIS, ONE WOULD THINK, MUST SURELY BE THE FRUIT OF GOETHE'S LIFE IN ITALY, OF HIS ASSOCIATION WITH THE MONUMENTS OF ANCIENT art. But though this play received its final form during the Italian sojourn, it had in fact been completed seven years before his departure. It is the first evidence of Goethe's turning to the classical ideal and style. Clarity and balance, moral restraint and serenity of soul—the qualities which Goethe found realized in the life of Charlotte von Stein—comprise the spiritual substance of his "Grecizing drama." Additional factors, from the artistic point of view, were his growing appreciation of Greek plastic arts and his attempts to comprehend their peculiar beauty by making sketches of classic forms. Goethe's attention was now also turned to the human body, even while carrying on his studies in natural science. In Jena, where the university institute afforded him opportunity, he pursued studies in anatomy, and at the small drawing school at Weimar he lectured on osteology.

Such is the moral and intellectual atmosphere in and out of which *Iphigenie* came into being and matured. The first version, written down in 1779, already exhibits the new style. It is still on the level of prose; but the prose, no longer the natural utterance of the earlier dramas, is now one which seeks to approximate the ideal of a poetically enhanced and yet not too deeply emotional expression. Shortly thereafter Goethe attempted to put the entire play into free verse and thus elevate it a degree. But the verse style was so unsuccessful that he rewrote it in prose. In this state he left it lying, a victim of the stagnation of his creative powers by which he was increasingly afflicted. His first experiences on Italian soil quickened his spirit. On his journey to Rome Goethe saw Raphael's picture of St. Agatha in Bologna. He admired the "healthy and sure virginity" of the figure, which was

[1] All men can hear it, / Born 'neath any sky . . . (*Iphigenie,* Act V, scene 3, translated by B. Q. Morgan.)

depicted without sensual charm but also without frigidity or crudeness. This was the ideal which he would impose upon his play; he would not allow Iphigenie to say anything that the saint might not utter. Here, as in the plastic art of the Greeks, he found purity and clarity of form, and external beauty as an expression of inner spiritual beauty. This was what he now sought, as man and as artist.

Euripides' *Iphigenia among the Taurians* supplied the fable. But the German's work transposed the ancient composition into a sphere so un-Greek and so modern that a thoroughly new drama emerged—new in content as in form. In the drama of the Greeks, man is subordinate to the superior power of the gods and of fate. Whatever he desires and whatever he does is subject to the intervention of higher forces. Fate is a force which follows its own logic without considering the wishes of the individual. This concept of man has nothing in common with that which the European writers after the Renaissance expressed in their dramas. Whereas the action of the new drama develops out of the character of the hero, and his destiny seems to be identical with his character and to arise out of his will, ancient tragedy (as Goethe later formulated it in his treatise *Shakespeare und kein Ende*) rests "upon an inexorable Should which is only sharpened and hastened by the counterirritant Would." Whereas the ideal of the modern world is the self-determining, free individual, the ancient dramas are dominated by a despotic necessity which crushes the individual whenever he ventures to challenge it. Nothing could be more alien to Goethe's current thought and feeling than the fatalistic pessimism of Greek tragedy. At no period of his life was faith in mankind and in the friendly constitution of the world clearer and surer. Iphigenie expresses this deep trust:

> For the Immortals regard with affection
> Far-flung races of men that are goodly,
> And then lengthen the fleeting existence
> Gladly of mortals, granting them gladly
> Time to share in the blessed enjoyment
> Born of gazing in reverence happy
> At their heaven, divine and eternal.[2]

[2] Denn die Unsterblichen lieben der Menschen / Weit verbreitete gute Geschlechter, / Und sie fristen das flüchtige Leben / Gerne dem Sterblichen, wollen ihm gerne / Ihres eigenen, ewigen Himmels / Mitgeniessendes fröhliches Anschaun / Eine Weile gönnen und lassen. (*Iphigenie,* Act I, scene 4, translated by B. Q. Morgan.)

Goethe's drama is intended to set forth what man can be if he accepts fate because he sees in it the higher will of friendly gods, if he tames the demons in his own breast and realizes his native potentiality for self-perfection. Pure humanity heals all human failings; the forces of fate retreat before the power of a steadfast and noble soul.

Euripides dramatizes a familiar legend, the myth of Tantalus and his unhappy race who must expiate the guilt of their presumptuous ancestor. Orestes slew his mother because she was responsible for the death of his father, Agamemnon. The ancient law of blood vengeance demanded this frightful retribution, and Apollo had also enjoined it. But the deed alone, and not its motive, is what counts. As the price for absolution from his guilt Orestes must fetch the image of Artemis, Apollo's sister, from Tauris, where it was worshipped by barbarians against the will of the goddess. Among the Taurians, Orestes and his friend Pylades discover Iphigenia, Orestes' sister who they believed had perished. She helps her brother steal the image of the goddess whom she served as priestess: the Greek is not obliged to extend to barbarians loyalty and truth. But the project would have miscarried if the *deus ex machina* in the form of Athena had not suddenly appeared and brought everything to a happy ending. Orestes is absolved and returns to Greece with Iphigenia.

Of this fable Goethe retains only the basic elements. In the hands of the modern poet the dramatized myth is transformed into a psychological drama. The curse, the guilt, the adventure of the abduction, all become a matter of inward life. Here man does not receive his law of conduct from without: he legislates for himself and struggles for the possibility of working out his law in freedom. In Euripides, fate has the effect of a curse which adheres to the race of Tantalus; to the modern poet the notion of tribal guilt is as intolerable as that of gods who exact unjust vengeance of individuals.

> For each man, be he good or evil, takes
> With him the just reward for what he's done.
> One can inherit blessings, not a curse.[3]

The curse under which Orestes labors lies within himself, in the state of his spirit; it is his deficiency in "moderation and wisdom and pa-

[3] Ein jeglicher, gut oder böse, nimmt / Sich seinen Lohn mit seiner Tat hinweg. / Es erbt der Eltern Segen, nicht ihr Fluch. (*Iphigenie*, Act II, scene 1, translated by B. Q. Morgan.)

tience." The Greek Orestes is pursued by the Erinyes; in Goethe's play these mythical avenging spirits are transformed into demons of "feverish delusion" in the soul of a noble man from whom too heavy a task has been required. Here, then, the curse too can be resolved by a spiritual act, by purging, purification, pacification. Man is redeemed by man; Iphigenie's pure humanity is the luminous power which vanquishes fate and banishes the spirits of delusion from the soul of her brother.

> O Holy one . . . Touched by thee,
> I found my cure.[4]

In the end her high humanity prevails even over "violence and cunning, men's proudest boast." For her there are neither barbarians and Greeks nor races and classes but only faith in the worth of all who bear a human countenance and live in the community of good will. Incapable of lying, she reveals to the barbarian king the secret of the captives and their complot. "Destroy us—if you think you dare." When Thoas bitterly rejoins that she must then believe that the barbarian would heed the voice of truth and humanity to which the Greek, Atreus, her wicked ancestor, did not hearken, Iphigenie replies with a profession of her faith in the universal validity of humanity. Of its voice she says:

> All men can hear it,
> Born 'neath any sky,
> In whom the source of life flows through the heart
> Unsullied and unchecked.[5]

For a moment Iphigenie's pure soul is disturbed by the old picture of the gods who were vengeful and demanded of men things contrary to the dictates of their conscience. But for her such authority would be intolerable. The boding tones of the song of the Parcae recall the horror of destiny which she has overcome, the feeling of desperate helplessness among dark powers. But the new, pure faith maintains its victory. Her heart which has retained its strength in prayer is in-

[4] Du Heilige . . . Von dir berührt / War ich geheilt. (*Iphigenie,* Act V, scene 6, translated by B. Q. Morgan.)

[5] Es hört sie jeder, / Geboren unter jedem Himmel, dem / Des Lebens Quelle durch den Busen rein / Und ungehindert fliesst. (*Iphigenie,* Act V, scene 3, translated by B. Q. Morgan.)

capable of deception, for it is through moral sensibility that the gods speak to men. The image which is here saved is not, as it is in the legend, the statue of Artemis, but the image of the gods in Iphigenie's soul, the ikon of her faith. Other poets, the French C. G. de la Touche, for example, had anticipated Goethe in remaking the ancient Iphigenia into a modern human being. But neither they nor their successors have given more beautiful and purer expression to the basic faith in humanity than Goethe has done in asserting that the man who trusts the divine over him and in him is capable of self-perfection, and that this achievement can be his. The ideal of noble simplicity and serene grandeur which German philhellenes admired in the art of the Greeks was here realized in the medium of modern language. Goethe's *Iphigenie* will always remain one of the purest manifestations of European morality and art. The German above all may point to this work as the noblest expression of his highest essence and success whenever his essence and his worth are questioned by himself and by the world. This is a modern, an un-Greek work, the product of an age which has been surpassed in moral culture by no other in the history of the West. Its ancient costume cannot disguise the fact that the humanity incarnated in Iphigenie is a synthesis of the ideal of Christian morality and the new, as yet quite sentimental, concept of Greek antiquity. In antiquity there were no "beautiful souls."

Here the natural is in a sense sublimated, a process only possible after centuries of Christian discipline. But the "moral beauty" (as Shaftesbury would say) is raised to such a pitch that a figure of priestly purity emerges. Can Iphigenie be imagined in love? Can her peace of soul be attained at a lesser price than total abnegation of the life decreed for man, as the being suspended between nature and spirit and forever struggling to retain an insecure equilibrium between them? Schiller judged Iphigenie as follows: "She is moral, and moral only; but in sensual force, life, motion, and all that gives a work a specific and genuine dramatic character, she is very wanting." Even in 1802, when the play was produced in the Weimar theater, Goethe found it "devilishly humane" and said that it recalled to him "a state more than past." He called it his "child of sorrow" and was almost apologetic about it; if he had known Greek antiquity better at the time, he said, he would not have written *Iphigenie*.

All life in this play proceeds from the soul; inward life is the true reality; inward movements constitute the action in this drama, which is poor in external happenings. As against the quiet working of a life which contents itself within a narrowly limited sphere, masculine activity and bold enterprise in the dangerous world without seem crude and bleak. The matriarchal quality of the ethical content is more closely akin to the saintly women in Raphael's pictures than to the powerful grandeur of Greek statues. But in the style of dramatic representation the manner of plastic art is dominant. As in Gluck's operas on classic themes, the *dramatis personae* confront one another like living statues and give expression to their inward life in fully formed utterances. Only at the climax, which comes precisely at the middle of the play, in the scenes involving Orestes, does the slowly mounting action become vigorous and explicit. Each act is dominated by a single person; in the first it is Iphigenie, in the second Pylades, in the third Orestes, then again Iphigenie, and in the final act Thoas. The small number of persons, the relegation of events to a locale off stage, the preponderance of dialogue over action, are all more in the spirit of French "high tragedy" than of the ancient drama. There is no chorus; its place is taken by monologues. Shortly before his journey to Italy Goethe had read the *Electra* of Sophocles. The "long iambs" of the Greek trimeter pleased him, and with Herder's help he attempted to appropriate their character. In Rome he transformed *Iphigenie* into a poetic form modeled on Shakespeare's blank verse; Goethe's play, along with Lessing's *Nathan* (1779), assured the dominance of the iambic pentameter in German drama for a century.

Only in one respect is Goethe's play related to Greek antiquity. As an entity, in spirit and structure, in the sublimity of its conception and its language, in its dramatic dynamism and its dialogue, it is the first of Goethe's works to demonstrate his new understanding of Greek art as Winckelmann had taught him to appreciate it. The clarity and regularity of form, the inner control and serene grandeur, which the German admired in the works of the ancients and of their modern followers, he attempted to attain in his own composition, not by imitation but by creation after his own manner. This drama does not copy Greek form and does not repeat ancient interpretation of the world and of life. It proclaims and glorifies an ideal of humanity in which the refined morality of the Christian West is united with longing for the beauty of Greek art.

A few years after the *Iphigenie* was first written, Goethe treated the theme of humanity in an epic poem which attempted to give a broad philosophic view. It is called *Die Geheimnisse* ("The Secrets"). In 1784 the first volume of Herder's main work, the *Ideen zur Philosophie der Geschichte der Menschheit* ("Ideas on the Philosophy of the History of Mankind"), appeared. Humanitarianism, it is here stated, is the concept of the noble vocation of man and attains its fairest flowering in religion. The unfolding of the natural tendency toward humanitarianism is the loftiest meaning in the development of the individual as in that of the whole race. Herder wrote: "From the beginning of life onward our soul seems to have only one task, the attainment of inward stature, of the form of humanity . . ." A similar sentiment had been previously expressed in Lessing's *Nathan*, which Goethe admired greatly.

To the realm of these ideas Goethe's *Iphigenie* belongs, as does this symbolic poem also. *Die Geheimnisse* was planned on too large a scale, however, and never reached completion. Only twenty-four stanzas were finished. In the spirit of the century, in which secret societies and Masonic lodges played so large a role, Goethe describes an order of noble knights. Lessing and other contemporary writers had proposed conjectures concerning the relationship of Freemasonry to the medieval order of Knights Templar. In the poem, twelve knights represent twelve religions, the worship of various ages and peoples. Their grand master is called Humanus. Each knight worships God after his own manner, but as a group they are united into a community by their reverence for this "elect" and by the contact which each of them upon his path has once had with him. In the sanctuary of the order there stands, as its high symbol, the cross; but the cross is surrounded by a garland of roses to give a friendly covering to the "harsh wood." The tale of the Rosicrucians, a Neoplatonic fraternity of the seventeenth century which existed only in the wishful dreams of Johann Valentin Andreae, was still current in Goethe's lifetime. He was acquainted with the most famous of Andreae's writings, the *Chymische Hochzeit des Christiani Rosenkreutz*. In the eighteenth century there appeared an order which called itself the Rosicrucian.

The principal symbols of the poem are not difficult to interpret. Here the faith of the great humanists of the eighteenth century finds its poetic transfiguration. It is a belief in the general religion of humanity, a universal morality and love, which, they felt, constituted the everlasting kernel of the positive religions, otherwise so diverse in dogma and creed. These religious beliefs appear as variants of an ideal basic form, which they approximate most closely in their highest representatives and in their periods of bloom. The cross, symbol of Christianity, the most important among the religions based on the mystery of transitoriness and redemption, is garlanded with roses. The emblem of beautiful life, of flourishing existence, is linked to the melancholy reminder of death; the two in combination constitute the whole of the religion of humanity. Humanus is an intermediary figure of the sort which appears in all religions. In him the knights can perceive their master, because his moral attributes are of the highest. His essence is nature sublimated: restraint of passions through intellect, free self-determination through self-domination.

> For every force forever forward presses
> To live and work unceasing everywhere,
> The while from every side we meet duresses
> Of life's great current, onward us to bear.
> In all this inward storm, these outward stresses,
> Our mind of one great truth becomes aware:
> That power which holds all beings fast and faster
> Man can escape if he himself but master.[6]

It is easy to see how closely related this is to Spinoza's doctrine of the correct love of God and of the power of intellect over the emotions.

Goethe's doctrine of humanity as a practical goal for the individual and for mankind, of advancing humanization through increasing control of the intellect over the natural emotions, is the ethical comple-

[6] Denn alle Kraft dringt vorwärts in die Weite, / Zu leben und zu wirken hier und dort; / Dagegen engt und hemmt von jeder Seite / Der Strom der Welt und reisst uns mit sich fort. / In diesem innern Sturm und äussern Streite / Vernimmt der Geist ein schwer verstanden Wort: / Von der Gewalt, die alle Wesen bindet, / Befreit der Mensch sich, der sich überwindet. (*Die Geheimnisse,* translated by B. Q. Morgan.)

ment of his pantheistic picture of the world. But the two concepts, the experience of an infinite God in nature outside ourselves and the constraint of nature within ourselves, are as yet unrelated to one another. When he became aware of the Roman environment and learned to appreciate ancient works of art and the Mediterranean way of life, Goethe realized that the idea of humanity, here proposed, required reworking. It seemed to him now that in the northern countries men frequently "have more of the ideal in them than they can use, than they can exploit," and that they are therefore inclined to exaggerations in emotions and in faith. In a letter from Rome he speaks of his pleasure in reading the newest volume of Herder's *Ideen*. Goethe, too, believed that humanity would conquer in the end. Yet he adds: "But I am afraid that at the same time the world will become a large hospital and that all individuals will become one another's humanitarian nurses." [7]

As introduction to *Die Geheimnisse* Goethe composed a poem, which he then removed and placed as a *Zueignung* ("Dedication") at the beginning of the first collected edition of his works, which he published in 1787. In the form of an allegorical story, it expresses his own concept of his mission as poet. As he wanders through nature in the early morning a goddess appears to him. She speaks to him and reminds him that she had been his comrade, aid, and comfort from his youth. When the poet recognizes her he renews his gratitude and vows that he will receive future happiness also from her alone. Her name? Everyone calls her his own, but to virtually every eye her aspect is unbearable; whoever serves her must enjoy his fortune alone.

> Ah! I had many comrades whilst I strayed—
> I know thee now, and stand almost alone.[8]

She admonishes him not to withdraw into a feeling of his own singularity, but "to fulfill the duty of a man." The poet replies with vigorous assurance of his readiness. He knows that he must transmit her gifts to his fellow men and be a helpful friend and guide to them.

[7] Nur fürcht ich, dass zu gleicher Zeit die Welt ein grosses Hospital und einer des andern humaner Krankenwärter werden wird.

[8] Ach, da ich irrte, hatt' ich viel Gespielen, / Da ich dich kenne, bin ich fast allein. (*Zueignung*, translated by W. Edmondstoune Aytoun and Theodore Martin, New York; Holt and Williams, 1871.)

In me the gift grows but to be partaken,
I can and will no more the talent hide,
Why did I seek the way with such endeavor,
If to my brothers I shall show it never? [9]

The goddess bestows upon him the gift which consecrates him to her service and now pronounces her name: she is Truth, and from her hand he receives the veil of poesy. To utter the truth of whatever he may be speaking is the task of the poet; this is his service to humanity. For other eyes the sight of truth unveiled is "pain"; only the poet can endure it. He must communicate it to humanity, veiled in images, similes, allegories, symbols. Employing the language of the senses, art produces something supersensual, something spiritual.

The veil of song, by Truth's own fingers given,
Of sunlight woven and the morning air.[10]

By doing this service, poetry and poetry alone relieves mankind from the heavy burden of life: "Day becomes lovely, night becomes bright." [11]

The Tragedy of the Artist

IN HIS YOUTH GOETHE SUFFERED FROM INWARD UNREST, FROM A LACK OF SPIRITUAL BALANCE, WHICH WAS THE PAINFUL CONSEQUENCE OF HIS EXTRAORDINARY genius. Now, in the years when his person attained the form and maturity of manhood, he discovered that an incongruity between himself and his environment nevertheless persisted. He understood that this was the consequence of insoluble dissonances between the requirements of a productive individual and the demands of society.

[9] Für andre wächst in mir das edle Gut, / Ich kann und will das Pfund nicht mehr vergraben! / Warum sucht' ich den Weg so sehnsuchtsvoll, / Wenn ich ihn nicht den Brüdern zeigen soll? (*Zueignung*, translated by William Gibson, *The Poems of Goethe*, p. 1.)

[10] Aus Morgenduft gewebt und Sonnenklarheit, / Der Dichtung Schleier aus der Hand der Wahrheit. (*Zueignung*, translated by W. Edmondstoune Aytoun and Theodore Martin, *Poems and Ballads of Goethe*.)

[11] Der Tag wird lieblich, und die Nacht wird helle.

Following the habit of his nature, he sought to obviate the danger which he saw implicit in this realization by taking flight "behind a picture." As he had written *Werther* to heal himself of the sentimentality which was the disease of his generation, so he neutralized the tormenting problem of his existence as an artist by giving it objectivity in a tragic figure and thus bringing it to a close. The story of the Italian poet, Tasso, which supplied the material for his new drama, appeared to offer a situation similar to the one which he must himself confront, to involve the same conflict as the one he must himself resolve. The attraction that drew him to this subject emanated from his innermost nature. "I can justly say of my work that it is bone of my bone and flesh of my flesh." *Torquato Tasso* was begun shortly after *Iphigenie*. Here, too, Goethe did not succeed in finishing the play straightway; not more than two acts were written, in poetic prose. In Italy the work was resumed, and it was carried on there as a new scheme and in a new verse pattern. Only in 1789 was the play finally completed, in Weimar, shortly after Goethe's return.

When, forty years later, Jean Jacques Ampère compared the hero of this drama to Werther, Goethe agreed and himself called him "an intensified Werther." The absolute quality of a passionate soul finds itself in conflict with the demands of the world, is incapable of reaching a solution, and is irresistibly drawn to its destruction. But whereas Werther's condition is morbid demoralization, which is intensified to so high a pitch by the special circumstances of a passing situation, Tasso's problem arises out of the inalterable composition of his nature. Other circumstances would not have changed his constitution. Only if he could lay aside what comprised his special worth, if he could cease to be a poet, could he avoid the conflict which leads him to his destruction. But this was to demand the impossible. The theme of this play is, as Goethe said, "the disproportion between talent and life." It is the tragedy of an artist that is here presented. *Tasso* is the first great work to deal with the problem of art and life, artist and society, a problem which has since played such a large role in the literature of Europe.

This drama objectifies painful experiences poetically. Goethe, during his first Weimar period, attempts to reconcile the egotism of genius, which demands unqualified realization, with the requirements of environment. Always and everywhere the artist exists in the dichotomy between fantasy and reality, idea and deed, freedom and law, the self-created world of poetic dreams and the assured world of general normal life. The sensitive women around him best understand why, even in the small circle of educated aristocrats which constitutes a kind of ideal audience, Tasso is unable to make a move without forever bruising both himself and his friends.

> But Tasso's eye scarce rests upon this earth;—
> His ear perceives all nature's harmonies;—
> . . . . .
> Oft he ennobles what seems mean to us,
> And sets at nought what we most highly prize.
> Within this magic circle wandering,
> The gifted man attracts, and draws us on
> To wander with him and to feel with him.
> He seems approaching—and approaches not;
> He seems to look on us, and spirits might,
> For what appears, be standing in our place.[1]

Solitude is essential to the poet; only when he is alone with his own spirit can he produce the works with which he favors the world. It appears as if he required nothing more than his own ego. But inasmuch as his work arises out of his contact with life, he requires an audience for whom to create. Art is communication. It is, as Goethe says, a work of man *for* man.

> Man's talent ripens in tranquillity,
> His character in battling with the world.[2]

Talent alone does not make a great poet, only talent plus personality. But how was Tasso to live with others, immoderate and intense as he was in joys and sorrows, in trust and distrust, longing for men

[1] Sein Auge weilt auf dieser Erde kaum; / Sein Ohr vernimmt den Einklang der Natur; / . . . / Oft adelt er, was uns gemein erschien, / Und das Geschätzte wird vor ihm zu nichts. / In diesem eignen Zauberkreise wandelt / Der wunderbare Mann und zieht uns an, / Mit ihm zu wandeln, teil an ihm zu nehmen: / Er scheint sich uns zu nahn, und bleibt uns fern; / Er scheint uns anzusehn, und Geister mögen / An unsrer Stelle seltsam ihm erscheinen. (*Tasso,* Act I, scene 1, based on translation by J. Cartwright, p. 10, London: Nutt, 1859.)

[2] Es bildet ein Talent sich in der Stille, / Sich ein Charakter in dem Strom der Welt. (*Tasso,* Act I, scene 2, translated by J. Cartwright, p. 16.)

with whom to share his feelings and yet always fleeing them again, bruised and beaten, to his own solitude?

Still another side of Tasso's character constitutes a problem to himself and to others. Has he any right to expect others to endure his difficult nature with tolerance and forbearance? What does Tasso contribute to the world? Does life require his art in the degree that he requires life? Social humanity confronts the self-confident individualist in the person of the Princess, who is a poetically enhanced image of Charlotte von Stein. When Tasso expresses the basic principle of unqualified freedom, such as the ego demands, in "what pleases is permitted" (in his *Aminta* the Italian poet had said, *S'ei piace, ei lice*), the Princess replies, "What is proper is permitted" (so Guarini in his *Pastor Fido* answered Tasso, *Piaccia se lice*). Another antagonist is the Duke, a cultivated man of the world, who masters life with wisdom because he is able to dominate himself. But Tasso's real antagonist, the figure who stands in the relationship of complementary, polar opposition to him, is Antonio, the man of practical understanding, of constant activity. Antonio embodies all that the poet lacks of being a true man capable of coping with life in all its aspects. Tasso and Antonio together make up the play of forces in the midst of which Goethe himself is poised and whose balance he seeks to find in order to attain peace in his own soul. But can the great poet ever hope actually to conquer that other aspect, represented by the prudent realist? When Antonio shows himself a friend in the hour of collapse and urges Tasso to turn outward to the world in order to gain as man what he would lose as poet, Tasso answers that a life in which he did not dream and compose would no longer be life to him.

> Dost thou the silkworm e'er forbid to spin,
> Because he spins himself more near his death? [3]

He is incapable of compromise, of abnegation; he can be no other than what he is. If these qualities set him apart from society, they alone make him capable of producing "great art." And it is through his work that he expresses the idea of the free, original personality which challenges ephemeral convention.

[3] Verbiete du dem Seidenwurm, zu spinnen, / Wenn er sich schon dem Tode näher spinnt. (*Tasso*, Act V, scene 2, translated by C. des Voeux, p. 187, Weimar, 1833.)

In the end Tasso stands alongside his new-found friend Antonio—an unexpected bond which is not altogether credible psychologically. Will this bond give the desperate man a new and serener existence? Goethe spoke of this drama as a particularly "consistent composition." But does he indeed dare carry consistency to its conclusion? Does not the poet rather recoil before the unveiled spectacle of destruction? Tasso says that the bark of his life is shipwrecked, that he has saved his bare life like the sailor who clings to the rock upon which he has foundered. Is that enough? Can it be enough for a man like Tasso? Along with the respect of his friends he has lost his self-respect, and along with this ideal circle of friends the hope of ever again finding a society for which he can dream and compose. "All that is tragic," Goethe later said, "rests upon an irreconcilable opposition. When compromise occurs or becomes possible, the tragic vanishes." [4] How could reconciliation be conceivable here? Thrice in this last scene Tasso says No to every hope.

> I am rejected, I am banished, yes,
> Myself I've banished . . . No! All is past! [5]

Nothing is left him to alleviate his situation but the very thing which was the cause of his misfortune: his poetic mission.

> And if mankind are in their torments mute,
> A God allowed me to tell the pangs I feel.[6]

How could the cause itself ever be removed? Again and again Tasso would demand the impossible of himself and others, driven by the demon who knows no accommodation, no compromise. "To live in the idea means to treat the impossible as if it were possible."

The historical Tasso sickened in soul at the end of his restless life. Did not madness await Goethe's hero? Schopenhauer seems to be of this opinion, and Richard Wagner so interpreted the end of *Tasso*. Such a catastrophe is not made explicit, but it is implicit in the nature of the artist in his inalterable incompatibility with society—implicit

[4] Alles Tragische beruht auf einem unausgleichlichen Gegensatz. So wie Ausgleichung eintritt oder möglich wird, schwindet das Tragische.

[5] Ich bin verstossen, bin verbannt, ich habe / Mich selbst verbannt . . . Nein, alles ist dahin. (*Tasso,* Act V, scene 5, translated by C. des Voeux, p. 206.)

[6] Und wenn der Mensch in seiner Qual verstummt, / Gab mir ein Gott, zu sagen, wie ich leide. (*Tasso,* Act V, scene 5, translated by C. des Voeux, p. 208.)

at least as a macabre possibility, which would become actual if ever circumstances would place a slight increment in the scale of misfortune. The "if" points to Goethe's individual case. In this play, as in *Werther,* the poet saves himself by making his poetic image pay the fatal price. *Ecce poeta*—the inclination to self-willed ruin is present in each of these two exponents of the problem of existence. But since this contradiction in them is inevitable, one is not justified in judging them from the moral point of view. Here, too, right (and also wrong) is on both sides. Without social humanity, which demands abnegation and discipline of the individual, peaceful communal life is not possible; without the extraordinary, the creative personality, all culture would stiffen and decay. Life requires the deeds of the man of action as much as the visions and works of the artist; but the world is not so constituted that both kinds of achievement can be realized in a single person. The contradiction cannot be adjusted. But the movement of life arises from oppositions and tensions.

Like *Iphigenie, Tasso* belongs to the type of spiritual drama which Goethe created. In its peculiar association of the lyric with the dramatic this type takes its own position along with the dramas of Shakespeare and Schiller. Action is reduced to the minimum so that the inner life can appear with greater purity and richness. In *Tasso* Goethe's diction attains even greater sublimity and maturity, if that were possible, than in *Iphigenie.* The clarity, truth, and beauty of expression are as perfect as the rhythmic progress, the melodic flow of the verses. A style which gives the individual obviously general applicability, so that the specific case stands for all cases, is truly classic; it reveals, in Walter Pater's expression, "the type in the individual." Hence the wealth of aphorisms which distinguishes this play. In them individual experiences are crystallized into a penetrating and universally valid insight which is set, like a fine gem, in a beautiful mounting. The characters themselves become representative of universal forces and attitudes in life; the action as a whole becomes the symbol of the polarized dynamism of the life process. Events are governed by a supreme necessity, and the whole is suffused by the clear light of inexorable truth; there is no accident, no caprice.

Italy

GOETHE'S RESOLUTION TO GO TO ITALY AROSE FROM AN URGE TO FREE HIMSELF FROM THE PROFOUND CRISIS WHICH HAD BEEN TROUBLING HIM FOR YEARS. It was the crisis of a mature man who had squandered the energies and ideas of his youth and was now besieged by an abundance of new insights and plans without being able to release in artistic creation the vital forces pent up within him. Goethe's first decade in Weimar is like a large building site covered with excavations, foundations for new enterprises, half-finished structures. *Egmont, Iphigenie, Tasso,* the dramatic fragment *Elpenor,* the great novel, the philosophic epic *Die Geheimnisse,* researches in natural science—not one of these works and enterprises then reached completion. His productive sap and energies were as vital as ever at this period; but the power to carry things through to completion failed. His creative spirit was in want of clarity and assurance because he lacked the knowledge which only new and basic experiences could procure him, experiences which were not to be had in the familiar and limited environment of Germany. Goethe himself now regarded what he had previously thought, known, and achieved as inadequate. The work he envisioned could not be developed out of what had gone before. Past achievements now seemed to him not true in idea and not pure in form, seemed arbitrary, confused, and bleak. "My titanic ideas were only figures of air, apparitions of a more serious epoch to come." He must make a new beginning, submit to a new period of instruction. Concerning the school to which he must go to restore his poetic productivity he had long been clear. Only the presence and the sight of the great works of ancient art could give him what he required. He must go where "the ground and the alpha and omega of all art" was still preserved; he must go to Rome.

It was in Weimar that Goethe first acquired a deeper understanding of ancient culture and art. He studied the classic work in which the new appreciation of Greek antiquity was presented, Winckelmann's *Geschichte der Kunst des Altertums* (1764). The "noble simplicity and serene grandeur" of Greek works was here opposed, as the norm of true art, to the pathos and the agitated style of the Baroque, as well as to the playful grace of the Rococo. The modern artist and poet, Winckelmann proclaimed, could become great and original only by imitating the ancients. Other critics of the century, Shaftesbury for example, had expressed similar convictions, but none with such decisiveness. The doctrine of imitation which had been much discussed from the Renaissance on pointed to the beauties of nature as a proper model for the artist, but Winckelmann maintained that something higher was to be found in the works of the Greeks—an ideal beauty, a "primal beauty," such as only the creative spirit of man could imagine. This perfect beauty could be experienced in the artistic works of the Greeks more quickly and in purer essence than in the phenomena of nature; compared to these, beauty which we find in nature is but as a shadow.

At the same time Goethe also read the writings of Raphael Mengs, who was a friend of Winckelmann and the most famous classicist among the painters of his time. Here too the new idealist doctrine (whose connection with the Neoplatonic tradition one should not fail to recognize) was presented. In pure beauty, divine perfection is visible; in nature such perfection is not encountered, but it is to be found in the works of the Greek artists. Hence modern artists must learn to look upon nature through the eyes of the Greeks. Among the earlier painters Mengs regarded as valid only those of the Italian Renaissance—Raphael, Titian, Correggio. This critical judgment left its impression upon Goethe. For him, too, Raphael was the culmination of Western art, whereas he regarded Michelangelo with many reservations.

His own viewpoint Goethe expressed summarily in a report on the treatise of the Berlin art critic, Karl Philipp Moritz, whose acquaintance he had made in Rome. Entitled *Ueber die bildende Nachahmung des Schönen* ("On the Imitation of the Beautiful in Art"; 1788), the treatise, as Goethe himself says, is the result of mutual discussion. Imitation, first laid down as a principle, is to be understood as vying, emulation. The beautiful is opposed to the useful; it has no need to justify its existence by usefulness, but exists for its own sake, "an entity existing for itself." In it as in a symbolic microcosm there is manifested to us an imitation of the highest beauty, which we might find realized in the whole of nature if we were capable of perceiving it.

The beautiful can hence be only an idea which we obtain from our limited experience of nature by perceiving it with "eyes of the intellect." It is this supreme model which the artist must emulate in his work. Only the consideration of nature and art as a single whole can lead to the correct comprehension of the beautiful; for it is such consideration alone which renders the artist capable of producing it in fact. The creative individuality is here allowed its basic worth; but its ideal goal now appears to be a striving to produce works whose validity shall transcend the personal. It remains indeed the expression of an individual force, but in such fashion that an object of universal validity is produced, and that by a process which conforms to the same norm and necessity which govern nature.

Genius, Goethe learned in his progress toward the classic style, is not capricious in its activity, but law-abiding and normative. It can attain perfection only in the reconciliation of nature and intellect, in cultivated humanity. Its manifest signs are serenity, clarity, harmony, and measure. "If Raphael and Albrecht Dürer stand supreme, is there anything a true disciple must avoid more than arbitrariness? When he picked up and examined a crab on the seashore at Venice, Goethe was filled with admiration at the impression of perfect suitability and correctness revealed in the organic form: "What an excellent and splendid thing is a living being! How appropriate to its condition, how true, how real!" [1] Here there is no caprice and no fantasy, but necessity in every detail, and regular and disciplined articulation of the whole. So must works of art also be constituted if they are to possess objective truth. But this excellence is only to be attained if the artist is ruled as individual and as creator by a spirit of synthesis of subject and object, synthesis of spontaneity and norm.

> This is the final law of all creation:
> Ungirdled minds will meet with sure disaster,
> Where they do strive to pure perfection.
> High aim demands profoundest concentration;
> And inner discipline reveals the master,
> Since law's and freedom's majesty are one.[2]

[1] Was ist doch ein Lebendiges für ein köstliches, herrliches Ding! wie abgemessen zu seinem Zustande, wie wahr, wie seiend! (*Italienische Reise, Venedig,* October 9, 1786.)

[2] So ist's mit aller Bildung auch beschaffen. / Vergebens werden ungebundne Geister / Nach der Vollendung reiner Höhe streben. / Wer Grosses will, muss sich zusammenraffen. /

Goethe spent the late summer of 1786 in Karlsbad, where the Duke, Herder, and Charlotte von Stein were also sojourning. From Bohemia he started on his great journey on the third of September. His departure was taken in the deepest secrecy, so that the journey seemed a sort of flight. Not even to his friend had he said a word about it, although he had escorted her part way when she returned to Weimar. He was rendered mute by a feeling that more depended upon this journey than he could put into words, even to his most intimate friends; there was also a superstitious sense that no one must know of his intentions if they were to succeed. Later he declared in letters that only the highest necessity had compelled him to this decision. For years, he writes to Charlotte, he had not been able to look upon any Latin author or any picture of Italy without suffering anguish. To the recriminations of the deeply annoyed lady he rejoins by insisting that this was a life-and-death crisis. "If I perish, I perish; I was in any case of no more use." He must regain his health, for his own sake, but for the sake of his friends also.

The thing he sought in Italy he called convalescence, cure from distressing pain and illness.

> I believed I could properly learn something here, but I did not believe that I should have to go so far back in my schooling . . . I am like a builder who wished to erect a tower but had laid a bad foundation; he becomes aware of it betimes and willingly stops work on what he has raised from the ground in order to make sure of his basis, and he takes pleasure in the prospect of the surer soundness of his structure.[3]

It was characteristic of him that the new insights which had begun to take shape as result of his study of books and pictures in the field of ancient art could only be sharpened to the maturity and clarity of intellectual mastery by visual perception. Historical knowledge was not enough. Without direct inspection, he says, he could understand nothing; only when he saw them did these things speak to him.

In der Beschränkung zeigt sich erst der Meister, / Und das Gesetz nur kann uns Freiheit geben. (*Natur und Kunst,* based on translation by Ludwig Lewisohn, *Goethes Gedichte und Sprüche in Prosa,* p. 127.)

[3] Ich glaubte wohl hier etwas rechts zu lernen, dass ich aber soweit in die Schule zurückgehn müsste, glaubt ich nicht . . . Ich bin wie ein Baumeister, der einen Turm aufführen wollte und ein schlechtes Fundament gelegt hatte; er wird es noch bei Zeiten gewahr und bricht gerne wieder ab, was er schon aus der Erde gebracht hat, um sich seines Grundes mehr zu versichern und freut sich schon im Voraus der gewissern Festigkeit seines Baues. (Letter to Charlotte von Stein, December 29, 1786.)

What was wanted was a sense impression, which "no book and no picture gives," an autopsy of Greek works, so that the foreknown truth might become certainty.

> If I had not taken the resolution which I am now carrying out I would have been ruined utterly and good for nought, so far had the eagerness to see these objects with my own eyes ripened in my thoughts. For with historical knowledge I could approach them no nearer; it was as if the objects were only a hand's breadth distance from me and yet were separated by an impenetrable wall.[4]

It was not as if he were seeing the things for the first time, but rather as if he were seeing them again, so ready was his spirit for new appreciation. But his imagination alone did not suffice.

Goethe stopped in Venice for two weeks. He had not the patience to linger in Florence. At the end of October he arrived in Rome. Here he moved in a circle of German painters whose most important members were J. H. W. Tischbein and the Swiss Angelika Kauffmann. He lived with Tischbein for some time, carefully preserving an incognito and avoiding all social life. Tischbein tells of Goethe's life in their modest dwelling: "There he sits during the morning, working at the completion of his *Iphigenie* until about nine o'clock. Then he goes out and looks at the great works of art here. You can easily imagine with what an eye and what understanding he sees everything, for you know how true is his thinking." In February 1787 Goethe went to Naples, and a month later to Sicily. On this journey he was accompanied by a German painter. Without seeing Sicily, Goethe found, one could not obtain a proper notion of Italy. "Only here is the key to all." At the beginning of June he was again in Rome, where he remained until his departure at the end of April 1788.

In the years of wholesome solitude in Italy he found himself again as artist and as man—so Goethe himself formulated the value of his sojourn. Information concerning the details of what he saw and experienced are supplied in the two volumes of his *Italienische Reise*. These were organized some thirty years later, but the principal mate-

[4] Hätt ich nicht den Entschluss gefasst, den ich jetzt ausführe, so wär ich rein zu Grunde gegangen und zu allem unfähig geworden, solch einen Grad von Reife hatte die Begierde diese Gegenstände mit Augen zu sehen in meinem Gemüth erlangt. Denn ich konnte mit der historischen Erkenntnis nicht näher, die Gegenstände standen gleichsam nur eine Handbreit von mir ab, waren aber durch eine undurchdringliche Mauer von mir abgesondert. (Letter to Charlotte von Stein, October 10, 1786.)

rial was drawn from letters and diaries. This work does not offer conclusions, the results of judicious retrospect, but rather presents the life of the past as a present experience. In the whole, as in important details, it preserves unaltered the actual experiences of the visit. Only "the insignificant events of the day" were eliminated. For the period of his second stay in Rome, for which there were not many letters, Goethe was forced to rely upon his memory in larger measure. But the whole work is filled to the brim with the lively immediacy and the wealth of things he had seen and thought and made his own in Italy. There are indeed traces of the mood of an aging man in Goethe's preparation of his original documents for the press, of a man for whom the past is something done with and who weighs profit and loss critically. But this note is hardly perceptible; it hovers about the description like a zephyr.

The *Italienische Reise* as it stands is one of the greatest books on the incomparable country of Italy, perhaps the greatest—significant not only for what Goethe sees, but for the manner in which he sees it. At its center are the ancient works, the pictures of the great painters of the Renaissance, and the buildings of the same period. To the architecture and plastic works of the Baroque Goethe closed his eyes. For him Raphael and Palladio were the greatest artists. He gained his acquaintance with the art of antiquity, as Winckelmann had before him, only from the statues which were preserved in the Italian museums, principally in those of Rome—the Vatican museums, and the collections of the Cardinals Ludovisi and Albani. He saw only a few original works of the Greek period; the rest consisted of Roman copies, for the most part produced by sculptors of minor importance. In addition there were the bronzes and paintings which had been newly found in Herculaneum. Winckelmann's interpretation of ancient art rested upon these works. He had never been in Greece, nor did Goethe's knowledge extend farther. Greek architecture he saw with his own eyes at Paestum, journeying there twice from Naples to see the famous Doric temples. This memory was "the last and grandest idea" which he took with him from Italy. On his Sicilian journey he also saw the temples at Agrigentum. We must realize how little all this is compared to what we know of Greek art and architecture today. Classical archaeology made its greatest finds only in the nineteenth century. Of the results of the excavations of cult sites in Samothrace, Delos, Olympia, Eleusis, Delphi, Crete, and on the Acropolis, of the ruins of Pergamon, Troy, and Mycene there was as yet no knowledge, and scarcely anything was known of the archaic period.

But to Goethe what he was able to see in Italy was a great abundance, and he called it "an unfathomable abyss of art." He believed he should approach these treasures in the attitude of a mere spectator, avoiding as far as possible any scholarly judgment. "I live here now with a clarity and serenity of which I have long had no feeling. My practice of looking upon and perusing all things as they are, my trust in allowing my eye to be my light, my complete renunciation of all pretension again stand me in very good stead and quietly afford me supreme happiness." [5] The art which addresses itself to the eye is by all odds the prime object of Goethe's interest. His letters from Italy are the reports of a plastic artist rather than of a poet. What he sees and what he examines everywhere reveal the eye of the painter and the sculptor.

He hoped that he would develop his own modest talent in painting, in this ideal world of art, to greater richness and assurance. Goethe had sketched from his youth and had time and again attempted to reach artistic achievement in this respect also. But if his journey to Italy was conceived as a path to the fulfillment of this old and quietly cherished dream, it did in fact lead to a result quite different. His experiences in Rome, his association with painters, taught him that he would never be able to produce masterly work in the plastic arts. "I am too old for the fine arts; so whether I botch a trifle more or less makes no difference." His attempts at sketching did indeed help him to see more precisely, did teach him to develop attention to details, and did satisfy his desire to comprehend by inspection. But in the retrospect of old age he recognized how basically perverse it was to desire to attain practical artistic mastery when natural gifts were wanting. "I lacked the proper plastic power . . . My copies were mostly vague intimations of some figure, and my figures were like the light phantoms in Dante's *Purgatorio* which themselves cast no shadow and recoil from

[5] Ich lebe nun hier mit einer Klarheit und Ruhe, von der ich lange kein Gefühl hatte. Meine Uebung, alle Dinge, wie sie sind, zu sehen und abzulesen, meine Treue, das Auge Licht sein zu lassen, meine völlige Entäussrung von aller Prätention kommen mir einmal wieder recht zu statten und machen mich im stillen höchst glücklich. (*Italienische Reise, Rom,* November 10, 1786.)

the shadow of real bodies."[6] Later he pursued sketching only as a comfortable avocation, "as others smoke tobacco." Upon occasion the urge to sketch again became pronounced, as it did for the last time in 1810 when he sketched a series of more than twenty landscapes. Considered as a whole, his production is impressive enough; he left more than two thousand sketches behind him.

The country and people in Italy he regarded with as much attention as sympathy. Everything Roman Catholic, however, remained utterly alien to him. The rites and ceremonies of the Church he found theatrical and untrue. But the air, the light, the blue of the southern sky, the lush vegetation of the Mediterranean landscape afforded him daily delight. All of his life Goethe was dependent upon climate, upon the favor or disfavor of weather and season. He never lost the feeling that the climate of central Germany which he had to endure at Weimar and the sparsity of nature there were a hindrance to his physical and artistic existence. In one of the *Römische Elegien* (the seventh) he complains of the gray sky, the colorless and formless world of the north. This child of the gay and generous country on the Rhine and the Main felt himself a climatic exile at Weimar all his life. On his visits home he speaks of Thuringia as the "northerly stretches," return to which always cost him an effort. When he later looked back upon his time in Italy it seemed that he could never relinquish its memory; he had had to rise up "from that great Italian banquet" and again find sustenance "at the northern cat-feed of leavings."

Aesthetic requirements of his nature played an imponderable role. In Italy he had come to understand to what degree the clarity and beauty of Greek forms and figures were products of Mediterranean landscape, and why northern artists were able to attain these qualities only by painful exertion. The public gardens at Palermo, the view to the mountains and the sea made Homer's description of the island of the Phaeacians a living presence. He reread that canto of the *Odyssey* and gave his travel companions an extemporary translation of it. "The clearness of the sky, the breath of the sea, the mist in which the mountains seem to fuse with heaven and sea into a single element," the luxuriant gardens of Sicily—all of this was for him the best com-

[6] Es fehlte mir die eigentliche plastische Kraft . . . Meine Nachbildungen waren mehr ferne Ahnungen irgend einer Gestalt, und meine Figuren glichen den leichten Luftwesen in Dantes "Purgatorio," die, keine Schatten werfend, vor dem Schatten wirklicher Körper sich entsetzten.

mentary on the verses of the ancient poet. Homer's lines ceased to comprise a poem; they seemed "nature itself." Out of these impressions emerged a plan for a Homeric drama, a tragedy of Nausicaä. Only a little of this was actually carried out. But among the fragments there are a few verses which, as Jacob Burckhardt thought, "belong among the most wonderful and lovely things that Goethe has said." Such is this magnificent description of the southern country:

> There blooms again press forth beside the fruits,
> And fruits change off with fruits throughout the year.
> The lemon, pomegranate shows itself
> 'Mid dusty foliage, and there the fig
> Follows the fig . . .
> There wilt thou stroll amid the lovely arbors,
> Rejoicing in the spacious, flowering meads.
> Beside thee ripples on the brooklet, led
> From tree to tree
> . . . . .
> A silver sheen rests over land and sea,
> And fragrant floats aloft the cloudless ether.[7]

Mignon's song of her lost homeland is a visionary anticipation of the enchantment produced by the Sicilian landscape, and spiritual echoes of that enchantment are the unsurpassed strophes in the Helena act of *Faust* in which the image of the Arcadian idyll is conjured.

None of his new insights seemed so important to Goethe as the view that art is a second nature, created by great men. So he now looks upon the art of the Greeks. "How the ancients followed nature and with what great spirit they followed it is inexpressible." [8] "All that is capricious, all that is fanciful collapses: here is necessity, here is God." [9] It is not that the Greeks were naturalists and sought to construct copies

[7] Dort dringen neben Früchten wieder Blüten, / Und Frucht auf Früchte wechseln durch das Jahr. / Die Pomeranze, die Citrone steht / Im dunklen Laube, und die Feige folgt / Der Feige . . . / Dort wirst du in den schönen Lauben wandeln, / An weiten Teppichen von Blumen dich erfreun. / Es rieselt neben dir der Bach, geleitet / Von Stamm zu Stamm / . . . / Ein weisser Glanz ruht über Land und Meer, / Und duftend schwebt der Aether ohne Wolken. (*Nausikaa,* Act I, scene 3, translated by B. Q. Morgan.)

[8] Es ist unsäglich, wie die Alten der Natur und mit welchem grossen Sinn sie ihr gefolgt sind.

[9] Alles Willkürliche, Eingebildete fällt zusammen: da ist die Notwendigkeit, da ist Gott. (*Italienische Reise, Rom,* September 6, 1787.)

of the forms of nature, but rather that they fashioned forms as did nature itself—forms both suitable and "true"—that is to say, created out of the feeling for organic wholeness. "I have a feeling that they observed the laws which nature itself observes, and upon whose track I am." [10]

Here in Italy he succeeded in acquiring a better picture of nature's own methods of producing her forms. He was no less alert and receptive in the presence of natural phenomena than he was in the presence of monuments of art. The secret of *Pflanzenzeugung und -Organisation* ("plant reproduction and organization") begins to be unveiled. The idea of an extremely simple basic form, an *Urpflanze*, suggested to him the type which regulated the process of morphological development as a schematic pattern. Individual varieties thus appear as variations on a theme; they are developed from a single simple primitive form according to a regular process. "The same law can be applied to all other living things." To discover this primitive type everywhere, and, with it as key, to understand the individual phenomena of nature's huge realm, now becomes the real substance of Goethe's study. The basic principles of morphology were discovered, and thereby the science of comparative morphology, as Goethe pursued it, was established. "Painfully sweet" he calls the feeling which this discovery evoked. Consciousness of being on the track of the secret of creative development, of the divine in action, and of having discovered the simple form "with which, as it were, nature seems constantly only to play, and yet in its play to bring forth manifold life," is attended by a religious thrill. For the first time, as he expresses it, after tedious spelling out of words, the book of nature was finally legible.

As an old man Goethe spoke of his time in Rome as if it were a lost paradise. Only there had he felt what it is to be a human being, only there had he been truly joyful and happy. When he attempted to follow the example of the ancient artists in his own country, he remarked with resignation that this could only be done "as well as it may in Thuringia." He discovered soon enough that such fulfillment could not be repeated, that one could not swim in the same river a

[10] Ich habe eine Vermutung, dass sie nach eben den Gesetzen verfuhren, nach welchen die Natur verfährt und denen ich auf der Spur bin. (*Italienische Reise, Rom,* January 28, 1787.)

second time. In March of 1790 Goethe again traveled south to upper Italy to await the Duke's mother, who was returning from Rome, and escort her home. He was very unhappy at leaving Weimar. His house finally had a young woman, Christiane, as its mistress; several months previously she had borne him his first son. He felt that he could no longer be alone, no longer live abroad. He had to wait in Venice for seven weeks. Longing for his beloved and for his comfortable house tormented him. The weather was rainy and cold, also, which made Venice particularly disagreeable—wet above and below alike. He could not summon up his usual enthusiasm for Italy; "the first bloom of inclination and curiosity" was withered. He complains of Venice's dirt and frivolity; he calls the lagoons a frog-pond, the magnificent city a warren of stone and water. As he waited and wandered about the city alone, wasting time and money, the life of the people and the pomp of the Church's Easter celebrations aroused more annoyance than interest.

> Fine is the country, forsooth! But nowhere see I Faustina.
> That's not the Italy which, broken-hearted, I left.[11]

But the weeks of discouragement were not without fruit. "I have seen, read, thought, composed, as never before in a year." What he wrote were sharp, bitter, witty epigrams, which he combined with other barbed fruits written before and after into a cycle: *Epigramme: Venedig 1790*. The object of his darts was in the first instance Christianity and the Catholic cult. He speaks sarcastically, like an apostle of the Enlightenment in the manner of Voltaire; never before or afterward did he depreciate Christianity to such a degree (much that was too audacious Goethe himself withheld). Another group of epigrams criticized the latest political event, the French Revolution, reflecting no slight distaste. The erotic verses were probably written in part at Weimar; they speak of the loss of his old and the acquisition of his new love.

> Once I had a love, dearest to me of all things!
> Ah, but now I have lost her, and do silently suffer the loss! [12]

[11] Schön ist das Land! doch ach, Faustinen find' ich nicht wieder. / Das ist Italien nicht mehr, das ich mit Schmerzen verliess. (*Venezianische Epigramme,* No. 4, translated by Paul Drysen, *Goethe's Poems.*)

[12] Eine Liebe hatt' ich, sie war mir lieber als alles! / Aber ich hab' sie nicht mehr! Schweig' und ertrag' den Verlust! (*Venezianische Epigramme,* No. 7, based on translation by Paul Drysen, *Goethe's Poems.*)

Long did I seek for a wife, and, seeking, I found only women;
Finally thee did I catch: woman, and thou wert the wife! [13]

Other verses in the series contain a complaint that as poet he is forced to waste life and art "in the worst of material," the German language; and also the *fin-de-siècle* remark on the close relationship of juggler and poet. Also among the Venetian epigrams we find the first attack upon Newton's theory of colors, the earliest indication of Goethe's interest in the field of optics. The artistic models for these essays in satire were the epigrams of Martial and those of the *Greek Anthology*, which he had studied under Herder's guidance.

Impudent I have become? I think it no wonder. Immortals,
You know, and not you alone, that I'm also docile and true.[14]

A poetic fruit of Goethe's Italian experiences and at the same time of his new life with Christiane are the *Römische Elegien* (in the manuscript they are called *Erotica Romana*). The Eros of these poems, which follow the elegies of Propertius and Tibullus in style, is not the sentimental love-genius of the Christian era, but the ancient god of joyous pleasure, knowing no shame, in whom body and soul are undivided. The direction of pleasure is from without to within. The enjoyment of the searching eye and the caressing hand raises warmth of heart and rapturous perception of beauty to a supreme harmony. Following the ancient mode, the small happenings and intimate situations of life with the beloved are depicted without restraint. Pictures which veil that which must either be looked upon uncovered or from which the eyes should be entirely turned away, says Goethe, are lascivious. The love poetry of the Greeks and Romans knows no lasciviousness, and in this respect Goethe's elegies too are antique. No impure feeling darkens natural pleasure.

Heartfelt loving unites us forever, and faithfullest yearning;
Change we know, but it dwells only in ardent desire.[15]

[13] Lange sucht' ich ein Weib mir, ich suchte, da fand ich nur Dirnen, / Endlich erhascht' ich dich mir, Dirnchen, da fand ich ein Weib. ("Venezianische Epigramme," manuscript version, translated by B. Q. Morgan.)

[14] Frech wohl bin ich geworden; es ist kein Wunder. Ihr Götter / Wisst, und wisst nicht allein, dass ich auch fromm bin und treu. (*Venezianische Epigramme*, No. 74, translated by B. Q. Morgan.)

[15] Herzliche Liebe verbindet uns stets und treues Verlangen, / Und den Wechsel behält nur die Begierde sich vor. (*Römische Elegien*, No. 13, translated by B. Q. Morgan.)

Emotion and sense, body and soul, are here made finally and equally happy in a single experience. For Goethe this was a pleasure long denied and a release from the painful tension which resulted from his abstemious passion for Charlotte von Stein. What he experienced in his adventures with Roman girls was repeated with greater earnestness and inwardness in the tie which he formed with Christiane Vulpius shortly after his return. Out of the stuff of these experiences the beloved of the elegies is formed; if she resembles Christiane outwardly, she is nevertheless essentially a creature of the poet's imagination.

New Life in Weimar

FROM ROME GOETHE HAD WRITTEN CHARLOTTE TO ASK THAT SHE MAKE HIS RETURN TO HER EASY. BUT WHEN HE HAD RETURNED IT SOON BECAME EVIDENT that the old confidence could not be restored. The patience with which he bore her angry recriminations could not delude her perception that the old love was dead, that Goethe no longer needed what she had to give. Uncompromising as she was in her ideals in general, and particularly in her demands upon the only man whom she had determined to love, she was unwilling to forgive. She could only love where she admired. His other Weimar friends, too, received Goethe more coolly than he thought he deserved.

In his mood of estrangement and loneliness during the first months after his return, an event occurred which disrupted his relationship with Charlotte completely. In July 1788 Goethe became acquainted with a girl of a petty bourgeois family, Christiane Vulpius, then twenty-three years old. She soon became his mistress and moved into his house with a stepsister and an aunt.

> Do not repent, my beloved, of having surrendered so quickly!
> Not any less for that do I esteem your love.[1]

[1] Lass dich, Geliebte, nicht reun, dass du mir so schnell dich ergeben! / Glaub' es, ich denke nicht frech, denke nicht niedrig von dir. (*Römische Elegien*, No. 3, translated by Paul Drysen, *Goethe's Poems*, p. 223.)

Goethe has described the girl in the fourth Roman Elegy and in the poem *Der Besuch* ("The Visit"). "I am married, but not by a ceremony"—so he himself designated his relationship to her. This was nothing unusual in an age when social classes were rigorously divided but when, in individual cases, the heart might claim its rights through such "marriages of conscience." Christiane loved the much-admired man with the warmth of a joyous, pulsing heart. She kept house for him and brought into his life the pleasantness and comfort which it had so lacked. The carefree, simple, "natural being" was well suited to the sensitive man of problems, who knew that we cannot avoid the contradictions in ourselves and that we must attempt somehow to reconcile them. Of the children whom she bore him, only the eldest, August, survived. Class convention excluded them from the social life of the court society. But Goethe's mother was liberal enough to receive her son's beloved with cordiality, as if she were his legitimate wife.

The poet's letters to his "little darling" everywhere show how warm and honorable was his feeling for her. They tell how he enveloped her with his protection and affection, how he always made an effort to show his gratitude for her devotion and loyalty through words and deeds, through assurances of his love, and by gifts, and with what free spirit he accorded this gay creature every pleasure, especially dancing which she so loved. Not many legitimate marriages, indeed, can have been as happy and as solid as this free relationship. From the poem *Die Metamorphose der Pflanzen* it might appear that Christiane shared in Goethe's intellectual life also. But of this there could be no question. "The realm of the intellect has no existence for her, she is meant only for housekeeping," Goethe is said to have remarked to a woman friend. But that she did not affect culture, but gave of herself and lived as her simple nature demanded, was not the slightest of Christiane's virtues. Weimar gossip was not kind to her; there was much talk of her strong inclination to wine. But no one dared cast aspersions upon her virtue. For Goethe, indeed, there must have been times when he wished for some companion other than the uneducated creature who spoke in the Thuringian dialect, and for other household arrangements. Schiller suggests as much in a very "correct" letter to a distinguished lady. He is of the opinion that Goethe is too weak and softhearted to dissolve the bond. "This is his only vulnerable spot, which hurts no one but himself, and even this is integral to a very noble part of his character." The misgivings of friends who saw danger to Goethe's poetic productivity in this alliance, and also the kindred feelings in his own bosom, evoked a response from Goethe in his elegy *Amyntas* (1797):

Shall I not cherish the plant, which, only my being requiring,
Quiet, but dauntless in force, eagerly clings to my side?
Thousands of branches took root, and with thousands and thousands of fibers
Into my being it grows, firmly entwined with my life.
Sustenance takes it from me: whatever I need is its joyance,
Thus at my marrow it sucks, thus does it suck out my soul.
. . . . .
Sweet is all prodigality: do not begrudge me the sweetest!
He who surrenders to Love, can he be niggard of Life? [2]

How spirited and resourceful "the little one" could be in an emergency she showed when soldiers of the French army, on a rampage of plunder after the battle of Jena, forced their way into Goethe's house. In a situation charged with danger, Christiane's presence of mind saved him and his property. This incident brought an "old resolution" to a head. Goethe married Christiane and thus, as he expressed it, he confirmed "his domestic happiness by legal forms." When she was taken from him by death in 1816 (she was only fifty-one years old) Goethe grieved for her deeply.

His new life with wife and child prevented him from sinking into complete human solitude during the first years after his return. To be sure, his tie with Christiane severed him from his old friends. But at the same time she enriched his life with a kind of happiness it had never known.

Oftentimes I have erred and later my senses recovered,
Never with fortune like this: fortune for me is this girl! [3]

[2] Soll ich nicht lieben die Pflanze, die, meiner einzig bedürftig, / Still, mit begieriger Kraft, mir um die Seite sich schlingt? / Tausend Ranken wurzelten an, mit tausend und tausend / Fasern senket sie fest mir in das Leben sich ein. / Nahrung nimmt sie von mir; was ich bedürfte, geniesst sie, / Und so saugt sie das Mark, sauget die Seele mir aus. / . . . / Süss ist jede Verschwendung: o lass mich der schönsten geniessen! / Wer sich der Liebe vertraut, hält er sein Leben zu Rat? (*Amyntas*, translated by B. Q. Morgan.)

[3] Oftmals hab' ich geirrt, und habe mich wieder gefunden, / Aber glücklicher nie;

It was hard enough for him to acclimatize himself to German conditions again. The state of literature in particular frequently brought him to despair. Literature was in a doldrum; Schiller had not yet appeared with his classic dramas, and the new romantic school had not yet begun to reform the aesthetic and philosophic education of the nation. In 1792 the Swiss painter and art critic, Johann Heinrich Meyer, came to Weimar. Goethe had made his acquaintance in Rome and had found in this scholarly expert an ideal partner for his aesthetic speculation and his preoccupation with classic art. But who else was there in the little town, or in all of Germany, with whose understanding Goethe could reckon if he should proceed to bring to fulfillment his views concerning the essence and character of art which had matured in Italy? And where were readers to be found for works in which his new artistic maturity would express itself? A letter of this period reflects the discouraged skepticism which threatened to stifle all his plans:

> The Germans are on the average upright and decent people; but of originality, invention, character, unity, and the execution of a work of art they have not the remotest notion. In one word, they have no taste. Needless to say, on the average. The cruder part is duped by fickleness and exaggeration, the more educated by a kind of smug propriety. Knights, robbers, the charitable, the grateful, a decent and honest third estate, a disreputable nobility, etc., altogether a well-entrenched mediocrity, from which at best a few steps ventured downward lead to a dead level of dullness, or upward to folly—for ten long years these have been the ingredients and the tone of our novels and plays.[4]

In the end nothing was left for Goethe but to go his way alone, to pursue his studies of nature and of ancient literature and art—as well as this could be done in Thuringia—and to follow these great models.

---

nun ist dies Mädchen mein Glück! (*Venezianische Epigramme,* No. 100, translated by B. Q. Morgan.)

[4] Die Deutschen sind im Durchschnitt rechtliche, biedere Menschen, aber von Originalität, Erfindung, Charakter, Einheit, und Ausführung eines Kunstwerks haben sie nicht den mindesten Begriff. Das heisst mit *einem* Worte: sie haben keinen Geschmack. Versteht sich auch im Durchschnitt. Den roheren Teil hat man durch Abwechslung und Uebertreiben, den gebildetern durch eine Art Honettetät zum Besten. Ritter, Räuber, Wohltätige, Dankbare, ein redlicher biederer Tiers Etat, ein infamer Adel pp. und durchaus eine wohlsoutenierte Mittelmässigkeit, aus der man nur allenfalls abwärts ins Platte, aufwärts in den Unsinn einige Schritte wagt, das sind nun schon zehen Jahre die Ingredienzien und der Charakter unsrer Romane und Schauspiele. (Letter to J. F. Reichardt, February 28, 1790.)

Goethe was probably never as lonely as he was in these years between his return from Italy and his friendship with Schiller.

Goethe did not resume his official duties, but circumstances brought it about that he took over the direction of the court theater in 1791. For twenty-six years he devoted much of his time and energy to this arduous business, especially after 1798 when a new and respectable theater building was at his disposal. With the limited resources of a small country, Goethe achieved great things. It was in Weimar and only in Weimar that an appropriate style of presentation was finally developed for the new verse drama. The Weimar style of producing Shakespearean drama, Goethe's own plays, and then Schiller's great tragedies soon became the classic model for all German stages. But to the lighter bourgeois pieces also, musical comedies and light operas, Goethe devoted the care which alone could make good performances possible. The director of the court theater often had to make his poetic talent available for special occasions. Goethe wrote a series of prologues, epilogues, and preludes for Weimar and for the summer theater at Bad Lauchstädt; he improved the German texts of Italian and French operas, composed new lyrics for them, attempted to write a continuation of *The Magic Flute,* and finally, translated Voltaire's *Mahomet* and *Tancred.*

But the most important and most difficult part of his duties was training the actors in the new style. In Germany of the time only the naturalistic conversational style in diction and acting was known, so that Goethe had to begin by teaching the actors that their task was to present not themselves but the character of their role. In *Wilhelm Meister* the actor Jarno says, "If a man can play only himself, he is no actor." To play together in an ensemble like the individual instruments in an orchestra, to speak verse rhythmically, to employ the devices of mimicry and gesticulation with a conscious discipline of style—all of these things they learned from Goethe to follow and to recognize as essential norms. Schiller assisted in this tedious and patient work. Caroline von Wolzogen, who witnessed rehearsals, reports: "Schiller concentrated on developing feeling and thorough understanding of the roles; Goethe on their presentation in life. Many times we saw how in four weeks he taught comprehension, speech, posture, deportment; like a magic wand his clear insight set petrified masses into charming motion." Eventually Goethe attempted to collect and formulate the elements of histrionic art in his *Regeln für Schauspieler*

("Rules for Actors"; 1803). The audience, too, had to be educated to the new demands. One facet of his experiences, which gave him a more intimate knowledge of the theater than that possessed by any other German writer of his time, Goethe has set forth delightfully in the *Vorspiel auf dem Theater* ("Prelude in the Theater"), prefixed to the first part of *Faust*. Here many a pregnant word is said concerning the inevitable conflict between the ideal intentions of the poet and the actual requirements of the theater, which has to reckon with the divergent interests of the crowd.

The French Revolution

THE OUTBREAK OF THE GREAT POLITICAL TEMPEST WAS NO SURPRISE TO GOETHE. HE HAD FELT THAT SOME CATASTROPHE OF THE SORT WAS IMMINENT; HE HAD foreseen that it would take place in France. But his correct prescience derived neither from mature political thought nor from historical speculation; it was rather through a single symptom, a single figure which, after his fashion, he sensed as a general symbol, that Goethe became aware how critical was the situation in Europe. When in 1781 the wonder-seeking and wonder-believing Lavater told him of the magic arts of the adventurer and charlatan Cagliostro, who was well known at the time, Goethe replied with grave words of warning:

> Believe me, our moral and political world is undermined, like a great city, with subterranean corridors, cellars, and sewers, and virtually no one takes thought of their implications or the plight of the inhabitants; only a man who has some information finds it intelligible when now the ground collapses here, now smoke issues from a crevice there, and strange voices are heard yonder.[1]

Four years later the prestige of the French court was very gravely compromised by a scandal (the so-called "Affair of the Queen's Neck-

[1] Glaube mir, unsere moralische und politische Welt ist mit unterirdischen Gängen, Kellern und Kloaken minieret, wie eine grosse Stadt zu sein pflegt, an deren Zusammenhang, und ihrer Bewohnenden Verhältnisse wohl niemand denkt und sinnt; nur wird es dem, der davon einige Kundschaft hat, viel begreiflicher, wenn da einmal der Erdboden einstürzt, dort einmal ein Rauch aus einer Schlucht aufsteigt, und hier wunderbare Stimmen gehört werden. (Letter of June 22, 1781.)

lace"), in which Marie Antoinette, the queen, and also Cagliostro were involved. Goethe was dismayed at the "immoral abyss of city, court, and state" which was revealed. Hatred, he later remarked, hurt no one, but contempt destroyed man's position. His friends would not believe him when he prophesied approaching woe from this sheet lightning. When the thunderstorm broke in 1789 he was nevertheless shocked; his first reaction was revulsion. His earliest expressions on the subject are in the *Venetian Epigrams*.

> Always I have disliked those loud apostles of freedom;
> Each, after all, only craved license and pow'r for himself.[2]

In the leaders of the Revolution he could see only demagogues. Instead of leading the crowd toward humanity, they deceived the people basely; they were irrational enthusiasts who imprinted the stamp of reason upon lies and folly. A man who, like Goethe, regarded gradual progressive development, as it occurs in nature and history, as the only wholesome and sound method, could have no confidence in an attempt to force a sudden change. Everything violent and sudden was deeply repellent to him, he later said to Eckermann in speaking of the Revolution, because it was not in accord with nature.

In his political thinking as in his general concept of the world and of humanity, Goethe was dominated by a conservative idea of regular evolution. "It is inherent in my nature: I would rather commit an injustice than tolerate disorder." [3] Many people have taken exception to this frequently cited sentence, although in practice it is the normal course of policy at all times. What Goethe means is something like this: the balance of forces and conditions which we call social order is of the highest value in the sense that it constitutes a prerequisite for all purposeful activity of the individual. If this balance can be preserved or restored, then even an action or decision which is in one respect unjust is permissible, if it assures order for the whole of social life, since order is the foundation of every thing. An injustice which achieves this is expiated by its wholesome results. But this does not exculpate tyranny and abuse of privilege and possessions. Goethe defended princely absolutism as little as he did churchly reaction. He

[2] Alle Freiheitsapostel, sie waren mir immer zuwider; / Willkür suchte doch nur jeder am Ende für sich. (*Venezianische Epigramme*, No. 51, translated by Paul Drysen, *Goethe's Poems*, p. 301.)

[3] Es liegt nun einmal in meiner Natur: ich will lieber eine Ungerechtigkeit begehen, als Unordnung ertragen.

knew very well that the upper classes in all countries had grounds to be apprehensive of "France's sad fate." Even the simple patriarchal conditions in the small German principalities he did not regard as just. It distressed him to see how the small ruling class, to which he himself belonged, devoured the marrow of the land and how "the poor folk always had to carry the bag."

But he was convinced that an intelligent prince could better procure what was good and just than could the demagogue with his misconceptions of liberty and equality. Pride of position is nowhere expressed in Goethe's works. In his later life, as in his youth, he was never lacking in understanding for "the classes of people . . . which we call the lower but which are surely the highest in the sight of God," in love for simple men, in admiration for their loyal and contented patience. His letter to Charlotte von Stein of December 4, 1777, provides evidence of this. And in a letter of 1786 we find: "A man who thinks highly of himself seems to have forfeited the right to condemn others. And what are we after all that we should dare exalt ourselves." [4] But in the wishes and deeds of the masses he had no confidence, now or later. Only of the sound-minded and well-intentioned individual did he expect any contribution to the advance of civilization. He was convinced that reason was to be found only in the minority. The masses were united by their prejudices and driven by their passions.

> The vulgar masses thou hast never known.
> They dawdle, stare, and gape, let others strive,
> And when they move, a luckless ending marks
> What planless and by chance they had begun.[5]
>
> Awhile with halting minds the masses go,
> Then ride the stream, wherever it may flow.[6]

The political ideal of his maturity Goethe set forth in *Tasso*. It is a state where the prince rules wisely and where everyone renders con-

[4] Wer auf sich etwas hält, scheint dem Rechte entsagt zu haben, andere gering zu schätzen. Und was sind wir denn alle, dass wir uns viel erheben dürfen.

[5] Die rohe Menge hast du nie gekannt, / Sie starrt und staunt und zaudert, lässt geschehn; / Und regt sie sich, so endet ohne Glück, / Was ohne Plan zufällig sie begonnen. (*Die natürliche Tochter*, Act IV, scene 4, translated by B. Q. Morgan.)

[6] Die Menge schwankt im ungewissen Geist, / Dann strömt sie nach, wohin der Strom sie reisst. (*Faust*, v. 10381, translated by Bayard Taylor, *Faust II*, p. 111, first American edition, Boston: Fields, Osgood and Company, 1871.)

scious obedience, believing that he serves only himself because nothing but what is right is enjoined upon him.

One piece of revolutionary history Goethe saw close at hand. When the armies of the Austrians and Prussians made their vain attempt to crush the Revolution from without in 1792, the Duke of Weimar participated in the campaign of the Prussian army. The Duke wished his friend to accompany him, and Goethe did so very unwillingly. He was little concerned, as he said, with the death of either the aristocratic or the democratic sinners. On the whole, he hated wars, and called them "the hereditary disease of the world." Among the German citizenry of the time there was in general no trace of the militarism and the glorification of war which played so great and fatal a role among the Germans of the following century. Of himself Goethe said: "I am a child of peace and desire to maintain continual peace with the whole world, since I have concluded peace with myself." [7] During the months which he spent in this unlucky undertaking he always tried to maintain the attitude of an onlooker. Where everyone was partisan, the poet, in his opinion, must remain completely unpartisan, in keeping with his nature.

But for that very reason he saw more clearly than those implicated in the partisan struggle what a "cycle of tragedies" must be released by the great collapse of the old order. On the evening of the battle of Valmy, in which the war was lost for the allies, Goethe understood what the officers could not see: that with this event a new era had begun. Much later (1822) he told the story of the one-year campaign in his *Campagne in Frankreich* ("Campaign in France") and the *Belagerung von Mainz* ("The Siege of Mainz"); together with *Dichtung und Wahrheit* and the *Italienische Reise* these comprise the whole of Goethe's autobiographical writings. He endeavored to while away the tedium of camp life and the uncongenial war atmosphere by productive work; while others fought he occupied himself with observations and studies in natural science. To the great work of destruction he opposed the quiet toil of the intellect. While the cannons roared for a decision at Verdun, Goethe explained his theory of colors to a German prince.

[7] Ich bin ein Kind des Friedens und will Friede halten für und für mit der ganzen Welt, da ich ihn einmal mit mir selbst geschlossen habe. (*Italienische Reise, Rom,* October 12, 1787.)

As soon as he could, he returned to Weimar and endeavored to draw about himself a circle "into which nothing but love and friendship, art and science, could enter." Situations in which he could not participate actively he abhorred. To preserve his productivity under such conditions he resolutely secluded himself from the superior forces which threatened to cripple him. He preserved this attitude during all of the troubled period which now began for Germany. When in 1794 he formed a friendly union with Schiller and Wilhelm von Humboldt, he described the goal of their common activity as follows: "We seek together to maintain ourselves in the aesthetic life as far as possible and to forget everything outside ourselves." [8] Soon thereafter he wrote: "All of Germany is divided into people who are malicious, timid, and indifferent . . . For myself, therefore, I find nothing more advisable than to play the role of Diogenes and roll my tub about." [9]

But the huge wave which waxed ever stronger and eventually flooded all central Europe penetrated every refuge. Several times Goethe attempted to come to terms with the Revolution by fixing its characteristic phenomena and effects in dramatic forms. But in none of the plays does the revolutionary power appear in gigantic stature, in none of them the triumphant figure of the goddess of liberty. The first of these dramas treats of the "Affair of the Queen's Necklace" under the title *Der Gross-Cophta*. It was first planned as an opera libretto (*Die Mystifizierten*), but in the end it became a comedy—an average society-piece which shows no awareness of historical implications and only repeats the familiar intrigue. Incidentally, the fashionable rage for secret societies is ridiculed. In this atmosphere Cagliostro, the Grand Cophta, is in his proper element. Goethe became interested in this demonic charlatan, collected reports about him in Sicily, and even visited his family (to whom he subsequently sent the honorarium which he received for the play).

Other plays sought to counter the political excitement which events in France had aroused among the German peasantry and bourgeoisie. In *Der Bürgergeneral* ("The Citizen-General"), a comedy in one act, Goethe advises the German peasants to leave the French to

[8] Wir suchen uns zusammen, soviel als möglich, im ästhetischen Leben zu erhalten und alles ausser uns zu vergessen.

[9] Ganz Deutschland ist in schadenfrohe, ängstliche und gleichgiltige Menschen geteilt . . . Für meine Person finde ich nichts Rätlicheres als die Rolle des Diogenes zu spielen und mein Fass zu wälzen.

their own worries and to trouble themselves about politics as little as possible. Everyone must begin with himself and set his own house in order; thus the interests of the whole would also be best served. For Goethe the reaction of Germans to the French Revolution was nothing more than tavern politics. The German middle classes were in fact in no way prepared, either spiritually or practically, for a libertarian alteration of the old feudal order; there could be no question of a genuine revolutionary movement at that time. Germany had its first revolution in 1848, when the French had already gone to their barricades for the third time.

The satiric title *Die Aufgeregten* ("The Excited") was given to another political drama (1793), which was never completed. It seeks to show how artificial the excitement in Germany was, however genuine the need for it may have been in France. According to Goethe's conviction, revolutionary insurrections of the lower classes were a consequence of the injustice of the upper classes. Nor is the nobility spared in this play. An aristocratic lady who has learned from events is made to say: "I will no longer be silent at any injustice, no longer tolerate any pettiness that pretends to greatness under a great cloak, even if I should be called the hated name of democrat." [10] But to the democrats, too, objection is made. "But if all such advantages as health, beauty, youth, wealth, intelligence, talents, climate, have validity, why should not the advantage that I am sprung of a line of brave, famous, honorable ancestors also have a kind of validity!" [11] In these plays Goethe is on the defensive against the Revolution. The phenomenon itself is not dealt with; only the spread of the movement to Germany is opposed.

Twice Goethe set about giving the incidents of the Revolution a more general, tragic aspect. Of the tragedy, *Das Mädchen von Oberkirch* (1795), only two scenes were presented. Its intention was to show how an innocent girl is destroyed by the fanaticism of the mob. The theme of the other revolutionary tragedy, *Die natürliche Tochter* (1804), deals with the significant personality in times of political

[10] Zu keiner Ungerechtigkeit will ich mehr schweigen, keine Kleinheit unter einem grossen Scheine ertragen, und wenn ich auch unter dem verhassten Namen einer Demokratin verschrien werden sollte. (*Die Aufgeregten,* Act III, scene 1.)

[11] Wenn alle Vorzüge gelten sollen, Gesundheit, Schönheit, Jugend, Reichtum, Verstand, Talente, Klima, warum soll der Vorzug nicht auch irgend eine Art von Gültigkeit haben, dass ich von einer Reihe tapferer, bekannter, ehrenvoller Väter entsprungen bin! (*Die Aufgeregten,* Act III, scene 1.)

chaos, the fate of the noble individual in the whirlpool of anarchic mass movements. In the *Mémoires historiques de Stéphanie-Louise de Bourbon-Conti* Goethe had read of the vicissitudes of an adventuress who was the illegitimate offspring of a duke of the house of Bourbon. Until the outbreak of the Revolution she had struggled in vain for recognition of her aristocratic privileges, and then with other members of the royal house she had fallen victim to the insurrection. The story of how a helpless individual was drawn into the rush of retaliatory proceedings and destroyed by them seemed to Goethe a symbol of the situation in which an individual, whether innocent or guilty, good or evil, finds himself in the midst of general upheaval. The grim contradiction involved in the fact that the value and dignity of personality, the things most precious in the gauge of culture, were no longer respected in the political movement, seemed to him the basis for a genuine tragedy. Eugenie, the heroine, was made to rise from childish naïveté to heroic greatness.

A dramatic trilogy was to represent the conflict of an individual struggling for free self-determination against "monstrous empiricism." Only the first drama was completed: *Die natürliche Tochter*. It takes place in the strained atmosphere before the outbreak of the tempest. A court conspiracy, instigated by the possibility that Eugenie might be recognized by the king as a legitimate heiress, attempts to dispose of her by violence. She is spirited away with the design of being deported to a colony. Eugenie is without guilt, pure and beautiful, a comely daughter of nature; and yet she must suffer for her birth. She can save herself by marrying a bourgeois husband, for thus she would lose her noble title and forfeit her claims. But this Eugenie will not do. In vain she looks about for help, to the court, to the church, to the people. She stands powerless and helpless, caught fast in the net of fateful circumstances and brutal intrigues. Only by abnegation and sacrifice, by yielding to power, denying her dreams, acquiescing in at least a sisterly marriage with a man to whom she is indifferent, and thus choosing the lesser evil, can she hope to save herself and sustain the hope of helping the royal house and the country she loves. The individual sacrifices to political necessity his right to his own free life, his claim to happiness. Would the sacrifice be worth while?

Even if we did not know Goethe's plan for the continuation, the tragic coloring of the piece would supply the answer: Eugenie must perish, if only because she cannot do anything but remain passive. In the general catastrophe, toward which the political struggle between despotism and revolution is progressing, there would be no freedom but only the brutal necessity which accompanies a natural catastrophe. The causes are only suggested in the drama; political conditions are discussed only generally. The play presents the fate of an individual, not a historical event in its causes and phenomena. The spotlight is turned wholly upon the figure of the heroine; the people generally manifest no independent activity. They do not speak; and when they are spoken of the tone is one of great skepticism.

With none of his great dramas did Goethe make less impression than with this, with none did he have more painful experiences. The nature of its action and style contributed even more to its failure than the content which ran counter to the partisan tendencies of the time. Goethe himself thought that its principal failing lay in the tendency to make its motivation overexplicit. In contrast to Schiller, he always supplied too much motivation in his dramas, and for the stage this was inappropriate. An important factor is that the action is so slight—even more so than in *Iphigenie* and *Tasso*—and its tempo rather that of an epic report than of dramatic action. Everything takes place in the souls of the characters, and each expresses his inward thoughts with complete clarity and without psychological implications.

The greatest difficulty in *Die natürliche Tochter* is its style, both that used in the portrayal of characters and that of their verbal expression. The effort of the classic artist to make what is universally valid apparent in the individual case, to make general truth perceptible in the particular, and to give the typical in abstract form instead of depicting naturalistically in colors which are true for the moment only—an effort which is evident in all of Goethe's dramatic works after the *Iphigenie*—all these tendencies dominate most clearly in this play. Here Goethe is farthest removed from Shakespearean drama. Perhaps the style of French classicism, with which shortly before Goethe had again become familiar through his translations of Voltaire, was not without influence here. Goethe did not seek in the substance of his thought alone to keep his spiritual distance from the distressing actuality of the political catastrophe; in the form and language of his drama, too, he endeavors to rise above the confusion of events and to expound reality by treating it as a symbol of general truth. With the exception of the heroine, the persons of this drama have no names and are designated only by their positions. They serve merely as typical representatives of political and social powers who wage war with one another. Nor does one find here reference to a definite country or to definite historical events. This idealistic drama undertakes rather to set forth the characteristic traits of a revolutionary situation in which everything that exists and is seemingly permanent begins to totter, and to show the fate of the individual who insists upon his own eternal rights in the midst of the general catastrophe. It does this by means of discourse rather than action.

In none of Goethe's dramas, not even in *Tasso,* does the dialogue have such terseness; in none is it so richly encrusted with pithy aphorisms. The style of pure poetry here reaches a maturity and beauty which could never be surpassed. *Die natürliche Tochter,* the last of Goethe's classic dramas, marks the end of his classic style; it is, as Schiller said, "wholly art": the poet could not advance further in this direction without becoming artificial and abstract to the point of unintelligibility. The art of this play was already too rarified for contemporaries, its incidents were too poor in the coloring of actual life. The audience found it pale and intellectual, like the linear outlines of Greek art which then played so large a part in Goethe's aesthetic efforts. It was general opinion that the play was as smooth as marble and as cold. But may we term it coldness when the spirit offers its highest power in order to transcend the sense of the overwhelming menace of chaos; when it seeks to raise actual conflict to the sphere of a poetic spectacle and to show that the struggle of the day is rooted in an eternal contrast? In such times there exists in the relations of social classes to one another not the relatively balanced cultural status, which Goethe had accustomed himself to regard as permanent, but a sharply defined and hostile Either-Or:

Thou must either mount or fall,
Thou must either rule and win,
Or submissively give in,
Triumph, or else yield to clamor,
Be the anvil or the hammer.[12]

[12] Du musst steigen oder sinken, / Du musst herrschen und gewinnen, / Oder dienen und verlieren, / Leiden oder triumphieren, / Amboss oder Hammer sein. (*Ein anderes,* translated by Edgar A. Bowring, *The Poems of Goethe,* p. 127.)

To tolerate violent overthrow as a means of historical development was, as has been said, thoroughly contrary to Goethe's conservative frame of mind. In his picture of social life the masses were not a positive element. But in his rejection of the French Revolution Goethe did not stand alone. The greatest German poet of the older generation, Klopstock, who first hailed the Revolution in solemn odes as the dawn of a freer age, was horrified by the bloody spectacle of the Jacobin terror. Schiller, the boldest opponent of German tyranny, whom the Paris National Assembly had named an honorary citizen of France, was not less repelled by the partisan fury which committed bestialities in the name of reason and justice. Despite his sympathy for the great ideas of the Revolution, Herder was also dismayed by the forms they took. Even among the young generation of romantics, initial enthusiasm turned to detestation of radicalism in action. Under the influence of Edmund Burke, who led the polemic in England against the ideas of 1789, they developed a conservative program of political reforms and an antirevolutionary, organic concept of history. In the complete picture of the German reaction, therefore, Goethe's negative attitude to the Revolution was neither abnormal nor unique. It was only that no one else had felt such decided distaste from the beginning as had he. Even in his old age he speaks of the Revolution as the "most frightful of all events."

And finally, if in his drama Goethe sought refuge from the politically actual in the generally human, he was not alone in this urge. When Schiller announced a new monthly, *Die Horen,* in 1794, he made it the principal point of his program that nothing would be said in it concerning politics, the "favorite theme of the day." For, as he thought, it was precisely in a period of excitement that it appeared necessary "again to liberate spirit by a general and higher interest in what is *purely human* and raised above the influence of the age, and again to unite the world, politically divided, under the banner of truth and beauty." A similar purpose was Goethe's when he dealt with a thoroughly real subject in a thoroughly unreal style.

The Friend

GOETHE FOUND UNEXPECTED RELEASE FROM THE ISOLATION WHICH ENVELOPED HIM AFTER HIS RETURN FROM ITALY IN HIS FRIENDSHIP WITH SCHILLER. THE decade of this union with the greatest poet whom Germany possessed after Goethe became the happiest period of his spiritual history. At first everything seemed to bode an unfriendly opposition rather than a union. Soon after Goethe's return, Schiller made the acquaintance of the quietly revered and much sought-after "great man." The first impression is described in a letter: "[Goethe] is of medium stature, bears himself stiffly, and has a stiff gait; his face is inscrutable, but his eye very expressive and animated, and one finds pleasure in his glance . . . His voice is entirely agreeable, his discourse flowing, spirited, and lively." But would Schiller be able to come closer to him?

At first Goethe rather withdrew from his discreet suitor. He had returned to Weimar with definite ideas of a pure, classic art, and was less inclined than ever to favor any form of naturalistic or extravagant expression. But the German public still preferred such pieces as Schiller's *Die Räuber* ("The Robbers"), in which "brainstorm" Goethe saw nothing but the aberration of an immature talent. Neither had Schiller's last work, *Don Carlos,* pleased him; nor had the essay "On Grace and Dignity," which was inspired by Kant. Schiller now lived near Goethe, in Jena. When they met upon occasion they were not cordial to one another. Schiller found Goethe's mode of thought not sufficiently definite, his entire attitude too sensual, too realistic. Then there was his private life, the free union with Christiane Vulpius, "who has a child by him," and whom he was going to marry—a fine stroke of genius!

Schiller's judgment was darkened by a concealed bitterness, disillusioned hope, a deeply offended pride. He knew very well that he could not measure himself against Goethe as a poet, certainly not in lyric poetry. "He has far more genius than I"—and more expertness, greater power of sensual imagery, a more refined sense of art. Schiller's humbled *amour propre* erupted in the only explosion of passionate distaste which the younger poet ever allowed himself against Goethe's person. "This man, this Goethe, stands in my way." He felt as Brutus must have felt toward Caesar. How agreeably fate had dealt with Goethe, and how harshly with Schiller! "Through a sad and bleak youth I strode into life." He had had to leave home without finding a safe harbor, had suffered deprivation, had been forced to rely upon the help of others—this proud man who valued nothing higher than freedom and independence. Now he must again fight for his existence, uncertain whether he would be able to marry his Lotte, and whether he could find some modest position, some small income. He was finally given a professorship of history at Jena; Goethe had helped procure him this place. But what sort of position was this? Work which was unsuitable to him, and no fixed pay. He felt deceived.

Year after year the two passed one another as strangers. Nevertheless, Goethe had several of Schiller's plays presented at the theater in Weimar. For his part, Schiller praised Goethe's *Egmont* moderately in a critical article, and on the appearance of *Iphigenie* said that Goethe's genius had nothing to fear from comparison with the Greek tragedians. In his aesthetic studies Schiller approached ever closer to the principles of the classic concept of art. Whereas Goethe remained rigid in his fixed views, Schiller inwardly moved in his direction. As far as he was concerned, it was a kind of secret contest: if his self-confidence was to assert itself he must in his own fashion attain the height upon which he saw Goethe above him. When he had matured sufficiently to become a friend, on an equal basis, and when Goethe's situation, if it was not to grow into a crippling crisis, demanded that he have such a friend—at that favorable moment the two men were brought together by a chance meeting. For Goethe the consequences of this encounter were so important that it might seem the work of a designing providence.

In July 1794 Goethe and Schiller took part in a meeting of scholars in the field of natural history at Jena. By accident they both left together and spoke of the report which they had just heard. Schiller said that "so fragmentary a manner" of regarding nature did not suit him. Neither did it suit him, remarked Goethe, but there was another, better manner: one must imagine nature as a single large organism. And now Goethe developed his doctrine of the "flexible law," in accordance with which nature produces its organisms—the idea of metamorphosis. Schiller rejoined in the terminology of Kant that this was not experience but an idea. Goethe was disappointed, but answered courteously that he could only be content that he had such ideas and was capable of imagining them so clearly. By means of this conflict, the two men discovered that behind their views there must lie a common, higher unity.

"Schiller's power of attraction was great; he attached to himself all that approached him," Goethe said at the end of the report in which he recorded this first serious conversation. Schiller took the next step, which was decisive in determining the future of their relationship. He wrote Goethe a letter such as Goethe had never yet received, filled with generous admiration, profound and correct in its remarks on Goethe's personality and artistry. Goethe replied in a similar spirit of generous candor. It was as if royal spirits had freely associated themselves in a noble accord whose principal article was the open recognition of the peculiar worth which each perceived and acknowledged in the other, plus the will to form an alliance upon this basis. For the first time Goethe could have the feeling that he was understood and approved by a poet of his own standing.

What Schiller had said of Goethe in his letter he developed upon a note of philosophic speculation in his brilliant essay *Ueber naive und sentimentalische Dichtung* ("On Naïve and Sentimental Poetry"). Here the question is propounded whether a modern writer can hope to attain the position of the great poets of antiquity who possessed innately the quality which modern man yearns for as it were a lost paradise, to wit, oneness with nature. The problem in cultural philosophy here posed has its hidden source in a very personal question: how could Schiller as a poet of ideas assert himself beside the realistic naturalness of Goethe's writing? The answer was supplied by the experience of life, which Goethe formulated as follows: "It is seldom that persons, as it were, constitute the halves of one another, do not repel one another, but join and complement one another." He further declared that pure enjoyment and true advantage could only be mutual. And so it came about. A fair give and take was the basis for establishing and maintaining an association which continued to be honorable and lively for a decade. Goethe was at once convinced that Schiller's friendly interest would quicken and enhance his productivity. It soon developed that in fundamentals they were at one, that their personal reactions, thoughts, and wishes coincided or were sufficiently alike over large areas. The intimacy of their intellectual communion was equaled by the intimacy of their external association. As long as he lived in Jena, Schiller came to visit Goethe frequently in Weimar; and when his regular visits took Goethe to Jena, he was in daily contact with Schiller. After 1799 Schiller too lived at Weimar, and this made an even closer association possible.

Although no reports of their conversations remain, their extraordinary correspondence provides a reliable picture of the character of their association and the subject matter of their discussions. Thus it forms a kind of compendium of German classicism. All questions of art and of the intellectual life are here dealt with; there are problems of technique and of creation which only artists could discuss with professional competence; there are questions concerning the literary life in Germany; and finally, others dealing with the profoundest artistic principles. One speaks to the other with freedom of his personal and artistic weaknesses, but also of the admiration which he feels for his friend. Goethe here confesses that he is filled with trepidation at the thought of writing a genuine tragedy and fears that the mere attempt would destroy him. Thereupon Schiller replies that he finds a tragic power and depth in all of his friend's works, and that this power would surely suffice for a complete tragedy. The two poets constitute a kind of ideal audience for one another, and even more, they release one another's productive energies. Schiller's critical remarks on *Wilhelm Meister*, which Goethe completed during the first years of their friendship, are the most pertinent and profound that have ever been made on that work. Without Schiller's constant prodding, *Faust* would probably have remained forever the fragment which Goethe had printed in 1790. Goethe expresses his gratitude in most generous terms: "You have given me a second youth and have again made me a poet, which I had virtually ceased to be." And Schiller, to whom Goethe discharged a similar duty of offering encouragement, thought that so sage and painstaking a friend was truly a gift of God. Where in the history of the world's literature are we to find such an exchange as this?

Once the friends combined their efforts for a poetic enterprise, which is as remarkable as a venture of this sort must inevitably be. It is a multifarious work whose unity is comprised in a common attitude and a common form, a cycle of epigrams. These epigrams, which they called *Xenien* (1796), are barbed verses, bolts and arrows discharged against all that was worthless, mediocre, and partisan in contemporary German literature, strictures against petty spirits, in which even greater men like Wieland, Herder, Jean Paul, and the romanticists were not wholly spared. Of this work Goethe later reported: "Frequently I supplied the thought and Schiller made the verses, frequently the reverse was the case, and frequently Schiller made one verse and I the other." This was rather a work of purgation and cure than an expression of personal repugnance.

Schiller was already a sick man when Goethe made his acquaintance, though he was only thirty-five years old. His sufferings constantly increased; his works were wrested from a body whose health was already seriously undermined. When he died he was forty-five. The leading periodical in Germany then spoke of him as "the best-loved, favorite poet of the nation." He himself had regarded Goethe as greater and had loved him, for, in keeping with his friend's saying, to such great merits there could be no response but love. Goethe later said that Schiller's death had blighted his life. It is certain that, second only to the Italian journey, Schiller most deeply affected Goethe's life. The world of the eighteenth century from which both derived, the great movement of ethical idealism, vanished together with Schiller. Contemporaries wondered that Goethe did not create a memorial to his friend. He answered: "How could I? I was ruined." But he did make an attempt. The sketch contains the famous verses:

Nights that he spent in vigil
Have made bright for us the day.[1]

A few months after Schiller's death a dramatic presentation of the *Glocke* was given at the summer theater at Lauchstädt. For this occasion Goethe composed an epilogue which is a deeply felt and eloquent threnody for his friend:

Meanwhile his mighty spirit onward pressed
Where goodness, beauty, truth for ever grow;
And in his rear, in shadowy outline, lay
The vulgar which we all, alas, obey![2]

[1] Seine durchgewachten Nächte / Haben unsern Tag erhellt. (Translated by Stuart Atkins.)

[2] Indessen schritt sein Geist gewaltig fort / Ins Ewige des Wahren, Guten, Schönen, / Und hinter ihm, in wesenlosem Scheine, / Lag, was uns alle bändigt, das Gemeine. (*Epilogue to Schiller's "Song of the Bell,"* translated by Edgar A. Bowring, *The Poems of Goethe*, p. 429.)

Goethe thought of completing the Demetrius tragedy which Schiller had left as a fragment. But such a project could not succeed. When he later told the story of his life he meant to include a detailed account of his complete association with Schiller. But this too came to nought; we have only a few notes which were published in an appendix to the *Annalen* (most detailed on the beginning of the friendship). Goethe never ceased speaking of Schiller in terms of the highest admiration. Schiller was, he said, the last aristocrat among the German poets, without fear or reproach. No vain word was ever heard of him. Goethe disapproved of the discussions which had already begun concerning the relative merit of himself and Schiller. Instead of quarreling as to which of the two is greater, he said, one ought rather rejoice that there were two such "fine fellows" about whom to quarrel.

The Problem of "Bildung"

AMONG ALL FORMS OF LITERARY COMPOSITION THE NOVEL HAS UNTIL THIS DAY HAD GREATEST DIFFICULTY IN MAINTAINING ITSELF IN THE FACE OF LITerary criticism. It is paradoxical enough that precisely the most popular of all forms and at the same time the form which possesses the highest market quotation in the literary commerce of nations must time and again struggle for its legitimate place in the realm of art. A half art, an incidental art, or no art at all, the most formless of all forms, the latest and most questionable species of literary development—such are the judgments of traditionalists among writers and critics concerning the favorite of bourgeois literature. In the name of lyric poetry (as the essence of pure poetry) and of drama (as the highest form of poetry), the novel is decried as an illegitimate competitor. Only the epic in verse is vouchsafed equal aesthetic rights. One may well inquire, with what right? Does verse alone transform shapeless material into a structure capable of satisfying the strict demands of traditional aesthetics? Epic in verse is virtually dead; it had its bloom in the Middle Ages and in the Renaissance. Everywhere its place has been taken by the novel. The youngest of modern literatures, such as the Russian, the Scandinavian, the American, straightway made their highest contributions in the form of the novel. It may nevertheless be that in the view of the sacred canon of traditional aesthetics the very supplanting of verse epic by prose narrative is a symptom that rigorous style and pure form have disintegrated—if one could prove that in form the modern novel is nothing more than loosely organized reportage, unsystematic psychological analysis, or masked autobiography. But can such degradation of the novel be taken seriously in view of the great examples of the nineteenth century, to say nothing of older examples of the highest rank, such as *Don Quixote*, the writings of the English humorists of the eighteenth century, or *Werther*? Here the novel is as genuine art as anything produced in lyric and in drama.

It may well be that denigration of the novel as formless rests upon a concept of form which is too rigid—as if stylized language and artistically ordered rhythms were the only elements of form. The novel (like the *novella*) is organized by what we have been wont to call, since Shaftesbury's day, "inner form"—a form which is not perceptible to the eye, not distinguishable to the ear. Out of the steadily flowing process of life, situations, figures, and incidents are selected, taken up, and compressed into the definite entity of an episode, which is made into the representative case, the microcosmic symbol, of the whole of life. Basically there is no other form here than that of composition. The possibilities of this truly Protean species seem limitless. Ever since it reached full development it has easily accommodated itself to attitudes of life and images of the world as they have undergone change in the course of history. It has approximated the lyric and also the drama, it has served fanatic devotion to truth and also free-ranging fantasy. In didactic eras the novel has been a means to affect the life of society. It has been open to the philosophic, psychologic, sociologic interests of the modern spirit. There appears to be no literary forum upon which the current questions of a day can be discussed with equal convenience.

Periods of classic art are inclined to establish rigid bounds for the various literary genres, and to maintain individual genres with their characteristic peculiarities unadulterated. What Goethe thought of this at this time he has said in *Wilhelm Meister* (in the seventh chapter of the fifth book, written in 1795). Here (in connection with

Hamlet) the distinctions between the novel and drama are discussed and the conclusion is reached that the novel must present above all convictions and incidents, the drama characters and deeds. Thus in the novel the hero must suffer rather than act. This gives rise to a process which is always slow, always retarding. Here we do not witness the painful spectacle of passion and will wrestling with fate and the environment and the resultant loss of happiness and of life. It is not conflict and struggle that the novel must present, but rather growth, development, accommodation, the friendly harmony and coöperation of man and universe, of will and destiny. Here the individual and life are linked to one another, are woven into a single web. The course of things indicates no irreconcilable disharmony in the nature of life, but rather a secret harmony. An adjustment is reached and arouses deep satisfaction, which is not the result of conscious strife and struggle. The hero does not live according to a preconceived plan. The hidden nature of life appears to manifest itself as a "purposeless expediency," which, as Kant says, is the essence of the beautiful. To make the bright and invigorating phenomenon of this hidden order manifest was more in keeping with the aims of the classic humanist than was the representation of irremediable opposition which is the subject matter of tragedy.

Wilhelm Meisters Lehrjahre reflects the prime interest of the idealist: the preoccupation with the question of personality, the essence of whose being resides within itself, and whose worth is its uniqueness. This excludes everything that might distract the author to representations of spiritual moods. It is no psychological novel. An event is portrayed—the development of an individuality—which shows the objectivity and teleological direction of an organic process, of a growth which proceeds according to its own laws. What this book purposes to show is the way the ego emerges from a given nucleus in a gradual, imperceptible, yet consistent process, and finally reaches maturity. In this development a balance is established between the individual who is forcing his way into the world and the self-contained, counteracting environment. At the end of the story the personality stands complete in its development, prepared to be a fellow man and to take a place in the life of the social whole. This process of maturation is the nucleus about which the colorful stories of the novel crystallize. We never arrive at anything that might be called a result. The most significant epoch in the life of an individual is the time during which it is in the process of development; thereupon begins its conflict with the world, and this can be interesting only insofar as something emerges from it—so says Goethe to Eckermann. It is with the decisive last phase of the process of development that the narrative begins; the story of childhood is recounted in allusions. And the novel ends at the threshold of manhood, where "conflict with the world begins."

The hero is not an extraordinary person. An exceptional case, a genius with his peculiar problems, a man like Tasso, could not serve as symbol, could not constitute a classic case, in the degree requisite for a formative novel of education. Decades later Goethe expressed himself in a conversation to the effect that Wilhelm was indeed only a "poor dog," but that only in such a figure could the ramifications of life and its diverse duties be clearly indicated, as they could not be in a definite, complete character. In the novel an individual capable of instruction and cultivation, a student of life eager for knowledge, is conducted through the multifarious experiences of the world. He is "Wilhelm Schüler [Student], who, I know not how, has surprisingly obtained the name of Meister [Master]"; a man who still has to learn the art of life. "To develop my individuality, quite as it is, was unconsciously from youth up my desire and my purpose." [1] Wilhelm's efforts become constantly clearer, more conscious, more definite—that is the path his inward development takes.

According to the substance of this book the progress of maturation is cultivation, the development of the hero into a civilized human being. This process is not the result of purposeful pedagogic efforts, as in older educational novels; it is consummated by the complicated interworking of incalculable forces and powers, like the processes of growth in the vegetative world. This is the first classical formative novel of the Germans—not the first of its kind in general (that position is held by Wieland's *Agathon,* which appeared thirty years before)—and the model for a long series of successors. Other nations, too, have similar novels of development or education; but only among the Germans did this genre attain such flowering and such perfection that it may be called the German species of modern novel *par excel-*

[1] Mich selbst, ganz wie ich da bin, auszubilden, das war dunkel von Jugend auf mein Wunsch und meine Absicht. (*Wilhelm Meisters Lehrjahre,* Book V, chapter iii.)

lence. This may be regarded as a weighty argument for the view that modern Germans are an individualistic people to a higher degree than other European nations. The English and French novels of the nineteenth century were to a far greater extent novels of society. Even a narrative with a similar motif, such as Stendhal's *La Chartreuse de Parme,* does not have the full development of the hero's individuality as its theme; it only tells how he learned great passion.

After the completion of this novel Goethe wrote to Schiller that the apparent, specifically stated results of the work were not its whole content. That is to say, they are not the whole of the narrative. For what is presented here is the *orbis pictus* of contemporary German life. Using as his example special German conditions, the author depicts the general situation of educated people in eighteenth-century Europe. Wilhelm is a child of the third estate, the bourgeoisie. He is driven out of the constraint of bourgeois limitations into the world of romance and into ventures of the spirit by his vague desire for an existence which would transcend the sphere of the useful and the commonplace, of trade and material possessions. "A prudent man finds the best education in travel." The traditional form of the novel of travel proved to be the most convenient for presenting the development of a personality, since the hero had to be brought into contact with diverse representatives of contemporary culture and the manifold spheres of social life.

The first part of the novel depicts Wilhelm's relation to the theater. In its first form (begun 1777, finished 1785), which extended only to the sixth book and was then broken off, the work bore the title *Wilhelm Meisters theatralische Sendung* ("Wilhelm Meister's Theatrical Mission"). In these parts Wilhelm appears to be fascinated by the idea that his efforts for a higher existence could best be realized through the medium of the theater. He feels within himself the power to step forward as actor and playwright and as reformer of the backward German theater, and from this lay pulpit to speak to the heart of his people. The conviction of his great mission gives wings to his spirit. The novel alludes to the period after the middle of the eighteenth century. It was the period of the great ascent by which the Germans, as the last of the older civilized nations, attained the heights to which other peoples better favored by history had been able to raise themselves previously.

The dream of a national theater was more than a romantic fantasy at the time. A national theater, in contrast to the court theater and the primitive mimes of wandering troupes, signified one which addressed itself to all who were capable of understanding the language of art. At the very time that Goethe began to write his novel, the Emperor Joseph had raised the *Burgtheater* of Vienna to the rank of national theater, so that serious drama might have a worthy seat. Lessing had favored such plans, and while connected with the *Nationaltheater* at Hamburg he had endeavored to promote their realization. The "sweet dream" was destroyed by the bitter realization that no national theater could be created for a people which was not yet a nation. But this was to misapprehend the situation. For the very reason that the Germans were torn apart politically like no other nation in Europe with the exception of the Italian, and because they possessed no national but only a cultural unity, a community of language, arts, and sciences, the theater was the appropriate place from which the voice of the collective spirit could speak to all the upper classes. In the period of transition to the "permanent theater," which was essential for the new drama created by bourgeois poets—a theater with a fixed cast, a fixed audience, and a distinguished repertory—the idea of the national theater was the star which indicated the correct way. Among the literary genres, drama is the most social. Like symphonic music it demands a group of performers, and it is intended to be taken up and enjoyed by an audience. The theater is an assembly which is representative of all society.

Wilhelm was right; if he wished to reach the educated classes, a national theater was the best medium in Germany. Even as a boy he had perceived in his marionette theater a higher world of fantasy. An actress was the first love of the bourgeois youth, who did not understand that the instruments of art have nothing to do with the ideal world which they help call into life for a brief hour. His next step was a connection with one of the traveling troupes which then gave rough-and-ready satisfaction to theatrical appetites of the cities. With these comedians Wilhelm arrives at the castle of a duke, where he writes an allegorical piece which meets with approval. But his pride of authorship is quickly dampened by an encounter which gives him his first proper notion of dramatic art. He becomes acquainted with Shakespeare's plays. Nothing that he had hitherto read or experienced could be compared with the impression these plays made upon him. This was great poetry, but it was more: "It is as if one were standing before the huge book of fate laid open . . . He seems to answer for us all riddles . . ." A new world was thrown open to him, an unfamiliar sense of true life uplifted him. He became dominated by a desire to enact the "incomparable Hamlet" with the troupe. Wilhelm wished to rehearse the tragedy and himself play the prince. More than ever he was convinced that his urge toward the harmonious cultivation of his nature and his need to affect a larger circle could both be satisfied only through the theater. Therefore, he joins the troupe, stating as his condition that *Hamlet* shall be produced. He had already begun to translate the play, and when he speaks of it we see how well he understands it. He makes an adaptation for the troupe, and in this version the play is rehearsed. The dramatic production itself constitutes the high point of Wilhelm's life in the theater.

But at the very moment of his intoxication with the happiness of success, a mysterious warning reaches him from an unknown source: "Flee, lad, flee!" The role which the theater could play in Wilhelm's education has ended. If he wished to remain in that sphere he must forfeit the higher possibilities of his existence. Another task awaits him, for which he can become adequate only in another school: "Vivre est le métier que je lui veux apprendre" (Rousseau, *Emile*). A duty which piety required him to fulfill leads to Wilhelm's departure from the troupe. A new phase of his student years, the last, begins.

At a castle he meets a small circle of active humanists. In them the most important powers that actuate human existence seem to be personified. Together they constitute the totality of an ideal personality, and they are guided by a common spirit. Wilhelm is inwardly prepared to accept what this elite has to teach him. He has had enough of theater management. All that he had attempted heretofore now seems aberration and confusion. When he hears one of his new friends declare it best for him to leave the theater entirely because he has no talent at all for it, he is ready to accept this sentence, though it wounds his self-love grievously. He does in fact take leave of the theater, and as guest of the Society of the Tower (as the circle of friends is called) he learns insights which give new direction to his life and form to his personal existence. If he has hitherto existed for himself, dominated by the urge to promote the development of his individuality, he now comprehends that when individual cultivation has attained a certain level a man must integrate himself into a community and learn "to live for the sake of others and forget himself in dutiful activity. Only then does he get to know himself, for it is in action that we really compare ourselves with others." [2]

Life has already in fact prepared a task for him which will bring all his confusions and dilettante efforts to an end. Wilhelm discovers that he has a son: Felix, the issue of his love affair with the actress Marianne. The child had been about him for some time without his realizing how closely they are related. What has been a badly managed aberration of his first unskilled steps into independent existence is now transformed by the genius of life into the fairest possibility for useful and purposeful activity. His apprenticeship is over. He himself must now become teacher and educator, must care for, provide for, sustain.

> He no longer looked upon the world like a bird of passage, or upon a building as a bower, hastily put together, which withers before it is deserted. Everything that he thought of initiating had to grow along with the boy, and everything that he produced had to endure for several generations. With this attitude his years of apprenticeship were ended, and with the feeling of a father he had also acquired all the virtues of a citizen.[3]

Life has yet another gift in store for him. He finds the woman who had appeared to him in his theater period as a helper in time of need and as a fleeting promise of future fulfillment. Natalie possesses the inner wholeness to which Wilhelm had aspired on the eagerly trodden paths of his education. This "beautiful soul" becomes his wife, and this is the highest confirmation of the worth he has now attained.

Of the end of the novel Schiller said that Wilhelm passed from an empty and indefinite ideal into a definite and active life without

[2] . . . um anderer willen zu leben und seiner selbst in einer pflichtmässigen Tätigkeit zu vergessen. Da lernt er erst sich selbst kennen, denn das Handeln eigentlich vergleicht uns mit andern. (*Wilhelm Meisters Lehrjahre*, Book VII, chapter ix.)

[3] Er sah die Welt nicht mehr wie ein Zugvogel an, ein Gebäude nicht mehr für eine geschwind zusammengestellte Laube, die vertrocknet, ehe man sie verlässt. Alles, was er anzulegen gedachte, sollte dem Knaben entgegen wachsen, und alles, was er herstellte, sollte eine Dauer auf einige Geschlechter haben. In diesem Sinne waren seine Lehrjahre geendigt, und mit dem Gefühl des Vaters hatte er auch alle Tugenden eines Bürgers erworben. (*Wilhelm Meisters Lehrjahre*, Book VIII, chapter i.)

thereby forfeiting his power of idealization. And so it is. Wilhelm's first striving is indefinite; his undeveloped individuality does not understand itself but appears to contain an incoherent multiplicity of urges. In this vague state, theater and acting are the right thing. Here all the possibilities of life and human existence are played with; but the actor is of necessity undifferentiated as an individual because he must have within himself the possibility for many roles. But life demands a different attitude—decision, limitation, action. Voluntary discipline and abnegation is the condition of all cultural achievement, individually as well as collectively. In the novel these decisive maxims are given epigrammatic expression: "Man cannot be happy until his unqualified striving sets a limit upon itself." [4] And again: "He who wishes to do or enjoy each and everything in his whole humanity, he who wishes to link all things outside himself to such a sort of enjoyment, he will only spend his time in a forever unsatisfying striving." [5]

It is the same thing that Faust desires:

To bare my breast to every pang,—to know
In my heart's core all human weal and woe,
To grasp in thought the lofty and the deep,
Men's various fortunes on my breast to heap,
And thus to theirs dilate my individual mind,
And share at length with them the shipwreck of mankind.[6]

Wilhelm Meister and Faust are polar opposites, complementary potentialities for giving life fulfillment. One is the man of culture who seeks adjustment and totality; the other, the heroic, absolute titan; in one we sense a dim but gradually prevailing demand for harmony of existence, and in the other a mighty will probing the limits of humanity; one is an individual who integrates himself into the common structure of human culture, while the other's lofty vision transcends

[4] Der Mensch ist nicht eher glücklich, als bis sein unbedingtes Streben sich selbst seine Begrenzung bestimmt. (*Wilhelm Meisters Lehrjahre*, Book VIII, chapter v.)

[5] Wer alles und jedes in seiner ganzen Menschheit tun oder geniessen will, wer alles ausser sich zu einer solchen Art von Genuss verknüpfen will, der wird seine Zeit nur mit einem ewig unbefriedigten Streben hinbringen.

[6] Und was der ganzen Menschheit zugeteilt ist, / Will ich in meinem innern Selbst geniessen, / Mit meinem Geist das Höchst' und Tiefste greifen, / Ihr Wohl und Weh auf meinen Busen häufen, / Und so mein eigen Selbst zu ihrem Selbst erweitern / Und, wie sie selbst, am End' auch ich zerscheitern. (*Faust*, v. 1770, translated by Anna Swanwick, London: Bohn, 1850.)

the mob and the mean; in one, the course of development leads through error and indecision to mature fulfillment, in contrast to the urge of the other which ascends to the infinite in mighty strides; one reflects bourgeois diligence, the other unexampled grandeur. These opposites, Wilhelm Meister and Faust, must be looked upon together if we are to perceive the entirety of human possibilities as Goethe conceived them. In the field of energy between these extreme poles lie the manifold modes of existence by which man may achieve a fulfilling sense of life.

To be sure, the element of the unusual also occurs in the novel; but all that can be called destiny appears here as a helping and serving rather than as a hindering and disrupting function. So friendly are the possibilities which destiny offers, so convenient the course of events, that it ultimately appears to depend solely on man whether he will come to a good end or not.

> The texture of this world is formed of necessity and accident; man's reason is interposed between them and understands how to control them. Necessity it treats as the basis of its being; accident it understands how to direct, to guide and to use, and only when reason stands firm and steady does man deserve to be called a god of the earth.[7]

But such practical wisdom can come only at the end of the process of individual maturation, not at its beginning. It is the fruit of education, not its premise. The man in process of growth can do no other than surrender himself to the external and internal forces which affect him.

> Everything that encounters us leaves traces behind, everything contributes imperceptibly to our education. But it is dangerous to desire to make an inventory of all this. Then we become either proud and negligent or humbled and spiritless, and the one is as hampering to the sequel as the other. It always is safest to do only the next thing that lies before us.[8]

[7] Das Gewebe dieser Welt ist aus Notwendigkeit und Zufall gebildet, die Vernunft des Menschen stellt sich zwischen beide und weiss sie zu beherrschen; sie behandelt das Notwendige als den Grund ihres Daseins; das Zufällige weiss sie zu lenken, zu leiten und zu nutzen, und nur, indem sie fest und unerschütterlich steht, verdient der Mensch, ein Gott der Erde genannt zu werden. (*Wilhelm Meisters Lehrjahre,* Book I, chapter xvii.)

[8] Alles, was uns begegnet, lässt Spuren zurück, alles trägt unmerklich zu unserer Bildung bei; doch es ist gefährlich, sich davon Rechenschaft geben zu wollen. Wir werden dabei entweder stolz und lässig, oder niedergeschlagen und kleinmütig, und eins ist für die Folge so hinderlich als das andere. Das Sicherste bleibt immer, nur das Nächste zu tun, was vor uns liegt. (*Wilhelm Meisters Lehrjahre,* Book VII, chapter i.)

The substance of the life to which Wilhelm matures is not education for the sake of education (*Bildung*), not passive self-enjoyment, and not contemplation. This is the first of Goethe's great writings in which he preaches the gospel of work which he never ceased proclaiming until his death. It combines the activism which is characteristic of the men of the West with the aesthetic and ethical ideal of education of classical humanism. Only a life filled with action is a true life for the cultivated man. "As long as one lives, one must be active." [9] In the "Hall of the Past," the wonderful museum which Wilhelm and Natalie visit, sarcophagi and funerary urns are so exhibited and decorated that the melancholy of the grave is replaced by impressions which lead to the present, to life. The tone is not *memento mori* but "Remember to live." But living is one with acting, working, as long as the day lasts. This is the positive dictum which is impressed upon Wilhelm not only once, but many times, and in many connections: "Doubt of any kind can only be outweighed by effective activity." [10] "To be active is man's first duty." [11] "Wherever you are, wherever you abide, be effective however you can, be active and amenable and let your present be joyful." [12]

It is only through action that the individual is linked with his fellow men; and it is only in and with the community that the individual can hope to realize the ideal of humanism. With specific reference to radically individualistic ideas of culture, Goethe states: "Only all men constitute humanity, only all forces taken together constitute the world . . . Every potentiality is important, and must be developed. If one man promotes only the beautiful, and another only the useful, only in combination do they constitute a whole man." [13] And so we read also in Goethe's autobiography "that only mankind taken as a whole is truly man and that the individual can

[9] So lang' man lebt, sei man lebendig! (*Maskenzüge.*)

[10] Jede Art von Zweifel kann nur durch Wirksamkeit gehoben werden. (*Wilhelm Meisters Lehrjahre,* Book V, chapter xvi.)

[11] Tätig zu sein, ist des Menschen erste Bestimmung. (*Wilhelm Meisters Lehrjahre,* Book VI.)

[12] Da, wo du bist, da, wo du bleibst, wirke, was du kannst, sei tätig und gefällig und lass dir die Gegenwart heiter sein. (*Wilhelm Meisters Lehrjahre,* Book VII, chapter viii.)

[13] Nur alle Menschen machen die Menschheit aus, nur alle Kräfte zusammengenommen die Welt . . . Jede Anlage ist wichtig, und sie muss entwickelt werden. Wenn einer nur das Schöne, der andere nur das Nützliche befördert, so machen beide zusammen erst einen Menschen aus. (*Wilhelm Meisters Lehrjahre,* Book VIII, chapter v.)

only be joyful and happy if he has the courage to feel himself integral to the whole."[14]

Wilhelm's path leads from artistic dilettantism and aesthetic dreams to practical diligence. At first he undertakes something for which his nature supplies no potentiality (as was the case with Goethe's sketching), and seeks cultivation where none was to be found. "An inward feeling warns him to abstain, but he is unable to attain clarification and is driven upon a false path to a false goal, without knowing how it comes to pass."[15] But it is not in his plans for the theater alone that he is a dilettante; his relations to women also are at first characterized by an unsure passivity and by false choices. He makes wrong turns everywhere. But the conclusion to which they lead is good. That is precisely the great truth of life which Goethe wishes to demonstrate by the example of his narrative: how it is possible "that all the false steps lead to an incalculable good." His case is like that of Saul, who went out to seek his father's she-asses and found a kingdom. So it is at the end of the novel. Error, aberration as the correct path, false striving as the inevitable and indispensable bypath to the correct goal: could there be a more positive view of the possibilities which life holds ready for proper effort? "It is by error that man is able to advance toward truth" (C'est par l'erreur qu'au vrai l'homme peut s'avancer—C. A. Helvétius).

This faith too, Goethe acquires from his trust in the moral pre-eminence of action, in the "primacy of practical reason." In a note for his autobiography he says that error as well as truth can be the motivation of activity. Since the deed is everywhere the prime consideration, something excellent may arise from an error in deed, for the effect of everything done extends to infinity. "So production is indeed always best, but destruction too is not without happy consequence."[16] Or, in a letter: "Every return from error edifies man mightily, in detail and in the whole."[17] The premise of this view is that action is

[14] . . . dass die Menschheit zusammen erst der wahre Mensch ist und dass der Einzelne nur froh und glücklich sein kann, wenn er den Mut hat, sich im Ganzen zu fühlen. (*Dichtung und Wahrheit,* Part II, Book IX.)

[15] Ein inneres Gefühl warnt ihn, abzustehen, er kann aber mit sich nicht ins klare kommen und wird auf falschem Wege zu falschem Zwecke getrieben, ohne dass er weiss, wie es zugeht. (*Annalen, Bis 1786.*)

[16] So ist das Hervorbringen freilich immer das Beste, aber auch das Zerstören ist nicht ohne glückliche Folge. (*Anhang II* to *Dichtung und Wahrheit IV.*)

[17] Jede Rückkehr vom Irrtum bildet mächtig den Menschen im Einzelnen u. Ganzen aus.

good in itself because even from a mistake something good may emerge in the chain of consequences, whereas inaction due to apprehension of error leads to nothing. Just as new life is summoned into being through destruction, so out of error recognized and rejected the most positive of consequences may follow. Later, in conversation with Eckermann (January 18, 1825), Goethe summarizes concisely the doctrine contained in Wilhelm Meister's story: "Basically the intention of the whole seems to be nothing else than that man, despite all folly and confusion, is directed by a higher hand and attains his happy goal after all." [18] This "higher hand" manifests itself in the somnambulous assurance, the dreamlike consistency, with which Wilhelm advances toward his goal, however many bypaths and wrong turns he takes. He is rather imperceptibly led to his goal than consciously desirous of it.

> Error will never desert us. A craving for what is ennobling
> Urges, however, our constantly striving minds gently onwards towards truth.[19]

But there is another factor which watches over Wilhelm's steps and warns and guides him at critical points of his journey without his being aware of it. A peculiar creation of the eighteenth century was the secret societies. The most important of them were the Masonic lodges which first appeared in England and then spread over the whole continent. In Germany the elite of the nobility and the intellectual bourgeoisie forgathered in them for humanitarian and charitable purposes. Frederick the Great, Lessing, Wieland, Herder, and Goethe belonged to Masonic orders, and Schiller composed his *Lied an die Freude* ("Song to Joy") for the use of the lodge brothers. In addition, there were other more obscure associations. The combination of practical humanitarianism and secret ritual gave them an aura of romantic idealism. Because of these qualities secret societies became a favorite motif in the novels of the time, popular as well as literary (Schiller's *Der Geisterseher,* and various stories of Jean Paul). In these

[18] Im Grunde scheint doch das Ganze nichts anderes sagen zu wollen, als dass der Mensch, trotz aller Dummheiten und Verwirrungen, von einer höheren Hand geleitet, doch zum glücklichen Ziel gelange.

[19] Irrtum verlässt uns nie; doch ziehet ein höher Bedürfnis / Immer den strebenden Geist leise zur Wahrheit hinan. (*Vier Jahreszeiten,* based on a translation by Paul Drysen, *Goethe's Poems,* p. 322.)

novels the secret emissary usually plays a large part; as protecting "genius," or sometimes as an evil destroyer, he mysteriously directs the destiny of the hero.

Goethe has given a refined expression to this motif in his novel. The emissary here is the Abbé who accompanies Wilhelm in his various wanderings and at the proper time sends him a prudent word. It subsequently appears that the sage mentor is a member of the Society of the Tower, an association of active humanists which had its seat in Lothario's castle. Jarno, a member of this society, also is another helper and warner. When Wilhelm discovers how these men have quietly taken his part, have observed the course of his life and recognized his errors, he asks himself why these invisible friends have not employed greater rigor in directing him, have not exerted their effect more directly. The reply gives expression to the doctrine of the pedagogical value of error which is the basic idea of the novel:

> It is not the duty of the educator of men to protect from error, but rather to guide the errant, even to allow him to drain his cups of error to the dregs—that is the teacher's sagacity. He who only tastes of his error abides with it for a long time, rejoices in it as with some rare fortune; but he who utterly drains it must come to understand it unless he is mad.[20]

In the nineteenth century already exception had been taken to this motif of secret societies, and certainly the modern reader will not accept it as readily as did the audience in an age when these lodges actually played so great a role. But we can easily perceive its function in the course of the action in *Wilhelm Meister* and understand why it is indispensable for the composition. It is a premise for the success of the experiment in education that there can be no inexorable and mechanical fate. What Wilhelm encounters from without dovetails with the striving which develops from within, in friendly coöperation and indeed so perfectly that the course of events approximates the wonderful providential character of a fairy tale.

The solution of the scene in which Faust stands resolute before Care is here anticipated; the important thing is to allow destiny no power over self. How else could it be possible to give one's life stead-

[20] Nicht vor Irrtum zu bewahren, ist die Pflicht des Menschenerziehers, sondern den Irrenden zu leiten, ja ihn seinen Irrtum aus vollen Bechern ausschlürfen zu lassen, das ist die Weisheit der Lehrer. Wer seinen Irrtum nur kostet, hält lange damit Haus, er freuet sich dessen als eines seltenen Glücks; aber wer ihn ganz erschöpft, der muss ihn kennen lernen, wenn er nicht wahnsinnig ist. (*Wilhelm Meisters Lehrjahre,* Book VII, chapter ix.)

fast value through the striving of one's own will? Every man forges his own happiness. One who is accustomed to find ineluctable caprice in the given necessity with which man must reckon, and to ascribe a rational sense to accident, forfeits the use of his reason and mastery over his inclinations. On these matters Wilhelm receives instruction from the Abbé at the very beginning of his wandering (in the seventeenth chapter of the first book). "We imagine we are devout when we loiter along without reflection, allow our course to be determined by agreeable accidents, and finally give the results of such a wavering life the name of divine guidance."[21]

These maxims of Goethe were perhaps intended at the same time to counter the mood of fatalism which began to spread over Germany at that time and then grew to such menacing proportions in romanticism. In the novel, according to Schiller's good explanation, the Society of the Tower took the place of the gods or of destiny. The notion of an autonomous fate taken over from antiquity is here rationalized, but it is not at the same time mechanized. For it is not a rationality proceeding according to its own unfeeling logic which plays the role of destiny in Wilhelm's life; rather it is the understanding and human participation of unselfish men who possess that same potentiality which, unknown to Wilhelm, resides in himself as well, a practical sagacity adequate to life. For them there is only one sort of incident which cannot be controlled, to wit, chance. But the man educated to consistent activity can make even chance serve his ends, and thus exorcise its demonic aspect. What can the art of life mean if not the capacity to transform all that life gives into the positive potentialities for a fruitful existence, accident and necessity, error and omissions? To be sure, the account will never exactly balance; it does so as little in this case as in the case of Faust. If man can neither remove nor expand the limits of his nature, he can nevertheless within these bounds enhance the force and raise the level of his activity. That is the goal of education.

Wilhelm's development is promoted not alone by the greatest and most important of his experiences, his apprenticeship in the magic

[21] Wir bilden uns ein, fromm zu sein, indem wir ohne Überlegung hinschlendern, uns durch angenehme Zufälle determinieren lassen und endlich dem Resultate eines solchen schwankenden Lebens den Namen einer göttlichen Führung geben. (*Wilhelm Meisters Lehrjahre,* Book I, chapter xvii.)

mountain of the theater. Every contact with the people who encounter him (and he has many such contacts) contributes to the process by which his ego is unfolded. The small world of the novel reflects the world of broader life to which character must be educated. The artistic means by which Goethe brings this about consists in his giving individual figures sufficient general significance to permit them to appear as typical representatives of attitudes and phenomena of life. This is not so obvious in the *Theatrical Mission* as it is in the second version, and there especially in the new later parts. When Goethe took the work up again he made notes which reveal this procedure clearly. Concerning the principal persons these notes say: "Wilhelm, aesthetico-moral dream. Lothario, heroically active dream. Laertes, unqualified will. Abbé, pedagogical-practical dream. Philine, present sensuality, frivolity. Aurelie, stubborn, self-tormenting perseverance. Mignon, madness of maladjustment." [22]

Each of these figures represents a single attitude, a definite state, a particular striving. For Wilhelm, who is to be developed and rounded off on all sides as his nature permits, who is to be educated aesthetically and morally at the same time, each of these figures opens up one side of life or one manner of human existence. Some of the figures merit special attention, in particular that of the mysterious girl who enthralls the imagination of the reader more than any other figure in the novel and who has affected the literature of the century following. Mignon appears to exist at the boundary where the soul is confused by the dark powers of madness. She is compact of suffering, and rigid in her pain. An enigma of some kind distinguishes her: she seems an epicene hovering between the sexes. When they wish to give her a girl's dress, she says, "I am a boy, I do not wish to be a girl." Those who do not like her call her androgynous. In the narrative her name sometimes bears the neuter article; in the same sentence she is once referred to as "he" and again as "she." In the *Wanderjahre* she is spoken of as a "boy-girl." Her history, her sad past, explains why she does not wish to be a girl and takes refuge in being a boy. A premonition tells her that her doom must be consummated as soon as she matures to woman-

[22] Wilhelm, ästhetisch sittlicher Traum. Lothario, heroisch aktiver Traum. Laertes, unbedingter Wille. Abbé, pädagogisch praktischer Traum. Philine, gegenwärtige Sinnlichkeit, Leichtsinn. Aurelie, hartnäckiges, selbstquälendes Festhalten. Mignon, Wahnsinn des Missverhältnisses.

hood. Begotten of incest, she is marked by guiltless guilt. She may not become wife or mother. Her sorrow is yearning: yearning for her lost native country, *Das Land wo die Zitronen blühn,* which for her is one with the lost paradise of childhood; yearning for salvation in protective love, which she seeks of Wilhelm. But all fulfillments are unattainably distant. Mignon lives only to the hour in which the first great agony of love makes her emotionally a woman. Now she has transgressed the bounds which have been set her; she cannot, she may not live longer. Her last song gives expression to her last yearning: yearning for redemption from the heavy life which she cannot comprehend and cannot endure. Here she speaks of the figures of heaven as of beings that are neither man nor woman. In Mignon's figure and destiny Wilhelm encounters the power and profundity of an incomprehensible sway whose cruel consequences he learns to avoid by determined discipline of his inward self and rational direction of the course of his life. In her that which society calls "guilt" is revealed as dark doom. The famous verses sung by the harpist, Mignon's father, cause and sharer of her destiny, speak of this matter:

> You lead us darkling into life,
> You let the poor one lose his worth,
> Then let him into misery fall:
> For all guilt is avenged on earth.[23]

In all the colorful movement of the novel and in the benevolent ordering of Wilhelm's career, these manifestations of dark destiny stand as representatives of the other, subterranean world, lawless and irrational. From them the path leads to the demonic sphere of romantic powers and figures. But that is not Wilhelm's path.

The female figure which stands in contrast to him is not the frivolous and pretty sinner, Philine, but Natalie the "Amazon." In her Goethe sets forth pure humanity, as he had in Iphigenie; but in this woman humanity does not appear as a quiet inwardness but as an active love directed toward the world. Goethe called Natalie the heroine of the novel and said of her that she deserved the name of a beautiful soul, for "her virtues arise from her nature, and her edu-

[23] Ihr führt ins Leben uns hinein, / Ihr lasst den Armen schuldig werden, / Dann überlasst ihr ihn der Pein; / Denn alle Schuld rächt sich auf Erden. ("The Bread of Tears" [*Wilhelm Meisters Lehrjahre,* Book II, chapter xiii], based on translation by William G. Thomas, *The Minor Poetry of Goethe.*)

cation stems from her character." She had what Wilhelm lacked; she was in possession of that to which he must be educated. Her nature demanded nothing but what society required; and thus she lived in natural accord with others because she lived in harmony with herself.

The concept of "beautiful soul" was known in medieval mysticism; it is also familiar to the eighteenth century: Wieland, Kant, and Schiller use it, and Rousseau speaks of the *belle âme*. From Plotinus, Shaftesbury adopted the thought that the soul must become beautiful if it is to perceive beauty and realize it. With Goethe this ideal of sensitive individualism acquires a new form. The internal and the external, soul and character, the force of conception and of action, have attained equipoise in the person of Natalie; aesthetic and moral education, the claims of the soul and those of the world, achieve pure reconciliation with one another. To this worldly piety, Christian asceticism is opposed in another female figure, whose autobiography is communicated in an insertion under the title *Bekenntnisse einer schönen Seele* ("The Confessions of a Beautiful Soul")—an unnamed figure who is contrasted to her niece, Natalie. In her the pietistic type which Goethe came to know in a pure form in Susanna von Klettenberg, the friend of his youth, is portrayed with psychologic genius. A girl whose morality is too sensitive, whose pure heart is too demanding to be satisfied with what others call love and life, who can find peace only in free and unqualified obedience to her conscience, finds herself reduced to her inward being as the only place where she may serve God undisturbed. These experiences and the realization of how easily the nature of man is drawn to sin alienate her from the world. Instead of acting and being effective in the world she withdraws into pure contemplation. The reading of these *Bekenntnisse* familiarizes Wilhelm with the value of a definite religious life which is not mentioned elsewhere in the novel. He admires the uncompromising attitude with which the pure soul responds to the effects of the world and endeavors to live according to its own law. But he also learns that a nature so delicate and attuned to so sensitive a conscience is led to an exaggerated cultivation, so that in the end the whole of life seems unattainable. Turning aside from the world, general abnegation, is the consequence. People of this sort, says Natalie, are models whom one must emulate in his own way while following his own path, but whom one must not attempt to imitate. For it is a misfortune for man "if he is induced to strive for something with which he cannot ally himself through some regular activity of his own."

The world of politics makes no appearance in this model picture of cultivated existence. Wilhelm is not educated to politics; indeed, the notion that his readiness and capacity for definite and rational dealing might include political activity also appears strange. We must remember that the novel takes place in a period when the middle class was kept in complete political passivity. But inasmuch as the educational ideal which is realized in the development of Wilhelm's personality finds its final form in the capacity to share in the creation of great communal works of culture, social phenomena and problems play no slight role in the process of development. A letter which Wilhelm writes to his brother-in-law, who wished to recall him to the bourgeois life of gain, gives concise and summary expression to Goethe's thoughts concerning the bourgeoisie and its position with reference to the privileged strata (Book V, chapter iii). Here Wilhelm speaks of his desire to develop his personality. But he thinks that in Germany this is properly the privilege only of the nobleman. An ordinary citizen might indeed distinguish himself personally by a special achievement, and in the end cultivate himself intellectually also; but his personality would be lost in the process. The nobleman, on the other hand, is a "public personage" by descent and position. If he plays his role worthily, he develops at the same time all of the qualities which give an individual personal culture. For him life is full of great possibilities; he is able to act and be effective as a unified personality. But the ordinary citizen is of significance only by reason of specific knowledge, competence, and possession. One who must make himself useful in a specific manner becomes a specialist. So the existing order of society demands; and neither Goethe nor his hero thinks of altering this order.

But for Wilhelm harmonious cultivation means everything. He too would like to be a "public personage," and to this end he would like to fashion his manners, his taste, his spirit. But as an ordinary citizen, he believes, only the theater can give him all of these things. What the actual "great world" is to the aristocrats, the world of illusion must be for Wilhelm: a school of culture. We see what importance is given to the social aspect. Social classes are estimated according to the possibilities which they afford for the education of the whole man. Cultivated personality is the highest, the decisive value. When in the end Wilhelm marries a noble lady who possesses all the advantages of her favored position, the consummation of his education is thereby assured. He succeeds in making the same transition which Goethe himself had completed at Weimar. However, the representatives of the nobility who play so dominant a role in the second part of the novel are ideal figures in a representation whose aim is to provide examples. In the Germany of the time, the nobility (in no other country except England was it so numerous) was by no means as significant culturally as would appear if we should take this portion of the novel as a true description. The life which the circle of the Society of the Tower lived was not typically aristocratic. In the first and more realistic portion of the novel, the presentation of the nobility is quite different. The society which Wilhelm comes to know at the Duke's castle is far more expert in proud enjoyment than in intellectual culture. The portrait of this society is unsparing enough.

Goethe was twenty-seven years old when he began *Wilhelm Meister;* he was forty-three when he set about completing it. In the interval came the decisive experiences of the years at Weimar and of the Italian journey, which brought about profound human and artistic changes. He had begun the novel in a style of vivid realism such as is displayed in no other of his prose works; the first six books are colorful and adventurous, filled with characteristic traits and figures of contemporary social life. The first version is autobiographic to an incalculable degree, in the sketches of the hero as in matters relating to the theater. As late as 1782 Goethe still speaks of Wilhelm as his "beloved image." When he resumed work upon it twelve years later he called the book a "pseudo-confession." The change in general concept corresponds to a far-reaching change in details and especially in the style of the narrative. All critics have been struck by the difference in the depiction of the figures of the second part. Realistic characterization is replaced by representation according to types; to such a degree have the principal figures become representative of definite attitudes toward life, of generally valid concepts and modes of relationship, that they seem to be rather symbols than individual characters. This lack of color appears most clearly in the case of female figures, such as Therese and Natalie.

Hence the novel as a whole acquires a stylistic dichotomy which is an inevitable consequence of its genesis but nevertheless fatal to its artistic effects. It is evident that the world of the theater, the sphere in which the hero moves during the years of his wandering, has in the interval become entirely alien to the author of 1794. We may conjecture that he would have chosen a quite different background if such a thing could have been done. It is possible that Goethe already felt what he expressed in 1823 in a conversation with the Chancellor von Müller. The conversation concerned the great success of Walter Scott's novels, and of how different was the situation of the English as compared to the German writers. Social and political conditions in Germany could only hamper and injure a work like *Wilhelm Meister*, but could not promote it. Goethe's expression of opinion is quite interesting:

> Scott's magic rests upon the magnificence of the three British realms and the inexhaustible multifariousness of their history, whereas in Germany there is no fertile field for the writer of novels anywhere between the Thuringian Forest and the sand wastes of Mecklenburg, so that in *Wilhelm Meister* I was forced to choose the most miserable material imaginable, itinerant comedians and miserable landed gentry, only to bring some movement into my picture.[24]

The circumstances of its origin brought it about that Goethe's greatest prose work, like his greatest dramatic composition, *Faust*, is a fusion of heterogeneous elements, if not in the same measure. Two halves are here joined, which to be sure have an inner connection because of Wilhelm's development, but between which there is a disharmony in form that is not always clearly resolved. The general character of the first part is description, that of the second part reflection. If the first part was composed by a writer whose intention was to recount the story of a maturing individual, the substance of the second part is general sagacity concerning life scattered with a generous hand. The tradition of the philosophical novel which goes back to Voltaire is of course effective even in the first part; but it is

[24] Scotts Zauber ruht auch auf der Herrlichkeit der drei britischen Königreiche und der unerschöpflichen Mannigfaltigkeit ihrer Geschichte, während in Deutschland sich nirgends zwischen dem Thüringer Wald und Mecklenburgs Sandwüsten ein fruchtbares Feld für einen Romanschreiber findet, so dass ich in Wilhelm Meister den allerelendesten Stoff habe wählen müssen, der sich nur denken lässt, herumziehendes Komödiantenvolk und armselige Landedelleute, nur um Bewegung in mein Gemälde zu bringen.

only in the portions written later that the tendency to instructive comment and maxims on the management of life get the upper hand.

However regrettable it may be that this obligatory model for generations of German narrators is not of a single mold and style, its superabundant freight of wisdom will always give the novel a high position among the great books of world literature. Out of it a compendium, unsystematic, to be sure, but spiritually comprehensive, of humanitarian faith and striving can be put together—an introduction to cultivated life according to the noblest of cosmopolitan ideas which the bourgeois culture of the West has produced. It is the idea of the man who develops the principal forces of his ego and unites them into the entity of a well-rounded form; who makes his own rules of conduct and as an independent member joins the society of those who toil for the never-ending work of human culture.

A Middle-Class Homer

WITH NONE OF THE WORKS OF HIS CLASSICAL PERIOD DID GOETHE HAVE SUCH SUCCESS AS WITH *HERMANN UND DOROTHEA* (1797). THE CRITICS OF THE OLDER AS well as the younger generation were at one in their enthusiasm for this epic. Schiller saw in it the pinnacle of Goethe's art, indeed of all German literature. A. W. Schlegel, the leading critic of the romantic school, called it a perfected work of art in the grand style, a book filled with wisdom and morality. Wilhelm von Humboldt, the scholarly humanist, was induced by it to write a book on classical aesthetics. He was of the opinion that the specifically poetic and epic manner seldom appeared in so pure and complete a form as in this masterly composition. Goethe himself long retained a special affection for this work. He willingly read it to friends and admirers, and we have evidence that it often moved him to tears. The fame of the work long survived. G. G. Gervinus, one of the great historians of the nineteenth century, thought that if an Attic Greek should return to life, *Hermann und Dorothea* would be the only poem in all modern literature which might be offered him without embarrassment as a specimen of Western art. But its immediate success does not determine the rank of a poetic work; only the duration of its effect can guarantee its worth. The ideal case in which contemporaries and posterity are equally enthusiastic, as is true of *Werther,* is the exception, not the rule. If we disregard its role as a school text, we may assert that of Goethe's classic works none has so faded as this. It has retained a place of honor, but its niche is in the temple of history, not among living compositions whose effects abide.

To rejuvenate the great epic was a favorite dream of the Germans in the eighteenth century. Klopstock's *Messias* was intended to be a Christian epic in classic verse, to surpass Milton's great model in subject and in spirit. But this pretentious work was to such a degree an expression of pietist religiosity that its popularity had to wane when sentimental devotion lost its power. Wieland's gallant and at the same time sentimental, witty, and entertaining verse narratives of knights and fairies, adventures of war and love, were a secular pendant which continued the romantic but not the ancient form of the epic. Taste for small descriptive narratives in the style of the classic idyll, and study of Homer, gave rise to the bourgeois epic *Luise* of J. H. Voss (1795), a story of a German parsonage told in Homeric rhythms. This was an idyll rather than an epic, but for that reason was more pleasing to educated readers. Not war and battles, not men and arms were sung here, but happiness within the limitations of a patriarchal style of life—the existence of the poor but cultivated middle class upon which the German culture of the time rested. In his book on *Hermann und Dorothea* Wilhelm von Humboldt declares that heroic epic was impossible in the present. Nothing remained to modern writers but to draw epic material "from the private life" of those classes who still lived "the natural, simple life of the ancients."

Hermann und Dorothea, too, is a bourgeois idyll. Again the work of another poet had aroused in Goethe the desire to react creatively to the impression which it made upon him. In a poetic advertisement he gives public acknowledgment to Voss for his inspiration. In addition, another source of inspiration was named, to whom Goethe felt even more obliged; he calls him the man

> . . . who, at last from the great name of Homer
> Freeing us boldly, now calls us with his glory to vie.[1]

[1] . . . der, endlich vom Namen Homeros / Kühn uns befreiend, uns auch ruft in die vollere Bahn. (From the poem *Hermann und Dorothea,* translated by B. Q. Morgan.)

The reference is to the great philologian, F. A. Wolf, who was one of Goethe's friends. Goethe valued, though with patient sighs and fortitude, his instructive association with this man who was always and everywhere belittling and choleric; he admired the caustic acumen of "Master Isegrim," but with some irony. Wolf had proposed the epoch-making hypothesis that *The Iliad* and *The Odyssey* were not the work of a single great poet but of a group of rhapsodes, a *familia Homeridarum.* If that were the case, Goethe wittily remarked, even the modern poet could without arrogance associate himself with the *Homeridae.*

And indeed *Hermann und Dorothea* is Homeric in verse, language, and narrative style. It adheres to the tone of Greek poetry more closely than any other of Goethe's classical works with the exception of his *Römische Elegien.* Actual imitations of Homeric structure and turns of speech are, to be sure, infrequent. The fact that a speaker is regularly introduced in the Homeric manner with a complete verse ("Then spake the goodly dame, and these were the words she uttered") seems almost unavoidable in a hexameter poem. It is a direct imitation of ancient usage when the poet apostrophizes one of his characters ("Wavering yet, dost thou falter, thou neighbor prudent"), or when he invokes the Muses. But the general tendency of the style is more important than these questionable details. With the material of a modern language and in accordance with his ideal of classical clarity and grandeur, Goethe attempts to reach the simple, unembellished sublimity of Homeric diction without actually copying that diction. When he names typical attributes of a character each time he speaks of him, that is of course a peculiarity of Homeric epic, but one which could be adapted to his own narrative style without affectation. The epithets themselves are Goethe's own creation, simple and beautiful, and appropriate to the bourgeois material and idyllic character of the German epic. So, for example, the modest "good" is a frequently used epithet. So, also, carefully chosen adjectives designate simple and pure qualities. This applies no less to descriptions of nature:

> . . . the glorious, spacious
> Landscape, which with its fruitful hills before us is winding.[2]

[2] . . . die herrliche, weite / Landschaft, die sich vor uns in fruchtbaren Hügeln umher schlingt. (*Hermann und Dorothea,* "Euterpe," translated by B. Q. Morgan.)

But, in addition, there are also compounds formed upon the Greek model, such as "all-destroying war," "garden-surrounded houses," mostly suggested by metrical requirements (the dactyls of the hexameter line), which produce an effect of strangeness. In general the meter gave Goethe much trouble. His scholarly friends "of strict observance," in particular Wilhelm von Humboldt, had convinced him that a correct imitation of the ancient scheme in the German hexameter was both possible and necessary if the rhythmic beauty of the Greek verse was to be attained. Thus the poet's feeling for language was misguided and he was led to accept compromises with false and devious views. Hence there is something hybrid about the language and rhythm of Goethe's epic; what was intended as an independent German counterpart to Greek works produces a bookish effect. Frequently the German is pronounced, so to speak, with a Homeric accent. In this fact contemporaries saw a nice confirmation of their belief in the basic relationship of the German spirit with the Greek, of German literary language with that of Greek poetry. Posterity has come to regard these metrical theories as delusions justifiable neither scientifically nor aesthetically.

The story of his poem Goethe took from a local event. He transferred to the present a simple incident in the history of the Protestant refugees who fled to Thuringia from Catholic Salzburg in 1732, among whom was a girl who after some difficulties married a young German. In his work the refugees are emigrants from the left bank of the Rhine who fled before the French armies of the Revolution. Into the love story and the peaceful mood of the small city, the impinging alarms of distant war sound a boding note. But this is only like summer lightning on the horizon, a dark background out of which the strong, wholesome figures of the poem rise to luminous clarity. The incident itself bears the characteristics of a typical story of courtship: the girl from a strange place seems more desirable to the man than the women of his own country, and she stirs his heart. All of the figures have the perfect simplicity of the type; they are ideal representatives of a wholesome bourgeois world, of which the poet wishes to give an exemplary picture of classic dignity. This work, too, belongs among Goethe's efforts to demonstrate to the Germans that neither their character nor situation gave them grounds to be infected by the revolutionary commotion. The epic closes with an appeal to his countrymen to stand steadfast in a period of uncertainty and to protect their possessions.

> It does not become a German to further this fearful commotion,
> And in addition to waver uncertainly hither and thither.[3]

At the time of the war of liberation these nationalist accents gave the work new popularity. The poet was asked for a continuation, but could not bring himself to write one. It was not in Goethe's character to repeat himself.

The artistic significance of this faded work will be found in the first instance in its consistently maintained classic style. In particular the generally significant is everywhere made apparent; here are the true forms of a natural, moral life. Over the whole, petty and straitened as the circumstances of commonplace bourgeois life may be, there shines the splendor of an exemplary existence. This is true even of the details. When, for example, Hermann harnesses his horses, he does so in a manner which conveys an impression of rightness and appropriateness. Men who know their business have always harnessed horses in this way, and always will, if it is done properly. But this perfection is not of a moral nature; there is nothing of the hero of virtue about these figures, indeed, nothing heroic. They are models by reason of their solidity, their diligence, the rich substance of their thoughts and actions, by reason of their appropriate humanity. Goethe attempted to give each separate figure and each separate incident the synthesis of individual character and ideal generalization which he admired in classic art. His figures, he said, must have sufficient individuality to stand by themselves, but, at the same time, they must all belong to the same race—to the race of sound and energetic people who pass their lives in constant activity. That even in their world a higher personal factor can assert its qualified right is demonstrated by Hermann's steadfast love.

In the course of the work Goethe, along with Schiller, sought to reach a philosophic understanding of the principal properties of the epic genre. But these opinions concern the pure form of the epic in contrast to that of the drama and have their being altogether in the

[3] Nicht dem Deutschen geziemt es, die fürchterliche Bewegung / Fortzuleiten, und auch zu wanken hierhin und dorthin. (*Hermann und Dorothea,* "Urania," based on translation by E. A. Browning, p. 113, Philadelphia: McKay, 1898.)

exclusive realm of aesthetic principles. In practice the conclusion was that the modern poet who wished to rejuvenate the moribund genre must confine himself to a definite historical specimen as his ideal model, and this was the epic of Homer. Goethe's artistic power did not avail to break free from the overwhelming constraint of this supreme authority. Klopstock in his *Messias* had been more independent. If historical knowledge and criticism had attained the level which it reached in the nineteenth century, Goethe would have realized how questionable must be the project of renewing the epic after the Homeric manner in so late an age as that of bourgeois culture. Homer's epic style belongs to the Greek middle period, an age of feudal aristocracy and of heroic mentality. The style perished along with the social class to which it belonged, just as the knightly epics of the European Middle Ages perished along with the chivalric society whose poetic illumination they provide. Goethe was sensible of this nexus; he had sought to subdue the lofty style of his bourgeois poem, to moderate the dramatic grandeur of Homer, by adding an idyllic element. In the German situation of the time this compromise form was viable. Goethe, however, realized that even then his readers were more attracted by the sentimental qualities of the material than by the bold innovations of the style. "In *Hermann und Dorothea* I have for once done the Germans' pleasure, as far as the matter is concerned, and now they are highly satisfied." We may surmise that in later periods also the popularity of this work rested more on its subject matter than upon the sciolistic attempt to renew the epic in an age whose soil was no longer able to produce such extinct plants.

The great success which this work enjoyed gave Goethe an incentive to further epic attempts. Some years previously he had recounted the classical animal fable of the Middle Ages, the legend of Isegrim and Reinhardt, of the wolf and the fox, in loosely formed hexameters (*Reineke Fuchs*, 1794). As model he used the prose account which Gottsched had published in the middle of the century. The "primitive world-child" appears here as a rogue in the latest political style.

> You say that in centuries past a poet sang of these matters?
> How can that be? Why, the tale deals with the things of today.[4]

[4] Vor Jahrhunderten hätte ein Dichter dieses gesungen? / Wie ist das möglich? Der Stoff ist ja von gestern und heut'. (*Xenien*, No. 242, translated by B. Q. Morgan.)

Other projects in epic form did not go beyond the planning stage. During his sojourn in Switzerland in 1797, Goethe became acquainted with the legend of William Tell. It seemed to him very appropriate for epic treatment. He thought of the hero as an energetic citizen, naïve and without self-consciousness, and of his antagonist Gessler as a comfortable, temperamental tyrant. But it was disastrous to the project that he asked Schiller about it. "One must never ask anyone, if one wishes to write something." Schiller suggested a plan for a dramatic treatment of the legend, but Goethe abandoned the whole idea.

Another plan was more ambitious. The idea of vying with the greatest epic poet on his own ground must have seemed to the German classicist a venture worthy of engaging all his artistic skill. Between Hector's death and the retirement of the Greeks from Troy there seemed to him to be place for a further "Homeric" epic. It would tell of the death of Achilles and of Hector. Fired by Schiller's interest, Goethe dedicated himself to this enterprise with great devotion. He wished to present Achilles in love with Polyxena, that is to say, as a sentimental lover of the breed of Werther rather than as a hero of Homeric cast. Only one canto of Goethe's *Achilleis* was completed, and it contains more talk than action. It is not surprising that this vision of classicistic and historical preoccupation would not take shape; it cannot be regretted that the enterprise did not succeed.

As by-products of Goethe's epic mood several ballads emerged, which are distinctly different from his earlier works of this character. The best of the earlier ballads, such as *Der Erlkönig* (1780) and *Der Fischer* (1779), were in motif and style still inspired by folk poetry. They are stories of the forces of nature, of mythical spirits of the elements which seize upon men, of elf-kings and water sprites. The new poems, on the other hand, are tales in verse. They do not recount instances of model morality, as do Schiller's ballads, but rather marvelous incidents in which some general insight or idea is given symbolic representation. *Der Zauberlehrling* ("The Sorcerer's Apprentice"; 1797) gives spirited treatment to the old motif of the presumptuous disciple who would play with the half-understood art of his master. The material derives from Lucian. *Die Braut von Korinth* ("The Corinthian Fiancée") also uses an old legend, the story of the "living corpse," of the vampire who draws her surviving lover down to her grave. Goethe has given the horrible incident deeper meaning by making the basis of the story the opposition between the natural piety of the Greeks and the ascetic spiritualism of Christianity. The third and best creation of this fruitful year was *Der Gott und die Bajadere* ("The God and the Bajadere"). The original Indian legend had long occupied Goethe's imagination. He gives it a form which makes it a magnificent example of faith in the innate yearning of man for the good and the genuine. Union with God awakens in the lost Bajadere the hidden spark, the capacity for true love. The light burns bright and strong in the defamed woman. When she preserves the loyalty of a spouse by voluntary immolation, God raises her purified to himself. "The deity rejoices in repentant sinners." Goethe has scarcely told a more beautiful story in verse. Our admiration must hesitate between the poetic mastery and the sublimity of the concept. The loving union of God and creature, of the ego and the All, is here celebrated as the mystery which is at the heart of all great religions of redemption.

Classic Poems

GOETHE'S LYRIC POETRY OF THE TWO DECADES AFTER HIS RETURN FROM ITALY DISPLAYS THE MASTER IN MANY FORMS AND KEYS. THUS THERE IS A GROUP OF poems, inspired by closer familiarity with the Roman elegiac poets, archaic in style, meter, and in many details. These are echoes or by-products of his epic attempts, written during the years when the hexameter was a familiar measure to him. *Alexis und Dora* recalls the mood of Ovid's *Heroides*, except that here the ancient style is completely transposed to the key of modern passion. The locale is Italian, the scenery southern, perhaps the Bay of Naples as it presented itself to Goethe when he embarked for Sicily. The beautiful pictures are evoked by yearning memories; the bittersweet recollection of hours of fulfillment and departure supplies the emotional content of the poem. The lover himself recounts the story of his love in a moving monologue. Everything is compressed into a single hour—meeting, profession of love, devotion, and separation. The fleeting rapture was enhanced to exquisite pain by the separation which was implicit in it—"woe and happiness" at once. As the boat carries the lonely man farther and farther away from his beloved, his longing grows to retain the brief happiness which had been so unexpectedly vouchsafed him, and to make it secure as bridegroom, as husband. But now anxiety is aroused, and jealousy, which threaten to rend his soul; and this constitutes a new and climactic intensification which drives him to despair, to death. A "poet's *envoi*" suggests mitigation, healing, but does not carry the story itself beyond the climax at which it breaks off. Past and future fuse in the almighty present, which for this single bittersweet moment exhibits the overwhelming power of an absolute. The poetic beauty of this little work is so great that it may stand with assurance beside the most important love elegies of Roman literature.

A kindred archaizing style is exhibited by the elegy *Euphrosyne*, a poem of deep feeling and beautiful eloquence in memory of a young woman, the eighteen-year-old Christiane Neumann. She was Goethe's favorite among the actresses at Weimar, intimate with him from her early youth, and educated by him. On his Swiss journey in the fall of 1797 he received news of the death of this charming girl. The opening of the poem depicts the Alpine scenery in a few majestic verses; painful memory evokes Euphrosyne's shade from Hades where she has been dwelling in the circle of famous women who have died young—those of whom Greek legend and drama tell, the circle of Antigone and Polyxena. In memory of the time when she played the princely boy in Shakespeare's *King John,* the shadow of the winsome child comes to life. And now the poet raises a lament upon the lot of man who alone among all creatures of the natural order is subject to uncertain fate.

Nature, how great and secure in all thy works thou appearest!
Heaven and earth both obey law that is fixed and eterne:
Year after year follows on, and spring receives from the summer,
As from the winter the fall, always a welcoming hand.
. . . . .
All this breath and this death is governed by law; but our human
Life, that treasure supreme, yields to a fluctuant fate.[1]

[1] Ach, Natur, wie sicher und gross in allem erscheinst du! / Himmel und Erde befolgt ewiges, festes Gesetz: / Jahre folgen auf Jahre, dem Frühling reichet der Sommer, / Und

The third elegy of this group is based upon the story of Glycera and the painter Pausias which Pliny tells. It presents spirited variations on an aesthetic theme: to wit, how the poet feels at a disadvantage to the painter when he has to reproduce sensual life. Can the warmth of emotion be expressed at all? "His words are but phantoms compared to your forms." [2] The solution is reached in a dialogue full of animated repartee which alternates regularly like the stichomythia of Greek drama; an ascending series of significant moments and of changing poses portrays the painter's beloved in all her beauty. In the end phenomenon and emotion, object and subject, appear to correspond to one another.

The song lyrics comprise the second and largest group of this period. To this group belong four poems which prove that Goethe was still as great a master of the tone of the folk song as in his youth, except that he now employed it more freely and with more conscious art. In three of the poems, *Kriegserklärung* ("Declaration of War"), *Schäfers Klagelied* ("Shepherd's Lament") and *Trost in Tränen* ("Consolation in Tears"), Goethe was inspired by folk songs and folk-song melodies; in the fourth, *Nachtgesang* ("Night Song"), his inspiration was the melodic flow of a well-made Italian song (*Dormi, che vuoi di più*). To the realm of the sentimental artistic song belong poems such as *Nähe der Geliebten* ("Nearness of the Beloved"), suggested by the inferior verses of Friederike Brun, a contemporary poetess, and by Zelter's beautiful musical setting of them; and *Gegenwart* ("Presence"), which also used the motif and the melody of a contemporary song. The graceful *Gefunden* ("Discovered") transcends the simplicity of popular poetry by the careful consistency of its symbolism. At this time also the best of Goethe's *Gesellige Lieder* ("Social Songs") were written, the fruit of his delight in cultivated society and in the musical entertainments which he loved to arrange in his house. They are far above the coarse jollity of university pastime, although some of them, like the genial *Ergo bibamus*, have become popular student songs.

If we look for a common denominator to which these various poems

---

dem reichlichen Herbst traulich der Winter die Hand. / . . . / Alles entsteht und vergeht nach Gesetz; doch über des Menschen / Leben, den köstlichen Schatz, herrschet ein schwankendes Los. (*Euphrosyne,* translated by B. Q. Morgan.)

[2] Neben deiner Gestalt bleibt nur ein Schatten sein Wort! (*Der neue Pausias und sein Blumenmädchen.*)

give expression, it is that they seek to make the general apparent in the particular, the eternally valid in the specific case. In *Alexis und Dora,* for example, we are made to feel what separation, separation unadulterated, so to speak, means. In *Euphrosyne* the basic theme is the lawless caprice, the unnatural arbitrariness, of death in the human sphere. *Dauer im Wechsel* ("Permanence within Change") treats of the general phenomenon of transitoriness, how it affects man in an infinite variety of manifestations, what a deadly peril it is to his beliefs, and how provocative a challenge to his desire for eternity. The songs themselves, insofar as they present a philosophic attitude toward life, express typical moods and emotions in a manner generally valid. We may take, for example, the pair of poems *Meeres Stille* ("Sea Calm") and *Glückliche Fahrt* ("Happy Journey"). Here impressions from the Italian period are formed in so superpersonal and objective a way that the pictures which emerge diffuse by imperceptible means a symbolism of many facets.

> It makes a great difference whether the poet seeks the particular for the general or sees the general in the particular. From the first procedure arises allegory, in which the particular is only an example, only a specimen of the general. But the second mode is properly the nature of poetry; it expresses a particular without thinking of the general or indicating it. He who grasps this particular in all its vitality receives the general at the same time, either without becoming aware of it, or else only doing so later.[3]

It is in such fashion that the poems of this period, each after its own manner, seek to make a general truth apparent in individual phenomena. They are not for this reason products of detached reflection but rather what Goethe's poems always are, "occasional poems," growing out of moments of quickened perception. For him there could be no poetic content which would not be "content of one's own life." But for him personal experience is merged into the generally valid. "All people who live side by side experience similar vicissitudes, and that which happens to the individual may serve as symbol for thousands" (*Der junge Feldjäger*).

[3] Es ist ein grosser Unterschied, ob der Dichter zum Allgemeinen das Besondere sucht oder im Besondern das Allgemeine schaut. Aus jener Art entsteht Allegorie, wo das Besondere nur als Beispiel, als Exempel des Allgemeinen gilt; die letztere aber ist eigentlich die Natur der Poesie, sie spricht ein Besonderes aus, ohne ans Allgemeine zu denken oder darauf hinzuweisen. Wer nun dieses Besondere lebendig fasst, erhält zugleich das Allgemeine mit, ohne es gewahr zu werden, oder erst spät. (*Maximen und Reflexionen*, No. 279.)

Principles of Classic Art

. . . Die Schule der Griechen
Blieb noch offen, das Tor schlossen die Jahre nicht zu.[1]

AFTER HIS RETURN FROM ITALY GOETHE MUST SOON HAVE REALIZED THAT HIS MATURED VIEWS ON THE NATURE AND EFFECTS OF HIGH ART WERE UNIQUE IN Germany. In the early years, before he secured Schiller's interest, he was paralyzed by a feeling of spiritual and poetic isolation. But subsequently his association with his new friend and the labors which he shared daily with the scholarly painter Heinrich Meyer strengthened and extended his Italian experiences through historical and aesthetic studies, and he conceived a strong desire to make the results of his apprenticeship in the paradise of art useful to the artistic life of Germany, and as counselor and educator to influence young painters and sculptors. He had brought with him the conviction that much more of the technical aspects of art could be taught and transmitted than was ordinarily assumed. A new sojourn in Italy was to procure him fuller knowledge and mature a plan which he had prepared with Meyer. They wished to collaborate on a book on Italy which should treat of that country's climate, physical aspect, inhabitants, culture, and art, in the past and in the present. Goethe assembled much material and many notes for this "strange work." His letters to Schiller and to Meyer often speak of it. But this project never reached realization, any more than did the second journey to Italy. Meyer went to Rome in the autumn of 1795, and Goethe wished to follow him. The plan was rendered futile by the disturbances of war in the two years following. Then Goethe lost the desire, and contented himself with a journey to southern Germany and Switzerland. On Meyer's return home in the autumn of 1797, Goethe met him at Stäfa and accompanied him to Weimar. The works of art and the new views which Meyer brought from Italy provided rich material for aesthetic speculation, in which Schiller eagerly took part.

[1] . . . The school of the Greeks / Still remained open; years had not barr'd up its doors. (*Römische Elegien*, No. 13, based on translation by E. A. Bowring, *The Poems of Goethe*, p. 361.)

The plan for a periodical with a strict program which had been discussed for many years now took shape. The first works of the romantic school which were then appearing, books like Wackenroder's *Herzensergiessungen eines kunstliebenden Klosterbruders* and L. Tieck's novel, *Franz Sternbalds Wanderungen,* which relates the story of a painter, strengthened the "Weimar Friends of Art" (as they called themselves after 1801) in their conviction that this was the fitting moment to set forth emphatically the classical standpoint. In 1798 the first volume of *Die Propyläen* appeared, with Goethe as editor. This periodical, he remarked, was "a true benefaction" for him, for it required him "to express the ideas and experiences which I have so long been dragging about with me." A Weimar contemporary tells us that "clarity" now became Goethe's favorite word. For him it was the highest ideal of art as well as of aesthetic speculation. The relationship between art and nature is now the chief concern of his thinking. Goethe clearly formulated his opinions on the subject in the *Einleitung in die Propyläen* ("Introduction to *The Propyläen*"). In the form in which they are expressed here, these ideas were immediately applicable only to his high-classical point of view, but they were retained later also in their essential principles.

First and above all problems of plastic art are dealt with, for here where Goethe himself was not a master he felt an urgent need for principles and general rules. In this respect, also, Italy had had most to teach him. The Greeks continued as before to be for him unattainable models of artistic perfection. Their works contained the rules and regulations of true art. From them he wished to derive these rules so as to save young German artists the detours by which he himself had been confused. It could not be a matter of imitating nature, but rather in emulation of nature to produce "something spiritual-organic," a work of man which surpasses nature. For the plastic artist study of the human figure must always be the first and most important task. Here he could learn much from comparative anatomy, which establishes the "ideal image," the type. To the painter it is likewise important to learn from the new discoveries of the physicists relating to colors (at this period Goethe's scientific research was increasingly concentrated upon optics).

But the most important problem for all artists was that of the suitable subject. This question had occupied Goethe insistently after his return from Italy. All modern artists, he thought, are at a disadvantage, as compared to the ancients, in that they have no clear concept of what subjects of themselves invite artistic representation and what subjects resist it. In contrast to the naturalist, the classicist is convinced that not everything in the reality of nature is suitable for artistic treatment; on the contrary, there are a limited number of subjects which "possess a certain ideality in themselves" and for that reason are to a greater degree than others "subjects for true works of art." To give these professions of faith the assurance of a scientific doctrine, to establish objective norms, was a principal design of the *Propyläen.* In Goethe's formulation this doctrine states that such subjects are best suited to pictorial or plastic representation which "determine themselves by their sensual existence," that is to say, which may be completely understood through sensual perception alone. "The ancients considered a picture as a finished and finite whole; in this space they wished to show everything so that the spectator should not think of something in connection with the picture, but should think the picture and see everything in it." [2] Greek works of art address themselves wholly to "cultivated sensuality." Only what has sensual significance and beauty should be set forth, and what is inward and moral should be presented only insofar as it can be communicated by figure and gesture.

The degree to which this theory is applicable to literature is defined by Goethe in his essay *Ueber epische und dramatische Dichtung* which grew out of his discussions with Schiller. The epic poet and the dramatist, this essay concludes, deal with similar subjects but in opposite ways. In the epic an incident is presented as altogether past, in the drama as altogether present. For both, the most suitable subjects are those which are, like the heroic legends of the Greeks, "purely human, significant, and rich in emotional content." Another distinction is drawn according to which the epic shows man as active, as affecting the external world; hence this form requires spectacular descriptions of broad sweep. Tragedy, on the other hand, presents man as suffering, as "being guided internally," and hence requires only a limited field for its action.

[2] Die Alten sahen das Bild als ein *ab-* und *ein*geschlossenes Ganze an, sie wollten in *dem* Raume alles *zeigen,* man sollte sich nicht etwas *bei* dem Bilde denken, sondern man sollte *das* Bild denken und *in* demselben alles *sehen.* (Letter to H. Meyer, February 27, 1789.)

Goethe's treatise *Ueber Laokoon* was written as a contribution to the *Propyläen.* Here the famous sculptural group so brilliantly interpreted by Lessing serves as a point of departure for general reflections on the relation of art and nature, on unity in multiplicity as the sign of beautiful form, and on the problem of the pregnant moment which was much discussed in the aesthetics of the eighteenth century. The essay *Der Sammler und die Seinigen* attempts to set up artist types and to elucidate thoroughly the central theme of "beautiful" art in distinction to "characteristic" art. A third contribution offers a translation of Diderot's *Essais sur la Peinture* and Goethe's commentary upon it, in which Goethe partly agrees with and partly refutes Diderot. Here, too, the principal subject is the relationship of art to nature. Goethe finds that Diderot is inclined to mingle or even to amalgamate the two. These essays, together with the somewhat older and less important paper on *Einfache Nachahmung der Natur, Manier, Stil,* constitute the most important sources for our knowledge of Goethe's classic theory of art.

The editors of the *Propyläen* also announced prize competitions (1799–1805). Each year they set German artists a specific theme; the choice of subjects was limited to Homeric poetry and Greek legend ("Aphrodite introduces Helen to Paris," "Achilles' battle with the rivers," "Ulysses and the Cyclops," and the like). But all these attempts to give classical principles currency among plastic artists and, following Winckelmann's precedent, to steer the art of the young generation into Greek paths, miscarried. For one thing, the number of young painters and sculptors in Germany was still small, but above all they were all carried along on the broad and strong current which streamed from the growing romantic movement. This was of their generation, and the young artists felt themselves a part of its spirit. Thus the effect of Goethe's programmatic periodical was confined to a very small circle. The number of copies sold was so small that in the winter of 1800 Goethe himself gave up the periodical. To Schiller, who shared his disappointment at the failure, he wrote with bitter resignation that this offered additional proof that men desired not "genuine theoretic insight" but only words. "We stand opposed to the new art," he remarked, "as did Julian against Christianity." When in 1805 a last exhibition marked the end of the efforts of the Friends of Art in Weimar, Goethe summed up his criticisms. He charged the romanticists with having placed feeling above intellect, and naturalness above art.

> Everyone has feeling, some have temperament, but genius is rare, art is difficult. Feeling has a tendency toward religion; a religious feeling coupled with artistic temperament will, when left to itself, produce only imperfect works; such an artist relies upon moral elevation to compensate for artistic shortcomings.[3]

But in art the moral may be expressed only in what is sensually most beautiful. Later (in a letter to Zelter dated 1813), he again asserts that the romanticists had rendered his efforts futile: "the fever of legends and saints" had driven "all true pleasure in life" out of plastic art.

Goethe gave expression to his classical doctrine again in a contribution to a collection of essays entitled *Winckelmann und sein Jahrhundert* (1805). This book is a magnificent monument to the great reformer who opened the eyes of his contemporaries to the grandeur and beauty of mature Greek art. Goethe's contribution is a landmark in the history of the critical essay; he himself had never written anything better in this genre. Winckelmann's life and work are here considered from the highest point of view. The clumsy scheme of traditional biography is transcended in a manner which puts Goethe's contribution on a par with the brilliant criticism and essays of the brothers Schlegel. In detailed brief characterization he speaks of Winckelmann's "essential nature," his potentialities, the forces and qualifications which constituted his productive personality, and the results of his efforts. The precious legacy of the Greeks Goethe again looks upon in its joyous worldliness and its oneness with nature and human totality. Winckelmann, he says, was himself "of such a classical nature." In Greek art he found "the responsive counter-images" of his own ideal striving.

The heart of the treatise is the chapter on beauty. The ascending series of natural forms strives toward beauty as an ideal goal; its final product is the beautiful human being. But only rarely is nature able to produce perfection, and she can never maintain it. In the proc-

[3] Gemüt hat jedermann, Naturell mehrere, der Geist ist selten, die Kunst ist schwer. Das Gemüt hat einen Zug gegen die Religion, ein religiöses Gemüt mit Naturell zur Kunst, sich selbst überlassen, wird nur unvollkommene Werke hervorbringen; ein solcher Künstler verlässt sich auf das Sittlich-Hohe, welches die Kunstmängel ausgleichen soll. (*Letzte Kunstausstellung 1805*, Nachlass.)

ess of morphological development there is no permanence, no static being. "For speaking precisely we may say that it is only for a moment that the beautiful human being is beautiful." In this respect nature is surpassed by art. In the *Propyläen* Goethe had said that man had set himself the task, "Let us make gods, images like ourselves." This implies what the essay now says: man draws upon all his "perfection and virtues" to produce a work that shall possess a higher ideal reality and, above all, permanence. The highest province of art is representation of the perfect human figure, produced out of the entirety of the creative forces of the artist. A beautiful work of art, "in that it gives soul to the human form," raises man above himself, completes the circle of his life and activity, and gives him the timeless perfection which is peculiar to the gods. "It is by such feelings that those were seized who looked upon the Olympian Jupiter . . . The god had become man in order to elevate man to a god." [4] It was this that Winckelmann perceived; this highest beauty, detached from time, resting upon itself in enduring perfection, revealed itself to him in the works of ancient art. There exists no higher embodiment of perfection, even of moral perfection, than this beautiful form fashioned of the spirit of man. It is the symbol of transcendent divine perfection. In the beautiful entirety of a work of art we have a symbolic image of that highest beauty which is otherwise incomprehensible to us. Here classical aesthetics merges into metaphysics.

The Romanticists

WHEN THE NEW SCHOOL OF THE ROMANTICISTS CAME FORWARD AT THE END OF THE CENTURY IT WAS AT FIRST NOT CLEAR WHETHER THERE WERE IRRECONcilable conflicts between its doctrines and Goethe's views. With Schiller it was otherwise. Whereas from the beginning he fell into disagreement with the romanticists, Goethe was at first inclined to recognize

[4] Von solchen Gefühlen wurden die ergriffen, die den olympischen Jupiter erblickten . . . Der Gott war zum Menschen geworden, um den Menschen zum Gott zu erheben. (*Winckelmann.*)

their contribution without prejudice. The spectacle of an entire group of new stars suddenly making its appearance in the firmament of German literature was in itself quite impressive. Furthermore, the innovators, who forgathered at neighboring Jena where Fichte taught, and who were otherwise so arrogant, took great pains to enter into friendly relationships with Goethe. Soon there were no more zealous prophets of his greatness. In brilliant essays and critical articles they proclaimed to the German public, from whose lack of understanding and aesthetic cultivation Goethe had suffered so severely, that he was the nation's greatest writer, and that his work was the pinnacle of all modern literature. In him they saw, as Novalis expressed it, "the true vicar of the poetic spirit on earth." Goethe had never had disciples and students, had never been able to count on producing a great effect through the works of his maturer years. But he could be well satisfied with the reception which the romanticists accorded his novel *Wilhelm Meister,* which was just then published. When in 1798 the new school entered the public forum with a periodical of its own, the *Athenaeum,* and Schiller deplored the presumption of the critical fragments published in it, Goethe rejoined that such a type of criticism might be productive of much good in the current state of German journalism.

> This general worthlessness, partisanship for extreme mediocrity, this toadyism, these cringing gestures, this emptiness and lameness, in which few good things get lost, have a fearsome opponent in such a hornets' nest as the "fragments." [1]

The most scholarly of these young literati, August Wilhelm Schlegel, praised Goethe for his translations from Shakespeare and Calderón. This "very good head, lively, energetic, and clever," seemed to be of one mind with Goethe in aesthetic matters. Schlegel wrote a highly complimentary review of *Hermann und Dorothea.* His wife, Caroline, made eager efforts to improve the relationship with the Weimar poet. Goethe did not have many admirers as enthusiastic as this spirited woman. He was treated with respect even by Friedrich Schlegel, the most self-assured among the young critics. The service

[1] Diese allgemeine Nichtigkeit, Parteisucht fürs äusserst Mittelmässige, diese Augendienerei, diese Katzenbuckelgebärden, diese Leerheit und Lahmheit, in der nur wenige gute Produkte sich verlieren, hat an einem solchen Wespenneste, wie die Fragmente sind, einen fürchterlichen Gegner. (Letter to Schiller, July 25, 1798.)

rendered in return was that the dramatic works of the brothers were produced at the Weimar theater. It appeared as if an alliance would be formed between Goethe and the young people which might eventually succeed in greatly raising the aesthetic level of the German public.

To one member of the Jena circle Goethe felt close spiritual kinship. Schelling, the precocious genius who had become professor of philosophy, at Goethe's intercession, at the age of twenty-three, produced a philosophy of nature which corresponded well with Goethe's view of nature. With Schelling Goethe discussed his theory of colors, for which he found little appreciation otherwise among contemporary scientists. For some years Schelling was a frequent guest at Goethe's house. What attracted Goethe was the imaginative coloring which distinguished Schelling's view of nature from Kant's conceptual abstraction, his confidence in the strength of the spirit in its struggle with the secrets of the organization of nature, and also the aesthetic rather than ethical mode of his thought. By instinct Goethe resorted to sensual observation, to the "detail of experience"; the speculative gifts of the young thinker helped him find his way from the particular to the general, from the individual case to the law, more easily. Furthermore, there was great agreement in detail and in principle. If Schelling says that there are not two disparate worlds but only a single world, that nature is visible spirit and spirit invisible nature, Goethe gives expression to the same thought in his verse

> For that is Nature's way throughout:
> What grew within, now holds without.[2]

Or when Goethe remarks that only "observation of an ever-creating nature," contemplation with the "eyes of the spirit," can give us access to the secrets of its creative acts, this corresponds to Schelling's doctrine of "intellectual intuition," of perceptive thought as the capacity to comprehend intuitively the general, the essential, which expresses itself in countless organisms. Schelling's remark, "Come you here to physics and recognize the eternal," was said in the spirit of Goethe. So also was the view of polarity as the efficient cause of all processes of life: "Only where there is opposition is there life." That is Goethe's faith too. Of Schelling's treatise *Bruno* (1803), Goethe

[2] Denn das ist der Natur Gehalt, / Dass aussen gilt, was innen galt. (*Zahme Xenien VI.*)

said that what he understood of it coincided with his "innermost convictions."

But the more the romanticists developed their own type of poetry, and then more particularly of painting, the more clearly visible did profound differences become to Goethe. How must it have struck Goethe when in 1805 Friedrich Schlegel recommended that ancient German art must be imitated, that its technical execution was more careful than that of Italian painting and that it had remained true longer to the "most ancient Christian Catholic images." In confidential letters Goethe now used strong words. He spoke of the "philosophic and religious caricatures who are now confusing even many a good head in Germany and yet eventually will lead to nothing but an esoteric form of conceit," of the "modern religious medievals," of the neo-Catholic sentimentality which was worse than any narrow-minded naturalism. He deplored the anarchy, formlessness, and want of technical precision in these innovators who were in themselves talented.

Riemer reports a conversation of August 1808 in which Goethe attempted to castigate the questionable elements in romantic poetry and art by comparing them with ancient art. Ancient art, he said, was sober and moderated; but modern romantic art was unchecked, Dionysiac. The ancients idealized the real by treating it in a large style and with taste, whereas the romanticists attempted to give the appearance of reality to what was impossible and unreal by means of fantasy. Ancient art was plastic and true; romantic art sought to bestow upon a subject in itself insignificant an element of the marvelous by means of coruscating colors. "The so-called romantic poetry is attractive particularly to our young people because it flatters their caprice, their sensuality, their propensity to license, in a word, the inclinations of youth." [3]

Statements made in a letter of the same period (to Zelter, October 30, 1808) bring us nearer to the principal points at issue. No longer is anyone willing to understand that the highest contribution of art, as of nature, is to give form, and that in giving form the condition is "that everything become, be, and remain something particular, some-

[3] Die sogenannte romantische Poesie zieht besonders unsere jungen Leute an, weil sie der Willkür, der Sinnlichkeit, dem Hange nach Ungebundenheit, kurz der Neigung der Jugend schmeichelt. (Conversation with Riemer, August 28, 1808.)

thing significant." The chief profit of his Italian experiences Goethe felt to be that he had finally freed himself from the merely subjective, from the dimly sensed or fancifully imagined, from precocious caprice, and from spiritual imprecision, and that he had achieved a clear insight into the objective norms of beauty, always looking toward the Greek models. For him it is a matter of freedom under law, of originality orienting itself by the norms of classical tradition. Now these young poets and artists again invoke free imagination, individual feeling, and inspiration.

In Wackenroder's *Herzensergiessungen,* which set forth the program of the new school of painting, classical antiquity is as little regarded as nature. All the more attention is given to the Christian piety of other days. A young man who was more familiar with the world of tones and of inner infinity than with the world of the eye, of figures and forms, here spoke of plastic art in a manner which revealed clearly enough that he possessed no notion of the problems of artistic creation, of the representation of a subject, and of technical mastery. He thought that art must not be learned but was a gift of intense feeling, of enthusiasm. Correct painting would emerge of itself if one sunk himself intuitively into the subject and relied upon inspiration, which was always a gift of heaven. Raphael had painted his pictures in a state of dream. Wackenroder further maintained that the sole genuine effect of art was the arousing of emotion and of pious feeling. Hence the subject was more important than the form, the mood in which the subject was apprehended more important than the manner of its representation. It is in his own soul that the artist must seek his inspiration, not in the world of natural objects and figures. Artless simplicity, finally, appeared to be the highest ideal; in early paintings "that childish good-natured simplicity and limitation" appeared at its most beautiful. It is of this simplicity that Friedrich Schlegel said that it was the primitive character of man, the lost paradise. The romantic painters did not limit themselves to this view; but in its bases and tendency their art never lost its connection with these origins.

For Goethe this program was unacceptable in every clause. The victory over obscurantist medieval Christianity, over transcendental mysticism and churchly dogma which was initiated by the Reformation, was in his view an inestimable advance upon the road to the pure and luminous clarity of modern thought. The demand to return to medieval Catholicism he found preposterous and spiritually reactionary. The sentimental worship of artless simplicity seemed to him equally reprehensible. If he too was as positive in his rejection of technical overrefinement, he nevertheless knew that the highest simplicity, the simplicity of great art, flourished not in ages of primitive beginnings, but only in periods of mature mastery. And finally, a doctrine which relegated the plastic artist to the formless world of emotion and of inward vision seemed to him the worst aberration.

The romanticists applied the same ideas to literature. Friedrich Schlegel declared that romantic poetry was progressive universal poetry and that its fundamental principle was that the poet's caprice could tolerate no constraining law. Nothing could be more repugnant to Goethe's matured classical view than this doctrine. Here nature was no longer valid as the great schoolmistress, nor was the world of Greek gods and heroes. It was demanded that the poet like the artist submerge himself in the infinity of religious feeling and in the boundless multifariousness of history. It must have irritated Goethe even more that the romanticists appealed to his own beginnings, to his and Herder's contributions to the period of Storm and Stress—to those very opinions and works which the classic poet now regarded as confused, subjective premonitions and preliminaries to his own mature achievements and ideas. But now that he believed he had found the correct road to great art, to true objective beauty, and wished to point this road to the gifted young poets, it turned out that no one was prepared to follow him. The failure of the *Propyläen* set the seal on his bitter disillusion. Schiller, Humboldt, his few like-minded friends at Weimar alone understood him and agreed with him.

But even in this situation Goethe retained his liberal spirit of conciliation and his open-mindedness. Despite the painful isolation, spiritual and artistic, in which he found himself after the death of Schiller, he was prepared to help the romanticists and to receive suggestion from their ideas and compositions. One owed such tolerance, he thought, to the higher standpoint which modern philosophy had attained. "We have learned to esteem the ideal though it may present itself in the strangest forms." Arnim's and Brentano's collection of German folk songs, the *Wunderhorn,* he welcomed with a friendly review. Nor, despite his dislike of the "tendency back to the Middle Ages," did he shut himself away from efforts to rescue ancient German poetry from oblivion. He showed benevolent interest in the brothers Grimm. Much that was invaluable, he acknowledged, came to the light of day through such scholarly devotion; this applied, too, to the *Nibelungenlied,* which he read aloud to his friends at Weimar. He said that it was worth while to understand the poem at its true value even though one must first disperse the mist which "Messrs. Görres and Associates" had spread over it. He found that the Nordic epic could hold its own with all "that we possess of excellence as poetry." But this was said under the impression of first acquaintanceship. In the end, according to Goethe's view, Homer was without rival. The Homeric epics remained for him the most important works in the literature of the world, the most perfect that poetry had ever produced.

We can demonstrate in two specific instances how Goethe reacted to significant specimens of romantic productivity—how he became clear in his mind as to what elements in the new he could find acceptable and what he must reject. First there is his encounter with Beethoven. Bettina Brentano had told him much about the great but lonely man. Goethe made Beethoven's acquaintance in 1812 at Bad Teplitz in Bohemia. He was struck by the compressed energy and depth of this self-willed man and understood why he must seem singular to the world. But to Zelter he admitted how much Beethoven at the same time repelled him: "A quite unrestrained personality, who is indeed not wrong in finding the world detestable, but who, to be sure, makes it no more agreeable thereby either for himself or for others." [4] He felt the same way about Beethoven's playing and about his compositions. "The yearning and restlessness which bursts all bonds and loses itself in the infinite" in this art gave him more pain than pleasure. When Felix Mendelssohn played the first bars of his C-Minor Symphony for him, Goethe thought that it was grandiose but for the reason that it could arouse only astonishment. "Beautiful and mad enough to drive one crazy"—so Goethe felt also about Beethoven's music later. Like his friend Zelter he admired it "with horror." The self-willed subjectivity in it, like its sublime pathos, were alike alien to him, even hostile, though he felt and acknowledged its power, its "majesty."

[4] Eine ganz ungebändigte Persönlichkeit, die zwar gar nicht unrecht hat, wenn sie die Welt detestabel findet, aber sie freilich dadurch weder für sich noch für andere genussreicher macht. (September 2, 1812.)

But Goethe's attitude toward Beethoven is governed by another consideration also—his general attitude toward music and his musical education. It is not to be denied that this "Augen-Mensch" had less understanding for music than for plastic art, both because of his nature and because of his education. But who dares call the greatest lyric poet of European literature unmusical? He was in close contact with the most important song composers of his age, above all with Friedrich Reichardt (who set 128 of Goethe's texts to music) and with Zelter. Both his contemporaries and later composers repeatedly set his poems to music. None of the romanticists or lyric writers of the following generations surpasses him in musical sense and melodic verse. One must "never read, always sing" his songs, he remarked. Many of his songlike poems were evoked by melodies which pleased him. He was unwilling to live without music. In 1807 he organized a small private orchestra and also a choir from among the members of the theater, and with the assistance of these groups he arranged concerts in his house over a period of several years. To these performances he invited the court and his friends. For the most part, old church music was presented. He loved vocal music best; to him the human voice was the most beautiful instrument. Thus song, chorales, and opera were always more important to him than instrumental music. In his early decades Goethe wrote libretti for operettas in the French style (prose dialogue with song interpolations), then in the style of the Italian opera (recitative and aria), and also texts for comic operas (*Scherz, List und Rache; Der Zauberflöte zweiter Teil*). Projects of this sort occupied him at a later period also. In Italy he was pleased with Cimarosa's *opera buffa,* but he saw the true master of opera in Mozart, whom he had heard as a seven-year-old prodigy in Frankfort in 1763. Later he made efforts to understand difficult piano music also and had Bach's works played to him repeatedly. In 1821 Mendelssohn, then twelve years old, appeared at Weimar and enchanted the old man. The visits were repeated and the impression which Mendelssohn's playing made grew ever deeper. It bordered, Goethe found, "on the miraculous." Two years later the playing of the beautiful Pole, Maria Szymanowska, did endless good to the sufferer during the days of his last agony of love. He thanked her for the "happiness of sounds" in the stanzas of his poem *Aussöhnung.*

In his old age Goethe's understanding of great music grew. We need only look at the part assigned to musical practice in the program of education of the *Wanderjahre*. Goethe now believed, furthermore, "that a sense of music must be associated with every artistic sense." He demanded competent performers, musicians like Zelter and Mendelssohn, who gave him access to difficult works. He knew well enough that he understood music better through reflection than through immediate experience. He called himself, with some exaggeration, "toneless and without a musical ear, though a good hearer," who must transform the sensual expression into concept and word in order to make it his own. "I know well enough that I am missing a third of life on that account." The less native gift for an art a man possesses, the more he is inclined to cling to what he was able to acquire of it in the years of his greatest impressionability. A man will always show himself most conservative in his taste when his understanding is limited by nature. This is true of Goethe's attitude toward music, and must be taken into consideration for a correct appreciation of his attitude toward Beethoven. If we look closer we shall discover an even deeper compulsion in Goethe's hesitation about contemporary composers. The music which he loved stems from the period when European culture had not yet become a problem to itself, from the ages of faith and of firm and tranquil spirit. But he found distasteful music in which the tendency to pathetic and sentimental expression was consummated and where technical complication took the place of monumental pristine simplicity and strength.

The other incident with which Goethe is always reproached is his attitude toward Heinrich von Kleist. First of all, we must note that Kleist was also unknown and unrecognized by the other poets of his time, and that Goethe did not know of Kleist's maturest work, the *Prinz von Homburg*, which was only published posthumously, in 1821. *Amphitryon* had already disturbed Goethe as a dubious symptom of the age. Whereas ancient treatment of the subject involved confusion of the mind, in the modern poet it is confusion of the emotions. Even worse was the impression which *Penthesilea* made upon Goethe. When Kleist presented the piece to him, "upon the knees of his heart," Goethe rejected it with a harshness which he did not often permit himself. "She comes of so marvelous a breed, and moves about in so strange a region, that I must take time to accustom myself to both." [5] But how could he ever accustom himself? Nevertheless, he presented *Der zerbrochene Krug* at Weimar, and it was not his fault that the venture miscarried.

For Goethe, more than a difference in artistic style or in aesthetic doctrine was involved in this case. Everything in the writing of the romantic generation that repelled him, everything that seemed to him problematic, unnatural, and unbeautiful in their works, here struck him more clearly and more compactly for the very reason that by his gifts Kleist was the mightiest of their dramatic poets. He could overlook much in Tieck's broad and variegated pieces, could even accept them on the whole with a certain irony. Zacharias Werner's dramas pleased him because they were suitable to the contemporary theater and because of the effectiveness which the forceful dynamism of their action gave them. For a long while he was deluded by the hope that the beginnings of maturer achievement were here displayed. All of these productions were, to be sure, outside the circle of his own art and of his own views, but not outside the sphere of what Goethe could find acceptable.

With Kleist it was different. We have no more detailed statement from Goethe about *Penthesilea,* but it is not difficult to imagine the kind of effect this play made upon him. He cannot have been unaware that here a man who was suffering from life, a spirit despairing of itself, was descending into an abyss of irreconcilable contradiction from which no way leads back to the faith which was so important to Goethe—the faith which he felt must be fortified in man by all means, even those of poetry, if his thoughts are to be right and his existence fulfilled; the faith that a kindly meaning may be found in life however much it wearies and degrades us by suffering, agony, and question-compelling accidents of all sorts. But *Penthesilea* gave voice to despair without restraint; for this despair there was no longer security of sense nor of reason; nay, the only certainty that yet remained and was designated by the equivocal word "feeling" proved delusion. The conclusion, so it may have seemed to Goethe, could only be destructive hopelessness. Did not the raving of the heroine indicate as much; did not her disintegration make painfully evident man's

[5] Sie ist aus einem so wunderbaren Geschlecht und bewegt sich in einer so fremden Region, dass ich mir Zeit nehmen muss, mich in beide zu finden.

animal origin and cause one to question the continued existence of the ideal of humanity upon which Western culture was based?

The unmitigated harshness with which Goethe rejected this work and its author probably has still another reason. We may surmise that Goethe did not dismiss only what was strange and unacceptable to him personally. So deep a disturbance must have a general reason. This work demonstrated to an acute degree the properties which in Goethe's view made romantic literature as a whole questionable. He feared that such compositions would exert a baneful influence on the spiritual and moral state of German culture, for which Goethe more than others had the right to feel responsible. The more literature attained a central point in culture, in the process of general secularization, the more it assumed, as "worldly gospel," the position which religion had possessed in the past, the more important it must be for it to discharge this eminent function in as positive a manner as possible. In pursuance of this function, poetry must give man a view of life and of his position in the world which should permit his spirit to raise itself in free contemplation above the dark and difficult constraint by which life sought to limit him at every step. In this sense great art in all mature cultures had been a means by which man assured himself of his spiritual as well as of his moral liberty. It gave him detachment from life, raised him above natural necessity. It is thus that he acquires the power to be master of his existence in thought and deed insofar as his potentialities permit. But how could a composition have this liberating and uplifting effect when it represented man as a fragile victim of dark demons within and without him, immolated to the needs of a being which appeared to know neither rational order nor intelligence? Here what was highest and most important was at stake—the function of literature in creating culture; and the importance of the case was increased by the conviction that this function was then threatened by the direction which German literature in general had taken. In Kleist the constantly accentuated problem of the spiritual situation was intensified to a pathologic state. More clearly than the work of others, his writings revealed the danger which, according to Goethe's conviction, this development hastened. The time had not yet come when pathologic phenomena were of large concern to European artists and when the problematic as such aroused an interest which was in itself no sign of cultural health. But to the man who had had much experience in association with the inward demon and with the dangers of the spirit of the time, a phenomenon such as Kleist seemed symptomatic of the crisis which had overtaken the spiritual and intellectual condition of the age. Later, works like those of the French romanticists and a phenomenon like Byron gave Goethe new occasion to clarify to himself the dangers of modern titanism. It was these dangers which brought him to the renowned and reprehended formulation that the classic is the healthy, the romantic the sick (Eckermann, April 2, 1829).

Nevertheless, it would be false to make the cleavage between Goethe's poetic work and thought and romanticism so deep as to render profitable interchange impossible. Just as the rich lyric of the romanticists is unthinkable without Goethe's poetry, so Goethe's post-classical works are full of ideas, figures, motifs, and themes which he adopted from the sphere of the romantic spirit and made his own after his fashion. This is true in particular of the *Wahlverwandtschaften*, the Pandora scenes, the *Divan*, and the second part of *Faust*.

At the same time Goethe's personal relations with the romantic poets developed in the reverse direction. He met the hesitant Zacharias Werner with fatherly friendliness; he produced Werner's plays and patiently endured his "sensual-hypersensual" activities in Jena and Weimar. But when his errant protégé then took refuge in the Catholic Church, Goethe dropped him as resolutely as he had dropped the convert Friedrich Schlegel. Similarly, he withdrew from the Brentanos after he had long yielded to Bettina's insistent enthusiasm. What was beneficial and invigorating in these stormy relations was given expression in the *Sonnets*. When Schelling was later on the point of being recalled to Jena, Goethe advised against it. The Christian "mysticism" to which the natural philosopher had turned in the interval was repugnant to Goethe. It would be in a way comical, he thought, "if for the celebration of the third century of the truly great gains of Protestantism we should see the old outgrown stuff reintroduced in a renewed mystic-pantheistic, abstruse-philosophic form, though one by no means to be despised in silence."[6]

[6] . . . wenn wir zur dritten Säkularfeier unseres protestantisch wahrhaft grossen Gewinnes das alte überwundene Zeug nun wieder unter einer erneuten mystisch-pantheistischen, abstrus-philosophischen, obgleich im Stillen keineswegs zu verachtenden Form wieder eingeführt sehen sollten. (Letter to Minister von Voigt, February 27, 1816.)

But it was of romantic painting that his rejection was and continued to be most constant and most decisive. Individual productions, to be sure, like Runge's allegorical and symbolic representation of the hours, Goethe valued for the sake of their beautiful detail, but even such pictures he numbered among the works which were "beautiful and mad enough to drive one crazy." To the artist he expressed his admiration for his "delicate, pious, amiable efforts," with the proviso that he could not wish contemporary art on the whole to proceed in the same path. Goethe was also able to appreciate the work of C. D. Friedrich, which, after Runge's, was the most talented of the new school, though he thought his "delicate, even pious" works were "not altogether to be accepted in a strictly artistic sense." Later his admiration for Friedrich's landscapes increased. Perfection, he now thought, must be valued highly even "when realized in a strange manner." That was indeed truly wise judgment. But then came another period during which he turned from such work with distaste. His attitude was the same toward painters like Peter Cornelius and J. F. Overbeck. Their sketches aroused "admiration, even astonishment." In extreme old age he spoke commendably of Neureuther, a pupil of Cornelius, and showed him marks of enduring friendship. But in all the romantic painters he found their archaizing primitivism, their imitation of old-fashioned simplicity, unintelligible and strange.

For the work of a bygone era to be imitated in later times there were, of course, precedents in the history of art. "But I know of no cases when artists transposed themselves with feeling, spirit, and mind into an earlier epoch to such a degree that they desired to make their own productions identical with those of their predecessors in invention, style, and treatment." [7] It is as if one would return to the womb to be born again (letter to C. H. Schlosser, September 21, 1813). In moments of just judgment Goethe's expressions concerning the "tendency back to the Middle Ages" were again more tolerant. He had passed through a similar stage in his own youth, and for the romanticists it was probably only a transition to higher views and productions.

[7] Aber ich wüsste nicht, dass Künstler sich, mit Gemüt, Geist und Sinn, in eine frühere Epoche dergestalt versetzt, dass sie ihre eigenen Produktionen an Erfindung, Stil und Behandlung denen ihrer Vorgänger hätten gleich machen wollen.

But ever and again the neo-mystic religious sentimentality repelled him. He expressed himself vigorously on the "mad Protestant-Catholic, poetic-Christian, obscurantism," a "premeditated barbarism," a plague which may not be stopped but must be allowed to exhaust its fury. Above all, he regarded as utterly misguided and corrupting the view, which had grown more prevalent since the critical writings of Wackenroder, Tieck, and Friedrich Schlegel, that modern painting could only be born anew out of Christian simplicity, out of a new feeling of Christian community of a mystic character. "Among the ancients during their best period the idea of the holy arose out of the beautiful as sensually perceptible. Zeus attained perfection only through the Olympian statue. Modern civilization rests upon the morally beautiful, to which, if one would have it so, the sensual is opposed." [8] Moral beauty had also been the dominant quality of his *Iphigenie*. Since he had learned to understand ancient art properly in Italy, his thoughts and feelings were different. How could the morally beautiful, the perfect figure, be produced where only the "mist" of inward, amorphous feelings and visions was recognized as the fertile field for begetting art?

For Goethe the world of visible phenomena of nature was the native heath of the plastic artist, but in it form was more important than color. For him plastic art remained the principal and basic art, and he was most concerned with the clarity and beauty of outline. It has often been noticed how poor in colors are his own classical compositions, as are the classicistic paintings of his age. From the ideals of the Weimar Friends of Art there was no road leading to the colorful pictures which the romanticists, following the models of the fifteenth and sixteenth centuries, created. But that these old pictures with motifs taken from Christian mythology should be models for the modern painter at all Goethe found preposterous. He would acknowledge the validity of only two teachers, nature and the art of the Greeks. He might be certain that he understood both better than did the romantic neo-mystics. But they would not suffer him to lead them from the mist of their "pious delusion" to the powers of clear day and to his sensually beautiful figures. This filled him with an

[8] Bei den Alten, in ihrer besten Zeit, entsprang das Heilige aus dem sinnlich fasslichen Schönen. Zeus wurde erst durch das olympische Bild vollendet. Das Moderne ruht auf dem sittlich Schönen, dem, wenn man will, das Sinnliche entgegensteht. (Letter to F. H. Jacobi, March 7, 1808.)

angry bitterness which in the end admitted of no understanding and no reconciliation. Even the instruction which he received, at first unwillingly, then with some embarrassment, from those experts in ancient German architecture and painting, the brothers Boisserée, and the impressions which he gathered from their magnificent collection of paintings, did not avail to alter his views.

He persisted in regarding the romantic efforts as a whole as did his *alter ego* in matters of art, the strict classicist Heinrich Meyer, who characterized them in his treatise on *Neudeutsche religiös-patriotische Kunst* ("Neo-German Religious-Patriotic Art"). Goethe had printed this outspoken essay in 1817 in his periodical *Ueber Kunst und Altertum*. The modern passion "for the respectable, naïve, yet somewhat crude taste" of the old masters, this essay says, would not renew art but only replace "the beautiful style of forms . . . clear and joyous representation . . . what is characteristic, diligent, forceful" by "meagerness" and "abstruse, dreary allegories." It was always safest and more reasonable "to occupy oneself exclusively with the study of ancient Greek art and what was linked to that art in modern times." In art "clarity of view, joyousness of reception, ease of communication" were supreme. But these qualities could be found nowhere in such perfection as in the works of Greeks. Hence the modern artist must take them as his point of departure and always refer to them. "Everyone should be a Greek after his own fashion, but a Greek he should be." Did not this, too, however, imply transposing oneself into an earlier epoch and returning to the womb of bygone views? But one must remember that for Goethe the Greeks were not a historical phenomenon along with others, but an absolute, removed from the vicissitudes of time; they were the eternally valid norm of the true, the correct, and the perfect in art. For him, therefore, there was not a multiplicity of historical styles of equal validity; there was only one good style, the style of true and conscientious representation of the "nature of things insofar as it is permitted us to recognize it in visible and perceptible forms." This is the decisive point, this was the issue of his polemic against romantic painting. Art which addressed itself to the eye must proceed from visible phenomena; it is not its function to represent emotions, inward moods, the formless life of the soul. Therein lay his irreconcilable opposition to the romantic school.

If we consider the fundamental bases of this opposition it appears that the principal cause of Goethe's resistance and his polemic was the transformation which had taken place in Italy of his view of the objective element in artistic production. Whereas in his youth he had fought against the abstract doctrines of the French theory of art and had opposed to them the native mastery of the inspired genius, now a reaction set in which went too far in the opposite direction. In his works the classic artist sought to vie with the objectivity of natural phenomena. This tendency was strengthened for him by the simultaneous development of his knowledge of the processes by which nature produced its forms. Far-reaching and firm laws, he now realized, regulate the endless process of the formation and transformation of organisms. From this principle derived the conclusion that the forms of art also must be produced in accordance with eternal laws if they are to be beautiful and necessary, objective and true. The fact that his aesthetic and his scientific views confirmed one another in this way gave rise to a conviction which was presented with the claim of an absolutely valid dogma. It made Goethe intolerant of the historical rights of the romantic movement and distorted his view of the value of the innovations which appeared in romantic painting.

For the romanticists the spirit of a historical mode of thought, of a modern renascence of the Christian Middle Ages, was fruitful. This was a manifestation of the great attention the new century directed to the world of history. Goethe did not share this new interest. He was dominated and limited by the normative unhistorical mode of thought of the eighteenth century, which he sought to restore in a new form. In literature, where he was master, his attitude was less dogmatic. But in the realm of plastic art, where he was and continued to be a dilettante, he shut himself up within an increasingly rigid system of rules and laws and thereby tried to remain right in principle against the only productive school of painting which then made its appearance in Germany. If his criticism is in many respects correct, particularly against the subjective exaggerations of early romanticism, he was on the whole refuted by the fact that the new classicism in plastic art which he sought to promote by his pedagogic efforts obviously was historically impossible. The facts contradicted his doctrine, however logically and clearly it may have been conceived and formulated. Thus arose the singular spectacle that in individual cases Goethe had to recognize what he rejected as a general direction according to the peculiar dogma he persisted in. He himself once said that even a great man was attached to his century by a weakness.

Seen from the point of view of the romanticists, there was an element in Goethe's attitude which embittered them more than anything else. When Goethe criticized their "neo-German patriotism," their enthusiasm for the German past, or when he reproached the sentimental subjectivity of their compositions as obscure and arbitrary, to them it appeared as if he thereby betrayed or rescinded the contributions and the ideas of his own origins. It was in the compositions of his early period that they had, so to speak, learned to read; through these works they had attained consciousness of love for what was German in the old genuine art. They believed they were the legitimate heirs of this outspokenly national mode of thinking and writing which had finally begun to spread among the Germans.

But Goethe in the meanwhile had found a second home in antiquity, Winckelmann's antiquity, which as artist he valued higher than the sphere of Nordic culture. For him antiquity had become, as Hofmannsthal expresses it, a magic mirror in which his own being and aspirations appeared in a strange and more illuminated form. While the romantics were going back to the Middle Ages, which were the Christian antiquity, and were making the idealized picture of the Catholic West the guiding model for their expectations, which were directed toward a Europe articulated into clearly differentiated nations, Goethe was willing to grant Christianity validity only as the basis of European morality. For art, poetry, and the formal cultivation of the individual, however, classic tradition remained for him the eternally fruitful soil, in the past and in the present. A synthesis of the ethical culture of Christianity with the aesthetic culture of antiquity, and a super-national world-wide humanity as the fruit of this alliance was the ideal goal for which, in his view, the creative spirits of all nations must collaborate. The romanticists, on the other hand (and indeed not all), renewed Christianity as a positive religion, restored the organization and authority of the Church, and in this community of faith wished at the same time to develop and strengthen the specific qualities of the individual nations.

In this opposition a conflict became evident which was never again resolved in Europe until it, together with other conflicts which arose later, was tragically eliminated by the great fratricidal wars in which the West turned to its own destruction. The national feelings and aspirations of the romanticists were not yet narrowed and cramped into particularism, not yet degenerated into nationalism. Their love for what was their own in history and culture was still pure and beneficent. In his youth Goethe had applied this tendency to himself and to the Germans. He had advanced, however, to an idea of culture in which national peculiarity was merged in a secular cosmopolitanism. But under the influence of the political events of the Napoleonic era there was developed an ever stronger patriotism which gave a particularistic direction to cultural striving also. In this tendency Goethe did not participate. His own development took the opposite direction. His differences of opinion with the romanticists contributed to making the divergent tendency of his own thought and his own production more definite and more explicit.

WISDOM

Sonnets

IN APRIL 1807 BETTINA BRENTANO APPEARED AT WEIMAR. FOR THE TWENTY-TWO-YEAR-OLD GIRL THE JOURNEY TO GOETHE WAS A PILGRIMAGE TO THE IDOL of her youth whom she had long revered at a distance. Many circumstances conspired to endow the encounter with the glamour of the extraordinary. Bettina was the granddaughter of Sophie von La Roche, Wieland's friend and a writer of reputation well known to Goethe personally in his youth. At that time he had called her his "dear Mama." Bettina's mother, the beautiful Maximiliane who had married the Frankfort merchant Brentano, was closer to him. The young woman was not happy in her marriage with her older husband. Goethe became the admirer and friend of the "suffering angel" at the time when he had separated from Lotte. It cost him much effort at that time not to become involved in a new passion. "Max's" children were Clemens and Bettina. The growing girl became a constant visitor at the home of Goethe's mother, who told her of the old days when Goethe and her mother had been friends. "The youthful story of her son flowed like refreshing dew from her maternal lips into my burning heart." What Goethe's mother told her she wrote down, and these notes of Bettina's were used by Goethe later on when he recounted the story of his youth.

Now she sat at the side of her idol, told him of Frankfort and his mother, recalled his youth, and at her departure received a ring as a gift. A correspondence initiated by Bettina made the tie closer. "And what is it that I wish? To tell how the generous friendship with which you received me has blossomed in my heart into a wild growth which violently suffocates all other life? To tell how I must always long for the time when I was *for the first time* happy?" At the end of the year she came to Weimar again. Now an exciting game began. The black-haired Mignon with dark eyes displayed a child's awed enthusiasm and the enticing charm of a woman glowing with passion in order to draw the poet closer to herself. At first Goethe warded her off, then was himself moved and showed a degree of intimacy and tenderness, but with reserve and without entangling himself in the dangerous net.

The relationship was spun out for three years in the correspondence which Bettina published after Goethe's death under the slightly coquettish title *Goethes Briefwechsel mit einem Kinde* ("Goethe's Correspondence with a Child"). Her letters are surely beautiful as an expression of her great love, and a unique item in Goethe's biography, which includes no other female correspondence of such quality. In his *Malte Laurids Brigge* Rilke has seen in them excellent testimony of the immeasurable devotion by which great lovers were wont to surpass their beloved. Rilke was also of the opinion that Goethe's attitude revealed the limitations of his greatness. "This woman in love was imposed upon him, and he did not face up to her." The description of an eyewitness, the philologist F. W. Riemer, who was Goethe's housemate at the time and had little sympathy for the "genial-baroque" character of Bettina, informs us how uncomfortable this emotional storm became to Goethe in the end. Later Goethe himself turned brusquely away in an epigram entitled *Den Zudringlichen* ("To the Importunate"): "What will not fit, bring not together!" But this was said after Bettina, who in the meanwhile had become the wife of Achim von Arnim, had, on the occasion of a new visit to Weimar, staged a fatal scene with Christiane which lost her Goethe's friendship. Goethe never again met her courtship halfway. In later encounters she was a nuisance to him. A letter to Karl August of the year 1826 says, harshly enough, that Bettina was repeating the old game which in a way became her in her youth; she spoke of nightingales and twittered like a canary, and this was now simply inconvenient.

In the same year in which he became acquainted with Bettina Goethe experienced another similar encounter. But here the roles were reversed. At the beginning of December 1807 he spent some time in Jena, as was his regular habit. Sojourning in Jena at that time was a romantic visitor, Zacharias Werner, and for some weeks he was Goethe's daily companion. Goethe was impressed by Werner's sonnets, which he read evenings in the circle of his Jena friends. "Sonneteering," the "quatrain-and-tercet" fashion, in which Goethe had not previously been interested, now engaged his attention. In the strictest and most formal of all genres he now again sought to appropriate an alien mode by reacting to it productively. But this enticement would not have been effective, the "sonnet rage" would not have seized upon him, had it not been reinforced by a new "raving of love." At the home of the Jena publisher, Frommann, Goethe met an eighteen-year-old girl, Minna Herzlieb, whom he had already known as a child.

> I did not start but kept up loving thought
> Of her whom once I carried in my heart,
> Then wisely thrust her from my thoughts apart,
> To whom again I'm close and closer brought.[1]

Minna possessed characteristics which Goethe loved more than anything else in woman, gentle sincerity and pure beauty. "More than was proper," he admitted to his wife five years later, he had loved this dear creature, who was indeed receptive to the homage of the great man, but who, bound by an unhappy love, could not think of responding to the Indian summer passion of a virtual sexagenarian. Abnegation was again Goethe's lot. It is from this concealed and painful emotion that the picture of the beloved which he paints in the *Wahlverwandtschaften* derives. But the lyrical fruit of this perturbation is a cycle of sonnets.

Bettina had maintained that the sonnets were addressed to her or evoked by Goethe's feeling for her. Individual phrases and turns of expression from her letters are in fact put into poetry here. And had not Goethe in his first letter asked her to write soon so that he should again have something "to translate," and had he not included two sonnets in this letter? Bettina had written:

> Just as the friend weighs anchor after long hesitation and at last must part; the last embrace seems to him what a hundred kisses and words have been, nay, more; the shores which he perceives in the distance are what the

[1] Ich fing nicht an, ich fuhr nur fort, zu lieben / Sie, die ich früh im Herzen schon getragen, / Dann wieder weislich aus dem Sinn geschlagen, / Der ich nun wieder bin ans Herz getrieben. (*Sonnet XVI,* translated by B. Q. Morgan.)

last glimpse was; and when at last even the blue hills vanish, his solitude, his memories are all that is left: even so is the nature of the loyal spirit which loves you, such am I!—who have been given to you by God as a dam over which your heart shall not float with the stream of time. It shall always remain young within you and always practiced in love.

These sentences served Goethe as poetic raw material for the two poems which he sent her. The first, which then opened the cycle, gives expression to the significance which the new passion has for his life, for the life of an aging man incessantly hastening onward, like the stream of ocean, to its end. Energetically Oreas, the mountain nymph, hurls herself against him, building a dam to check the flow to the sea in which the eternal stars are reflected—"a new life," a new youth of the heart. Then comes the sonnet *Abschied* ("Parting"), which takes up and intensifies Bettina's image of the departing vessel.

In the same fashion other sonnets also are evoked by Bettina's letters. But nothing more. The whole cycle is addressed neither to her nor to the other whom he actually loved, Minna Herzlieb, whose name serves as theme in the concluding poem *Charade*, which he wrote as a counterpiece to a sonnet of Zacharias Werner. The content is rather comprised in the feeling of a new life in new love which was aroused in Goethe by the two encounters with youth which followed one another with such rapidity. Bettina's passionate glow and Minna's gentle beauty flow together to form the ideal figure which is the beloved of these seventeen poems. The sonnets do not reproduce the circumstances of concrete situations; the reality in them has the perfection of poetic creation, of ideal wish-images, and is altogether a product of the imagination for which life has furnished only the material. Thus, in his usual manner, Goethe disposes with the aspects of these encounters which might be a dangerous temptation.

As motto for the cycle he set the words:

Love by loving I will laud;
Every form, it comes from God.[2]

A lover praises the rejuvenating power of passionate emotion and thus raises the tormenting actuality of concrete experience to the liberating generality of the essential. Every form, even the long-avoided,

[2] Liebe will ich liebend loben; / Jede Form sie kommt von oben. (Translated by B. Q. Morgan.)

strict form of the sonnet, is able to produce the effect of removing what is difficult from the material of life and affording redemption from life's sorrows. Thus nature becomes art and the anguish of necessity is transformed by spirit into freedom which may sometimes even dare be playful. This uplifting is expressed also in the style of Goethe's sonnets and in their language, which is joyously relaxed in a sovereignty all its own. The language moves lightly, as Platen later said in its praise, in full rhymes. Here a mind expresses itself which has mastered the heart's urge without bitterness—as is seemly for a man grown wise.

Pandora

Wer sie erkannt, der darf sie nicht entbehren.[1]

DURING THE TIME THAT GOETHE WAS COMPOSING HIS SONNET CYCLE HE WAS OCCUPIED WITH A LARGER WORK, A SOLEMN AND RICHLY EMBELLISHED PLAY. THE material derives from the cycle of Prometheus legend. Ever since his youth, when Prometheus had become for him the mythical incarnation of the titanic and rebellious feelings of creative man, this figure had attracted him. In 1795 he had thought of writing a "Prometheus Unbound" in the style of the Greek tragedy. Some years later, returning to this theme, he began a new work, which he originally intended to call *Pandorens Wiederkunft* ("Pandora's Return"). Finally entitled *Pandora,* the play which he wrote transforms the classical material into a symbolic myth in Plato's manner.

Greek legend knows nothing of a return of Pandora. For Goethe, Pandora is now not the daughter of Prometheus (as she was in the work of his youth), but a divine being, sister of Zeus. Once, marvelously endowed by the gods, she descended to Prometheus. The mysterious vessel which she brought with her released a stream of seductive phantoms which proved intangible when men pursued

[1] Who once has known her cannot rest without her. (*Faust,* v. 6559, translated by Anna Swanwick, London: Bell, 1879.)

them. Prometheus rejected her, but his brother Epimetheus received her tenderly. In a glorious dreamlike fulfillment, Epimetheus held the divine emissary in his arms. But the goddess could not remain in the archaic world of the Titans, for at this stage of history there was as yet no bond between gods and men. When Pandora separated from Epimetheus she took one of their daughters, Elpore or Hope, with her, while the other, Epimeleia or Sorrow, remained behind with her father. Ever since, Epimetheus has been consuming himself with yearning for the return of the incomparable one, and now the hour is near when she is actually to arrive. The play opens on the night which precedes her return, a night filled with Orphic expectation, mysterious premonition.

Upon the stage, in the style of the classical landscapes of Poussin, two worlds are opposed to one another: Prometheus' crude and powerful world of cliffs and caves, and Epimetheus' simple, sober house, a wooden structure patterned after the most ancient temples, comfortably furnished and surrounded by cultivated gardens. In classical fashion, Epimetheus introduces himself in a monologue. He is, as Prometheus terms him, the "man filled with sorrows, the man of heavy brooding." His nature is to reflect upon what is lost, to wish the return of what has passed. His opposite is Prometheus, the active man, the *homo faber*, who esteems not night and the happiness of dreams, not ideas and love, but day which challenges to creation. He prizes that which is practically possible, useful work, the conquering deed. The arms-forging smiths are in his service.

Another pair appears, the loving children of the estranged brothers: Phileros, the passionate and impetuous lover, and Epimeleia, the soulful and care-filled daughter of Epimetheus. Jealous rage drives the blinded young man to extremes. In him is still the crudeness of the earliest ages, and in his fury he wounds his beloved, thinking her faithless. Driven out of the community by Prometheus as a penalty, Phileros hurls himself into the sea, and Epimeleia is on the point of seeking death in flames. A general war threatens to break out. But the play is not intended to develop into a tragedy. Morning dawns majestically; Eos ("Dawn") banishes the night of horror and proclaims that in accordance with the will of the gods and of life the loving pair shall be preserved for the day which is now beginning and which will bring Pandora back with new and undreamed of gifts. This is the extent of the fragment. The arrival of the goddess is not described.

Before we inquire into the meaning implicit in the figures and action of the play, it is fitting that we first grasp the poetic content of the portion completed. This is contained primarily in the scenes with Epimetheus. We see him sunk in mournful recollection, filled with the aftertaste of the happiness which he has experienced in union with Pandora, and hopeful of her return. This constitutes the lyrical element of the composition. One will not fail to notice, says Goethe, that here (as in the *Wahlverwandtschaften*) the painful feeling of denial is given expression. In splendid verses Epimetheus seeks to expound to his brother what Pandora has meant to him. Beauty incarnate has manifested itself to him in her perfect form, so majestic that no praise can do her justice and no praise is required. In comparison with her all other values—esteem, wealth, power, wisdom—appear negligible. What substance could all existence have without perfecting and perfected form?

> To us in a legion of forms she descendeth,
> She floats upon waters, on meadows she wendeth,
> In sacred dimensions she gleams and resounds,
> And form that ennobles gives content its bounds,
> To it and herself lends a power supreme.
> To me as a woman in youth did she seem.[2]

There can be only a "reflection," for it is not vouchsafed man to look upon prototypes themselves. He can only look upon that which is illuminated, it is here said, not upon light itself. In later writings we read: "Truth is godlike; it does not appear directly; we must divine it through its manifestations." [3] Or: "Truth, which is identical with the divine, never can be directly apprehended by us: we perceive it only in a reflection, in illustration, in symbol, in separate and related manifestations; we become aware of it as life incomprehensible, and yet cannot help wishing to comprehend it." [4] It is to this view that

[2] Sie steiget hernieder in tausend Gebilden, / Sie schwebet auf Wassern, sie schreitet auf Gefilden, / Nach heiligen Massen erglänzt sie und schallt, / Und einzig veredelt die Form den Gehalt, / Verleiht ihm, verleiht sich die höchste Gewalt. / Mir erschien sie in Jugend-, in Frauengestalt. (*Pandora,* translated by B. Q. Morgan.)

[3] Das Wahre ist gottähnlich; es erscheint nicht unmittelbar, wir müssen es aus seinen Manifestationen erraten. (*Maximen und Reflexionen,* No. 619.)

[4] Das Wahre, mit dem Göttlichen identisch, lässt sich niemals von uns direkt erkennen: wir schauen es nur im Abglanz, im Beispiel, Symbol, in einzelnen und verwandten Erschei-

the verses in the poem *Zueignung* ("Dedication") refer: "The veil of song, by Truth's own fingers given."

Vis superba formae—beauty's proud might! Nowhere outside the Helena scenes of *Faust* has Goethe invoked it in such powerful words and so praised it as in this hymn. In the years before the writing of *Pandora,* he had been occupied with the teachings of the "ancient mystic," the Neoplatonist Plotinus. To his friend Zelter he sent (on September 1, 1805) his translation of the clauses of the *Enneads* which treat of the manner in which man is able to apprehend the beauty of the world spirit and the manifestations of it. The human spirit, with its capacity for formulating ideas, first gives form to matter. The beautiful is produced by the form-fashioning spirit of the artist. This is done not by imitating sensual perceptions of nature but by "returning to the rational principle underlying nature and according to which nature operates." According to Plotinus' doctrine, however, the idea is not thereby merged with individual figures of nature and of art; it retains its transcendent independence of perfection in the face of matter. On this point Goethe held a different opinion. When the spirit appears in concrete form, it is not thereby curtailed or diminished. To Goethe, the absolute, whatever it might be in the theoretical sense of metaphysics, appears adequate and entirely comprehensible in the highest manifestations themselves. In them the mysterious is "revealed."

It is of this supreme experience, when the suprasensual is perceived in sensual phenomena, that the ecstatic Epimetheus speaks. It is in the form of the beautiful that the idea communicates itself to man in the only manner suitable to him. In the highest manifestations of nature, and even more explicitly in those of art, we perceive, as Goethe wrote at this time in the prologue for the inauguration of the Weimar theater,

> Reflection of yon primal light above,
> Which though unseen illumines all the world.[5]

This view is finally stated emphatically at the beginning of the first act of the second part of *Faust*. As a scientist Goethe held the same

---

nungen; wir werden es gewahr als unbegreifliches Leben und können dem Wunsch nicht entsagen, es dennoch zu begreifen. (*Zur Meteorologie.*)

[5] Abglanz jenes Urlichts droben, / Das unsichtbar alle Welt erleuchtet. (*Vorspiel zur Eröffnung des Weimarischen Theaters,* translated by B. Q. Morgan.)

view of nature. In the transitory he thought he saw that which is permanent, in the individual phenomenon the protophenomenon or type, in eternal change the normative idea. A comparison with the famous allegory of the cave in Plato's *Republic* shows that the view which makes every phenomenon a reflection of an idea, a symbol of something transcendental, is quite in the tradition of Platonic thought. But Goethe does not distinguish between unity and multiplicity, between becoming and being; for him there is no perception of pure ideas, of transcendental *logoi.* The eternal appears in the visible, and only in the visible; the idea manifests itself in things which exist in time and space. Only by proceeding from the sensually perceptible appearance of things can we attain to the idea, only by proceeding from the reflection to the "prototype." In this sense all reality is symbol, everything transitory is simile.

The idea of the universally prevalent form which alone gives substance its highest and most effective realization, so that only substance thus fashioned achieves true being—this idea, Epimetheus says, had appeared to him most excellently in Pandora, in the youthful and beautiful female form.

> Who sees her, of his wits is dispossessed.[6]

This is also the feeling of the passionate lover Phileros. At once shuddering and ecstatic he asks:

> . . . Who gave to that form
> The force of a peerless and terrible storm? [7]

He does not know whether the form comes from Olympus or from Hades, from the world of light or the world of death.

As Riemer reports of a conversation he had with the poet in 1809, Goethe's own manner of experiencing the ideal, especially in his old age, "was to conceive it in feminine form." In Goethe's poetry spiritual values, even the highest moral values, are incarnated in sensual perfection. In describing the impression which Helena, "the form of all forms," makes upon Faust, Goethe has expressed this conception as an objective dramatic incident. In the *Marienbader Elegie,* the last of his

[6] Wem sie erscheint, wird aus sich selbst entrückt (*Faust,* v. 6485, translated by Bayard Taylor, revised edition, Boston: Houghton Mifflin, 1883.)

[7] . . . Wer gab der Gestalt / Die einzige furchtbar entschiedne Gewalt? (*Pandora,* translated by B. Q. Morgan.)

great love poems, he states the same idea explicitly: the gods, he says, have tried him by giving him Pandora, which is to say, deepest despair along with highest fulfillment. For, as Faust says of Helena,

> Who once has known her cannot rest without her.

In his autobiography Goethe says that nature appears to desire that one sex become sensually aware of what is good and beautiful in the other. For him, this is the mystery of supreme love, which contains as much earthly pleasure as serene piety, the twofold happiness of the senses and of the spirit, both in one as is appropriate to our twofold nature. The happiness of which Epimetheus speaks in rapturous recollection and his loss are Goethe's own supreme pleasure and denial. These lyric arias which fill the scenes of *Pandora* are superfluous for the action. They are confessions of the poet, painful words of parting, and at the same time words of gratitude, uttered from the suffering heart of the aging man who takes leave of life in its abundance and yet fears nothing more than final loss.

> Whoso is damned from the fair one to sever,
> Flee, nor his gaze e'er divert from his track!
> Seeing her, flames all his soul as in fever,
> Ever she draws him, nay, snatches him back.[8]

For, alas, everything is transitory, even the beautiful form. Only for an instant, so Goethe says in the essay on Winckelmann, is the beautiful human being beautiful, only for a fleeting hour do the rose and the lily bloom in full splendor. So too the fulfillment of life is transitory. Prometheus, the unsentimental, says:

> To bliss of youth, I ween, is beauty close akin:
> On mountain summits neither one is wont to bide.[9]

And Epimeleia, suffering the first anguish of love, contrasts the ephemeral destiny of man with the phenomena of ever-renewed nature:

[8] Wer von der Schönen zu scheiden verdammt ist, / Fliehe mit abegewendetem Blick! / Wie er, sie schauend, im Tiefsten entflammt ist, / Zieht sie, ach! reisst sie ihn ewig zurück. (*Pandora*, translated by B. Q. Morgan.)

[9] Dem Glück der Jugend heiss' ich Schönheit nah verwandt: / Auf Gipfeln weilt so eines wie das andre nicht. (*Pandora*, translated by B. Q. Morgan.)

Ah! why, ye gods, is infinite and endless
Everything, and only bliss is finite!
Starry shine and high exalted moonlight,
Somber shade and waterfall and murmur,
Infinite, and only bliss is finite.[10]

In 1810 Rahel Levin acutely observed to her friend Varnhagen the depressing effect which *Pandora* exerted upon her: "I understood at once what it means to be old at that time. One also becomes old suddenly. Old age too unfolds suddenly like a blossom from the bud, though the whole of youth must be a preparation for it." But irrecoverable loss is not accepted by Goethe in a spirit of helpless agony. The concluding verses of *Pandora* declare that the authority of the gods must be accepted.

What's to wish for, ye on earth can feel it;
What's to give, the powers up yonder know.[11]

If these portions give the fragment, for such it is, poetic substance, the poet's intention was nevertheless not to compose a lyrical drama but a play in which a grand subject, the origins and basic forces of mature culture, should be treated symbolically. The opposition of the mythical brothers in itself indicates the theme. By the side of Epimetheus, the contemplative, soulful dreamer and lover, stands Prometheus, the realistic activist. He has procured for men the elements of civilization, has provided them with fire, has taught them handicraft, agriculture, fishing, and commerce. From him they have learned to forge tools and weapons, the useful works of peace and the violent implements of war. He is concerned only with what is useful and knows nothing of the joys and sorrows of the inner life which guide his idealistic brother.

Yet the conflict between Prometheus and Epimetheus is not exclusive but polar; the tendency is toward consonance, toward over-all adjustment. In this polarity Goethe sees the basic structure of life; he has represented it repeatedly in the contrasting figures of his

[10] Ach! warum, ihr Götter, ist unendlich / Alles, alles, endlich unser Glück nur! / Sternenglanz und Mondes Ueberschimmer, / Schattentiefe, Wassersturz und Rauschen / Sind unendlich, endlich unser Glück nur. (*Pandora*, translated by B. Q. Morgan.)

[11] Was zu wünschen ist, ihr unten fühlt es; / Was zu geben sei, die wissen's droben. (*Pandora*, translated by B. Q. Morgan.)

dramas. The scheme for the continuation of the scenes which he had worked out—there are only catchwords—indicates a solution by which this opposition would be reconciled. The age of beginnings, when individual giants functioned as founders of civilization, is past; the era of violence is closed. Gods and men will now unite. The returning Pandora will bring gifts which will serve as the basis for a mature and tranquil civilization. Happiness and abundance not for selected individuals alone but for all, prosperity and learning, art and religion in a glorious ensemble: this is the vision which was to be given shape in symbolic figures and incidents. A rejuvenated Epimetheus was to be "elevated" with Pandora and to become the good genius of the consummated age. At the same time, Phileros and Epimeleia, the enthusiastic son of the active brother and the soulful daughter of the loving brother, were to become the first human pair of this new aeon. The formative and restraining power which is made manifest in Pandora's figure would now give existence its perfection. So may Goethe's intentions be conjectured from his laconic notes.

The *Pandora* scenes show Goethe in transition from the strict classical style—which had attained unsurpassable maturity in his *Natürliche Tochter*—to a new mode of presentation which was similarly concerned with "the general" but at the same time was more definitely symbolic. Lesser works, like the interlude *Paläophron und Neoterpe* (1801) and the *Vorspiel* of 1807, are attempts in the same direction. The style of Greek tragedy serves as a guiding star when Goethe, going on from the balanced harmony and serene beauty which Winckelmann extolled in classic art, now endeavors to rise a degree higher to a "grandness" of expression which approaches sublime pathos without actually falling into it—a grandness, that is to say, which is kept within the limits of classical restraint. Just as he mastered the epic verse of antiquity in *Hermann und Dorothea,* so here he undertook to imitate the principal meter of Greek drama, the iambic trimeter, and thus to give his dialogue the dignity of that of classical Greek tragedy.

The rhythms of classical drama elevate the language of Goethe's drama to a like level. Word forms are rugged and compact. There are coinages which attempt to renew in German the characteristic usage of Greek formations.

All-fairest, all-endowed, she moved sublime
Toward th' astonished one . . .[12]

In shining braids the wondrous growth was neatly coiled,
But, loosed and free, fell serpentine and touched her heels.[13]

People thought that such formations sounded like translations from the Greek. And what if that were true? If the Greek style had served to give the German poet the notion of and capacity for new formations of an artistic character, the innovations were the result of bold exploitation of possibilities already inherent in the German language and awaiting anyone able to seize upon and utilize them. The possibilities of a language are determined only by the individual able to exploit them. The creator of language, the great poet, is just such a man. Everywhere he augments language; he does not use it conventionally. The new expression, the new beauty which the poet, inspired by a foreign model, contributes to the existing stock is pure and incalculable gain. It was only after Goethe's *Pandora,* and because of it, that it became possible to employ in the German language a style which, like that of Greek drama, combines enhanced grandeur and beauty. In the Helena scenes of *Faust* Goethe has carried this style to its height.

In another respect, also, the Prometheus scenes are a preparation for the Helena sequence, for in them another element of style makes its appearance and is superimposed on the classical style. Greek meters are made to rhyme. In *Pandora* there are lyrical monologues in which the form of operatic aria is given new stylistic grandeur. There are songlike portions and choruses which serve the function of the ancient chorus; these are not to be declaimed rhapsodically, however, but are to be sung, as in an opera. The art of rhymed strophes is developed with great richness. Thus this work, which was first published in a romantic periodical, approximates the form of the romantic drama in which lyrical meters and structure are combined, words and music are united, and the whole approaches the form later called *Gesamtkunstwerk* ("total work of art"). *Pandora* is Goethe's first classic-romantic drama.

[12] Allschönst und allbegabtest regte sie sich hehr / Dem Staunenden entgegen . . . (*Pandora,* translated by B. Q. Morgan.)

[13] In Flechten glänzend schmiegte sich der Wunderwuchs, / Der, freigegeben, schlangengleich die Ferse schlug. (*Pandora,* translated by B. Q. Morgan.)

Elective Affinities

MANKIND HAS NEVER CEASED TO DREAM OF A PERFECT ORDER AND A PERFECT AGE IN WHICH THE DIFFICULTIES OF EXISTENCE WOULD BE RESOLVED AND LIFE'S anxieties banished—a Golden Age or a Kingdom of God, peace eternal or an era in which all men might live with one another freely as brothers. In the centuries of modern civilization which have been destitute of myth these dreams have been attached to individual historical phenomena or figures, and to them has been attributed the joyous abundance of life which is denied to the many. Whole cultures have been transfigured into ideal incarnations of human potentialities. Greece, as Winckelmann and his disciples imagined it; the noble savage, as Rousseau envisaged him; the medieval man, as he seemed to the romanticists. In the nineteenth century individual artists were similarly transfigured: Mozart was thought of as a light-hearted favorite of the gods; Goethe as a sublime Olympian who, like a god, was superior to the dark destinies which make the life of man bleak and dreary.

The picture of Goethe as an ever-young demigod moving in brightness did not inspire unadulterated reverence; it also evoked unfriendly feeling and was used to emphasize Goethe's limitations and weaknesses. So Hebbel said that Goethe knew beauty only *before* dissonances set in, envisioned only the dreamlike quality of beauty which is unaware, and is determined to remain unaware, of grim destiny and tragic complications. This is as little true of Goethe's life as it is of his work. In order to appreciate how distorted and untrue the image of the joyous Olympian is, we need only read his utterances in old age, when he looks back upon a long life and balances profit and loss. In his whole life, the septuagenarian says, he had never had a four-weeks' period of "real comfort." Other of his remarks are even more dismal and bitter: mankind en masse is a pitiful lot, silly and abject; he said that he had no faith in the world, and has learned despair. In 1816, after reading *Werther*, the gloomy work of his youth, he confesses to his friend Zelter that he himself could not understand how a man who had already found the world so preposterous in early youth could have tolerated it for another forty years. How such skeptical and melancholy expressions are to be judged, and how they may be related to other statements made during periods of confidence in life, we shall not consider in this place. Another and related problem, however, requires our attention when we approach the work which alone among Goethe's later productions concerns itself with the gloomy and irremediable aspects of life.

Goethe had declared to Schiller that he was not sufficiently acquainted with himself to know whether he was capable of writing a true tragedy; he recoiled from the mere thought of so doing and was almost convinced that the bare attempt would destroy him. Even in extreme age he repeated a similar thought (to Zelter, October 31, 1831): pure tragedy must be irreconcilable; he was himself, however, conciliatory by nature, and "in this world which was in general so utterly commonplace" irreconcilability seemed to him preposterous. It almost seems as if he intended to say that the difficulties of life should not be taken seriously. But was not *Werther* of the very stuff of which tragedy is made? Not in the sense of Greek tragedy, indeed, in which the catastrophe does not grow out of the quality of life itself. What is true of *Werther* is true also of *Clavigo* and of *Stella*. But what of Tasso, the "enhanced Werther"? In Goethe's later thought it may be that changing circumstances play too large a role. In speaking of Goethe's distaste for Kleist, Nietzsche is of the opinion that because of his conciliatory nature Goethe recoiled from the irremediable view of nature which confronted him in Kleist's tragedy. It would be more accurate to say, the irremediable aspect of human existence. In nature, Goethe did not find the gloomy contradiction with which tragedy has to deal. But that a poet of his rank perceived human life in its fundamentals and recognized the insoluble conflicts which comprise man's profoundest problems is proven clearly enough by what he said to Schiller. Yet to recoil from the dark mystery of life is natural for one whose existence reposes on trusting belief in and love of God.

Nevertheless, Goethe did once create a genuine tragedy, the novel *Die Wahlverwandtschaften* ("Elective Affinities"). He was sixty years old when he undertook the venture. The meaning of this work Goethe himself has indicated. There is no line in it which he had not experienced—experienced in the sense which he implies in calling all of his compositions fragments of a single large confession. He had taken up only what his own experience offered him as an urgent problem which he must conquer and reduce to poetic form. He also said that this novel was the only one of his works of considerable size in which he consciously attempted to present an idea. But we must remember another of his dicta in order to avoid taking the work too philosophically, as a mere product of intellect. Goethe says that the *Wahlverwandtschaften* gives expression to the painful feeling of self-denial, of abnegation. One may perceive that here a deep and passionate wound is loath to mend and cicatrize, a heart is fearful of recovery. A personal experience deeply felt, a clearly recognized and general situation, transformed into an idea and presented as something universally valid—that is the source and the achievement of this book as of Goethe's other mature works. Of this novel Goethe has also said that more was contained in it than could be apprehended at a single reading; the book must be read three times. One who knows the work will find that he might have said ten times. The book is written in the clearest prose, and it begins unpretentiously, even carelessly; but step by step the reader is led to a depth where the mind, unaccustomed to the half-darkness, is at first powerless.

In the announcement of the book Goethe pointed out that, as the title suggests, a chemical concept would be employed as symbol for human relationships. This was legitimate, he thought, because in the end everything was of only one nature, and even in the realm of intellectual freedom there are apparent "traces of murky passionate necessity" which man cannot by his own power banish. The phenomenon of chemical affinity had been observed and described some decades before by the Swedish scientist, Torsten Bergmann. If two compounds, *a-b* and *c-d,* react upon another, the reaction is either no change or a separation and new combination, *a-c* and *b-d.* Alkalies and acids which are in polar opposition to one another seek most definitely to enter into union with one another. In the novel the phenomenon is described in a manner which permits its symbolic meaning to emerge: "Here a separation and new combination has taken place, and we feel justified in using the word *Wahlverwandtschaft* because it actually appears as if one relationship is preferred to the other, one selected rather than the other."[1] But it only seems so.

[1] Hier ist eine Trennung, eine neue Zusammensetzung entstanden, und man glaubt sich nunmehr berechtigt, sogar das Wort Wahlverwandtschaft anzuwenden, weil es wirklich

Where a law of nature is operative there can be no question of choice. Choice exists only in the province of the chemist who brings these bodies together. "But once they are together, God help them!"—so Goethe expresses it, with meaningful seriousness.

But how can the chemical simile apply to human relationships? This, too, is discussed in the conversation which is placed at the beginning of the book and sets the key for its principal theme. Man, a mature and disciplined woman replies, is higher than the simple elements. We may speak of choice and *Wahlverwandtschaft* if we are at the same time aware that man alone is able to escape from the necessity of nature and to exercise free power of decision. Charlotte adds, without realizing that her statement gives expression to the web of conflict which is to be woven: "Unfortunately, I am familiar enough with cases where sincere and apparently indissoluble unions of two persons are annulled by the chance addition of a third, whereby one of the two who had been so beautifully united is thrust out into free space."[2] If a fourth is added, similar attraction and combination take place crosswise, and in this process of repulsion and attraction a sort of will and choice becomes apparent as if there were some mysterious intelligence at work. What if natural necessity exercises fuller control than we are aware over the relations of men to one another, even in the realm of love where we imagine that we exercise free choice through the individuality of our ego? It is the dogma of materialistic determinism which is under discussion: as a dependent member of a total natural causality man is implicated in the gigantic tissue of the law of necessity, and his belief that he acts and chooses freely is nothing more than vain delusion.

Accident brings the four actors of the drama together: the husband and wife, Charlotte and Eduard, the friend of the husband, and Ottilie, the young girl. Accident? There is much logical method in the manner in which this union is brought about. Demonic forces seem to intervene, fatal demons which hasten destiny as well as helpful demons which attempt to interfere by hint and premonition. Should one not rather speak of fate or of some sort of higher necessity?

aussieht, als wenn ein Verhältnis dem andern vorgezogen, eins vor dem andern erwählt würde. (*Die Wahlverwandtschaften*, Part I, chapter iv.)

[2] Mir sind leider Fälle genug bekannt, wo eine innige, unauflöslich scheinende Verbindung zweier Wesen durch gelegentliche Zugesellung eines dritten aufgehoben und eins der erst so schön Verbundenen ins lose Weite hinausgetrieben ward. (*Die Wahlverwandtschaften*, Part I, chapter iv.)

Rather, was it not wise arrangement that Eduard is not at once united with Charlotte as he wished to be, and that Charlotte herself had planned him to have Ottilie? Out of friendly interest the married couple invites the captain; with no special intention Eduard suggests that the girl be invited. At the end of the ominous conversation concerning "elective affinities" Charlotte decides to carry out the suggestion, and this forms an introduction to the doom which follows. Then there is the blindness of the participants' belief that they can return to their earlier peaceful state after they have just taken a further stride on their fatal way. Even striking warnings, like the death of the child, are unable to loosen the ramifications of the relationship, to break the magic circle. When the wise woman at last determines to yield, it is too late. And there are many similar strands which point to the inevitability of the conclusion and show man in the power of a superior necessity. "But once they are together, God help them!"

The strongest effect is exercised by the affinity between the husband and Ottilie. Eduard is a self-indulgent man of moods who can deny himself nothing, more because of selfishness than because of strength of character. His only interest is amateur gardening, precisely the avocation which Goethe discussed with critical acumen in his sketch on dilettantism. Gardening involved indefiniteness, he there said, because it is undefined and unlimited in its idea. It promoted sentimental and fantastic nothingness and diminished what was lofty in nature. This amateur interest was exactly appropriate to the prevalent state of mind which sought to be unconstrained and lawless in aesthetic matters, which desired to give free reign to whimsical fantasy and not to submit to discipline. Eduard is of the breed of romantic theorists, a dilettante of life, but more virile than Werther, and amiable and childish enough to please the ladies. His inclination to unconstrained passion, a failing from the moral point of view, makes him at the same time a seductive lover. He himself knows that his love for Ottilie is his first serious experience. Though he might be a bungler in all other respects, for love unqualified he believes that he possesses genuine talent. But he is by no means able to withstand the elemental force which waylays him so vehemently. Morality and conscience, consideration for the feelings of others, self-denial are no longer of any concern to him. Without resistance he yields to the overwhelming force, and it is his lack of moderation which in the end brings on the catastrophe. Nor does suffering purify him; he has no talent for martyrdom. It is only that the helplessness of his love unto death is sufficiently moving to arouse the sympathy of the spectator and appease moral sensibilities.

Ottilie is of a different and nobler mold. All light is centered upon this character, all the magic of beauty, innocence, and lovableness. This pure figure is constructed out of the passionate emotions which Minna Herzlieb had aroused in Goethe. Inexperienced, not properly conscious of self, she who was intended to be happy and to make others happy becomes involved in the issue of destiny. No one is as vulnerable to the mysterious force of elective affinity as she, for to a greater degree than the others she is vulnerable to the secret effects of the forces of nature. The intellectual clarity of worldly experience is not given her. Her intellectual development has proceeded slowly. She appears to exist in a state of semiwakefulness, and her knowledge comes rather from premonition than from rational comprehension. Since she lives inwardly, her expressions are demure and awkward. She is quiet and unobtrusive in her active attention to others; her step is so soft that she is never heard.

In order to indicate her proximity to the invisible forces of nature, Goethe employs a motif fashionable in contemporary science, the so-called "animal magnetism." Under the influence of Schelling's philosophy of nature, the electrical phenomena discovered by Galvani and Franz Anton Mesmer's hypnotic experiments were interpreted as the operations of nonmaterial cosmic forces in the human body. Through them the physical organism of man was thought to be most intimately linked to the whole of nature. In the "magnetic sleep" of somnambulists, romantic scientists and physicians believed they recognized a state in which the soul possessed a higher activity and a clearer consciousness than in the waking state. In this clairvoyant state the individual was thought to possess a heightened sensitivity to stimuli which could not otherwise be apprehended by the senses. In such a state, it was believed, men could develop an understanding for the "night side of nature" which had been obscured by the rationalistic culture of modern times. Goethe knew the writings of the physicist Johann Wilhelm Ritter on these phenomena, and through Schelling and Hegel he knew of the experiments which Schelling and other romantic philosophers of nature had set up at Munich. Both now and later he avoided delving deeper into these phenomena and thought it wicked to evoke them arbitrarily merely out of experimental curiosity, but he had no doubts that such powers did reside in men. "Where I cannot see clearly, cannot operate with definiteness, that is a sphere for which I have no vocation. I have never desired to observe a somnambulist." [3]

In the novel the phenomena of magnetism are treated neither for their own sake nor in order to decorate the narrative with a sensational motif. They are nothing more than a means of characterization, in that they indicate Ottilie's unconscious link with the forces of nature. She can detect the presence of hidden metals as does a divining rod; occasionally she falls into states of semiwakefulness in which she nevertheless understands the conversations of those present. The effect which her lover exercises upon her corresponds to that of the mesmerizer upon his medium. Whether Ottilie's remarkable sensitivity and susceptibility lie within the bounds of spiritual health or belong in the area of the morbid is obviously of no great importance to Goethe. What in this respect gives the impression of being unusual, exaggerated, or even problematic belongs within the limits of man's natural potentialities, as long as it is not artificially produced. And in any case, what meaning can words like sickness or health have when a young person is able to withstand the first great trial of life in so exemplary a manner? By these special gifts and reactions Ottilie demonstrates how true a child of nature she is and how, for that very reason, she is more subject to the attraction of affinity than are others. The conflict between the necessity of nature and the human need of self-determination must break out in her all the more vehemently, and all the more magnificent is the victory she achieves as a moral personality.

For she is no romanticist, no dilettante of life. Her moderation in food and drink indicates an instinctive will to self-control. The sense of what is proper is native to her. But she is carried powerfully along by the momentum of the strange emotion against which, at first, she has no weapons. Intense desires, bold hopes, blind her ever and again.

[3] Wo ich nicht klar sehen, nicht mit Bestimmtheit wirken kann, da ist ein Kreis, für den ich nicht berufen bin. Ich habe nie eine Somnambule sehen mögen. (Conversation with Chancellor von Müller, February 10, 1830.)

It is only after repeated skirmishes and under the pressure of great shock that she achieves power for self-denial. How could it be otherwise? As she expresses it, God must first open her eyes in a fearful manner for her to realize in what guilt she is involved. But along with clarity comes the plan for complete abnegation and repentance. That all is not yet well is not her responsibility. But Eduard is unable to renounce; he will not give her the peace which is necessary if fate is to be averted. She must come to realize that "the monstrously urgent powers" cannot be appeased by repentance and forbearance. Some greater sacrifice is demanded. She must now employ against herself all the energies which she has mustered in order to destroy herself. She no longer speaks, and she silently ceases to take nourishment. "I have gone off my course and I am not to return to it." [4] The rest she must manage alone, the last and most difficult she must achieve by herself, must die her own death. Joyful and tranquil she lives among her friends and yields serenely to the "indescribable, almost magic power of attraction" which she cannot escape feeling but which no longer involves danger for one steadfast in her renunciation. Her character ascends to dignity, to solemnity. A hard and clear word concerning the sixth commandment, accidentally spoken in her presence, finally occasions her death. Thus she becomes the victim of a destiny which it is not given her to overcome but which she now realizes as a moral being.

In this novel, marriage only supplies the motive in connection with which and through which the much broader and more general theme constituting the ideal nucleus of the story is treated. Marriage rests upon control of elemental urges, and is therefore the basis of civilization and its highest achievement. But it has been wrested from nature, and in consequence must constantly be defended against nature. Furthermore, nowhere does the individual's demand for satisfaction of his strongest emotions, his vehement appetites, come into such violent conflict with the claims and the necessities of society. In Goethe's novel this motif also applies to contemporary conditions. Romantic subjectivity, the glorification of passion and of a way of life based upon it, had led to a degree of freedom in sexual relations which threatened marriage as an institution. Mme de Staël, who was familiar with the

[4] Ich bin aus meiner Bahn geschritten, und ich soll nicht wieder hinein. (*Wahlverwandtschaften*, Part II, chapter xvii.)

romantic aberrations in marriage, has said: "In Germany love is a religion, but a poetic religion only too ready to tolerate what sentimentality can excuse. Surely the ease of divorce in Protestant regions endangers the sanctity of marriage. Spouses are changed as calmly as if it were merely a matter of arranging the incidents in a drama."

But the intent of Goethe's novel is neither didactic nor polemic. He knew well enough what it costs to deny highest passion and to sacrifice the heart's emotional claim in order to respect the demands of conscience and the duties of social morality.

> To break our word is too inviting,
> So hard our duty to fulfill.[5]

With all his respect for marriage, he was unable to find the solution which might have satisfied himself and his friends alike. At the very time that this book was being written it again happened that he was forced to muster all his strength in order to follow his "well-recognized duty."

> Whom befool not eye and lip
> Breath and voice enchanting? [6]

The view stated in the novel by the rigorous Mittler (Part I, chapter ix) is certainly Goethe's view as well. But this is only half the truth, the demand of morality which only together with the opposing claims of nature and the heart can comprise the whole of the problem of practical duty which must be solved each time anew.

The conflict between unqualified passion, which desires only to fulfill itself, and matrimony as the basis of moral civilization is the concrete instance in which a larger opposition becomes apparent. The story of an unhappy love, already told a hundred times, serves as the segment of real life in which the comprehensive problem is brought to the surface: How can man, a being placed between nature and super-nature, maintain himself and harmonize his contradictory demands? The natural force by which the two pairs are drawn to each other operates with varying power in each individual. The force of resistance also varies in strength, coresponding to the differences of

[5] Zu lieblich ist's, ein Wort zu brechen, / Zu schwer die wohlerkannte Pflicht. (*Abschied*, translated by Paul Drysen, *Goethe's Poems*, p. 54.)

[6] Wen betört nicht Blick und Gruss, / Schmeichelhafter Odem? (*Faust*, v. 12030, translated by Bayard Taylor.)

natural character and moral maturity. The narrative is shot through with phenomena which stand to one another in the polar relationship, of thesis and antithesis. The antitheses are related to one another, they strive toward one another, because only with one another can they achieve an equipoise, construct a whole. Affinity is only one particularly explicit case of this omnipresent phenomenon in which Goethe perceived the great driving force of nature, the pulse-beat of life itself. What else is true passion, love however vehement, if not the attempt of a sympathy implanted by nature in these partners to come to realization? Thus true love is a force as inexorable in character, as far beyond good and evil, as any other force in the realm of the great cosmic order.

The consequences of this position are of high significance. To men of Christian civilizations love is the most individual emotion; they believe that they determine the choice of their beloved according to the wishes of their own character, their own individuality, more freely than in any other human concern. But this book demonstrates that it is only after the attraction of affinities has set up a relationship in accordance with the will of nature that the properly human, the moral and personal, task is posed. Man is framed not to obey blindly, but himself to choose. Acting independently, he must decide whether to accept or to reject the relationship which nature has desired. Alas for him, if the struggle within him between nature and super-nature, between morality and the elemental urge, is so powerful that he cannot allay it; if he cannot achieve equipoise between the unequal members in the basic polarity by which his existence is determined, the equipoise upon which the soul's peace and life's happiness depend; if the demands of the two realms upon him assert themselves as an irreconcilable either-or, and if he must deny the commandment of the moral law in order not to prove disobedient to nature. This contradiction appears in most inexorable terms when the characters of the persons involved, and the course of life, so frame conditions that guilt is inevitable. Schelling, in speaking of tragedy, says that it is the greatest imaginable misfortune "to become guilty by fate without true guilt." That is Ottilie's guilt.

Here, more than in any other of his compositions, Goethe appears to approximate Schiller's tragic view of the world. But the dualism of the powers by which man's existence is determined is of a different character in Goethe's narrative, and his resolution is also different. For Schiller the claims of nature always retain an element of hostility; she appears minded, along with "the impishness of fate," to subject to herself our spirit which is designed for freedom and to destroy the dignity of the individual. But in Goethe's work the urge of nature has the same sacred necessity as the moral law. For the idea which is expressed in "affinity" belongs not to the realm of disorder and unreason but to the law-governed order of all things, the great order by which the world spirit finds realization. "There is necessity, there is God." Man's existence, and his alone, is problematic because the forces which elsewhere produce and maintain life and lead it gently into new manifestations can appear in it as hostile and disruptive powers. This places him in situations in which he can save his soul only by letting his physical existence be destroyed.

There are, to be sure, ways of avoiding the disruptive forces, by using moderation, restraint, forbearance. Goethe's work, in particular that of his later classical period and of his old age, is replete with recommendations of such an ascetic attitude. Nothing can be finer than for inclination to be directed by reason and conscience. But once a conflict has broken out there is only a single means left for deliverance, and that is abnegation. Goethe has nowhere set forth more beautifully the greatness that may be implicit in abnegation, the quiet heroism by which man glorifies himself, than in Ottilie's struggle against the passion through which the necessity of nature attacks her so overwhelmingly. This heroism seems more appropriate to woman than to man. But in Ottilie's case the power of fate can no longer be restrained at the cost of abnegation. It is only by immolating her life that Ottilie can burst the magic circle in which the four players are held as though under a magic spell and thus can regain free self-determination. In her very destruction she glorifies man's ability to remain true to the "Divine" in him (as Goethe described it in the hymn *Das Göttliche*). This tragedy does not end with a lesson, not with depreciation of nature as something suspect or as the great enemy. Until the macabre conclusion of the narrative, nature's order remains sacred necessity and the indisputable basis of existence. Nor does the attraction of affinities cease to operate until the end.

The conclusion is not tinged with despair but with a sort of mournfulness which contains both pain and acquiescence. Goethe has been blamed for having take place at Ottilie's bier miraculous cures such as those which occur in Christian legend. But this he does not do. What he describes are the effects of suggestion, which are not supernatural, and of spiritual revivification. The symbolical intention is beyond doubt. What Ottilie has suffered and what she has achieved is as great as any deed, for the sake of which the great perseverers in loyalty, the heroes of the Christian faith, have been revered. She has made the supreme sacrifice of which man is capable, has consecrated love and life in order to keep faith with that which constitutes man's status in accordance with his purest understanding of himself. "Perfection is the norm of heaven, desire for perfection is the norm of man." [6] No one can ascend higher.

Autobiographical Writings

MAN IS LED TO HISTORY THROUGH THE NEED TO RETAIN THE PAST BY RECALLING IT. THIS IMPLIES A CONVICTION THAT THERE IS A VALUE IN PRESERVING THE significance of what actually belongs to the past, and, furthermore, a realization that the present, for whose sake history is written, has a connection with what has gone before, and hence that knowledge of the past may be useful for the present. Knowledge of yesterday has been regarded as prerequisite for the correct understanding of today ever since men have grown accustomed to regard history as a continuous process in which everything that makes its appearance today grows out of yesterday, so that constant growth is as universal there as in the realm of nature. What has come to be, it seems, can best be comprehended in its peculiarity by examining the conditions which preceded its rise. The historically minded man comes to regard his own life in the same manner. And this procedure is most applicable where an individual has produced, in the successive phases of his existence, manifold works which nevertheless constitute a single whole. "And

[6] Vollkommenheit ist die Norm des Himmels, Vollkommenes wollen die Norm des Menschen. (*Maximen und Reflexionen,* No. 828.)

so I divide myself, dear friends, and am always one and the same."[1]

To describe the stages of this metamorphosis according to its peculiar character and its diverse results, and at the same time to comprehend and demonstrate the inalterable individuality, the nucleus which remains constant in change—for such an enterprise the great poet may well believe himself better endowed than any other. Accustomed by vocation and training to comprehend and interpret the life of the spirit and of the soul in its complicated unity, he is likely to have a new and deeper view of himself, of his inward life, of his relationship to his environment, to men and to ideas, to poets and thinkers who were his predecessors and contemporaries, in a word, of his "author's life," which he assuredly possesses the right to express and to hold up to his readers and critics. Difficult as it may be to understand onself, it is also a question whether it is easier to understand the individuality of another. Hindrances and errors are as great in the one instance as in the other. In the case of the artist, of the poet, there is the further factor that everything which he has to say concerning his work constitutes the most authentic commentary on it, in the sense that his explanations tell us directly and authoritatively what he intended to say and do in his works, what meanings he gave them, why he completed them so and not otherwise. But on the questions of where he is great or greatest, and of where he has succeeded in realizing his intentions, there indeed the poet himself cannot be the supreme judge.

The literature of the last century is rich in autobiographies of great thinkers, artists, poets, but it is remarkable that it is not even richer. Scarcely one of the greatest artistic figures has undertaken to recount his own life. Religious confessions constitute a considerable portion of this category of literature; among secular autobiographies Rousseau's *Confessions,* Alfieri's memoirs, and Chateaubriand's *Mémoires d'outre-tombe* are the most brilliant examples. But none of these documents of highly intensified modern self-preoccupation is to such a degree a work of genuine historical interest as is Goethe's autobiography. Here the author, unlike Rousseau, shows no inclination to investigate with penetrating analysis the secret corridors of his soul. Goethe is no theorist of life who wishes to confess or to justify himself, and who,

[1] Und so spalt' ich mich, ihr Lieben, / Und bin immerfort der Eine. (*Zahme Xenien,* VI.)

at every experience, finds his ego sufficiently interesting to treat it as a remarkable special case. Nor is it his primary intention to attain clarity about himself by following this bypath; he does not recall only to understand himself. To be sure, the tendency to reflect upon his own nature was not alien to him; this is shown clearly enough by his correspondence with Schiller and by many another document. But in his autobiography "know thyself" is an incidental motif, not the prime motive.

A great man here attempts to set forth the development of his ego as a specimen case of human growth. An individual of vigorous independence wishes to give reality to the form of life exemplified in him by showing himself as he acts on and reacts to his environment. The notion of organic evolution which dominated Goethe's scientific study also governed his examination of his own life. He once attempted to give abstract expression to the most important traits of his being in a short outline (*Selbstschilderung*, 1797). In this sketch he says that an incessantly active urge to poetic production, operating intrinsically and extrinsically, constituted the central point and basis of his existence. This poetic productivity was maintained because of the effect which "immediate experiences" exercised upon it, so that he found it constantly necessary to maintain activity by assimilating or rejecting, whether he dealt with books, people, or social groups. He always had either to work in active opposition or to attempt to produce something similar. Only this untiring maintenance of production was possible for him.

This abstract scheme may serve as a kind of sketch for the execution of his biography, as the formula which characterizes his constant attitude in all individual practical cases. When Goethe finished the first three volumes of *Dichtung und Wahrheit* he acknowledged that he had wanted to construct the whole work according to the rules which govern the metamorphosis of plant life. In the first volume, he says, "the child was to send forth tender roots in all directions and develop but few germinal leaves. In the second, the boy, with more vivid green, was to send forth, by stages, more complex branches; and in the third bed, this vitalized stalk was now to hasten to bloom in spikes and panicles and represent the hopeful lad." [2] This plan was not precisely

[2] . . . sollte das Kind nach allen Seiten zarte Wurzeln treiben und nur wenig Keimblätter entwickeln. Im zweiten der Knabe mit lebhafterem Grün stufenweis mannigfaltiger gebildete

followed in the execution of the book, but it served as a hidden framework for the whole.

Goethe also said that in old age a man willingly speaks of his past and his achievements. He was sixty years old when he thought of writing the story of his life. At such an age a man is justified in assuming that his work is on the whole done, that the contribution vouchsafed him has been made, and that he can no longer count upon a new harvest. But the primary purpose of this book was not to render an account of what had been completed. Though the historian may be primarily interested in results, the biographer (as Goethe says in the same unpublished preface) will have another aim. His concern must be to present in essence the personality and its epoch. "Biography should set forth life as it exists by and for itself and for its own sake."[3] Biographies are written and read because for man nothing is more interesting than man, than an individual in his living growth. The biographer offers a life of the past as something present, and affords us the singular pleasure of becoming its contemporaries. So Goethe himself had the liveliest interest in biographies from youth on. To comprehend great personalities and to share their lives was for him the only attraction of history. Caesar, Mahomet, Götz, Faust, and Egmont are the heroes of his youthful compositions. Later he translated the autobiography of Benvenuto Cellini, and in his essays on Winckelmann and the painter Philipp Hackert he described the individuality of artists. Now the time seemed to him to have come when he might venture to do for himself what he had previously done for others.

Goethe had yet another design in writing this book. It was to be at the same time an introduction to his creative life, as well as a path to his works. It was indeed a poet's life that was here narrated. In 1806 a new edition of his works began to appear which included everything that he had previously written, though not in chronological order. The things here presented as individual items, each independent and without recognizable connections, taken as a whole did constitute the fruit of a single individuality. But who could establish the relationship of the early works of the Storm-and-Stress period, to which Goethe him-

---

Zweige treiben, und dieser belebte Stengel sollte nun im dritten Beete ähren- und rispenweis zur Blüte hineilen und den hoffnungsvollen Jüngling darstellen. (Unpublished preface to *Dichtung und Wahrheit III.*)

[3] Die Lebensbeschreibung soll das Leben darstellen, wie es an und für sich und um sein selbst willen da ist. (Unpublished preface to *Dichtung und Wahrheit III.*)

self granted only historical validity, with his classical works or with those of his last period? Furthermore, Goethe had little confidence in the judgment of the public and the wisdom of German critics; he had had his experiences with them. An additional factor was that the new edition appeared precisely at the time when the old Germany was collapsing under the blows of the Napoleonic armies. A long era of peace, an age which (as Goethe knew) would never return, was coming to a violent close. But it was Goethe's age; in it he had lived his life, done his work. In the summer of 1808 he resolved to tell the story of his life; a year later he began to collect material; and from 1811 to 1813 he completed the transcription of the first three volumes. Then a long pause intervened. The following volume was to present, among other things, his relationship with Lili Schönemann. But Lili was still alive and it seemed tactless to tell the old love story in public. This was one of the reasons which made Goethe hesitate to write the continuation. He concluded the fourth volume long after Lili's death, in the year of his own demise—under constraint, one must say, in view of its fragmentary form. It was a year after Goethe's death before this volume appeared.

In the twelfth book Goethe says that it is one of his fundamental convictions that of most importance in all works of literature is their basis, their inward sense, their direction. For herein resides their truth, original, valid, and incorruptible by time and by external influences. It is this "basic truth" of his existence, as he calls it, that he wishes to present in the sections of his biography. He designates it also as "what is held true by the inward sense." This special intention is indicated by the title *Dichtung und Wahrheit* ("Poetry and Truth"), the meaning of which Goethe explained in a letter to Zelter (February 15, 1830). The public, he wrote, has always entertained certain doubts concerning the veracity of such biographic attempts. In a sort of contradictory spirit he had therefore wished to indicate even in the title that his book was not to be measured by the gauge of chronological exactness but to be taken as an artistic composition true in a sense higher than the factual, though all actual events are communicated without change. "A fact of our life is valid not insofar as it is true, but insofar as it has some meaning," he wrote to Eckermann. "Basic truth" is to be recognized only in recollection; if one seeks to set it forth he must allow it to be affected by poetic fancy. "All of this, which goes with narrator and narrative, I have here comprehended under the word *Dichtung*, in order to be able to employ for my own purposes the truth of which I myself have been conscious." [4]

The guiding principles which Goethe adopted in the execution of the book he states in the fictive letter of a friend which he prefaced to the work. His poetic works were to be treated here in the order of their composition; but in addition the circumstances of external and internal life which provided material for these works, the persons and the models which influenced the poet, the principles which guided him, were also to be communicated. The principal duty of every biographer was "to present man in his times and to show how far they oppose him, how far favor him, how out of them he shaped his ideas about the world and men, and how, when an artist, poet, or writer, he then reflected them in his creations." [5]

It is these ideal functions that Goethe wishes to carry out as his own biographer. From the nucleus of his own individuality man affects the outer world, and from without the world reacts upon his inward self. The product of this polar dynamism is the life of the individual and his contribution to the world. From this concept spring the total plan of the book and also the details of its composition and its inner unity as that of a growing organism. The process of growth, as a whole, and its separate stages are the necessary product of the ego and the world, of the individual and of given conditions. The constitution of the person who is here the subject is not stated in schematic characterization. The *curriculum vitae* enlightens us on these matters incidentally; incentives and achievements become perceptible when they are brought out by interrelations with the environment. In the course of this procedure the historical world is observed and comprehended only when and insofar as it has significance for the development of the individuality.

As is appropriate for a biography of this character, the hero is the measure and means of the narrative. Thus his parental home is described at once, but his native city only at the stage when the boy be-

[4] Dieses alles, was dem Erzählenden und der Erzählung angehört, habe ich hier unter dem Worte "Dichtung" begriffen, um mich des Wahren, dessen ich mir bewusst war, zu meinem Zweck bedienen zu können.

[5] . . . den Menschen in seinen Zeitverhältnissen darzustellen und zu zeigen, inwiefern ihm das Ganze widerstrebt, inwiefern es ihn begünstigt, wie er sich eine Welt- und Menschenansicht daraus gebildet und wie er sie, wenn er Künstler, Dichter, Schriftsteller ist, wieder nach aussen abgespiegelt. (Foreword to *Dichtung und Wahrheit I.*)

comes aware of his broader environment. Or similarly, literary conditions in Germany are set forth as they had developed up to the time when the young poet himself began to participate in them productively. The development of the hero appears as an unfolding of the germ, as a development of the seed, as the growth of the monad; in the story of youth, the beginnings and the signs of later manifestations are already indicated. In the dim desires of the boy and of the young man, the inclinations and strivings which will eventually crystallize into character are foretold. Wishes appear as premonitions of capacities innate in him, predilections as preludes to more serious interests. Goethe's story of himself, finally, is conceived of as a model case of the development of an individual, and as such it is commented upon in general observations on basic moral and psychological problems and phenomena. Thus this autobiography is rich in philosophical and pedagogical reflection; it addresses itself to readers who are informed about man and life, and who wish to be aroused to further reflection. It rests upon the faith that even upon critical examination a good meaning may be perceived in the life of man and a friendly order in the conditions of existence.

To the title Goethe subjoined the phrase, *Aus meinem Leben* ("From my Life"). This indicates the fragmentary character of the book, which presents nothing more than the story of his youth until his removal to Weimar. Nor are all the works of this period treated; *Faust,* for example, is not. Several times Goethe made plans for a continuation, but only certain installments were completed. The *Italienische Reise* appeared under the title *Aus meinem Leben: Zweite Abteilung;* the accounts of his participation in the campaign in France and in the siege of Mainz appeared in 1792. Goethe told of his "first acquaintance with Schiller" in his writings *Zur Morphologie* (1817). We also possess a sketchy account of his interview with Napoleon. Information concerning later decades is supplied in the *Annalen* or (as the title originally read) *Tag- und Jahreshefte als Ergänzung meiner sonstigen Bekenntnisse* (1830), which Goethe worked at intermittently from 1817 onward. This work contains a summary chronicle of events, of his relations to people, of poetic and scientific works, all arranged by years. These "annals, memoirs, and confessions" brush, as Goethe says, "upon world history, or if one will, world history brushes upon them, and so they move from insignificant details to the most important generality." Greatest detail is devoted to the period from 1795 to 1822, with which latter year the work closes. If its attitude is more objective, its style of presentation more impersonal, than that of the autobiography, and if it makes no claim, as the autobiography does, to novelistic form, it is nevertheless, in keeping with its purpose, an inexhaustible source of instruction and illumination for anyone desirous of a precise understanding of Goethe's thought and work.

Finally, we may include the correspondence with Schiller among the works which present us portions of Goethe's biography. Goethe himself had this most important body of his correspondence published (1828–29), having perceived its significance as a testimony for a period "which is past, which will not return, and which nevertheless continues to be operative to this day and reveals a mighty living influence, not upon Germany alone." Furthermore, this correspondence manifests the degree to which the labors of the two friends constituted an inseparable whole and to what an extent, during the period of their association, the one is not to be understood without the other.

In the Years of the German Liberation

IN MAY 1811 THERE APPEARED AT WEIMAR A YOUNG MAN WHO HAD COME FOR THE PURPOSE OF FINALLY CONVINCING THE GREATEST POET OF THE GERMANS that romantic enthusiasm for the Middle Ages and for ancient German art was more than "silly rubbish" and uncritical zeal. His name was Sulpiz Boisserée, and he had grown up in Cologne in the Catholic Rhineland. From youth, he and his brother Melchior were strongly attracted by the monuments of medieval architecture, the cathedrals on the Rhine and in Belgium, their father's home. In Paris they made the acquaintance of Friedrich Schlegel, became his pupils, and won him over to their interests when he followed them to Cologne. Their taste for the artistic monuments of the fifteenth and sixteenth centuries became increasingly practical. In a period of general secularization when numerous monasteries were abolished, Catholic churches closed, ancient altars and pictures disrespectfully handled, cast out, and destroyed, the means of the young merchants were sufficient to buy up and collect such examples of ancient German art which had been given over to destruction. They were possessed by a bold dream. In Cologne the most magnificent architectural work of the Gothic age, the ancient cathedral, stood uncompleted. They procured the ancient ground plan, which had been preserved. It now became the highest goal of their life to present to the eyes of their contemporaries "this so sadly interrupted monument of German grandeur," to urge its completion, and to start construction on its way.

In these years, Germany, defeated by French armies, lay crushed to earth. The greater the national misfortune, the more depressed the situation of the fatherland, the more important was this gigantic project for whose execution the energies of the entire nation were demanded. The first step was to gain public interest in the enterprise. What if Goethe's favor could be won for it? His disapproval of the return to the Middle Ages, his rejection of romantic art, were well enough known. Nor was it a recommendation in the sight of Goethe if anyone approached him as a pupil of Friedrich Schlegel. If the risk was desperate, so the reward to be won was incomparable. Sulpiz sent several sketches of the cathedral to Weimar. They made an impression upon Goethe; he found them "inestimable," sketches of a "Tower of Babel on the banks of the Rhine." Upon his invitation Sulpiz Boisserée came to Weimar and brought additional sketches and plans. For ten days he explained the architectural drawings and his intentions. He had also brought sketches of the most modern school of painting.

At first Goethe showed little desire to re-educate himself in his old age and to capitulate to youth. But what did it avail? Boisserée describes the course of the spiritual struggle with the "old pagan" and classical absolutist. "He roared on Tuesday when I was alone with him with the sketches, sometimes exactly like a wounded bear; one could see how he struggled with himself and brought himself to judgment for having overlooked something so great." The personality of the visitor surely played some role in the interview. Boisserée's "truly faithful historical and critical sense" was impressive. He found the correct tone, was respectful, tactful, understanding, without yielding in the convictions for which he stood, staking all the resources of his own independent personality and his expert's knowledge. He won, and left Weimar with the happy feeling "of having seen one of the first minds return from the error by which he had become unfaithful to himself." A relationship was thus initiated which soon became more intimate, and Sulpiz became something of a younger friend to Goethe. The letters which the old gentleman henceforward wrote him were pitched in a key of cordial sympathy and complete confidence. And the experienced man of the world was helpful to the hermit of Weimar in many affairs elsewhere, particularly in the negotiations which Goethe had to conduct in the 1820's with the publisher Cotta concerning the definitive edition of his works. In these negotiations Sulpiz functioned as a confidential agent with full powers of attorney and brought matters to a successful conclusion. When Goethe later attempted to strike the balance of this relationship, he acknowledged to his young friend how much benefit he had always derived from their association. It is indeed a rare and remarkable thing that two persons so different in age and in point of departure should agree in all principal matters, "even though the periphery of circumstances and intellect at first directed them to divergent paths."

In the years following, the Boisserée brothers' collection of pictures grew constantly. What they brought together was at that time without peer in Germany—a gallery of first-class works of Nordic and Christian painting (as they were called at the time). If Goethe was to be brought to an understanding and recognition of these monuments of older German, Dutch, and Flemish art also, he had to see the originals. The magnificent collection (it was later purchased by the king of Bavaria and deposited in the Munich Pinakothek) was then in Heidelberg. Goethe was now urged to visit his home country again and upon this occasion to familiarize himself with the pictures. Goethe was not unprepared for the encounter. Sketches and engravings of Schongauer, Dürer, and their contemporaries were to be found in the rich collection which he himself had assembled. But aside from such works of Dürer and Cranach he had never seen old German paintings.

In the course of his journey to Frankfort and Wiesbaden Goethe arrived at Heidelberg in September 1814. For two weeks he studied the Boisserée collection day after day. The impression it made was great, and Goethe was not backward in his expression of admiration.

So an old man has, in self defense, carefully shut himself off from youth which comes to overthrow age, and, in order to preserve balance, has tried to guard himself from all impressions of a new and disturbing character; and now suddenly there appears before me a quite new and hitherto quite unknown world of colors and forms which forces me out of my old rut of views and feelings—a new and eternal youth: and even if I should wish to say something here, a hand would reach out of a picture and strike a blow at my face, and this I should well deserve.[1]

In front of an altarpiece Goethe is said to have remarked, "If I were not such an old heathen this picture would have converted me."

As victories over Napoleon greatly intensified the patriotism which the romanticists had so diligently nurtured by their writings and other efforts, the fair and lovely hour of the full happiness of liberation began, when hope ran high and a new and better life seemed about to be inaugurated in all German-speaking countries. Goethe could not detach himself from this mood, and it helped strengthen his own feeling of a new and richer life. In Weimar he set himself to elaborate the impressions he had received from the Boisserée collection and to acquire a more accurate conception of the historical development of ancient German art. In the summer of the following year he again journeyed to the Rhine. This time he went to Cologne also, to inspect the cathedral. For several weeks Sulpiz was his constant companion. In their conversations (preserved in the young man's diary) questions of art had a large place. Goethe was as little inclined to yield to neo-romantic Christianity as to play off older German art and poetry against the Greek. One must not, he said in a short poem, compare Van Eyck with Phidias; in order to love the one properly, one must be oblivious to the other.

That is the world, and that is art,
That each in turn will swell the heart.[2]

Even now he found no revision necessary in the views he had acquired in Italy, except that they were too one-sided. He summarized the

[1] Da hat man nun auf seine alten Tage sich mühsam von der Jugend, welche das Alter zu stürzen kommt, seines eigenen Bestehens wegen abgesperrt, und hat sich, um sich gleichmässig zu erhalten, vor allen Eindrücken neuer und störender Art zu hüten gesucht, und nun tritt da mit einem Male vor mich hin eine ganz neue und bisher mir ganz unbekannte Welt von Farben und Gestalten, die mich aus dem alten Gleise meiner Anschauungen und Empfindungen herauszwingt—eine neue, ewige Jugend, und wollte ich auch hier etwas sagen, es würde diese oder jene Hand aus dem Bilde herausgreifen, um mir einen Schlag ins Gesicht zu versetzen, und der wäre mir wohl gebührend. (*Erinnerungen von J. B. Bertram,* September 26/October 9, 1814.)

[2] Das ist die Kunst, das ist die Welt, / Dass Eins ums Andere gefällt. (*Modernes,* translated by B. Q. Morgan.)

impressions of his first journey to his friend Knebel: "I have feasted at the Homeric as well as at the Nibelungen table, but I have found nothing more suitable for myself than Nature, broad and deep and always vital, to be found in the works of the Greek poets and plastic artists." [3] The art which is appropriate to his own individuality, which has enriched his own productivity, and which has confirmed his own view of the world, Goethe places above all other art, however great or historically important it might be. If this is prejudice, he grants others the privilege of similar one-sidedness. "As individuals, indeed, we never wholly free ourselves from a single aspect, and it is therefore our duty to regard others according to their own aspect in order to know and love them." So he writes to Sulpiz Boisserée (November 19, 1814).

If the romantic enthusiast had hoped to draw Goethe over to his side, he was finally forced to realize that such success could not be counted upon. Goethe was prepared to recognize and admire "Nordic" art, but he was not prepared for a change of faith. He did not think of acceding to the romantic view and of recognizing in old German and Flemish pictures the true models for contemporary German painters. To him this was and continued to be a fatal aberration. So far as the poetry of the Middle Ages was concerned, Goethe expressed to Eckermann (October 3, 1828) his definitive views as follows: One should interest himself in it for a period, but only to become acquainted with it and then leave it behind. For the modern man it had no cultural value. "Man in general is already sufficiently depressed by his passions and his vicissitudes; he needs not acquire gloom from the darkness of a barbaric past." Clarity and joyousness are what is wanted; and these can be found only in civilizations "in which excellent men attain to perfect culture." For him Greece and not the north remained the native heath of highest values and guiding images. By this faith he wished to live and to die.

The political events which led to the fall of the French Empire, to the liberation of German countries, and finally to the development of new national feelings and aspirations, found Goethe unprepared. He

[3] Ich habe an der homerischen wie an der nibelungischen Tafel geschmaust, mir aber für meine Person nichts gemässer gefunden als die breite und tiefe, immer lebendige Natur, die Werke der griechischen Dichter und Bildner." (November 9, 1814.)

did not at first recognize their significance, nor did he believe in their power. Goethe's admiration for Napoleon prevented him from taking an independent attitude toward these events. For the German poet the gigantic phenomenon who bore the name of Napoleon possessed a rank which placed him above the ordinary moral or patriotic level. Like others of the Weimar circle, Wieland, for example, and Herder, he had, toward 1800, expected great and beneficial things of Napoleon, in particular the reorganization of Europe in a new and more wholesome spirit. A man who had been powerful enough to put an end to the mob terror of the Revolution and the fanaticism of Jacobin ideologists, and to establish a new order broad enough to mobilize for effective action the best abilities of his people, such a man also had the right, nay, even the mission, to deliver the *coup de grâce* to the miserable "Roman Empire of the German Nation" of 1200 sovereignties which had so long been languishing in mortal illness. Of what concern to Goethe was this ruin which no longer possessed any political effectiveness? Why should he grieve for Prussia which had so long displeased him and which was now collapsing so ingloriously? The countries of southern and western Germany, which the conqueror had united into a *Rheinbund*, and to which, after the fall of Prussia, the Duchy of Weimar was joined, seemed to him the nucleus of a new Germany which could be fitted into a comprehensive continental organization.

Around 1800 there was no patriotism based upon the notion of a people or a nation, but only the local patriotism of the individual state. Lessing had already said of this regional loyalty that it had to give way to a consciousness of world citizenship based on a higher community of spiritual and moral interests. For the citizen of the eighteenth century the nation represented a community of opinion and aspiration which expressed itself not by political activity but by cherishing and augmenting the total store of cultural values. This was particularly true for the bourgeois class in the Germany of that time, which was rent into political and religious fragments and governed by numerous absolute princes. What the educated German thought of when he spoke of the common fatherland was identity of language, identical striving for an ever purer humanity, and creative activity in science, art, and literature. In their own peculiar way the Germans sought to coöperate in bringing about the rise of a culture which even

Europe was too small to contain and for which only the world, humanity itself, seemed to offer sufficient scope. The seductive vision of a future utopia was the picture of a peaceful community of flourishing peoples. How, in backward countries ruled at best by a rational authoritarianism, could educated Germans expect anything from politics when they themselves had no share in political power? It was part of Lutheran tradition to suffer authority patiently. The social and spiritual premises were lacking for the crystallization of a will to revolution, but only few lamented this fact. Coöperation in the task of cultivating superior and loftier moral and spiritual values seemed so noble and demanded so much energy that it was easy to forgo participation in political life.

The Germans of the eighteenth century were a nation unified by culture, not by a federal state. They believed, as Hölderlin said, that it was the state's duty to protect cultural productivity, that the state was nothing but "the wall about the garden of human fruit and flowers," and that the individual was the freer in having less experience and knowledge of the state, "whatever its form." They had but one attitude toward authority: mistrust. Nothing good could come of it. It is surely significant that the thought, "power is necessarily evil," was formulated in Germany. One need only observe the hostile suspicion with which power and those who succumb to it are treated in Schiller's plays, or the distaste for political activity expressed in Hölderlin's *Hyperion*. In the light of later developments, this disproportion between spirit and power, between individual culture and politics, stands out as one of Germany's great misfortunes. But to the historian it seems an inevitable consequence of the distinctive conditions in Germany during the eighteenth century. Only the events of the Napoleonic age, the humiliating experience of political impotence and the jubilant exaltation of the wars of liberation produced a change. Now, with Hegel's identification of state and power, the trend was too definitely toward glorification of power and Machiavellian nationalism. It is a peculiar and special misfortune of German history that the relationship between the views and ideals of its greatest period and those of modern generations was not ultimately one of continuation, of adaptation of traditions to new conditions of life—a process which necessarily takes place always and everywhere—but one of opposition which corrupted the nation's spiritual and moral culture. Neo-German nationalists and imperialists could invoke the spirit of the Augustan age of their people only by falsifying history; and this applies to the romanticists also. Any German poet or thinker at the end of the nineteenth century who still spoke in behalf of the great tradition necessarily became a critic and opponent of the German present. The struggle continues and will continue. If reconciliation is not achieved, then their world of great poetry and philosophy will become for the Germans a curiosity of the past, a lifeless display in the museum of national history.

But in regard to these matters Goethe's position was somewhat different from Kant's, Herder's, or Schiller's. To be sure, the experiences of the epoch of revolution did not make a nationalist or even a mere patriot of the citizen of the world. In a letter of 1799 he says: "At a moment when people are everywhere busy making new fatherlands, the man who thinks without prejudice, the man who can lift himself above his own time, finds his fatherland nowhere and everywhere."[4] In the *Xenien* he says:

> Germany? Aye, but where is it? I know not where I should seek it.
> For, where the learned begins, there the political ends.[5]

The idea which Schiller expressed in 1801 in the sketch for his poem *Deutsche Grösse* was also Goethe's view. Political misfortune does not affect the worth of the German. "German Empire and German Nation are two different things." The worth of the German rests upon his culture and his moral character, "which is independent of his political fate." His function is "to work upon the eternal structure of human civilization." Accordingly, Goethe refuses to indulge in the laments over the loss of a "whole which no man in Germany has ever seen in his life, much less troubled himself about" (to Zelter, July 27, 1807). The thing which alone gave contemporary German culture its rank and dignity had grown and flourished without reference to politics, petty or great; it was the work of thinkers and poets. Therefore, it could not be affected by the loss of political independence. It existed in its own sphere, above the events of the day. The greatest

[4] In dem Augenblick, da man überall beschäftigt ist, neue Vaterlande zu erschaffen, ist für den unbefangen Denkenden, für den, der sich über seine Zeit erheben kann, das Vaterland nirgends und überall.

[5] Deutschland? Aber wo liegt es? Ich weiss das Land nicht zu finden. / Wo das gelehrte beginnt, hört das politische auf. (*Xenien*, No. 85, translated by B. Q. Morgan.)

spiritual and artistic contributions which the Germans had achieved heretofore had been produced in the very period when Germany was in process of political dissolution and collapse. Representatives of a period of cultural greatness could hardly be expected to believe that political reorientation in the west and south, or the defeat of Prussia, would crush the essential spiritual force of the Germans and destroy their future. What they had created was their own work, not the work of those politically weak or politically powerful; what still remained to be done they could also hope to accomplish under the new conditions. Napoleon's new Europe was not founded on slavery and terror, the *Rheinbund* was no totalitarian state. There was enough left to them—art, science, humanity, work upon the "eternal structure of human civilization." Could there be anything more worthwhile for those who truly loved their fatherland and people than this striving?

But if in 1800 or 1806 Goethe was no German patriot according to the fashion then taking shape, his attitude toward Napoleon still distinguished him from other representatives of German intellectual life such as Kant, Herder, and Schiller. Here too he sought a point of vantage which would permit him to gain a higher and at the same time more realistic view of the age and its master. The concepts of general morality and national interest did not seem sufficient. Though as a German citizen he might belong with the sufferers in the mighty drama, as a poet he refused to allow his vision of the "protophenomenon" to be clouded even here. The French hero confirmed his conviction that everything great and fruitful in history had been produced by individual creative personalities and that there was no other historical greatness than that of the creative personality. Again the world was taught that he alone is a true prince who is capable of being one, that that man is sovereign "whom none can hinder, whether he pursue evil or good." For Goethe, Napoleon was the extraordinary, the virile man, the man for whom danger, struggle, and victory are the natural element of life. Great, unlimited strength which sets its own standards alone can represent the highest idea of genius. The spirit of the poet, for whom beauty is a goddess to be served in ever yearning love, here bows in admiration before the genius of great action, the complementary opposite whom he can never hope to equal. He knows that the productivity of this genius is higher than that of art because it forms and transforms reality. "In the beginning was the deed"—that is the alpha and the omega of human greatness. It is through such giants of action that a higher, unfathomable necessity carries out its purposes. Goethe attempts to designate this extraordinary quality by giving it a mythical name; he calls it the "demonic." Napoleon is an instrument of higher purposes, unconsciously entrusted with a mission greater in importance than his own purposes. In the light of this exalted view, distinctions between good and evil, like those between times and peoples, are nonessential.

Goethe's statements about Napoleon belong to the period after the Emperor's fall. Napoleon, Goethe said, had the greatest understanding that the world had ever seen; he was above all great in that he was always the same in every situation, "always clear and decided about what was to be done," capable of meeting any emergency, one of the most productive men who ever lived. In a conversation with Eckermann in 1828, Goethe said:

> The darkness and enlightenment of man make his destiny. The demon ought to lead us every day in leading-strings and tell us and direct us what we ought to do on every occasion. But the good spirit leaves us in the lurch, and we are lax and grope about in the dark.
>
> Napoleon was the man! Always enlightened, always clear and decided, and endowed at every hour with sufficient energy to carry into effect whatever he considered advantageous and necessary. His life was the stride of a demigod, from battle to battle, and from victory to victory. It might well be said of him that he lived in a state of continual enlightenment. On this account his destiny was more brilliant than any the world has seen before him, or perhaps will ever see after him.
>
> Yes, yes, my good friend, that was a fellow whom we cannot imitate.[6]

Even as an octogenarian Goethe declared that he would not suffer himself to be deprived of his "concept of Napoleon" by the petty spirits who now despised the dead hero, because it had cost him too

[6] Des Menschen Verdüsterungen und Erleuchtungen machen sein Schicksal! Es täte uns not, dass der Dämon uns täglich am Gängelband führte und uns sagte und triebe was immer zu tun sei. Aber der gute Geist verlässt uns und wir sind schlaff und tappen im Dunkeln.

Da war Napoleon ein Kerl!—Immer erleuchtet, immer klar und entschieden, und zu jeder Stunde mit der hinreichenden Energie begabt um das was er als vorteilhaft und notwendig erkannt hatte, sogleich ins Werk zu setzen. Sein Leben war das Schreiten eines Halbgottes von Schlacht zu Schlacht und von Sieg zu Sieg. Von ihm könnte man sehr wohl sagen, dass er sich in dem Zustand einer fortwährenden Erleuchtung befunden, weshalb auch sein Geschick ein so glänzendes war, wie es die Welt vor ihm nicht sah und vielleicht auch nach ihm nicht sehen wird.

Ja, ja, mein Guter, das war ein Kerl, dem wir es freilich nicht nachmachen können! (Eckermann, March 11, 1828.)

much to reach his view—a formulation implying the confession that he himself had not quickly and easily achieved appreciation of this manifestation of greatness.

Once Goethe was in the presence of the Emperor. This was in October 1808, when, at the diet of princes at Erfurt, Napoleon, as the master of Europe, received the homage of four kings and thirty-four other German princes and concluded an alliance with Tsar Alexander, who was also present. Napoleon had expressed the desire to see Goethe. The poet himself wrote a short and sketchy report of the interview, but this was sixteen years later. However, the principal points in the conversation are reliably reproduced in Goethe's account, as is shown by older reports from other hands, particularly that of the Weimar Chancellor von Müller. It is certain that at the beginning of the conversation the Emperor said of Goethe, "Vous êtes un homme," or even, "Voilà un homme." Of Goethe's works Napoleon apparently knew only *Werther*. That book was in the small library which he had taken with him to Egypt. He had studied it carefully, "as a judge in a criminal court studies evidence," and now he criticized the motivation of Werther's end in a manner with which Goethe thought he might agree. Napoleon also made some critical observations on French drama. Some days later Goethe again met the Emperor at a reception in Weimar, but this time Napoleon conversed more with Wieland. Both German poets were given the order of the Legion of Honor; Goethe wore his decoration with pride even during the war of liberation. The impression which the conversation with the Emperor made upon Goethe is indicated in a letter to the publisher, Cotta: "I will gladly confess that I could have had no higher and more pleasing experience in my life than to stand before the French Emperor, and in such a manner." Never had a prince so received him, never had one shown him such esteem. Goethe did not dedicate a poem to the Emperor, but he did dedicate one to Napoleon's young wife, the daughter of the Austrian monarch, when in 1812 she came to Karlsbad, where Goethe was sojourning at the time. These verses, however, in which the poet speaks for everyone, for Europe, are an expression of the expectations which centered about the great man. The campaign against Russia had begun, yet Goethe's solemn stanzas are devoted to the theme of "peace." Napoleon is lauded as the vanquisher of revolutionary chaos: "The confusion made by thousands one man has dissolved." The man who achieved this and who possesses the power of desiring all things will also "with gentle hand close the temple of Janus" and desire peace.

Did Goethe actually believe that this insatiable man would ever be able to rest? In his *Divan,* the destruction of the "tyrant of injustice" is praised in the poem *Der Winter und Timur,* written in 1814. Timur (Tamerlane) was the scourge of the Orient in the fourteenth century and had conquered India; but his armies were destroyed by the cold of winter. Winter is represented as addressing the conqueror:

> Thou dost kill the soul, thou freezest
> E'en the atmosphere; still colder
> Is my breath than thou ever wert.[7]

In Timur's story, Goethe himself says, contemporaries could "perceive the reflection of their own fate." But in the later edition of the *Divan* Goethe inserted another strophe, *Timur spricht* ("Timur Speaks"). Here triumphant mediocrity is rejected, and the stature of the great personality is again affirmed:

> Had Allah destined me as worm,
> As worm I should have been created.[8]

If we are to believe Eckermann, Goethe found the captive of St. Helena worthy of sympathy, and even a tragic figure in his humiliation. But at the same time he added that if one considered how the conqueror had trodden underfoot the lives and happiness of millions, his own fate was very mild. "Napoleon furnishes an example of how dangerous it is to raise oneself to the absolute and to stake all on the execution of an idea" (February 10, 1830). But Goethe does not say that it is not an admirable thing to act according to the unqualified greatness of one's nature, to remain true to one's demon. The contradiction cannot be eliminated; it belongs to the fabric of life which is woven of necessity and freedom, of good and evil, of creation and destruction. Another poet of the age, also a member of a subjugated people, the Italian Alessandro Manzoni, wrote an ode on Napoleon's

[7] Tötest du die Seele, kältest / Du den Luftkreis: meine Lüfte / Sind noch kälter, als du sein kannst. (*Divan,* translated by Edgar A. Bowring, *The Poems of Goethe,* p. 384.)

[8] Hätt' Allah mich bestimmt zum Wurm, / So hätt' er mich als Wurm geschaffen. (*Divan,* translated by B. Q. Morgan.)

death. Goethe translated it in 1822; it is his last poetic statement about the Emperor. Does Napoleon merit true glory? The poem answers:

> . . . Let future worlds
> Decide this point! We yield ourselves,
> With lowered brow, to the mightiest,
> Creative one . . .[9]

In Goethe's opinion the Germans had never been significant politically; their achievement was that they produced in the arts and sciences great works out of all proportion to their strength. This was Goethe's view between 1806 and the beginning of the revolt against Napoleon. At that time he made the scornful remark that Germany was nothing, but that the individual German was much. "The Germans, like the Jews, must be transplanted and dispersed throughout the whole world, if they are to develop completely, and for the benefit of all nations, the mass of good which lies in them" (conversation with Chancellor von Müller, December 14, 1808; the same idea was expressed in a conversation with Wilhelm von Humboldt, November 17, 1808). The year 1813 did not find him ready to change his attitude. He spent four summer months at a spa in Bohemia; it was a restless and uncomfortable period. He believed that Napoleon would deal successfully with this new crisis. He is reported to have said to the young Theodor Körner, who entered the Prussian army as a volunteer: "You may all rattle your chains; the man is too big for you; you will not break them." Such skepticism was widespread, and it was not without foundation. Modern historians have held that the Battle of the Nations, at Leipzig, which brought decisive victory after indecisive battles, was won rather by Napoleon's hesitation than by the military art of the Allies. Ten years later Goethe convinced himself that Blücher's brute strength brought the campaign to a successful conclusion only with the help of the ingenious strategists of the Prussian army. "The case is probably unique in world history: a kind of crude Timur (for 'Forward' was also the battle cry of the Mongols), surrounded by the most highly educated general staff; this is unique, has not been before and will not be again."[10]

[9] . . . Die künft'ge Welt / Entscheide dies! Wir beugen uns, / Die Stirne tief, dem Mächtigsten, / Erschaffenden . . . (*Der fünfte Mai,* translated by B. Q. Morgan.)

[10] Der Fall ist wohl einzig in der Weltgeschichte, eine Art von rohem Timur zu sehen (denn "Vorwärts" war ja auch die Losung der Mongolen), aber umgeben von dem allerge-

Goethe was least pleased with the part of the Russians. The Cossacks, who appeared at Weimar also after the battle, dampened his joy. He feared that the remedy was worse than the disease, that the Russians would now become the new political masters in place of the French, and that this would be at the expense of German civilization. And as for the unity of the Germans—did it consist of anything but hatred of Napoleon? Wilhelm von Humboldt, who had become a German patriot after being a humanistic citizen of the world, complained bitterly that Goethe was unwilling to make the same change. "He belongs altogether with those natures which are indifferent to anything political or German. Egotism, pusillanimity, and a contempt for mankind, which is largely justified but which must not be applied in such manner, combine to produce this attitude."

Goethe fled to mineralogical studies, "from his age into the primeval world," and to remote and exotic pursuits such as the study of Chinese books. "An opiate for the present," he called it. His confidence in the reliability and strength of the German elite which took the field against the oppressor developed only gradually. He refused to grant his own son permission to volunteer. Heinrich Luden, the professor of history at Jena, recorded a conversation which he had with Goethe in December 1813, two months after the battle at Leipzig. Goethe is reported to have said that one had no right to assume that the great ideas of freedom, race, and fatherland were matters of indifference to him; science and art were a poor comfort, if a man could not be conscious of belonging to a great and strong people. Moreover, Goethe did believe in the German future; Napoleon was right: the destiny of the Germans was not yet fulfilled; each individual had the responsibility of preparing the way for that destiny by augmenting, strengthening, and broadening the culture of his people according to his own gifts and position.

Seventeen years later Goethe again justified himself in a conversation with Eckermann (March 14, 1830). How could he have written war songs in 1813 without participating in the war, he asked, songs of hate written at a desk, when he did not hate the French—"though I thanked God when we were rid of them." To him, only culture and barbarism were important; the French were still one of

---

bildetsten Generalstabe; das ist einzig, war nicht und wird nicht sein." (To Karl August, November 14, 1824.)

the most cultivated nations, and he owed them a large portion of his own culture. National hatred belonged only to a primitive stage of civilization and vanished at a higher stage, when one was in a sense above the nation and shared alike the happiness and the unhappiness of neighboring peoples. "This stage of civilization was appropriate to my nature." And it was so indeed. Goethe would have had to be different in character, origins, and aspirations to be anything else than a passive spectator in an age dominated by war and political decisions. The "child of peace" was made solely for works of peace which (according to his own words), like everything truly great and good, belong not to a single people but to the whole world. He may have sensed even in the pure and sound love for one's own people, which at that time was first making its appearance among the educated bourgeoisie as a powerfully active impulse, that potential nationalistic isolation which subsequently became the curse of Europe. He answered critics by asserting that the great poet is also a warrior for freedom, though in a different field.

Set up fine monuments for me
As for your hero Blücher;
From Frenchmen he has set you free,
I from Philistine future.[11]

In Goethe's judgment it was not the affair of the citizen to work for German political unification. He regarded without confidence and without real sympathy the nationalistic efforts of students and liberals during the disturbed period of peace which followed the liberation. He might have been more interested in striving for a moral, spiritual, and perhaps even religious unity, but he himself lacked the necessary faith. He considered the Germans incurable particularists and individualists, even in cultural matters, incapable of recognizing one another's merits.

This weakness of the Germans, their standing in one another's way, if one may really call it a weakness, this peculiarity is certainly not to be discarded, for it derives from a virtue which the nation possesses and of which it may well boast without arrogance: namely, that perhaps in no other nation are born so many excellent individuals to live side by side with one an-

[11] Ihr könnt mir immer ungescheut, / Wie Blüchern, Denkmal setzen; / Von Franzen hat er euch befreit, / Ich von Philister-Netzen. (*Zahme Xenien, VII*, translated by B. Q. Morgan.)

other. But because each significant individual has trouble enough to complete his own education, and because each younger man adopts the culture of his own times, a culture more or less alien to middle-aged and older people; and because the German recognizes nothing positive and is constantly changing (without ever reaching a final form): such a range, not to say gradation, of cultural variations arises that the most thorough etymologist could not determine the origin of our Babylonian idiom, nor the most faithful historian trace the course of our eternally self-contradictory culture. A German does not need to grow old to be deserted by his disciples; no kindred spirits duplicate his growth. Everyone, aware of his own uniqueness, starts at the beginning, and who has not the right to that awareness? Thus, because of age, because one has a sense of belonging to a special faculty or province, because of interest vacillating in so many respects, everyone is at each moment kept from making the acquaintance of his predecessors, his successors, even his neighbor.[12]

These are the bitter words of a solitary man. One must correctly evaluate in its entirety this skepticism toward the nation, if one wishes to understand why, during these years, Goethe attempted to draw about himself a small magic circle within which he could pursue his quiet occupations, so that "the sacred fire" might be preserved for the next generation. His inward flight from his age was not prompted by timid egoism, but was a necessity for him because it was the means of preserving the force without which he could not create. Only by creation could he be great unique, incomparable, only thus a benefactor of his people.

In May 1814, Goethe was invited by Iffland, the great actor who was then director of the Berlin theater, to write a play to be presented

[12] Dieser Fehler der Deutschen, sich einander im Wege zu stehen, darf man es anders einen Fehler nennen, diese Eigenheit ist um so weniger abzulegen, als sie auf einem Vorzug beruht, den die Nation besitzt und dessen sie sich wohl ohne Uebermut rühmen darf, dass nämlich vielleicht in keiner andern so viel vorzügliche Individuen geboren werden und neben einander existieren. Weil nun aber jeder bedeutende Einzelne Not genug hat, bis er sich selbst ausbildet, und jeder Jüngere die Bildungsart von seiner Zeit nimmt, welche den Mittleren und Aelteren mehr oder weniger fremd bleibt, so entspringen, da der Deutsche nichts Positives anerkennt und in steter Verwandlung begriffen ist, ohne jedoch zum Schmetterling zu werden, eine solche Reihe von Bildungsverschiedenheiten, um nicht Stufen zu sagen, dass der gründlichste Etymolog nicht dem Ursprung unsers babylonischen Idioms, und der treuste Geschichtschreiber nicht dem Gange einer sich ewig widersprechenden Bildung nachkommen könnte. Ein Deutscher braucht nicht alt zu werden, und er findet sich von Schülern verlassen, es wachsen ihm keine Geistesgenossen nach; jeder, der sich fühlt, fängt von vorn an, und wer hat nicht das Recht, sich zu fühlen? So, durch Alter, Fakultäts- und Provinzial-Sinn, durch ein auf so manche Weise hin und wieder schwankendes Interesse, wird jeder in jedem Augenblicke verhindert, seine Vorgänger, seine Nachkommen, ja seinen Nachbar kennen zu lernen. (Letter to F. B. von Bucholtz, February 14, 1814.)

in celebration of the return of the Prussian king. After some hesitation Goethe declared himself willing, and expressed thanks that the opportunity had been given him to make known to the nation that he had always shared in its sorrow and joy, and that he continued to do so. The play was finally presented in Berlin on March 30, 1815, on the occasion of the first annual celebration of the capture of Paris. It is an allegorical drama in which the evil demons—War (who utters Napoleonic sentiments), Cunning, and Oppression—confront the good geniuses, Love, Faith, and Hope. The material, provided by the Greek fable of Epimenides, tells how "by strange circumstances, a wise man favored of the gods slept away a large part of his life and thereby gained greater powers as a seer." The play is called *Des Epimenides Erwachen* ("The Awakening of Epimenides"). Peace and unity are the principal themes of the appeal which the poet, speaking in allegories, addresses to the nation—unity of a free people, within itself and with its princes, and grateful enjoyment of liberation from so many sorrows.

The sleep of Epimenides during the "night of grief" surely denotes Goethe's own remoteness during the years of oppression. The tone of personal confession is unmistakable in the lines of the second act in which Epimenides says he is ashamed of the "hours of rest," that he feels others by their sufferings have become greater than he. But the play must at the same time be understood in a more general sense: Epimenides embodies the forces of civilization which withdraw into themselves in a period of disturbance and anguish, just as the Christians once took refuge in catacombs to preserve themselves for the new day of peace. Epimenides is thus acquitted of all guilt.

> Chide not the immortals' will,
> If many a year thou'st lived secure:
> They have kept thee close and still
> That now thy feeling may be pure.[13]

It is to peace and its works that the creative spirits of the nation should dedicate themselves, not to war and the rule of violence. This general meaning of the play was also a justification of the attitude of the

[13] Tadle nicht der Götter Willen, / Wenn du manches Jahr gewannst: / Sie bewahrten dich im stillen, / Dass du rein empfinden kannst. (*Des Epimenides Erwachen*, translated by B. Q. Morgan.)

poet, whose voice the nation wanted to hear when peace demanded the creative deeds of civilization once again.

> Many a boon our culture yields
> Fell to nought in war and strife;
> He who keeps and saves and shields,
> Holds the fairest lot in life.[14]

In the summer of 1814, when the countries of the Main and Rhine were again free, Goethe turned to the west instead of taking his customary journey to the spas of Bohemia. He had not been in Frankfort for seventeen years. Now the aging man was impelled to visit the scenes of his origin and youth, which he had lately described in retrospect in his autobiography. One of his periodical rejuvenations recurred, and he felt a desire for intellectual adventure, a longing to make a living present of what had become a remote memory. But the inner urge would probably not have sufficed to move to this venture a man who had grown comfortable and had become loath to stir himself had Boisserée not repeatedly urged Goethe to come and inspect with his own eyes architecture and pictures from olden times. Moreover, Zelter, Goethe's closest friend, was going to Wiesbaden for the cure. He left in advance and procured quarters.

Goethe spent six weeks in Wiesbaden, passing happy days in Zelter's society. He made excursions in the Rhine valley to Mainz, Rüdesheim, and Bingen, where he participated in the folk festival in celebration of the consecration of the restored chapel of St. Roche. Then followed ten days in Frankfort. The high point of the journey was a two-weeks' stay at Heidelberg, where he studied the collection of the brothers Boisserée. Then, after a second sojourn in his native city, Goethe returned to Weimar, arriving there on October 20. In his conversations with Sulpiz Boisserée there had been talk of Goethe's writing an essay about the efforts of the art-loving brothers and about their collection so that they might become known in Germany. But it was not until the following year that this plan matured. This time Goethe would have preferred to go to Karlsbad, fearing the exertion of the journey and disorder along the "restless Rhine," particularly

[14] Manches Herrliche der Welt / Ist in Krieg und Streit zerronnen; / Wer beschützet und erhält, / Hat das schönste Los gewonnen. (*Kunst: Beschildeter Arm,* translated by B. Q. Morgan.)

since Napoleon's return had again brought war. But shortly after he had arrived at Wiesbaden, the new confusion ceased and final victory was won.

At the court of the Duke of Nassau he met the generals of the Allies and the greatest of the Prussian statesmen, Freiherr vom Stein. During a visit at vom Stein's estate on the Lahn, a joint expedition to Cologne was decided upon, in the course of which the cathedral was inspected. Bonn and Coblenz were also visited. In August, Sulpiz Boisserée came to Wiesbaden and remained as Goethe's constant companion; his diary gives us a precise account of these weeks. This time the high point of the trip was a sojourn at banker Johann Jakob Willemer's country estate, *Gerbermühle,* situated on the Main outside the gates of Frankfort. In the preceding year Goethe had already spent some days with Willemer and his young wife, Marianne. Now he remained a month, caught in the grasp of a sudden passion for Marianne. Then he returned for a time to Frankfort, which was then very gay because of the autumn fair. "From morning till evening things are lively under my window; all day I go about town to see people and collections. Frankfort is crammed full of marvelous things" (to Christiane, September 12, 1815). At that time he met Astolphe, Marquis de Custine, a young French diplomat of Talleyrand's entourage, an admirer of Friedrich Schlegel and a friend of Rahel Varnhagen. In a letter to Rahel, De Custine describes the impression which Goethe made upon him. The account is little known, but gives so lively an impression of Goethe's appearance at the time that it must be cited here:

> You have not seen Goethe for a long while; he is now sixty-four years old; his countenance is still splendid; it is, as you say, the head of Jupiter, or rather of Homer. When his visage is not lively, it expresses a noble sadness: one could believe that he was looking upon a hero of antiquity who is succumbing to the weight of our misery. This century in which things burlesque are dominant is a burden to him; there is deep tragedy on his brow and in his look. When he becomes animated, he sparkles with *esprit.* And when he allows himself to smile, he is full of charm. What strikes me particularly in his lineaments is the harmony of the whole: never have I yet experienced so much consonance in combination with such multiplicity; all human feelings and all human thoughts are stamped upon his face; his countenance, full of life, is the mirror of a world and at the same time the expression of a character: from *Werther* to *Faust,* and even to the *Contributions to Optics*—all can be read

there. It is a universal spirit; science and poetry are enthroned upon this brow which embraces everything. One might believe that it was for him that the expression was coined: Man is the essence of the universal . . .

Although his constant dignity may seem somewhat stiff, there is a certain simplicity about him and one might consider him childlike; he is nevertheless infinitely remote from all naïveté; everything about him is will, and consciousness of his will . . .

He is master of himself, he is prepared to endure the reverses of destiny; he is the first great man whom I have found resolutely willing to accept all the misfortunes of genius without complaint; he is unhappy because he is alone; but he is willing to be alone because he has come to realize that he must be alone.

Goethe concluded his journey by spending two weeks in Heidelberg, where the Willemers followed him. A glorious Indian summer illumined this oppressive yet sweet period of love and resignation which saw the completion of *West-östlicher Divan,* the precious fruit of the two journeys. Departure was difficult and painful. The heart of the grievously suffering man was torn by the feeling that he had to end a bliss which would never be repeated. He did not venture to return again to Frankfort, as he had promised. Boisserée accompanied Goethe, who was in a state of profound emotional turmoil, as far as Würzburg. By the middle of October Goethe was again in Weimar.

On this second journey the plan for an essay on the monuments of the Rhine and the Main and on the collection of the brothers Boisserée assumed a more fixed form. According to the terms of the peace, the Rhineland was annexed to Prussia. It was hoped that the new and active administration would do something to preserve and collect precious monuments of a great past. Stein had induced Goethe to lend his influence to the enterprise and to submit to the Prussian minister Hardenberg practical suggestions in a memorandum. Goethe was now prepared to accede. Instead of a confidential memorandum he worked out a series of travel reports describing the art treasures of the oldest regions of German culture, those which were in private collections, and those which were public monuments, according to individual cities. The first collection of these studies appeared in the summer of 1816 under the title *Ueber Kunst und Altertum in den Rhein und Main Gegenden* ("On Art and Antiquity in the Rhine and Main Regions"). In the next year two more issues followed.

In one of these essays Goethe describes the St. Roche festival at

Bingen and the monasteries, churches, and castles of the beautiful Rhine valley between Wiesbaden and Rüdesheim, as he himself knew them from his visit of 1814. There follows an account of the visit to Cologne and a description of the uncompleted cathedral, along with an appreciation of the efforts of the brothers Boisserée. Goethe asks whether a favorable time has not now come to think of the construction "of this wonder of the world which had unfortunately remained only an intention." There is mention of other art collections on the Rhine, and a discussion of whether it would be advisable to establish an art academy at Frankfort. Mention is also made of the scientific institutes of the cities on the Main and in Hesse. Finally, there is an essay on Boisserée's collection of old paintings, at that time kept in Heidelberg; in this essay Goethe also expresses his thoughts on the relationship between the Christian religion, the Church, and fine arts—the principal theme of romantic aesthetics and art. As a son of the Lutheran city of Frankfort he had never felt at home with the Catholic tradition of German art. Under the influence of the romantic tendencies of the time, he had, in the *Wahlverwandtschaften* and in his autobiography, made many just observations on the subject, however determined his basic hostility to any modern renewal of an older Christian civilization might have been. Only his association with Sulpiz Boisserée had given him a better understanding of Catholic Christianity and its cultural achievements in earlier centuries. The *Divan* shows how ready Goethe was at that particular time to give every expression of true piety all the consideration it deserved, however unsuitable such piety might be for himself. But no conversion to the romantic ideal can be read into these benevolent reflections, which represent only Goethe's attempt to acquire a better understanding. He interprets in his own fashion what the study of old German painting has taught him and concludes with the admonition that one tendency and mode of thought must esteem others and allow them validity. "In this way we will cheerfully honor German art of the fifteenth and sixteenth centuries, and the froth of overvaluation, which has already become objectionable to expert and amateur, will gradually disappear." In these same fascicles he indicated very clearly through his friend Heinrich Meyer that he was not prepared to do more than recognize the historical worth of these older buildings and pictures, that even now he rejected Gothic architecture and any modern renewal of pious simplicity and technical primitiveness.

The periodical was continued with the shortened title *Kunst und Altertum.* The last fascicle appeared in 1832, after Goethe's death. The periodical served as a mouthpiece for everything which Goethe wished to communicate to the German public in the last decades of his life. Discussions of works of art, ancient and modern; of the literary novelties of the German and European book trade; articles and critiques by Goethe himself, by Heinrich Meyer, and occasionally by other like-minded men; glosses and short notes on general problems of the spiritual, moral, and aesthetic life; and reflections, aphorisms in verse, poems, and translations—such varied riches fill the pages of the carefully edited periodical. In it appeared almost all the important essays and criticism which Goethe wrote after 1816. No other of his later works gives so good an idea of the range of the aging poet's educative efforts.

West-Eastern Divan

AFTER THE COMPLETION OF THE SONNET CYCLE AND IN 1809 OF THE *WAHLVERWANDTSCHAFTEN,* GOETHE'S FORCE WAS CHECKED; FOR FIVE YEARS HE COULD PROduce no poetic work of significance. He had told the story of his youth, had reviewed his life in retrospect like a man uncertain whether the fountain of inspiration would ever flow again, like one who felt that it was a good thing to render an account of his work as if it were a finished whole. Only some new experience mighty enough to plough up his profoundest depths could again quicken his creative force—something which would assail the whole inner man, spirit and heart. The first journey to his old home induced the change; but that was only the second phase of the new productivity. It had begun shortly before, in an unexpected manner. The strangest thing imaginable, a poet of an unknown, vanished civilization, bringing poetry from a remote world that had perished, suddenly appeared on Goethe's horizon and obliged him to come to terms with him: the Persian poet, Hafiz.

The tradition of the East, to be sure, had always been an effective element in Goethe's spiritual life. From his youth he had had an interest in the culture of the Middle East as well as that of Greece and Rome. The Koran he had studied as a young man, and among the dramatic fragments of his early period was one intended to celebrate Mahomet as a religious genius. The vogue for things Chinese, which flourished in France particularly, left him untouched. Herder had given him a new picture of Jewish history based upon deeper understanding. But all of these inclinations and incitements waned when his Italian experiences made Greek antiquity his highest norm. Then, after the turn of the century, new incentives arose out of the movements of the time. In their search for "the primeval world" the German romanticists turned to the realm of Indian civilization, of which French and English scholars had first given broader knowledge. Friedrich Schlegel's treatise, *Ueber die Sprache und Weisheit der Indier* (1808), was the first book which revealed this new science of Oriental antiquity to Germany. In ethnographical history, Schlegel thought, the inhabitants of Europe and Asia should be regarded as members of one great family; one must know the history and literature of both if one were to understand the whole. The unlocking of the as yet unknown regions of earliest antiquity where the origins of Greek and Christian religion were being sought, and the discovery of the relationship of the ancient Indian language, Sanskrit, with European languages were the beginnings of scientific study of India in Germany and constituted the spiritual atmosphere which favored Goethe's new understanding of Oriental literature. To be sure, he did not seek, as did Friedrich Schlegel, "the supremely romantic" in the East. His relations to Indian culture did not go beyond the stage of eclectic appreciation. Kalidasa's ancient drama *Sakuntala* aroused his admiration as a document of the pure East, as he called it. But one who saw in Greek plastic art the embodiment of the divine most appropriate to man could only enter "with a sort of dread those boundless spaces where misshapen figures assail us and shapeless forms elude us and vanish" (to Windischmann, April 20, 1815). In the *Zahme Xenien* he had given quite definite expression of his detestation of the "beasts in the hall of the gods." On the other hand, he was ready to accept the poetic works of Indian antiquity as testimony of an effort which led from what was abstruse to genuine poetry. Yet all of this was only a passing interest, checked by Goethe's feeling that it was important to keep fantasy from being drawn into the formless and the misformed. For him the sun rose at another point in the East.

In the summer of 1814 Goethe read the first German translation of Hafiz, which had been published shortly before by the Viennese orientalist, Joseph von Hammer-Purgstall. A new world was opened to him, an unknown great poet was revealed to him. "I had to respond with productivity, because otherwise I could not have stood up to this imposing figure" (*Annalen*, 1815). The unexpected encounter found Goethe inwardly prepared. A desire to get started again, a late-summer longing for a new and higher existence, portended a new epoch of rich productivity for the aging man. How near was this alien poet to his own current situation, to the outward one as well as to that of his inner self! An old man had made these poems; they showed the dark colors of a late love and the quenched glow of a joy in life which rested upon the tranquil ground of mature wisdom and free piety. In addition to sharing common spiritual and moral attitudes, both poets experienced a common historical fate. While kingdoms collapsed about him and usurpers sprang up, Hafiz imperturbably sang of nightingales and roses, of wine and love. This poetry was like a mirror which reflected to Goethe the image of his own situation in the transfiguring illumination of a great past. From the impinging present and its crippling unrest Goethe could take refuge in the spiritual realm of this remote art. Before him was an example of how a great poet could at any time, even the most unfavorable, raise himself above the moment into the realm of timeless values. And the German poet followed this example.

North and West and South are splitting,
Kingdoms tremble, thrones are falling.
To the morning-country haste,
Patriarchal air to taste!
What with love and wine and song,
Chiser's spring shall make thee young.[1]

Thus Goethe's *West-östlicher Divan* begins. From the painful present he flees to an ideal remoteness and so becomes able in his own way

[1] Nord und West und Süd zersplittern, / Throne bersten, Reiche zittern: / Flüchte du, im reinen Osten / Patriarchenluft zu kosten! / Unter Lieben, Trinken, Singen / Soll dich Chisers Quell verjüngen. (Translated by J. Weiss, *Goethe's West-Easterly Divan*, p. 3, Boston: Roberts, 1877.)

to hope that he may gain a new and rejuvenated life. This poem at the opening of Goethe's *Divan* is called "Hegira," the name given by the faithful to Mahomet's flight from Medina. It was no flight into exile and frustration: a man called to greatness sought conditions which would permit him to inaugurate his work. Goethe's flight from the paralyzing present is also a hegira. The poet of the Christian West, the disciple of Homer, is certain that he too can find God and his works here in the East, "the land of faith and of revelations, prophecies, and promises." Goethe found the piety of the Persian poet acceptable because of its deep and basic earnestness. This was something different from the "characterless and actionless yearning," the transcendentalizing mysticism, which was so repulsive to him in the romantic artists and poets.

God is of the East possess'd
God is ruler of the West;
North and South alike, each land
Rests within his gentle hand.[2]

In an old book, a translation of the Persian poet Saadi which the German, Adam Olearius, had published in the seventeenth century, Goethe found a prayer which expressed with simple piety his own faith that polar opposition was the source of all of life's events. The prayer speaks of the drawing of breath, in the alternating rhythm of which the believer shall recognize the symbol of world structure and gratefully acknowledge God's wisdom. Always and everywhere the One is presented along with the Other, however the opposites may be called at any given time, and through their antithesis the processes of life are made operative.

Favor twofold in breathing see:
The air we draw, then set it free;
One is constraint, the other bliss:
So wondrously life mingled is.
Thank God, when he constrains thy will
And when he frees thee, thank him still.[3]

[2] Gottes ist der Orient! / Gottes ist der Okzident! / Nord- und südliches Gelände / Ruht im Frieden seiner Hände. (*West-östlicher Divan,* translated by Edgar A. Bowring, *The Poems of Goethe,* p. 274.)

[3] Im Atemholen sind zweierlei Gnaden: / Die Luft einziehn, sich ihrer entladen. / Jenes bedrängt, dieses erfrischt; / So wunderbar ist das Leben gemischt. / Du danke Gott, wenn

Goethe's book is rich in gnomic verse; indeed, reflective poetry dominates it. This was appropriate to the poet's years; it was likewise the manner of the Oriental poets, who, Goethe thought, lacked the vivid sense of imagery of the Greeks. Taking his position above both, Goethe wished to combine old and new, thought and perception, idea and reality. This creative synthesis is nowhere more magnificently successful than in the symbolic utterance of the poem *Selige Sehnsucht* ("Spiritual Yearning"), which constitutes the mighty closing harmony of the first book. The title first read *Selbstopfer* ("Self-Immolation"), and then *Vollendung* ("Consummation"). The poem speaks of the yearning of the ego for exaltation by surrender, of the mystery by which self is transformed, and its own power enhanced, as it merges with another being.

Tell it no man but the sages,
Since to scorn mobs oft are turning:
Life I'll praise on all my pages,
That for death in flame is yearning.

In the cool of nights of loving—
Getting thee as thou begettest—
Feelings strange o'er thee are moving,
Where the quiet light thou settest.

Thou'rt no longer in the mazes
Of a darksome obscuration,
And a new desire upraises
Thee to higher procreation.

Thou art hindered by no distance,
Comest flying, spellbound, turned
To the light without resistance—
In the flame thou, moth, art burned.

Till this thought has thee possessed:
"Die and be born over!"
Thou art but a sorry guest,
On this earth a rover.[4]

---

er dich presst, / Und dank' ihm, wenn er dich wieder entlässt. (Translated by J. Weiss, *Goethe's West-Easterly Divan,* p. 7.)

[4] Sagt es niemand, nur den Weisen, / Weil die Menge gleich verhöhnet, / Das Lebend'ge will ich preisen, / Das nach Flammentod sich sehnet. // In der Liebesnächte Kühlung, /

Goethe adopted from a *ghazel* of Hafiz the motif of the first stanza—the simile of the soul burning like a taper in the fire of love—and the metaphor of the moth. It is in the surrender of the ego, in its union with a Thou, that man gains experience of the highest rapture vouchsafed him in this life; and at the same time he achieves an enhancement of his own individuality which may be attained in no other way. The supreme moment of the rapture of love symbolizes this experience which is valid for all stages and all realms of our being. The soul, the moth, seeks redemption from the strait limits of its individual existence; it desires to dissolve in union with something infinite. One who has courage for this mystic venture will discover that in this merging the ego is not extinguished but, by metamorphosis and transformation, enters into a higher, supersensual mode of being: to die and to be reborn is one. Even what we call physical death is merely such a transition to other modes of being. Hence the mystic union of the soul with the divine and infinite gives us a foretaste of bliss even during life.

The pendant to this poem, in which enhanced rebirth by the surrender of the ego is in intimation praised as the highest mystery, is the poem *Wiederfinden* ("Rediscovery") in the *Buch Suleika*. Goethe's own experience at the time, his separation from his beloved and his reunion with her, is again a special case which becomes a symbol of life universal. The pulse-beat of the world is the desire of the separated for union with the whole, for each individualized thing evolves from an entity which distributes itself in polar opposites, only for each then to reunite with its complementary counterpart. This last truth Goethe communicates by recounting after his own fashion the story of creation—how cosmos arises out of chaos, how earthly forms and colors proceed out of the primitive polarity of light and darkness. So it is also with the love of man and woman.

Die dich zeugte, wo du zeugtest, / Ueberfällt dich fremde Fühlung, / Wenn die stille Kerze leuchtet. // Nicht mehr bleibest du umfangen / In der Finsternis Beschattung, / Und dich reisset neu Verlangen / Auf zu höherer Begattung. // Keine Ferne macht dich schwierig, / Kommst geflogen und gebannt, / Und zuletzt, des Lichts begierig, / Bist du Schmetterling verbrannt. // Und so lang' du das nicht hast, / Dieses: Stirb und werde! / Bist du nur ein trüber Gast / Auf der dunklen Erde. (*Selige Sehnsucht*, translated by B. Q. Morgan)

And in haste they seek each other
Who would each to each belong.[5]

The two become one. The frequently quoted poem in which Suleika and Hatem reach an understanding concerning the "highest happiness of the children of earth" speaks of the same thing. Is this happiness to be sought in the determined assertion of the ego? The lover knows that this is not the full truth:

All of earthly bliss united
In Suleika lives for me.[6]

However highly each individual, slave or ruler, values a sense of his own strong and inimitable personality, only in community with a complementary Thou, only in the feeling that a man is "single and double," can he attain the highest intensification. Only both experiences together, as a sort of systole and diastole, constitute the whole of life. The themes of "Spiritual Yearning" and "Rediscovery" are here given variation in a lighter tone. We can see how decisive Goethe regarded this experience.

The powerful art of *Wiederfinden* is not characteristic of the general style of the *Divan.* Taken as a whole, the language displays the mild maturity and restrained strength of an old and noble wine. The aging master is now in complete control of his art, in complete control also of the inward life which finds expression in poetry. A social spirit is here everywhere apparent. Emotions and thoughts are uttered in a relaxed, frequently conversational style. The love poems are written in alternating responses, the traditional form of amoebaean song. Incomparable is the art by which general truths and practical maxims are comprehended in simple, clear forms. The problem of philosophic poetry, always difficult, here finds an ideal solution.

But the *Divan* is not merely a book of lyric wisdom; it is also a compendium of late, mature love poetry. The invigorating incitement derived from the encounter with Hafiz was supplemented and enhanced by the mightily burgeoning feeling of a new youth. Like

[5] Und mit eiligem Bestreben / Sucht sich, was sich angehört. (*West-östlicher Divan, Wiederfinden,* translated by B. Q. Morgan.)

[6] Alles Erdenglück vereinet / Find ich in Suleika nur. (*West-östlicher Divan,* translated by B. Q. Morgan.)

the landscape round about, the landscape of his native country, so life itself responds to the rejuvenated man with fresh brilliance and bouquet. The past comes to life again and becomes a happy present.

> And there the wonted fragrance lingers
> As in days when love we suffered.[7]

New life, new love: that is the persistent basic melody of the *Divan*, manifold as are the poems here bound together.

> Through me once again there rushes
> Breath of spring and summer's flame.[8]

Meeting Marianne again set his heart on fire. Marianne, of Austrian origin, appeared as a dancer at the Frankfort theater when still half a child. Johann Jakob Willemer, a respected Frankfort banker, cultured and intelligent, took the young girl into his family and educated her with his own daughters. She then became the widower's beloved. When Goethe visited him in 1814, Willemer had just married her. For the young woman, glowing with life and spirit, the love of the great poet was a fulfillment to which she thought she could only respond by the gift of her heart. And for Goethe, as the motto to the *Buch Suleika* declares, the sun unexpectedly arose. A woman loved him, the aging man, a woman who could hold communion with his spirit. Both knew that they could give themselves to this love only at the price of denial, and they behaved accordingly. In the ideal sphere of poetry they could indeed become one. The core of the *Divan*, the *Buch Suleika*, contains the expression of their communion, the duet of the loving pair. Four or five of the poems superscribed "Suleika" are by Marianne. They are the most emotional. Goethe polished them off and gave them the perfection which he alone was able to give. He was able to do this without having to alter style or meaning. Through him Marianne was awakened as a poetess; in love, she shaped her image in the spirit and tone of his poems, and thus consummated the surrender which circumstances denied in any other form. In Goethe's love poems her own emotions and nature were re-

[7] Und da duftet's wie vor Alters, / Da wir noch von Liebe litten. (*West-östlicher Divan*, "Im Gegenwärtigen Vergangnes," translated by B. Q. Morgan.)

[8] Und noch einmal fühlet Hatem / Frühlingshauch und Sommerbrand. (Translated by J. Weiss, *Goethe's West-Easterly Divan*, p. 121.)

turned to her enhanced, and so received the purest possible expression of gratitude. "Thou hast awakened this book in me, thou hast given me it." Never has a woman received fairer homage from a great poet, and the great closing poem of the *Buch Suleika* is supreme homage.

Goethe never saw Marianne again. In July 1816 he set out with Heinrich Meyer upon a third journey to the Rhine and Main. Two hours out of Weimar "the most awkward of all drivers" caused their carriage to overturn. The axle broke, and Meyer was slightly injured. It was as if higher powers had made a warning gesture. Goethe returned to Weimar and never again took the westward road. But he never ceased belonging to Marianne inwardly. Letters were exchanged until the end, gifts, and words of grateful recollection. One of the last of his poems, *Dem aufgehenden Vollmond,* written at Dornburg in 1828, which begins "Wilt thou straightway forsake me," is an additional fruit of his constant love for the woman to whom he owed the purest happiness of his old age. When, after the completion of *Faust,* he set about putting his house in order, he returned to Marianne her letters, requesting her to leave the packet unopened "until the unspecified hour." The hour was not long in coming, and Marianne found among the letters another word of gratitude, a last poem of her beloved, dedicated to her. He speaks of their brief days together as the "fairest time of all."

The general intention of the western-eastern book of poetry is to combine in easy style the manner of the Orient as revealed in Persian poetry with that of modern Western civilization. It is not a question of mere imitation. The poet appropriates the spirit of the foreign material in a productive manner; if he playfully decks himself out in Oriental costume, he does so in order to veil what was contemporary and in the nature of a confession, and in order to remove every personal element to a softening distance which at the same time would stimulate interest. The style of Eastern poetry is not imitated either, but is freely and masterfully transposed to Goethe's own manner. The form of the *ghazel,* the Persian poem of praise, is employed in only a few poems, and even then is not strictly imitated.

The *Buch der Parsen* penetrates most deeply into the Eastern world of faith. In it Goethe presents a picture of ancient Persian fire-worship, which is to him still a noble and pure natural religion, the later degeneration of which he blames on Zoroaster (Goethe regards Zoroaster as the author of the Avesta). He uses this ancient religion to express his own reverence for light:

> If ye piously in each burning lamp
> See the nobler light's resplendent gleam.[9]

In full and solemn tones Goethe expresses the most inward motifs of his faith. It is the faith of an old man who has overcome the restlessness of life and the uncertainty of ever-changing human destiny, who has won that peace which is the fruit of mystic union with Him "who is, ever has been, and ever shall be." In the middle of the poem, in a passage emphasized by special type, Goethe stated a doctrine which epitomizes the final consequence of pure love of God, highest revelation embracing all other revelations within itself; he calls this doctrine a "sacred legacy," and communicates it to his brethren in the compressed phrase: "The daily performance of strict duties." What really matters is constant activity, productivity. This is the fruit of genuine piety. The endless toil of life carried out hourly and daily and always linked with eternal, unwearying labor directed toward the world and devoted to the world—such is the way in which man can fulfill his destiny in a manner most pleasing to God. For it is not vouchsafed him (as we read in preceding stanzas) to become directly aware of the absolute and eternal with effortless spirit, any more than he can tolerate the sight of the sun. But to work on untiringly in the light of the sun, for that is man destined, for that made. Other sayings from Goethe's last period similarly declare this the highest wisdom: "What then is thy duty? The demand of the day." To satisfy the demands of the moment loyally and strenuously means to proceed step by step upon the path which leads to our Father's house. *Chinesisch-Deutsche Jahres- und Tageszeiten,* a cycle of poems written later, concludes with a kindred doctrine:

> Desire for far and future things to quell,
> Work here and now with what is capable.[10]

Even those who have no desire to concern themselves with things Oriental will not be disappointed by the *Divan;* the most important

[9] Werdet ihr in jeder Lampe Brennen / Fromm den Abglanz höhern Lichts erkennen. (Translated by E. A. Bowring, *The Poems of Goethe,* p. 399.)

[10] Sehnsucht ins Ferne, Künftige zu beschwichtigen, / Beschäftige dich hier und heut' im Tüchtigen. (Translated by B. Q. Morgan.)

portions of this rich work require no commentary. To those who are annoyed by the exotic, Goethe says:

> Any west or eastern nation
> Has pure joys for delectation.
> Quit your whims and things external:
> Sit down to the feast eternal.[11]

But for those desiring full understanding the poet has provided "Notes and Discussions." Their intention is to explain, to interpret, and also to cite Goethe's sources for those readers "who have only slight acquaintance with the East, or none at all." Moreover, Goethe gives an account of his lifelong interest in Near-Eastern civilization, Jewish as well as Mohammedan. All together, these parts are an introduction to the history, religion, and literature of Oriental peoples in the light of contemporary knowledge.

> Who the poet would understand
> Needs must seek the poet's own land.[12]

Goethe says that the general characteristic of Oriental poetry is "what the Germans call *Geist,* the dominance of higher guidance." What is meant is that ripe intellectuality of an aging epoch which usually expresses itself as wit and irony. Under the superscription *Künftiger Divan,* Goethe gives a summary view of the individual books of his work; at the same time he declares that he does not regard it as completed and that he desires to carry it forward gradually. Thus a *Buch der Freunde* was planned, but never executed. Among the Notes there are scattered aesthetic and critical opinions of a general character: for example, the important ideas on the three basic types of literature and on literary genres, and on various methods of translation.

The *Divan,* including the poem cycle and the Notes, appeared in 1819, in Goethe's seventieth year. After Goethe's death Riemer and Eckermann published further *Divan* poems under the title *Aus dem Nachlass.* These are pieces which were written later, and also some which the poet himself had not wished to publish.

* * *

[11] So der Westen wie der Osten / Geben Reines dir zu kosten. / Lass die Grillen, lass die Schale, / Setze dich zum grossen Mahle. (*Aus dem Nachlass,* translated by B. Q. Morgan.)

[12] Wer den Dichter will verstehen, / Muss in Dichters Lande gehen. (*West-östlicher Divan,* based on translation by E. A. Bowring, *The Poems of Goethe,* p. 373.)

An old man to whom the vigor of his prime was momentarily restored wrote the *Divan*. A man tried by life but not discouraged, a sagacious man, whose deeper insight has not made him a skeptic, speaks in it. Unexpectedly life is restored to him and grants him a last intensification. Once more love and the sense of full existence raise him to a state in which devout wisdom and the fire of passion interpenetrate and achieve unique fullness and wholeness. Recollection evokes the mood of life's early spring, the past merges with present exaltation. Spirit is here the clear force of cosmic comprehension, not practical rationality, nor yet metaphysical speculation. The admixture of prudence, even of irony, is strong enough to endow the spirit with detachment and sovereign freedom, but it is not so strong as to be capable of disturbing the bliss of the unique instant. Thus Goethe attains the supreme, a soaring of the soul into the sphere where the tormenting cleavage of spirit and sense is healed, where the tension between yearning and wise resignation is resolved in a unification of opposites—something man can achieve only in rare moments and which he has never been suffered to retain. It was this that Goethe admired in Hafiz: "Contented in straitness, joyous and wise, taking his own portion of the world's abundance, looking from afar into the secrets of the Godhead, but on the other hand rejecting alike religious practice and sensual pleasure . . ." [13] Intense delight in life keeps the spirit from becoming heavy and gloomy. And the love poems are given a perfection by the ever present rationality, always sure of itself, a perfection which is the symbolic expression of the fact that here the marriage of form-fashioning consciousness and infinite passion has been consummated. Devout joy in the beautiful as it is revealed in the spectacle of stars, in the pleasure afforded by the brilliant colors of nature and by the form of the beloved—this joy endeavors to compete with these experiences; now the poet himself tries to bring forth artistic images of equal beauty. The result is a work of singular abundance and sublimity. Wisdom and piety, the happiness of the senses and of the heart, love and beauty, lordly play of spirit and reverent earnestness are in it combined into an image of perfection.

[13] Im Engen genügsam, froh und klug, von der Fülle der Welt seinen Teil dahin nehmend, in die Geheimnisse der Gottheit von fern hineinblickend, dagegen aber auch einmal Religionsübung und Sinnenlust ablehnend, eins wie das andere . . . (Notes and Discussions to *Divan, Hafis*).

Last Poems

IN THE *BUCH DER BETRACHTUNGEN* OF THE *DIVAN* THERE IS A SHORT POEM IN WHICH THE AGING POET CONVERSES WITH HIMSELF. THE VOICE OF SKEPTICISM, of resignation, is heard. How much of life's abundance headlong time has already taken from him!—the pleasures of the senses, free movement in the realms of nature and of the spirit, even enjoyment of fame and wide influence. Indeed, his joy in creative activity is no longer unalloyed, now that the bold venturesomeness of his prime has gone. What is then left to make life rewarding? Another voice gives the answer: "For me enough is left! Idea and love are left!" The inward world is left to him, everything that does not belong to time and space, that is not measured by calculating reason, by calendar and clock—in a word, everything that comprises the permanent basis of personal existence: the native capacity of spirit to adequate itself to the organization of nature by creative concepts, and the power by which the heart is directly linked to the world and to life. This twofold power the years cannot take, and so enough is left to make life worthwhile. Idea and love, the highest capacities of the spirit and the heart, still grow in old age and are ever more clearly and definitely concerned with what is permanent and essential in the phenomena and forms that emerge from or disappear into the stream of time. "The older a man grows the more everything becomes generalized" (letter to Schelling, January 16, 1815). The poems of the last two decades of Goethe's life are expressions of this attitude. They represent the order of nature and the cosmos in a new, completely symbolic manner and elevate the most elementary emotions to a sphere which lies above the concrete moment and the personal reference. Spirit and heart seek to become aware of the general in the particular, of what is permanent in change, of what is eternal in the moment.

Goethe collected in the last edition of his works under the title *Gott und Welt* ("God and World") the bulk of his poems devoted to the interpretation of nature. What distinguishes these two concepts in analytical thought is of no importance for the believing mind. The world is the divine made real; God exists only insofar as he actualizes himself in the world, and only in the world can man become aware of him. The individual poems are the fruit of reflection upon this "revealed mystery." They are diverse paths to one common goal: perception of creative divinity. At the time of his optical studies and his association with Schelling, Goethe thought of setting forth the organization of nature in a long poem. What he had essayed in concise form in the two poems on the metamorphosis of plants and animals was to be treated generally and in more detail. He considered using as his model the didactic poem in which Lucretius sets forth Epicurus' picture of the world. Goethe had become thoroughly familiar with this work about 1799 when his friend Knebel translated it into German hexameters. His own plan seemed colossal indeed. Goethe discussed it in detail with Schiller, and considered executing it in collaboration with Schelling; then he had misgivings, and left the young philosopher to undertake this adventure of the spirit alone. But Schelling did not carry it out. Later Goethe endeavored to realize the project by treating individual themes in separate short poems, complete in themselves but together offering a picture of the organization of nature in its principal features.

This series of nature poems opens with *Proömion*, a solemn overture. The God in whom Goethe believed is invoked: the uncreated, who from eternity is creative both in nature and in the spirit of man. Everything of which we have awareness, all reality, is the actualization of his spirit, but himself, the Absolute, we are not capable of perceiving directly. Only in our highest sensual experiences do we approach the eternally unknown. Then the phenomena of fleeting reality become simile and symbol of hyper-reality. For one who attains so far, the passage through the boundless realm of nature becomes a never-ending path to the mysteries of the divinity. Two separate stanzas are appended to the poem. The first contrasts the concept of an extramundane God with the idea of the God who is one with the world, who permeates, preserves, and moves all things, who is at once matter and spirit, energy and form, being and becoming. The second stanza speaks of the operation of the divine in man. The human being is a kind of small universe, a microcosm. In his inclination toward the good and toward intensification and perfection of his ego, he himself has always envisioned the divine and has made his own gods accordingly.

The oldest poem in this group is *Weltseele* ("World Soul"), published as early as 1803 under the title *Weltschöpfung* ("Creation of the World"). It expresses the enthusiasm evoked by the vision of the divine life in the universe. Philosophers since Plato had spoken of an *anima mundi;* the concept still plays a role in the aesthetic pantheism of Giordano Bruno. Goethe became acquainted with the concept of such a general spiritual principle through Schelling's treatise *Von der Weltseele* (1798). This spirit permeates, so Schelling assumes, the organic and the inorganic worlds, unites them in a common organism, and constitutes the inner unity of all natural forces. Intuition envisages this universal creative principle in its infinitely manifold operation. From the lowest phenomena it reaches upward to man. In him the All-Life rises to consciousness, in him the "loving strife" of polar powers reveals its original unity.

The poem, *Dauer im Wechsel* ("Permanence within Change"), also transposes philosophic thought to the sphere of lyric expression. The theme of transitoriness is here dealt with in connection with Heraclitus' saying that one can never enter the same stream twice. Where is there anything permanent? Wave follows upon wave; the buds of spring and leaves of summer come, and then the wind wafts them away. In incessant change something new forever arises and perishes in its turn. And so we ourselves constantly see the world in new ways, and our bodies, too, quickly change. But the close of the poem raises us above the image of constant change by the insight that for mankind there is one fixed point in transitoriness: in the process of transformation our spirit becomes aware of what is permanent, in passing away we learn what is eternal. By virtue of our creative force we ourselves are capable of producing something which does not perish with the instant.

Eins und Alles ("One and All") and *Vermächtnis* ("Legacy"), both written in the twenties, supplement one another. The first poem again speaks of the general creative force which fills the world's space with countless individual existences, and which nevertheless, coming to rest in no individual, is as limitless in potentiality as it is in its activity. To yield to the feeling of this infinity, to surrender to it, is the highest peace attainable by the incessantly striving individual. But here too there is no arrest. Precisely through this experience our spirit is strengthened for higher achievement and for comprehending more intimately the operation of the creative world soul. There is an echo of "Die and Become," the motif of *Selige Sehnsucht*. The same unlimited striving which we see everywhere active in nature operates in man also. In man as in nature there is no rest, no pause, but eternal creation and activity, formation and transformation. "The eternal stirs in all things."

To the poetic description and glorification of metamorphosis, *Vermächtnis* opposes as the other complementary truth consideration of what is permanent in change and eternal in the cosmos and man. The title makes it clear that the poet here wishes to utter an ultimate confession of greatest importance. Being is eternal in its process of constant development and disintegration, for that is the order of the universe. Thus the wisest of the sages have taught from antiquity downward; from Aristarchus of Samos down to Copernicus they have perceived and taught the truth about the organization of the universe. Our inner universe is similarly an ordered microcosm whose center of gravity, as Kant says, is formed by the moral law within us. "How can man confront the infinite as if he had assembled in his innermost profoundest self all spiritual forces which divagate in many directions if he asks himself: Can you think of yourself at the center of this eternally living order unless within yourself there is not similarly a sovereign moving element circling about a pure center?"[1] But, in contrast to Kant, Goethe finds that even our sensual perceptions provide true knowledge if only our intellect is capable of correct interpretation. "The senses do not deceive; judgment deceives." The last stanzas point the way to correct conduct of life: moderate enjoyment of the gifts of life; joy of life tempered by reason; the instant of fulfillment as something undestroyable by the process of time; and, finally, the supreme test: "What is fruitful, alone is true." This dictum is the concisest formulation of Goethe's pragmatism. It is not a question of the speculative value of truth but of its practical validity, that is to say, of what it contributes to life. Only its fruits legitimize it as truth. As Goethe says in a book review, it has the marvelous effect "of opening our eyes and our hearts, and of encouraging us even

[1] Wie kann sich der Mensch gegen das Unendliche stellen, als wenn er alle geistigen Kräfte, die nach vielen Seiten hingezogen werden, in seinem Innersten, Tiefsten versammelt, wenn er sich fragt: darfst du dich in der Mitte dieser ewig lebendigen Ordnung auch nur denken, sobald sich nicht gleichfalls in dir ein herrlich Bewegtes um einen reinen Mittelpunkt kreisend hervortut? (*Wilhelm Meisters Wanderjahre*, Book I, chapter x.)

in the field where our work lies to look about us in similar fashion and to draw fresh breath for renewed faith." But what is false is dead and sterile. It is recommended at the end of *Vermächtnis* that we should unite with those who are similarly minded and who act in similar ways. What are the creations of thinkers and poets other than works of truth in this sense? And by virtue of this they are also works of love, intended to serve all noble spirits as stars that point the true path.

Certain slighter poems express the fundamental principles of Goethe's view of nature in the form of compact apothegms. *Parabase* speaks of the principle which governs Goethe's work in the comparative morphology of plants and animals—how nature produces its manifold forms in accordance with a single basic form; how all individual forms ("each according to its own nature") are variations of a prototype from which they diverge more or less but from which they are never completely removed. The short cycle, *Howards Ehrengedächtnis* ("In Honor of Howard"), is dedicated to the English meteorologist, Luke Howard, whose theory of cloud formation pleased Goethe because it reduced the alterations of clouds to a basic principle and so "defined the indefinite." *Epirrhema* and *Antepirrhema* (the Greek titles are technical terms in Attic comedy signifying "address" and "intermediate speech") are concerned with the fundamental mystery by which in nature there is no internal element distinct from external form because all things are manifestations, because all forms actualize the type, because idea and phenomenon only exist coördinately with one another. "What else are the externals of an organic phenomenon than the eternally changing manifestation of what is within it?" The identical idea is expressed with polemic acerbity in the poem *Allerdings* ("Indeed"). It is directed against a dictum which had attained wide currency in the preceding century and which even Lessing and Herder had repeated. In 1730 the great natural scientist, Albrecht von Haller, had said in a philosophical poem:

Ins Innere der Natur dringt kein erschaffner Geist,
Zu glücklich, wann sie noch die äussre Schale weist!

No creature Nature's inner secrets knows;
O'erjoyed, if she at least the outer shell disclose.

To this "litany repeated *ad nauseam*" (as Hegel called it), against which Kant had already made protest, Goethe responds with his apodictic "Nature has neither kernel nor husk."

The theme of the tercets on Schiller's skull (*Schillers Reliquien*) places it among Goethe's nature poems. Whereas the other members of this group of poems are formulations of Goethe's views and insights concerning God, the world, and man, delivered in grand and solemn tones of religious emotion and composed in hours of calm reflection so as to embody generalized truth, this poem alone retains the color of the moment of its origin. It is the most personal piece in the group. Its occasion and the specific reference to its author are, to be sure, not revealed. Goethe gave the stanzas no title; we know only from his biography and from the reports of others that the skull whose examination gave rise to the magnificent verses was a relic of his friend Schiller. Through a chain of circumstances which cannot be detailed here, it happened that Schiller's remains were exhumed in 1826, together with those of twenty-two other deceased persons who had been buried in the same crypt at Weimar. How was Schiller's skull to be identified, how were the portions of the skeleton to be differentiated, so that they might be given a new and worthier resting place? Goethe believed that he knew how to pick out the skull. Would not the dessicated hull reveal the "divinely vouchsafed trace" of the living spirit which once resided in it? Here surely, as everywhere in nature, it must be true that the outer form was shaped by the inner. All forms are sensual phenomena of the one creative spirit which everywhere actualizes itself solely in individuation. Boundless as the sea is nature's creativeness, and its possibilities are infinite; yet it creates from norms, and its ever-changing forms stream forth according to fixed rules. All individual forms are variations of basic types which are retained even in the most fanciful modification. All of this is revealed and confirmed for the spiritual eye of the poet as he holds his friend's skull in his hands. With surging power the magnificent tercets express the profound emotion of the moment when the supreme mystery of "God-Nature" reveals itself. In reverence the worshiper acknowledges this mystery, bows before "the mysterious primal source of all things." In the concluding formula the mystery is indicated with laconic conciseness rather than expressed:

from form to form, from figure to figure, the creative spirit strides forward to ever higher patterns, from life to death, from destruction to new creation. To one who is capable of comprehending this image, the dead relic which is otherwise always and everywhere the sign of transitoriness becomes the symbol of eternal creation.

Finally, the ballad *Paria* (1823), in which deep religious experiences are symbolically expressed, must be included in this series. It is a triptych: two prayers of the pariah, petition and thanksgiving, are the altar wings which frame the powerful central piece, the legend itself. Goethe had read the story in Pierre Sonnerat's *Voyage aux Indes* forty years before and had never been able to forget it. "To me it seemed the fairest treasure to see such worthy pictures frequently renewed in the power of imagination, for they were constantly transformed, yet they did not alter but rather ripened to a purer form and more definite representation." Even now he could hardly bring himself to reveal the treasure cherished in secret, anxious lest he might thereby forfeit "the peculiar, pure figure."

The poorest of the poor, a pariah, turns to Brahma in the opening prayer. He beseeches Brahma, whose presence not even the noble and the just can endure, for a god who shall serve as intermediary between his own kind and the lord of powers. Then the "Legend" tells of the genesis of the pariah-goddess. The heart of the story is the singular incident of the transposed heads, which plays a significant role in Indian legend. The guiltless guilt of unexpected passion is expiated in death and resurrection by the pure, all too pure, and blameless woman. Her noble head is placed upon the body of a wicked woman, and the result is a monstrous creature, hybrid of the basest and highest in eternal cleavage, pure in desire but dissolute in action. The gods were pleased to let this hideous thing take place; from them seduction came, in the shape of the majestic and irresistible manifestation of a handsome and youthful god. This confounded the emotions of the pure woman, fired in her highest spiritual pleasure and sensual desire alike. The dangerous, equivocal magic of beauty of form! Who is strong enough to endure such a trial? And yet it comes from the gods, who alone know the wherefore. Now God and Lucifer, heaven and hell, are joined together in insoluble conflict within the ambivalent figure, and it will always

With its head in Heaven abiding,
Feel the downward drawing passions
Of a pariah of this earth.[2]

But for that very reason she cannot be wholly lost. For both belong to God, the elemental and sublime, the murky and the bright; all life is a mingling of both. Thus also the gruesome hybrid being can become the goddess who mediates between the higher and the lower. She becomes the voice of all creatures compounded as she herself is. With desperate lament and humble petition she will stand before God, accusing him even while loving him, and will beseech of his grace that all who suffer from the insoluble conflict of life shall be born anew.

In some such way as this is the meaning of Goethe's profound poem to be interpreted. Its symbolism points to the inexhaustible problems of human existence: man's relationship with time and eternity, with God and devil, with heaven and earth. The deeper meaning so magnificently given to the ancient legend is wholly the work of the poet; his Indian source has nothing of it. In these verses thought and language are welded into the closest amalgam. Goethe himself thought that the poem had appeared to him "as a Damascus blade forged of steel wire."

Urworte. Orphisch (1817) is a group of five stanzas, the story of whose genesis explains its striking title. Among classical philologists of the period there was a romantic group whose members concerned themselves with that Greek cosmogony which antedated the Homeric Olympus. In the Orphic poetry of the early period, when poets were still priests who expressed in symbolic images the religious mysteries, they thought they had discovered the primitive religion of the Greeks, dark myths of orgiastic and Dionysiac cults with which Winckelmann and his disciples had not troubled themselves. In the "sacred utterances" of hierophantic poetry there seemed to be preserved primitive images deriving from Oriental and Egyptian concepts. The Roman Macrobius tells of a doctrine of the Egyptians according to which four divinities—Daimon, Tyche, Eros, Ananke—gave assistance to each

2 . . . mit dem Haupt im Himmel weilend, / Fühlen Paria dieser Erde / Niederziehende Gewalt. (Translated by William Gibson, *The Poems of Goethe*, p. 24.)

new-born infant. Acquaintance with these "Orphic darknesses" opened up for Goethe a new realm of ancient wisdom, though one he found a "strange world." He did not concern himself with the historical aspect of the scholarly discussion. But he did wish to excavate from the historical rubble whatever of generally valid truth "the hoary magical sayings about human fate" contained, to renovate them "on a basis of his own actual experience," and to express them in his own fashion. It was impossible, he thought, to resist the charm exerted by "every universal." That is the meaning expressed in "Urworte." These laconically phrased utterances are intended to present pregnant symbols and formulas of ultimate, significant ideas. They are more closely akin to the spirit of Platonic than of Orphic wisdom.

The first stanza, "Dämon," concerns the problem of personality, the characteristics "whereby the individual is differentiated, however great his similarity, from all others." Thus Goethe himself expounds its meaning in an essay which comments upon this cycle. It is his peculiar character which constitutes a man's demon, Heraclitus says. For him, demon signifies mortal destiny. The Stoics distinguish an original ideal personality from the empiric one. That man's native individuality has fateful significance for him is one of Goethe's oldest convictions. "No one can new-coin himself, and no one can elude his fate." In his autobiography he shows clearly, reviewing his own development, that do what he will man will always be brought back to the path which his nature has prescribed for him. "What belongs to a man he cannot be rid of, even if he should cast it away."

As, on that day which launched thee into being,
The sun related stood to every planet,
Thy life commenced; and, with that doom agreeing,
Obeys till now the impulse which began it;
Such must thou be, thyself thy fate decreeing:
Thus did the Sibyl say, the Prophet sang it;
Nor time nor force that inwrought type can sever,
Which, through thy life, unfolds itself forever.[3]

[3] Wie an dem Tag, der dich der Welt verliehen, / Die Sonne stand zum Grusse der Planeten, / Bist alsobald und fort und fort gediehen / Nach dem Gesetz, wonach du angetreten. / So musst du sein, dir kannst du nicht entfliehen, / So sagten schon Sibyllen, so Propheten; / Und keine Zeit und keine Macht zerstückelt / Geprägte Form, die lebend sich entwickelt. (*Urworte. Orphisch*, "Dämon," translated by Frederick H. Hedge, *The Christian Examiner*, vol. XXXVII, p. 247, Boston: 1844.)

It is no astrological superstition that Goethe here defends; he had repeatedly rejected such superstition. He refers rather to the sense of an interrelated cosmic order revealed in astrological speculation in order to set forth in all its force and peculiarity the significance of the innate individuality as the first and most important element of fate. "That inwrought type . . . which, through thy life, unfolds itself forever"—not rigid husk, but something which progresses in accordance with the original, fixed mold, which comes to realization in collaboration with the forces and circumstances implicit in the situation of the individual's life, and yet which does so in such a way that the nucleus is carefully preserved even as the prototype is always preserved in species of animals and plants. Nor power nor time is able to destroy native character: not time, for through the generations it is preserved as a hereditary characteristic in ever-new individual forms.

If necessity is the dominant force in the sphere of the innate here spoken of, there is another and different accessory power which resolves and alters, and that is Chance ("Tyche"). The "conjuncture of earthly things," the entire complex of external conditions under which the individual is developed, everything that facilitates or hinders him, is designated by this symbol: happiness and unhappiness, the circle of his fellow men, the special circumstances of his social and historical situation, everything with which the living individuality must come to terms.

Next comes Eros: he lights and brings to full glow the flame of life, the entire realm of emotion from mere predilection to passion forgetful of self. "Here individual Daimon and seductive Tyche are united with one another." Will and passivity, choice and seduction, become inextricably linked. "Here there is no boundary to aberration." But under this very pressure the ego achieves self-awareness, realizes that it possesses freedom of self-determination, and also the freedom to unite with another being. Thus pairs, families, peoples are formed, in whose commonality the individual feels and operates as a member—all in accordance with the way and force by which the cosmic Eros forms chaos into a universal whole. In this process a noble personality will not become lost in the general but will find himself strengthened and enhanced in his preference for and loyalty to the definite and particular. But as one advances in life the ego, striving for free self-determination, everywhere encounters an objective and resistant element: Necessity and Law. All that remains is to accept with free consent what one must accept. In the end we learn through renunciation how delusive our feeling of freedom is. Duty constraining us from within and fate constraining us from without determine our wishes.

Up to this point Goethe's cycle follows ancient charms. The fifth stanza, "Elpis," invokes the friendly deity who loosens all constraint and banishes all boundaries, the goddess "Hope." In Goethe's poetry and writings this life-giving genius is repeatedly mentioned. From youth on she was his inseparable companion and comforter, the good spirit of limitless potentialities. How could a living being survive without it? "The dead are without hope." Out of the dark clouds of misfortune and fate Hope emerges like the ever-renewing day and upon wings of confidence and courage bears us to confront the future. Between the basic forces which are invoked and celebrated in these "hoary sayings" there are mysterious connections and affinities. They stand to one another in the relationship of polarity, of complementary opposition: Daimon and Tyche, Daimon and Ananke, Daimon and Elpis, Ananke and Elpis. And they follow one another as the ages in the life of an individual connect one with the other. Each is the dominant genius for a definite stage of life; only Hope accompanies us from our first step into the world until the end.

Since 1780 Goethe had belonged to the Masonic lodge at Weimar. It was closed in 1782, however, and was only reopened in 1808. It was to this group that he delivered the speech in memory of Wieland (1813). His son's participation in the activity of the lodge inspired Goethe to demonstrate his interest in a number of songs of solemn character. *Symbolum* (1815) sets forth the attitude of the Freemason in the context of general life. The most significant of these poems is the one dedicated to the lodge celebration of 1825. It refers to the semicentennial jubilee of the reign of Karl August. Here are the magnificent stanzas which express in perfect form the ethos which governed the life of the aged poet—an ethos of activity firm and faithful, of consistent and progressive striving which can alone give permanent substance to our existence, abiding force to our personality.

Let go the all-too-transitory!
It cannot help you in your needs:
What's goodly lives in ages hoary,
Renews itself in noble deeds.

And so it is that what is thriving
Through cause and action gains new force,
For constancy of thought and striving
Gives humankind a far more lasting course.

This solves the great interrogation
As to our second fatherland;
For whatsoe'er we do that has duration
Insures that we eternally shall stand.[4]

In accordance with the scriptural text, Goethe remarked in a letter of September 1823, much must be forgiven him, for he had loved much. That he was capable of rejuvenating himself periodically, that his senses, heart, and spirit could then be newly entranced by beauty of form and the charm of youth, that passion could ever and again seize upon him and rock him—only a moralist will be distressed by these things. The extraordinary man lives according to his own law. Men of genius, says Goethe, "experience a *repeated puberty*, while other people are young only once" (Eckermann, March 11, 1828). One who understands how to take at their true value the works in which such extreme intensification is expressed and resolved will be so grateful for their beauty and grandeur that he will lose all desire to deride or reproach. If, looked upon superficially, it was folly and material for a comedy—Goethe remarks jestingly: "An old uncle who loves his young niece too ardently"—nevertheless the victim himself paid the bitter price of spiritual torments even while enjoying the happiness which, according to the notions of conventional judgment, was no longer appropriate to him. In the end we shall have to choose whether we would rather forgo the dubious spectacle of an

[4] Lasst fahren hin das Allzuflüchtige! / Ihr sucht bei ihm vergebens Rat: / In dem Vergangnen lebt das Tüchtige, / Verewigt sich in schöner Tat. / / Und so gewinnt sich das Lebendige / Durch Folg' aus Folge neue Kraft; / Denn die Gesinnung, die beständige, / Sie macht allein den Menschen dauerhaft. / / So löst sich jene grosse Frage / Nach unserm zweiten Vaterland; / Denn das Beständige der ird'schen Tage / Verbürgt uns ewigen Bestand. (*Zur Logenfeier des 3. Septembers 1825*, translated by B. Q. Morgan.)

old man in love, or the poems which that love occasioned. Obviously, one can be had only together with the other. This is true of the *Divan*, and it is also true of Goethe's last great love poem, the *Trilogie der Leidenschaft*.

During his summer visits to the Bohemian spas Goethe several times met a beautiful young woman, Amalie von Levetzow. He had already encountered her previously and in his diary had given the charming creature the significant name of Pandora. In 1821 he met her in Marienbad. She had her daughters with her; the eldest, Ulrike, was now a grown girl of seventeen. Ulrike pleased Goethe, and he occupied himself with her and told her of his works. He took leave of the entertaining circle with "some regret." In the following year he found the Levetzows at Marienbad again. To the mother he confessed that he wished he had another son who might be married to Ulrike, and that he would be glad to do something for her education. But as yet his interest took the form of fatherly affection and aesthetic satisfaction. In the winter he wrote Ulrike a letter in which he assured her that "her loving Papa thought of his pretty daughter always." It was only the third encounter that was decisive.

In 1823 he saw the girl, now nineteen, in Marienbad again, associated with her daily, and courted her with gifts and verses. Her greatest satisfaction was in the intellectual advantage which she derived from close association with the great and admired man. "No, it was not a love affair," she later insisted. For her it was less; for Goethe, it was much more. This passion, this last, shook him to the core. Some months previously he had barely passed through a serious illness. Death had come very near to him. But then he returned to life with new energy, gay and rejuvenated. He had not enjoyed such good health for a long time. And now this new passion also came—as if everything had to happen that way. It mounted to a pitch of unreasoning blindness, of bold hope. Things went so far that the Grand Duke on behalf of his friend asked Frau von Levetzow in due form for Ulrike's hand and offered the entire family an assured position in Weimar. The sensible woman tactfully refused. The adventure of the old poet became a kind of public sensation. His son and daughter-in-law were much perturbed, and Goethe's friends spoke of the matter in their letters. When the Levetzows traveled to Karlsbad, Goethe followed them, stayed in the same hotel, and was Ulrike's constant companion. On the eve of his seventy-fourth birthday the old man danced with the young women and girls. He writes to his son with satisfaction: "A Polish lady invited me to dance the closing polonaise; I glided through the dance with her, and as partners were changed I managed to get hold of most of the pretty girls." A week later a "tumultuous farewell" ended the happiness stolen from pitiless time. And forever. Goethe never saw the girl again. Ulrike never married, though she had plenty of suitors.

Goethe's first letter, written on the return journey and addressed to the mother, requests in discreet words that his "darling" might remember the feelings of her friend. He hoped, too, that she would agree "that it is a nice thing to be loved, even though the friend might sometimes be inconvenient." To the girl herself he sent a small poem "from the distance," of which the closing lines are:

> For, bearing thee so wholly in my heart,
> I grasp it not that thou art otherwhere.[5]

As he sits in his traveling carriage, leaving everything behind him, as each hour takes him farther away from his beloved, he is overwhelmed with pain. From his anguished bosom arise the majestic stanzas which have made Goethe's last love unforgettable for all time. The period of possession, the moment of fulfillment when all yearning for the highest was satisfied by her beauty, flashes upon the inward eye. It was paradise from which a cherub had ejected him. After this the world seems unable to offer anything more; neither the beauty of the landscape nor contemplation of "supernal grandeur," of ever-creating nature, cheer him. Delicate, vanishing clouds in the blue ether and even the beauty of nature only evoke the image "of that loveliest of lovely forms," graven upon his heart with "letters of flame." Is this feeling, expressed with constantly growing power, merely love as the enchantment of sex? Goethe feels how his whole being, how senses, heart, mind, and soul are supremely stirred and translated to a state which can be suggested only in language from the sphere of religious emotion, in words like "the peace of God." It is not instinct or desire which is at the heart of this bliss, but the most sacred and comprehensive of all emotions.

[5] Denn wie ich dich so ganz im Herzen trage, / Begreif' ich nicht, wie du wo anders bist. (Translated by B. Q. Morgan.)

> Within our bosom's pureness stirs a striving
> To give ourselves in gratitude unbidden
> To something higher, purer—whence deriving?
> Unriddling for oneself Him ever hidden;
> We call it worship!—In such bliss commanding
> I feel a share, when I'm before her standing.[6]

This kind of supreme love, a pious withdrawal in the contemplation of the divine in beautiful human form, is the substance of the elegy. No possession, no fulfillment could be higher (this idea is rephrased again and again), and hence no loss could be more painful. Final incurable despair shakes the old and wise man;

> To me the All, and e'en myself is lost,
> I who but now was favorite of the gods.[7]

Like a wounded animal he wishes to hide his pain in solitude. Like Tasso, the wretched man has left only the consolation that a God has enabled him to give utterance to his suffering.

What a spectacle! The great man in tempestuous turmoil to the point of annihilation; all the wisdom of a firm spirit tried in life, the feeling of his own worth, the consciousness of his own achievement, the world of light and action which was his possession—none of these things could resist the assault of despair. Of old age the poem says nothing; what Goethe feels is timeless. Even if only a man of much experience can suffer so deeply and speak of his suffering in such a way, these are the plaints of a man who feels for everyone, who suffers and expresses in magnificent and restrained verses that which torments everyone, namely: the transitoriness of bliss and happiness; all that is separation, loss, self-denial, ever recurrent, and penetrating our entire lives; that suffering whose highest degrees are death and the loss of what is loved—

> They urged me toward the lips that would enjoy me;
> They separate us now—and thus destroy me.[8]

[6] In unsers Busens Reine wogt ein Streben, / Sich einem Höhern, Reinern, Unbekannten / Aus Dankbarkeit freiwillig hinzugeben, / Enträtselnd sich den ewig Ungenannten; / Wir heissen's: fromm sein!—Solcher seligen Höhe / Fühl' ich mich teilhaft, wenn ich vor ihr stehe. (*Trilogie der Leidenschaft,* translated by B. Q. Morgan.)

[7] Mir ist das All, ich bin mir selbst verloren, / Der ich noch erst den Göttern Liebling war. (*Trilogie der Leidenschaft,* translated by B. Q. Morgan.)

[8] Sie drängten mich zum gabeseligen Munde, / Sie trennen mich—und richten mich zu Grunde. (*Trilogie der Leidenschaft,* translated by B. Q. Morgan.)

Pandora's name is invoked. In the drama which bears that name the same experience had already been given expression: "Whoso is damned from the fair one to sever . . ." The sphere and stream of life are infinite; only our happiness and our existence are finite. Reason may capitulate to this inevitability, but our emotion never. For feeling demands eternity.

To the *Elegy* Goethe joined two other poems. The trilogy begins with the poem *An Werther*. It was written last, in March 1824, and served as foreword to the new edition of *Werther* which appeared in commemoration of the fiftieth anniversary of the first publication of the famous book. The poet addresses the shade of his hero:

My doom to stay, while yours was separation.
You went ahead—not greater your deprivation.[9]

The friend of life had not often spoken so bitterly. The wound bled afresh, the anguish was renewed, and as he surveyed his life, weighing profit and loss, the one most painful motif sounded out, drowning all else—farewell, separation, loss. "Separation is death!" But by comparison with the vehement lament of the following *Elegy* this overture seems restrained and prudent.

The third poem, *Aussöhnung*, was written first. In Marienbad Goethe had met the Polish pianist, Maria Szymanowska. The playing of this "incredible" artist had been beneficial to his excited state. He confessed to his friend Zelter that music then exerted enormous power over him. Once again, at the end of the trilogy, the principal theme is again sounded—"Oh, that it might abide forever!"—muted now, and with gratitude for rich happiness, no longer a hopeless lament. For art, in Goethe's conviction, "when allied with pain, must only arouse it in order to assuage it and to resolve it in loftier feelings of solace."

But the closing tone of reconciliation was the product of the creative artist. Life itself did not treat the lover so gently. Wilhelm von Humboldt, who was visiting in Weimar in November, found Goethe in a pitiable state, torn and suffering. The feeling of new youth was gone; the body was paying for the brief upsurge; disease of the soul made him also physically ill. The poem now became a solace to the poet in this mood. Zelter totted the sum of the great

[9] Zum Bleiben ich, zum Scheiden du erkoren, / Gingst du voran—und hast nicht viel verloren. (*Trilogie der Leidenschaft*, translated by B. Q. Morgan.)

crisis and found the correct answer: "The period was difficult, but the divine fruit was there; it lives and will live, and will bear its spirit's name beyond zones of space and aeons of time; and it will be called love, eternal and almighty love." Memory removed the shadows and transfigured the gain of the bittersweet experience. Four years later Goethe sent Ulrike a last word of gratitude: "How happy were the hours I could count off on those dear fingers."

Poems which are philosophical in character make up the bulk of Goethe's lyrics written in old age; but in addition to them and the *Trilogie der Leidenschaft* there are a number smaller in scope from his last years. They, too, speak of nature and of man in a mode of enthusiastically intensified perception and thought. Finally, there are a few love poems. First should be mentioned the much-cited verses inspired by an allegorical picture. This picture showed an angel hovering over the globe with one hand pointing down to earth and the other upward—obviously an intermediary, a bridging genius. This figure utters the following majestic verses:

If by day, in lovely far light
Airy mountains draw my dreams,
Nights the o'erabundant starlight
Overhead in splendor gleams—

Every day and night I ever
Think of man and praise his fate:
If he thinks aright forever
He's forever fair and great.[10]

The world of day with its abundance of colors and forms is evoked by the motif of azure distance which delights the emotions and arouses a longing for the beauty and joy of earthly existence. The other motif, the star-studded heavens above us, suggests the huge and never-failing order by which the infinity of the cosmos itself is circumscribed and held together. "The sacred laws become visible," as a

[10] Und wenn mich am Tag die Ferne / Luftiger Berge sehnlich zieht, / Nachts das Uebermass der Sterne / Prächtig mir zu Häupten glüht— / / Alle Tag' und alle Nächte / Rühm' ich so des Menschen Los: / Denkt er ewig sich ins Rechte, / Ist er ewig schön und gross. (*Schwebender Genius über der Erdkugel,* translated by B. Q. Morgan.)

poem of C. F. Meyer puts it. For Goethe, these are supreme and rapturous experiences.

> Man's life appears to share a glorious fate:
> The day so lovely, and the night so great.[11]

On the wings of this lofty emotion the poem soars to resounding fullness. Man is praised as the being in whom time and eternity, nature and spirit, encounter one another. It is vouchsafed him to ascend to true grandeur if he comprehends the two worlds in thought and emotion and unites them into a single whole. In most concise form and in briefest compass supreme truths and general ideas are compressed into a symbol of the dignity and mission of man. The ultimate and most personal of Goethe's mature wisdom is here uttered in a few basic words.

Once again and for the last time the lover speaks in two poems. One is called *Der Bräutigam* ("The Fiancé"). The heart recalls the period of fresh life, the betrothal time of first love when life oscillated in a happy rhythm of desire and enjoyment, of yearning and fulfillment. Day and night, activity and slumber, everything was then penetrated by the passion without which there was no life. The picture of the lovers, hand in hand, gazing at the setting of the sun and confidently and hopefully awaiting the return of light in the morning, reflects a state of the soul on which the shadow of transitoriness and death has not yet fallen. At the end the old man speaks. In the silence of night he recalls luminous youth; but before him he sees death, into which his beloved (or is it the vigor and beauty of his whole life?) has already entered. But faith in the beauty and grandeur of existence is strong and alert in him, and so is confidence that his passing will be like the setting of the sun, which never ceases to send forth its light. Do not the stars in the heavens stand even in the night as emissaries of eternal light? Consciousness of the eternity of all life asserts itself, and the melancholy of transitoriness is impotent against it. Thus the poem closes with surrender and gratitude, with complete affirmation of life.

There is a similar tone and meaning in Goethe's last poem to the moon, *Dem aufgehenden Vollmond,* written in the summer of 1828.

[11] Des Menschen Leben scheint ein herrlich Los: / Der Tag wie lieblich, so die Nacht wie gross! (*Trilogie der Leidenschaft,* translated by B. Q. Morgan.)

He had once promised Marianne to think of her in the nights of the full moon. For a sublime moment the emotion that had gone is relived in the present, and once again the man nearing eighty feels the full happiness of existence. Everywhere in these last poems the world of light shines forth in mighty triumph: by day the beautiful world of color and form which is produced by the sun, by night the light of the moon and the "love glance of the stars." In these delights of the eye Goethe experiences the beauty and grandeur of nature. They confirm and strengthen his faith that life is basically good, however otherwise it might appear in hours of darkness. Ever and again night is supplanted by light, death is swallowed up by life. Light and its works are for Goethe the most valid revelation of constantly creating divine nature. Legend reports that his dying words were "More light."

Chinesisch-Deutsche Jahres- und Tageszeiten, written in 1827, is the name of the last cycle of poems which Goethe composed. The title indicates an encounter of the sort which gave rise to the *Divan.* But in compass and substance this small work is much less important. At that time Goethe had studied works of Chinese literature. He was particularly pleased with a novel, the story of the flowered paper. Goethe found a moral quality in the account of how sensitively sympathetic and highly cultivated people appreciated an idyllic nature, the different seasons of the year, the alternating times of day, and felt that he could mirror his own mode of life in this setting. Sensual joy in the spectacle of natural phenomena and the calm wisdom of a ripe understanding penetrated in the Chinese writings to the eternal law which lies at the base of colorful multiplicity, and this was very closely related to his own mode of thought. In Goethe's poem only a few properties are Chinese; there is occasional mention of Oriental flowers and animals. The most important piece in the cycle is the beautiful poem of evening, *Dämmrung senkte sich von oben* ("Twilight Descended from Above"). Here everything is movement, and everything, even the coolness of the air, is perceived by the eye. The bulk of the cycle consists of short epigrammatic poems in the style of the *Divan.*

In any case, the inspiration which derived from the Oriental gnomic poetry was not exhausted with the *Divan.* Until the end, Goethe constantly wrote short apothegms in rhyme; these he called *Zahme Xenien* ("Tame Xenia")—"tame" in contrast to the polemic

Xenien of 1797. But there are many barbed verses among them, and frequently enough his "old wild nature" shows itself in all its strength. The principal objects of these hard-hitting verses are the character and degeneration of the *Zeitgeist*, and ridiculous or absurd utterances of contemporaries. In addition, there are others expressing the poet's general insights and views concerning God and the world, time and eternity, man and himself, and also occasional stanzas lyric in character. The whole is a work of great variety, a unique treasure of truths beautifully expressed and of satire acutely formulated, an inestimable compendium of the wisdom of Goethe's old age. Whatever thoughts and observations, principles and symbols had been broadcast in the poetry, essays, and scientific works of the final decades are here compressed with energy and clarity into striking formulations. There is many a word of practical wisdom in this colorful mélange, addressed not only to Goethe's time but to all ages.

Whoso with life will play
Can nothing have;
Who will not himself obey
Will e'er be a slave.[12]

Wilhelm Meister's Travels

Thinking and doing, doing and thinking, that is the sum of all wisdom.[1]

ALL OF HIS LIFE GOETHE PROTESTED IN HIS THOUGHT AND IN HIS WORK AGAINST THE IDEA THAT POETRY OFFERS INSTRUCTION FOR THE PRACTICAL CONDUCT of life. The literature of the eighteenth century was didactic. The eminently pedagogical spirit of the Enlightenment had claimed even belles-lettres for its purposes; belles-lettres, too, had to justify their existence by showing what they were capable of contributing to the

[12] Wer mit dem Leben spielt, / Kommt nie zurecht; / Wer sich nicht selbst befiehlt, / Bleibt immer ein Knecht. (*Zahme Xenien, VIII*, translated by B. Q. Morgan.)

[1] Denken und Tun, Tun und Denken, das ist die Summe aller Weisheit (*Wilhelm Meisters Wanderjahre*).

cultivation and strengthening of practical reason. Everything was to serve in educating for purposeful and rational action. The generation to which Goethe belonged had rebelled against this conception of the nature and the mission of poetry. The new gospel of the omnipotence and the irreplaceable worth of nature led, in the realm of literature, to the view that the first and most important significance of poetic art lay in its capacity to be a symbolic expression of emotion and an untendentious representation of life. Goethe defended the naturalistic objectivity of *Werther* by saying that if one must speak of the utility of a literary work, he thought the "clinical history" which he had written here, and which contained no specified moral or practical application, much more effective than any demonstration of virtue, however well meant. What was important was representation, not instruction. "One who does not learn it from the story will certainly not learn it from theory."

This is the attitude which is the premise to Goethe's early writings. In the works of his middle period, to be sure, a spirit of humane culture does find utterance. But even if these works exert a humanizing effect, they were not written for that purpose. Examples are presented, by means of figures, actions, and sentiments, examples of a culture whose aim is the well-proportioned whole of a cultivated personality. Proper desires are here the free and spontaneous consequence of pure feeling and thinking; they are not to be dictated by specific doctrines and commandments. None of the works of Goethe's middle period was written to demonstrate definite maxims of conduct, however praiseworthy. It was among his firmest convictions that the art of the poet must subject itself to no demands made upon it from without. It is autonomous and obeys only its own laws, the laws of unqualified and timeless truth and beauty. This applies to content as well as to form. In the first Wilhelm Meister novel there is a beautiful passage (in the second chapter of the second book) in which Goethe sketches a picture of the true poet. Just as God stands above the world, with which he is at the same time one in essence, so the poet stands above the desires, actions, and perplexities of men, sharing the sufferings and joys of every individual destiny and reflecting them in his creations, but in such a way that his glance disentangles and interprets everything. Awake, he lives the dream of life; he watches unself-conscious activity as teacher, helper, and soothsayer, as a friend of gods and of men.

Like a bird he hovers over the world. Thus the poet is exalted above everything particular, definite, and limited; to his comprehensive view the interwoven texture of life reveals itself in its basic lineaments and its significance. It would be folly to demand of him that "he should at the same time tug at the plough like the ox, follow a scent like the dog, or perhaps even, fastened to a chain, protect a farm by his barking."

In the tapestry of life the moral element is only one thread, not the entire fabric. So it is, too, with the useful. But poetry must set forth the whole. It makes the sovereign nature of life visible, its transcendence of good and evil, purpose and utility. In a letter (to H. Meyer, June 20, 1796) Goethe criticizes a work of Herder's adversely because it repeats the half-true Philistine maxim that the arts must acknowledge the moral law and subject themselves to it. "They have always done and must do the first, because like the moral law their laws spring from reason; but if they should do the second they would be lost." For then they would drop to dull utility. It is the business of philosophy and religion expressly and intentionally to affect morality. The Muse accompanies life, but cannot guide it. True poetry presents a higher reality. Measured by natural reality, it is illusion; but it is at the same time a work of the intellect which comprehends and understands reality, which is capable of taking an independent stand toward life, and thus redeeming man from life's burden and duress. "Like a balloon it lifts us with all the ballast which clings to us into higher regions, and causes the confused mazes of the earth to lie disentangled before us in a bird's eye-view." The reader's own musings are to be reflected in these clarified images, and the reader himself shall seek out the doctrines implicit therein. But in his work the poet must have no other goal than to shape his product as artistically and impressively as possible. If he works only for effect and has a limited, practical purpose, even though this purpose be noble and moral, he will produce only a degenerate kind of poetry, an intermediate thing between poesy and rhetoric. Effect is in any case no gauge of the artistic worth of a poetic composition. "The worst work has been effective, as well as the best . . . but they are not all works of art."

One may wonder, anyway, whether Goethe ever thought of the effect of one of his works when he was writing it. Certainly he felt himself to be a communicator of truth, and wished to transmit what he had discovered to "the brethren." "Art for art's sake" was for him no true principle, at least not in the sense which that formula acquired at the end of the nineteenth century. But Goethe said repeatedly that his compositions sprang not so much from the urge to communicate and to effect as from an innate need for productivity. The artist, he said, works from within outward, and in the end he would never bring anything but himself to light. What readers do with his works is not his affair but theirs. And so Goethe seldom produced anything with an eye to the situation and needs of the time. Only in his youth did such intentions play a part, in such works as *Götz* and *Werther;* but this was no longer the case even in the writings of his classical period. Schiller was different in this respect. He had the most definite views concerning the educative function which poetry must exercise in the present, and of the kind of poetry suitable for that purpose. Considerations of this character play a great part in the theory and practice of his writing of tragedies. But Goethe never believed that he must become a cultural leader and educator, even though he had the clearest awareness of his own historic position and achievement. His poetry is full of pictures and models. But it neither teaches nor demands. It touches upon the sphere of the will only indirectly, by clarifying and deepening the understanding of life. Here the elements of the moral world stand forth in their true significance, but so do all other forces and spheres of life.

In the last decades of Goethe's life this attitude changed. His more frequent activity as a critic, developed above all in the fascicles of *Kunst und Altertum,* arose from a need to counteract the hermitlike character of his external life, the isolation of his existence at Weimar. Limiting himself on general principle to recommendation and assent, he called attention in these essays to new phenomena of the literary and scientific life, or was induced by them to take some stand. In addition, in the *Divan,* the rhymed *Xenien,* and the *Maximen und Reflexionen,* he reacted polemically as well as productively to everything which touched his active mind: old and new works in all fields, historical as well as current phenomena and problems. In this continuous production of aphoristic and critical works he gradually produced something which, taken as a whole, has considerable significance.

Nothing is falser than the notion that in his old age Goethe was an egotistic individualist who looked down indifferently from his mountain heights upon the activity of his contemporaries, untroubled by the course of events and wrapped up in the mantle of self-assured wisdom. Goethe had indeed learned to be skeptical concerning the possibility that the course of things could be influenced by advice, admonition, or warning. Of this we shall have more to say. But the urge to productive discussion and the noble need for participating actively in the current life of the time were so strong in him that he could not refrain from letting his praise and blame, his Yea and Nay, be heard. While all that he wrote became more difficult in language and style, and he had less and less regard for the taste and understanding of the general public, in content his writings developed rather in the opposite direction. It is precisely his latest works which have immediate relationship to the present, to its positive as well as its negative tendencies.

This is particularly true of Goethe's last great prose work, the novel *Wilhelm Meisters Wanderjahre*. Here he is at the same time more didactic than anywhere else. It is a work reflecting concern for the present and offering criticism and instruction; a work intended for and addressed to an age in which the transition to new conditions was being consummated in ever increasing tempo, and in which many signs foretold an approaching crisis. In this situation Goethe believed that for once he should utter more directly and magisterially what he, now hastening toward his end, had to offer the present and the future as his legacy.

At the close of the *Lehrjahre* the hero of the story stands forth as a personality whose education is completed. The years of maturation are at an end, and the connection with Natalie inaugurates the next phase of his life, that of his manhood. Henceforth he must no longer be concerned with himself alone but must think of others, live with others, work for others; he must be husband, father, fellow citizen. Schiller had already said that "years of apprenticeship" is a functional concept whose necessary corollary is mastery. At that time Goethe had rejoined that he was indeed inclined to continue the story. The end of the *Lehrjahre* contains the motif of a continuation, and certainly not by accident. For without such a prospect the abrupt conclusion would hardly be tolerable. Wilhelm stands ready for a journey. It is not granted him to enjoy his marriage with Natalie. He must tear himself away from her at the moment when she has become his. The society of his humanitarian friends demands that he accompany the Marquis, the brother of the harpist, on his journey to Mignon's home in Italy, and that he take his son with him. This constitutes the link with the sequel.

The new novel shows Wilhelm on his travels. His friends have imposed the condition that he shall not stay in any place longer than three days. Thus he is always in motion, getting to know new conditions and new people, without being tempted to let himself be determined by accidental circumstances. After he has visited Mignon's home, that condition is annulled. Wilhelm's life now becomes a wandering without a definite goal. But the story of Wilhelm Meister the wanderer is not the principal matter in this book. His further development is also dealt with, to be sure, and this motif has its significance for the ethical meaning of the whole; but Wilhelm's story is no more than a portion of this whole, and not even the most important portion. He ceases to be the actual "hero." His story provides a framework for many pictures and teachings which are unfolded before the reader (and the book does count upon serious and persevering readers); the story itself is "a sort of continuing thread" by which the most diverse pieces are tied together. Goethe himself called his book a "queer opus" and anticipated the criticism, for which he must have been prepared, by throwing overboard, so to speak, any claim to form. Such a "collective labor" as this, he said, in which utterly disparate details are united in a structure which is rather an "aggregate" than a whole, was a questionable undertaking. But, he added, if the book was not all of one piece it was nevertheless all one in meaning. And that it certainly is. Here the details are more important than the whole; but they are all diverse expressions of a mind of the greatest definiteness and unity, of the wisdom of Goethe's old age.

Wilhelm has yet to learn to become a member of society and to be active in a way that is useful to the community. The result of the first stage of his life was called education. But it is not enough to be an educated man. That is the premise, not the purpose, a means to the goal, not the goal itself. Wilhelm has as yet acquired no practical competence which would enable him to do something definite in the right way. He must choose a calling. In this way, of course, he will limit his activity, but at the same time he will give it consistency and effect. The dreamer who had gone forth to renew the theater and to address the entire nation from this pulpit now becomes a modest specialist, a surgeon. But modest as this calling is, it is useful in an immediate and unproblematic way. To send back quickly into active life healthy people who are exposed to the accidents and mishaps of a vigorous existence is a task quite in harmony with that spirit of everywhere maintaining and augmenting energy which the works of Goethe's old age glorify and proclaim. The novel closes with Wilhelm employing his skill to bring his own son back to life. Could there be a finer confirmation of the fact that he has chosen the right calling? At first it seems as if Wilhelm were making his choice not without some resignation. He recognized and accepted the necessity for a man to address himself to a limited skill and a specific activity if he would be active among the active, useful among his fellow men.

The Society of the Tower, which had taken him in at the close of his apprenticeship and had sent him forth into the world, is called in the *Wanderjahre* the Brotherhood of the Renunciants. The word occurs in the very subtitle of the novel, as a programmatic designation of one of its chief motifs. To learn renunciation appears here as the moral foundation of a useful life. It includes the voluntary limitation of willing and action, control of impulses and emotions, purification of selfishness to reach social selflessness, and finally the subjugation of dreams, yearning, and of the melancholy feeling that all is transitory. It also implies relinquishing the senseless struggle against the inevitable. Moderation in matters of choice, diligence in matters of necessity—that is the goal. It is solely to the present, the demand of the day, the necessities and possibilities of the moment that the active man should address himself. The point is not to shake off the burden of life and to withdraw into oneself as into a monastery, but to make oneself more capable, stronger for the tasks of life, to summon all of one's forces for a definite undertaking. He whose efforts are generalized comes to nought. Only voluntary limitation leads to significant achievements. But activity is not demanded for activity's sake; man is not reduced to a mere *homo faber*. Clear awareness and energy of mind are assumed as the fruit of that cultivation of the ego which is the first goal to be achieved. When Wilhelm asks the maturer Jarno (who is here called Montan because he has become a geologist and miner) what the important thing in life is, he is told: thinking and doing, doing and thinking. That, says Jarno, is the sum of practical wisdom. Life must oscillate in an alternating rhythm of contemplation and activity, a rhythm which must be like exhalation and inhalation. Even the most positive of the emotions, love, must weave itself into all willing and acting.

And thy striving, be't with loving,
And thy living, be't in deed! [2]

Nor is the beautiful banished from this activistic world; only it is the end, not the beginning, of education. The right way goes from the useful through the true to the beautiful. The young man, whatever his calling is, must begin with a handicraft, with training in a practical skill, in life as in art. Dilettantism is the greatest of evils, because it excludes genuine education as well as genuine achievement. To the theoretical and aesthetic intellectualism of his age Goethe opposes, with stark one-sidedness, conscious limitation, practical specialization, as the better pedagogical principle: "To know and practice *one* thing correctly produces better education than a smattering of a hundred things." And still more decisively: "Your general education and all provisions for it are poppycock. That a man understand something quite completely, achieve something excellent, such as no other in his immediate environment is likely to do, that is what counts." And something else is needed: "the greatest respect for time as the highest gift of God and nature." Prudence is demanded and praised as the conduct which distributes time intelligently and manages to utilize every hour. "Something must be done every moment, and how could that be if a man did not heed both his work and the hour?" These principles and properties are represented by the persons who belong to the worshipful order of the Renunciants.

The Renunciants are individual, particular people, educated rather in the manner of the eighteenth century than of the new age, even though they are "renouncing" individualists, living in and active for society. But now they pass over into another, larger group. This new society no longer possesses the character of an elite, but consists of a large number of competent workers, practical men of the new, specialized type, organized artisans. The age of industrial production and

[2] Und dein Streben, sei's in Liebe, / Und dein Leben sei die Tat! (*Wilhelm Meisters Wanderjahre*, Book III, chapter i, translated by Thomas Carlyle, *Wilhelm Meister's Apprenticeship and Travels*, vol. II, p. 224, Boston: Cassino, 1882.)

association is being ushered in. As yet the individual is economically independent, relying upon his own power to work, his individual competence. But separation from the soil, social deracination, has already begun. The individual must now associate with others of his kind to form a guild in which the old class distinctions no longer play a part, an organization based upon work and achievement, not upon possession. This group plans an undertaking which can only be carried out communally because it exceeds the powers of the individual. The small company is the nucleus of a new society which is founded upon the organization of labor. Goethe calls the coöperative "the band." What he describes is an association of workers in which each can stand on his own feet because he is expert in a specific trade which corresponds to his special gifts. The forms of production of the industrial age, with its masses of workers, are as yet beyond the horizon of Goethe's world. But a condition is already imagined in which the individual can no longer master the new economic and social tasks but must seek association with others and subordinate himself to systematic planning and direction.

Where will such a coöperative find the land, the space, in which to make its new guild a reality? Old Europe's soil has long been cultivated and is in firm hands. But even here, perhaps in the east, there are broad spaces which are waiting to be colonized. And beyond, across the ocean, waits the New World. The most vigorous members are to set themselves in motion to found a new home in a young, free country. The pioneer spirit which conquered America finds expression here in the saying: "Where I can be useful is my fatherland!" Even in the *Lehrjahre* Wilhelm is invited by Jarno to go to America with him. Out of the Society of the Tower, we read, a company is to go forth, spreading to all quarters of the world. The *Wanderjahre* was written at a time when the great wave of emigration was beginning. The difficult economic situation after the long years of war, and the social unrest, which seized upon the most active elements in Europe, gave a mighty impulse to this movement.

To give room for wand'ring in it
Therefore is the world so wide.[3]

[3] Dass wir uns in ihr zerstreuen, / Darum ist die Welt so gross. (Based on translation by Thomas Carlyle, *Wilhelm Meister's Apprenticeship and Travels,* vol. II, p. 229.)

With Goethe this is not meant to be "Europe-weariness," which was also beginning to be a fad in literature. Goethe was convinced that the Old World with its traditions would remain the venerable motherland of culture. But the spirit which was active among the most competent and strenuous representatives of Western venturesomeness was striving to traverse the limits of the Old World. Goethe admired this spirit and in this last of his prose works (as in the closing act of *Faust*) he gave it his blessing. The magnificent spectacle presented by the conquering and colonization of another continent across the Atlantic Ocean by the activistic spirit of Europe engaged his imagination intensely during these years. He thought it worthwhile to look into such a growing world. The new, bolder plans which could not be realized in the old lands seemed to be offered boundless possibilities over there. Goethe's admiration for America is expressed in his familiar apothegm. In it the New World is praised because it is young earth, free from historic traditions, and not burdened by the barren conflict of inherited ideologies. In a conversation with Eckermann (February 21, 1827), Goethe commended Alexander von Humboldt's view that a canal should be constructed at Panama as a great and necessary project for the future, and predicted the colonization of the west and the establishment of cities in California. At the close of the novel we are summarily told that the company of artisans is really departing for America. Among them are Wilhelm's friends, and also his wife Natalie. It is not expressly stated that Wilhelm will follow them. But we know that he hopes to find in America greater and less hampered possibilities for his anatomical studies.

A different kind of education is presupposed by the new ideal of a type of person who is more social and practical than the intellectually and aesthetically cultivated man, and more "socialistic" than the representatives of the enlightened ruling class of the preceding century (which is here represented, favorably enough, by Herzilie's uncle, whose estate Wilhelm visits: Book I, chapter v). Goethe attempts to sketch the principles and practices necessary in a school designed to educate the new working men. One of the most significant chapters of this colorful novel describes the ideal form of such an educational institution. This was in keeping with the taste of the time. Problems of pedagogical theory, school reform, and the methods of instruction became subjects of more and more lively discussion after the close of the eighteenth century. Pestalozzi's doctrine in particular had found adherents everywhere in Germany. Goethe held himself critically aloof (see what he said in his conversation with Sulpiz Boisserée on August 5, 1815). But one main tenet in Pestalozzi's theory appealed to him: that vocational training, education for work, must go hand in hand with theoretical instruction; and that the view that humanity is advanced by encyclopeditis is a delusion.

Goethe was interested most in experiments like those of the Fellenberg Institute near Bern, into which he had inquired. In this school, located in the country, pupils were educated more by practical activity than by theoretical instruction. Its guiding principle was preparation for a practical vocation. Such experiments formed the point of departure for Goethe's own reflections on an education which could satisfy the requirements of the new century. He accepts the principle, long prevalent in Anglo-Saxon countries, that boys (he does not speak about education for girls) should no longer be educated in the home but with other children of different types. Goethe's ideal school has nothing in common with the German academic school, the Gymnasium. His is a boarding school, in the country, where teachers and pupils together constitute a community for life and work. Indeed, this "pedagogical province" is a small independent state, with its own constitution and its own economy. All pupils must participate in the agricultural work.

Among the means by which the inner personality is to be cultivated, while a practical skill is being acquired, the most striking is the role assigned to music. At every task the boys sing in chorus. In this manner community of activity is raised and strengthened into a community of feeling. But at the same time each boy is allowed to dress according to his individual taste. "We are entirely opposed to the uniform; it conceals character and hides more than any other disguise the individual traits of the children from the eyes of their masters." Languages are learned by practical use; only one language is spoken in a given month. A boy who shows a special liking for a particular language is thoroughly instructed in it. In poetry the pupils begin with the lyric, which is then taken up along with music in order to develop the feeling for rhythm. In the plastic arts workmanlike skill is first developed according to fixed principles. So the pupils also learn to make epic poems themselves; they are told myths and legends which they then reproduce in the style of epic poetry, while at the same time the young painters vie in representing these legends and myths in their pictures. In dramatic poetry, on the other hand, no instruction is given. This striking provision is based on the idea that drama presupposes an idle crowd of onlookers, for whom there is no place in this educative state, wholly devoted as it is to unflagging activity. If a pupil has histrionic talent, he is sent to one of the great theaters. In all these activities the role of the teacher is limited to ascertaining the natural inclinations and tendencies of the students and supervising the development of the individual. Each one must be allowed to find for himself what is suitable for him, what he is capable and incapable of, but he must at the same time be helped to shorten the way to the correct development of his nature. In doing so the teacher must avoid the errors by which fathers are wont to ruin their sons: their despotic interference with the boys' development and demands that their sons achieve what they themselves never succeeded in doing.

But the educative work of this model school is not completed with the mastery of manual and intellectual skills. The best and most important thing is still lacking. In order that doing and ability may acquire the assurance, steadfastness, and meaning which affects the whole of man—soul, spirit, and character—a general attitude must be developed in the young men: an attitude which is rooted in their own relationship to the invisible and the superhuman and at the same time constitutes a moral basis for the active life, a spiritual element which provides determinants and rules for all activity. Everything depends upon this, so the educators say, if the individual is to be a human being in every respect. And yet no man possesses this element by nature. Only the potentiality for it is innate: *Il y a une fibre adorative dans le coeur humain* ("There is a fiber of worship in the human heart"). To develop this potentiality is the most important task of education. The name of this decisive quality is "reverence." It is the awe of something exalted, which transcends our ego, and to which we bind ourselves by this voluntary subordination.

The doctrine which Goethe presents here (Book II, chapter i) is one of the best-known passages in all the work of his old age. And rightly so, for it contains one of the most profound and fruitful motifs of his humanitarian wisdom. There are three kinds of reverence, he says, which must be developed. First, reverence for what is above us—devout acknowledgment of God as the epitome of the perfect and the exemplary, from whom all earthly authority derives. The second reverence involves that which is below us—the earth and the life upon it. Thirdly, reverence is demanded for what is beside us—our fellow men. For in each individual the species is made real in a particular way, and only all combined constitute humanity, just as only all combined can do the work of life. Over one who has attained to this attitude hatred and enmity, arrogance and brutality, cruelty and tyranny can never again have any power. More than that: one who feels reverence will at the same time overcome fear, and thus attain to real culture. For, so we are taught, the natural man knows only fear; he is afraid of the elements, of the demons, of unknown powerful beings. In his relationship to the divine, primitive man wavers between victory and defeat, without ever being able to make himself free. From this unfree state, reverence raises man to that level of culture which alone corresponds to his dignity.

> To be afraid is easy, but burdensome; to cherish reverence is hard, but comfortable. Man resolves to be reverent unwillingly, or rather, he never resolves it at all; it is a higher sense which must be imparted to his nature and which develops spontaneously only in especially favored individuals, who have for that reason from the oldest times been regarded as saints, as gods. Here resides the dignity, here the proper sphere of all genuine religions.[4]

There are only three genuine religions, he goes on, and none of them is founded on fear: "With the reverence which a man allows to hold sway within him he can retain honor by giving honor." The first or ethnic religion depends upon what is above us. All so-called pagan religions belong to this group. They occur at the stage where mankind first freed itself from the fear held by primitive peoples. The second religion Goethe calls the philosophic. For him this means the conviction which the individual man of independent thought has shaped for himself. It is founded upon reverence for that which is like ourselves and arises out of the realization of man's peculiar position between what is above and what is below. "For the philosopher who

[4] Sich zu fürchten ist leicht, aber beschwerlich; Ehrfurcht zu hegen ist schwer, aber bequem. Ungern entschliesst sich der Mensch zur Ehrfurcht, oder vielmehr entschliesst sich nie dazu; es ist ein höherer Sinn, der seiner Natur gegeben werden muss, und der sich nur bei besonders Begünstigten aus sich selbst entwickelt, die man auch deswegen von jeher für Heilige, für Götter gehalten. Hier liegt die Würde, hier das Geschäft aller echten Religionen. (*Wilhelm Meisters Wanderjahre,* Book II, chapter i.)

places himself in the middle must draw down everything higher and draw up everything lower, and only in this intermediate situation does he merit the title of sage." As the highest achievement of this piety which embraces at once the universe and humanity, Goethe designates an inner state in which man "in the cosmic sense" lives in the truth. The third religion is based upon reverence for what is below us. It is the Christian religion. Nowhere else does Goethe speak of it with such approval as here. It is he says, an ultimate to which mankind could and had to attain.

But think of what it meant [for Christ] not simply to leave the earth lying beneath him and to claim the prerogative of a higher birthplace, but to recognize lowliness and poverty, mockery and contempt, ignominy and misery, suffering and death as divine, aye, to regard even sin and crime not as obstacles, but to revere them as furtherances of the Holy and even give them love! [5]

Traces of this attitude are to be found in other religions, but nowhere else is it the essence and the goal. Civilized humanity can never again retreat from it, and therefore the Christian religion can never disappear. An earlier passage of the novel says that it was the arduously attained goal of a long historical road that mankind had learned to be gentle to the guilty, forbearing to the criminal, humane to the inhuman. "Surely it was men of divine nature who first taught this doctrine, who spent their lives in making possible and accelerating the practice of it."

Wilhelm asks to which of these religions the educators give allegiance. They answer him, to all three, because only in combination do they constitute the true religion. Devout reverence for something transcendentally divine, but also the realization of the divine in the universe and in man, and devout acceptance even of what is dark, lowly, and transitory—only in combination do these constitute for Goethe the religion adequate to the whole of human existence and to the destiny of man.

Out of these three reverences arises the supreme reverence, reverence for oneself, and the former again develop out of the latter, so that man reaches

[5] Aber was gehörte dazu, die Erde nicht allein unter sich liegen zu lassen und sich auf einen höhern Geburtsort zu berufen, sondern auch Niedrigkeit und Armut, Spott und Verachtung, Schmach und Elend, Leiden und Tod als göttlich anzuerkennen, ja Sünde selbst und Verbrechen nicht als Hindernisse, sondern als Fördernisse des Heiligen zu verehren und liebzugewinnen! (*Wilhelm Meisters Wanderjahre*, Book II, chapter i.)

the highest of which he is capable, that he may regard himself as the best that God and nature have produced, nay more, that he can abide upon this height without again being drawn down into the commonplace by conceit and egotism.[6]

Anyone who professes the Christian creed, Goethe thinks, professes this triune religion. What else is the Trinity but the symbol of this highest unity? One might ask why love is not named instead of reverence. But love cannot be taught. It must and will be the fairest flower of reverence, because it is based on the purest spontaneity of the heart.

It has often been maintained that Goethe's program of education shows a resemblance to the most important Utopia of antiquity, the chapters on education in Plato's *Republic*. But the similarity is limited to a very few details: that body and soul must be equally cultivated (Plato says this is to be done by gymnastics and music), and that each individual must master one definite calling thoroughly, and only that one. In all other respects and above all in the human type of person that is to be achieved by education, Goethe's plan differs from that of the Greek in the most decisive way. Goethe cares nothing for selecting the choicest pupils, nothing for good stock. His education is not intended to develop an elite of "guardians" and philosopher-kings, but a medium type, that of the practically competent, which has made the basic values of Western humanity its own and recognizes them as the religio-moral foundation of its labor-directed existence. And finally, in Goethe's plan education is not in the hands of the state but of middle-class society; it is administered by cultivated, practical humanists. In it politics is neither premise nor goal. Nor are warriors or state functionaries to be trained, but only peaceful, independently acting citizens. Goethe's program is in many respects more practical than Plato's, and, if one will, much more democratic.

For the rest, the doctrine of reverence as here presented is in no need of elucidation. One most important, final word is uttered here with the perfect simplicity which only the sagacity of a great spirit

[6] Aus diesen drei Ehrfurchten entspringt die oberste Ehrfurcht, die Ehrfurcht vor sich selbst, und jene entwickeln sich abermals aus dieser, so dass der Mensch zum Höchsten gelangt, was er zu erreichen fähig ist, dass er sich selbst für das Beste halten darf, was Gott und Natur hervorgebracht haben, ja, dass er auf dieser Höhe verweilen kann, ohne durch Dünkel und Selbstheit wieder ins Gemeine gezogen zu werden. (*Wilhelm Meisters Wanderjahre*, Book II, chapter i.)

can achieve. This is the confession of the faith to which Goethe, viewing, thinking, and apprehending, had lifted himself in the course of his long life. How differently things would have gone in Europe if the Germans and other peoples of Western civilization had risen to the height of this feeling and willing or had at least striven for this attitude, this practical humanity. Goethe foresaw the catastrophe as little as did any of his contemporaries. It is only after the middle of the century that the prophets of calamity are heard. But we know that premonition and anxiety troubled him, that he was tormented by a presentiment of danger and crisis. When he clings to the advantages of European culture, to the standpoint of a humanity based upon universal reverence, and phrases them in words which are admonitory with all their clear simplicity, he expresses, along with faith in the dignity and the potentiality of mankind, concern for the fate of European humanity. Goethe's words as to the true religion, the one founded upon universal reverence, are the legacy which he bequeathed to the peoples of Christian civilization. They were uttered at the moment when a new and different age began to emerge, an age whose evil end was as yet unknown to anyone.

That Goethe was oppressed by the feeling of an approaching change is also revealed in other parts of the *Wanderjahre*. Repeatedly handicraft is praised as the best kind of skilled work. Furthermore, industrial production is already depicted. In great detail (in too great detail, most readers will think), Goethe describes the cotton spinning which was carried on in Swiss mountain villages as a home industry. This he regards as the only sound kind of mass production. But during the very years that he was writing the second version of his novel, the new machine form of production was developing more and more markedly in the new factories. Goethe visualizes with concern the consequences this change must involve for handicraft and home industry, for the economic as well as the social life of the individual. "Increasing mechanization torments and frightens me: it rolls forward like a storm, slowly, slowly; but it has taken its direction, and it will come and strike." [7] What can the individual do against it? He must either yield to the new or "seek a more favorable destiny across the

[7] Das überhand nehmende Maschinenwesen quält und ängstigt mich: es wälzt sich heran wie ein Gewitter, langsam, langsam; aber es hat seine Richtung genommen, es wird kommen und treffen. (*Wilhelm Meisters Wanderjahre*, Book III, chapter xiii.)

sea." How, in the age of the machine, when the individual will have to sell his labor and mass production will give rise to a mass existence, can the individual retain an independent existence and the possibility of collaborating productively in his own way toward the great goal of a self-stabilizing humanity?

Similar concern is felt for the role which property must play in an industrial civilization. Without being able to envisage the coming epoch of extreme capitalism, here too Goethe foresaw changes which must dissolve the old standards of morality. To be sure, he thinks it just that the spirit of individual enterprise should have free scope. Everyone should endeavor to retain and increase his possessions as his situation and opportunities permit. But while his own power is expanding he must be mindful of letting others share in his possessions and his profits. The man of property may only be an egoist for the sake of being able to conserve and distribute—not by giving his wealth to the poor, but by feeling himself a steward and conducting himself accordingly. Wealth must be communal possession. Everyone must aspire to profiting both himself and others. This, Goethe thought, was more than advice; it was the dictum of life itself. All forms of the state and all orders of society have their good and their evil. The state seems less important in the face of the world of coöperative labor. It is best to accept the existing order and to develop in society the "general good will" which alone makes common action, common labor, and common enjoyment possible.

In the social and economic views which Goethe presents here, conservative thinking is linked with ideas of true progress. But he confines himself to the laconic formulation of principles. He teaches no comprehensive theory and no social dogma. Just as little does he attempt to prescribe for specific social and economic situations. Nor does he claim to know the course world history will take. It is only of basic convictions and attitudes that he speaks. Goethe addresses a generation which, as the first socialistic efforts in France showed, was on the way to a new social ethic and to new organizational forms of economic production, but which at the same time in other countries, above all in Germany, was running the risk of separating spiritual life from the sphere of work and action and of making the separation ever greater. What the Germans needed was less speculation and more energy, Goethe says to Eckermann. In its entirety and in individual statements, the *Wanderjahre* opposes abstract spirituality and isolated aesthetic cultivation. The point is to make the young man accustomed to and competent for the conditions under which one can exist in the world and its particular departments. The commonalty of the active, constituted by persons so educated, has definite practical purposes and goals; in order to attain these, this community organizes itself into associations of workers. But more important to the poet is spiritual and moral attitude; everything depends on that. What Goethe wishes to teach and to praise is the frame of mind from which action arises, the spirit of a resolute sense of reality. But he knows that it is essential that the humane individual, who had been developed in the preceding centuries, be preserved amid the denser throngs and the quicker tempo of the new age, so that Europe should not succumb to the barbarism of an unleashed mass activism.

The combination of ethical humanism, which only the good will of the individual can make a reality, and the new spirit of a society founded upon labor, in a word, a humanitarian socialism, appears in the discussions and teachings of this pedagogical book as the principal task of the age. Always the individual remains the basic social unit from which our social, moral, and entire cultural life derives its powers. Neither state nor society can command, still less guide, the life of the individual; only he himself can do that. There can be no true commonalty, no healthy society, when the individual is sacrificed and is transformed into a functionary of a people, a class, or a workers' union. Upon the natural and special endowment of the individual, on his personal skill and initiative, depends the worth, the achievement, the hope of the commonalty of workers which Goethe endeavors to present in his model society. The important thing is to find the proper balance between the claims of the individual and those of the producing community, which, to be sure, must be more rigidly organized than the old society. Goethe's teachings are marginalia for an age which was on the point of making the portentous move toward mass activity. They seek to hold fast the old truth of the irreplaceable worth of the individual and to reconcile it with the necessities of the new social era.

But above the sphere of labor, of society, of usefulness and purposes, there arises yet another and higher sphere which adds the hyperreal to the practical, the eternal to the temporal, and only thus moves into the correct perspective. Even above the present and its immediate problems the stars follow their orbits according to eternal laws. This highest stratum is represented in the *Wanderjahre* not by speculation or doctrine, but by a human being, a wise woman, named Makarie, because even here on earth she is blessed. Though suffering, she nevertheless takes the most decided interest in the life of others, actively counseling and helping. In her the attitude of renunciation finds its purest realization, and she demonstrates that true piety is at the same time of the greatest service to life. She is capable of penetrating all masks and of gazing into the inner nature of every individual. She possesses the priestly exaltation and tranquillity of a soul which has become one with the will of the Eternal. By means of premonition and intuition she is in sympathetic contact with the forces of the universe. It is said of her that her soul accompanies the course of the solar system as an integrating part.

Here Goethe's most esoteric ideas concerning the connection of the human microcosm with the universe are suggested. The monad upon which our individuality rests moves along with the great course of the constellations; but while it thus constantly shares in the whole, it never oversteps the limits of the All. Participation in the supermundane does not denote in this case a mystic surrender of self, but a supreme strengthening for the deeds which are to be done upon and for the earth. What is said of Makarie's sidereal visions, to be sure, is so bold that one must suspect an element of irony in these passages. Riemer points this out. It is as if Goethe wished incidentally to ridicule the speculations of a science which had degenerated into a too fantastic mysticism, such as that pursued by Schelling's disciple, G. H. Schubert. But the intentionally serious significance of raising Makarie's figure to the level of myth is unmistakable: she signifies the connection of earthly life with that of the universe, of human activity with the forces which move the cosmos. And of these supreme mysteries she speaks in the only way in which they can be spoken: symbolically.

In order that his compendium of teaching and wisdom might not lack a poetic element and imagination not go empty-handed, Goethe inserted nine stories which for the most part had already been written (from 1807 on) and published before he ever organized the novel into a single entity. Several of them, for example, *Die neue Melusine* or *Die pilgernde Törin* (a translation from the French), are little stories and fairy tales which he had long had in mind. Some are related in motif, and as a group have in turn an inner relationship to the spiritual substance of the novel. In them characters are depicted who in the struggle with their passions attain to the stage of renunciation. *Sankt Joseph der Zweite,* inspired by Dürer's "Life of the Virgin," presents the motif only as a suggestion. *Die pilgernde Törin* shows a father and son as rivals in love, a theme which is treated more seriously and with maturer artistry in the most significant of the stories, *Der Mann von fünfzig Jahren.* This story tells how an aging man is involved by opportunity and circumstances in the madness of a passion for a young girl; how he endeavors to simulate the appearance of youth which he no longer possesses; how he falls into dissension with himself; and how, at last, he is snatched from his unseemly dream just in time, when he discovers that he is the rival of his own son. How painful his own externally aroused excitement appears in contrast to the true passion of youth! But this complication is not analyzed. The poet emphasizes his intention to abstain from entering into the details of the spiritual action.

The reader who is accustomed to the skillful psychological revelation and omniscience of modern novels will find Goethe's reserve strange. But let us not be deceived as to the reasons for it. A writer of Goethe's stature was no more ignorant of psychology than are modern storytellers. If he refrained from giving the entanglement in all its complexity and kept to the level of general observation and pure narrative, he did so not because he had no more to give. To enter into complicated and dubious matters would not have been appropriate to the style of this untragic narrative, would have destroyed its artistic effect. In this work inner states were not to be analytically explored, but spiritual and moral conflicts were to be dramatically represented, and moral decisions were to be narrated as results of spiritual processes. The moral of the story is: "The sensible man needs only to restrain himself, and then he will also be happy."

A "queer opus" this novel surely is. It is composed of such numerous and diverse elements that there can be no question of a finished product, of well-rounded form. Many sorts of people, activities, ages, and spheres of life are depicted—the colorful multiplicity of an era in rapid transition from conditions which had long obtained to situations of altogether different character. In the realm of thinking and willing there is a correspondingly large diversity of views and attitudes, all of which, however, point to a common center. These elements, disparate as they are, could have been bound together all the same by the framework of a firm composition. But this was not achieved. Or shall we say, it was not attempted? Goethe himself thought that he was only offering an accumulation of details, which possessed no other unity than that of a fundamental standpoint and a didactic intent which permeated the whole. Once he had forgone organizing this plenitude of material into an artistic whole, he took every liberty that suited him. Basically the entire book consists of episodes. There are gaps and mighty leaps which astonish the reader. Some conversations are only sketchily reproduced. At one time the author appears as the narrator, at another time as the editor of others' papers or as mere reporter. More frequently than in any of his other works, the poet addresses his reader directly and gives reasons for his procedure; yet he breaks off wherever it suits him, promises subsequent explanations, which are never given, and is otherwise careless. A certain affectation of mystery is unmistakable. Sometimes the author hoaxes the reader in a manner which is not unfriendly but which does impose upon the reader's good will. Some of these stories are not narrated to the end but merge with the main plot. Toward the end the narrative grows increasingly laconic. Important events are condensed and reported in bare summaries. To make matters worse, the whole novel is interspersed with observations, so that stretches of the narrative are completely overrun with the author's own reflections. Any fragments and aphorisms which could not be accommodated in the novel itself are annexed in two separate collections (made by Eckermann).

Goethe did not find easy his labor on this last of his works in prose. Publication had been announced as early as 1810, but it was 1821 before the first version appeared. The author himself was not satisfied. Among readers the book evoked more disapproval than assent. An unexampled scandal occurred. Between 1821 and 1828 a pastor with the grotesque name of Pustkuchen, concerned over pure faith and virtue, published an "Anti-Meister" under the same title as Goethe's book, and in no less than five volumes. In this work, figures taken from Goethe's novel appear and censure their author in the severest way in their dialogue. Goethe's later style is also parodied. Other parodies followed. One called itself *W. Meisters Meisterjahre.* Goethe had the feeling that he was partly to blame for these unhappy occurrences because of the fragmentary character of his first version. He therefore resolved to expand his book—reluctantly and groaning at the burden which he had thus taken upon himself. But when he was finally done (in the year he turned eighty), he took a deep breath as if he were free from a nightmare. "Not everything that an excellent man does is done in the most excellent way." It was thought both then and later that even the second, revised version showed all too plainly the symptoms of a flagging of creative power. A patient reader will find that he is compensated for the artistic shortcomings by the treasure-store of wisdom which he will find lavishly displayed in precisely this heavy, unwieldy, and ill-joined book. The *Wanderjahre* is an extraordinary work, in its strength as in its weakness, and it requires extraordinary readers.

Lesser Fiction

AKIN TO THE *LEHRJAHRE* IN SPIRIT AS IN THEME ARE CERTAIN TALES WHICH WERE WRITTEN DURING GOETHE'S WORK ON THAT NOVEL. THESE FORM THE *Unterhaltungen deutscher Ausgewanderten* ("Recreations of German Emigrants"; 1795). The framework is like that of the *Decameron;* German refugees who have been driven across the Rhine by the French armies tell one another stories. These tales contain strange occurrences "which for a moment reveal to us human nature and its hidden mysteries." As in the Italian novella, the *Unterhaltungen* does not treat of extraordinary people, but of remarkable individual incidents, which bring about a decisive turn in the lives of those affected. Among them is an episode from the life of a celebrated cavalier of the period of Henry IV of France, Marshal François de Bassompierre, from whose memoirs Goethe learned the story; he adheres closely to the account given there. Hofmannsthal made a colorful tale out of the same incident. All the stories in the collection are only by-products of the epic mood in which Goethe was at the time. And yet, with them begins the German *Novelle.* From this insignificant seed grew the many-branched tree of this favorite form of modern literature.

The independent concluding piece of the cycle is *Das Märchen,* a symbolic story reminiscent of Voltaire's philosophic narratives. In it things happen as in a dream; everything is familiar and clear, but at the same time strange and mysterious. The action seems to point to some hidden meaning which can be apprehended in individual details but not grasped as a whole. Many as have been the attempts at interpretation of this piece, none is satisfactory. For here the reader's imagination is supposed to be aroused to endless activity by images and ideas, and his reason at the same time playfully enticed into a maze from which there is no exit. Schiller has preserved a remark of Goethe's in which he said that it was his concern to represent symbolically "the mutual assistance of forces and their re-reference to one another." And so we read in the *Märchen:* "No individual gives help but the one who unites with many at the proper time." The conclusion seems to express this: force, semblance, and wisdom rule the world, but the rule of love is still more certain, its influence more primal and more general. "Love does not rule, but it molds, and that is more." So it is in the order of nature, and only works of this sort can endure. Like Goethe's narratives, this small, mysterious dream-story stimulated the romanticists to attempt similar creations.

The series of Goethe's stories ends and culminates with one which is called simply *Novelle* (1828). This work, most carefully executed and most painstakingly polished as it is, is nevertheless more than a brilliant display of artistic mastery. Goethe himself remarked that one could not fail to realize that this work had issued from the deepest depths of his being. Here, too, as in other cases, a long process of quiet crystallization precedes. The plan for a story under the title *Die wunderbare Jagd* ("The Wondrous Chase") went back thirty years. At that time Goethe had discussed with Schiller and Humboldt the possibility of treating the material in the form of an epic in hexameters, or perhaps more briefly as a ballad. His friends' misgivings had spoiled his pleasure in the execution of it. But now the old interest returned, and it appeared that unobtrusively the right form had developed. By its title this short narrative claims to be a model specimen of its kind. A *Novelle,* Goethe remarked in his conversations on the subject with Eckermann, tells of an unprecedented event. A more concise definition has hardly ever been found for this much discussed genre. An individual occurrence, unusual to the degree that it is still in the realm of what is actually possible (for otherwise it would be a fairy story or a legend)—is not this what comprises the substance of the ideal *Novelle?* In the style of the tale Goethe intends to vie with the finest models, the novellas of the Italian Renaissance. He does not enter into description and analysis of the inner life; it is all epic report, pure representation of external happenings, but still not mere reporting. The inner life is revealed in words; everything spiritual is made vividly present and thus comprehensible.

The remarkable and unparalleled event which occurs (a tiger and lion hunt in a German setting) takes place not for its own sake; the whole apparatus of exciting, outlandish incident appears to have been constructed in this tale only in order that at a critical moment a decisive truth might meet the eyes of certain persons, above all of one person, the young hero of the story. Honorio's fate is at stake. A passion which might easily become fatal for him—a hopeless love for the young princess—appears to have become more real than ever as a result of the first event, the killing of the tiger. But the second turning point (and such unexpected turning points have always been peculiar to the novella) removes this danger completely. What a humiliation when the "heroic deed" proves unnecessary: the tiger, which had escaped from a side show at a fair, was a tame creature which could easily have been caught. But it is this mortifying experience from which the decisive turn unexpectedly develops. The lion which has similarly escaped is tamed, soothed by a boy's fluting and song. But the unusual incident is gloriously surpassed by an event which belongs to the spiritual world. The steadily rising action culminates in a solution which has the radiance and the power of the miraculous. Old sagas and legends from the youthful era when man, nature, and God were linked with one another in loving communion are revived, the stories of Daniel and of Androcles. Now as then the eternal truth is revealed that piety and love alone are capable of overcoming the intractable and destructive elemental forces. Where strength operates against strength, where human wit and will are in hostile opposition to nature, the end can only be destruction.

But love, the devout feeling of unity with the divine order and its forces, is victorious in a higher sense. The elemental is not destroyed; it is appeased by the "peaceful will" which also lies hidden in it as a spark of the universal harmony. It is aroused by man's will to love, which acts in accordance with the ancient, true faith in God's omnipotent love.

For on earth His power's asserted,
And His eyes rule sea and world;
Lions are to lambs converted,
And the wave is backward hurled.
Shining sword is stopped while smiting,
Faith and hope fulfillment yield;
Love in wonders is delighting,
As it is in prayer revealed.[1]

The flute-playing boy, the singer of this song, and his parents, the warder and his wife, stand for a sort of humanity which confronts the representatives of modern society as archaic, strange, and yet superior. These children of former days speak in the solemn language which is natural to the patriarchal epochs of religious cultures. And they understand how to use the peaceful power which slumbers in music, whereby it has served mankind from of old, to assuage the elemental. But all of this appears to come about only in order that Honorio, the silenced "hero," may draw from it the power which is now the central issue, the power of renunciation. As he thus restores the unity of his soul he is restored to himself, to active life. This is what the episodic story is intended to narrate, and nothing more is demanded. For it is easy to imagine what these people, whose lives we have looked into for one eventful hour, will do now. In the works of Goethe's old age this small, beautifully fashioned story stands before us as the work in which he glorifies, with less qualification than elsewhere, the piety which Christianity (but not Christianity alone) has made actual in its noblest representatives: the feeling of fearless confidence in God who is mysterious but who reveals himself to genuine desire, whose gracious will permeates and unites the realms of reality.

[1] Denn der Ew'ge herrscht auf Erden, / Ueber Meere herrscht sein Blick; / Löwen sollen Lämmer werden, / Und die Welle schwankt zurück. / Blankes Schwert erstarrt im Hiebe, / Glaub' und Hoffnung sind erfüllt; / Wundertätig ist die Liebe, / Die sich im Gebet enthüllt. (*Novelle*, translated by B. Q. Morgan.)

Goethe in His Old Age

THE SEPTUAGENARIAN POET CALLED HIMSELF A HERMIT. HE LIVED IN HIS CELL, HE SAID, BUT ALWAYS HEARD THE ROAR OF THE SEA. TO STAND ABOVE LIFE, in order to be able to surrender himself undisturbed to inner visions and reflections, but still to view the activity of the age, so that his thinking and writing should not lose connection with the progress of affairs—such was the attitude which grew ever stronger in him, as the one appropriate to his advanced age. Externally considered, Goethe's existence seemed rather that of a prince holding court than of a hermit turning away from the world. By withdrawing into himself he enticed contemporaries to come to see him and pay homage to him.

The house in which he lived had the character of a modest residence of state. But this was true only of the portion which looked out upon the world. While the public rooms were furnished with works of art and handsome furniture, the rooms in which Goethe lived exhibited the greatest simplicity. To live in magnificent, showy chambers, he thought, was the affair of princes and the wealthy, because such surroundings make a man placid and inactive. But for him this would not do. A simple dwelling and furnishings that were if anything uncomfortable comprised the right environment for a spiritually productive man. But the house on the *Frauenplan* in Weimar was spacious enough to accommodate in addition Goethe's son and his family. After Christiane's death August's young wife, Ottilie, looked after Goethe's comfort. She never ceased to demonstrate deep reverence for her father-in-law. But she was not the "expert cook" and thrifty daughter whom the old widower would have needed most. On the contrary, she was unstable, flighty, and capricious, though entertaining and cultivated. Together with her friends, Ottilie issued a private journal called *Chaos,* which had outside collaborators also. Goethe himself took a hand in this witty enterprise. The character of the young woman, odd sometimes to the point of eccentricity, called for patience. In the wise old father her restless spirit found understanding and composure in the stormy crises arising out of her unsatisfactory marriage.

Her younger sister, Ulrike von Pogwisch, often lived as a guest in the joint household. Ulrike knew how to entertain the old gentleman with cheerful friendliness and amusing bits of gossip. Despite all domestic contretemps and tensions, the presence of the two young women was very beneficial. Then there were the three grandchildren, two boys, and after 1827 a girl. Goethe, who had always been fond of children, loved them and took a friendly and active interest in them. They brought light and laughter into the great house. To be sure, the position of the son in this domestic community was difficult enough. How could this mediocre man have maintained himself in comparison with his overpowering father, on whose very rank and influence the civil existence of the son depended? Goethe did nothing, it appears, to increase these difficulties. He patiently endeavored to mitigate and counterbalance what was unalterable in the life of his beloved, only son. August helped him considerably with the labors entailed by his superintendence of the scientific and artistic institutions at Weimar and Jena. After 1823 he bore the title of Privy Councilor. The son's chief activity, insofar as he was not engrossed by small offices at court, consisted more and more in serving his father as executive assistant in all private and official affairs. All his energies were devoted to this service.

The inner realm of Goethe's life, his productive career, demanded assistants of another type—cultivated and scholarly men who were capable of assisting in the composition and publication of his books. The eldest of these collaborators was Dr. Friedrich Wilhelm Riemer, an erudite philologist, an expert in ancient languages and literatures, who had lived in Goethe's house for almost ten years as August's tutor, and had then remained in Weimar as teacher in the Gymnasium. He also accompanied Goethe several times on his journeys to the Bohemian spas, and on these occasions functioned as secretary. But above all Riemer took an active part in Goethe's literary and scientific labors, and collaborated in the editions of Goethe's works by making stylistic corrections and performing practical editorial duties. Wilhelm von Humboldt said of him that he was the proper "assistant of the great man" and was in the habit of saying "we" when he spoke of their joint labor. To what degree this man was dominated in his own thinking and producing by the spirit of the master (insofar as he was capable of grasping it) is shown by the *Mitteilungen über Goethe* which he published in 1841. Goethe appointed him, together with Johann Peter Eckermann, administrator of his literary remains.

Eckermann had come to Weimar quite late, in 1823, and had been readily accepted as collaborator by the poet, who was in despair at his excessive load of work. Eckermann was not as learned as Riemer, but more sensitively organized and more highly gifted. This "very good, sensitive, and intelligent" man "cultivated himself up to" Goethe and also wrote a book about him. Modest as his position in Weimar was, and many as were the personal sacrifices which it demanded, the possibility of remaining so near the adored great poet and of serving him was a happy dispensation for this delicate, effeminate man. Goethe's friends thought him only a sort of "faithful little subaltern of a man" with modest talent (so Sulpiz Boisserée calls him). But his master knew well that his shyness concealed a "simple pure soul, which would likewise prefer to be pure with itself and the world." His true worth was not quickly or easily revealed. It is to the devotion of this faithful servant that we owe the book which is without parallel in all the world's literature, the *Gespräche mit Goethe in den letzten Jahren seines Lebens* ("Conversations with Goethe in the Last Years of his Life"; 1836).

With Goethe's consent Eckermann had begun to write down his conversations with the poet as early as 1824. It then took nine years before the material for the two first volumes was in shape. He himself said that the work was to be regarded rather as Goethe's, as a spoken work, than his own. But even as a literary achievement Eckermann's book may claim acceptance as an original production. The genuineness of the whole is not to be doubted, even though the individual reports are not reliable in the same degree. These failings are to be explained by the history of the book's genesis. Clumsy at writing, easily blocked by personal and material difficulties, Eckermann did not make his notes into a coherent work until two years after Goethe's death. From unused remainders a third, weaker portion was published (1848); for this volume Eckermann also used the notes of others. Not everything is faithful reproduction. Sometimes conversations are reconstructed from memory on the basis of fragmentary notes; some of the material is actually original, poetic imitation. But in some fashion or other, nevertheless, everything pertains to the spirit of the poet. The receptive disciple is so steeped in that spirit that he is even able to speak in the manner of the master. To be sure, Eckermann painted his own subjective portrait of Goethe, and it is this which he wishes to transmit to posterity. It is the portrait of a sublime Olympian.

The principal business of the poet's last decade, in which Eckermann, Riemer, and other collaborators assisted, was the preparation of the definitive edition of Goethe's works, which had been in progress since 1824. From 1827 on this edition appeared in regular installments. It was not only to include a complete collection of all his writings, even minor and forgotten ones; by its arrangement it was also "to bring into clear view the author's make-up, education, progress, and manifold experiments in all directions." The great undertaking was not completed until ten years after Goethe's death, under the supervision of Riemer and Eckermann. It comprises no less than sixty volumes. Goethe had chosen as its title *Vollständige Ausgabe letzter Hand* ("Complete Edition"), for everywhere in it the final corrections were made, and for each individual work the definitive version was fixed which the author wished to remain unaltered in all future editions. Several works, for example, the second version of the *Wanderjahre* and the second part of *Faust,* were completed especially for this edition.

Two other men belonged to the circle of Goethe's intimates and regular visitors, though not to the group of permanent collaborators. They, too, left notes of their conversations with Goethe. Frédéric Soret, a young scientist from Geneva, had come to Weimar in 1822 as tutor to Prince Karl Alexander. He came into close contact with Goethe chiefly because he was the only man in the Weimar circle with whom Goethe could have technical discussions of his geological interests. Soret translated into French Goethe's treatise on the metamorphosis of plants. The notes which he had written concerning his conversations with Goethe were used by Eckermann for his collection. But when combined with Soret's letters these notes in themselves make an interesting and important book, giving the account of an intellectually independent young man who was better able to observe and to judge impartially and critically because he derived from a different cultural environment.

Even more important than Soret's notes are those of the Weimar Minister of Justice, Chancellor Friedrich von Müller. During Goethe's last decades von Müller visited him regularly and wrote down their conversations immediately. He too was an independent thinker, who,

Neue Pinakothek, Munich *Photograph by Hanfstaengl*

JOHANN WOLFGANG VON GOETHE, 1828

BY JOSEPH KARL STIELER

with all his reverence for the great man, ventures to see and to reproduce him in all his human aspects. In several respects von Müller's *Unterhaltungen* merit preference over Eckermann's collection. The vigorous, practical personality of the Chancellor was by nature more adequate to its phenomenal subject. But Eckermann, on the other hand, has a finer sense for the really productive aspects of Goethe's nature. Therefore he managed what von Müller could not do: by his intelligent sympathy, as Goethe gratefully acknowledged, he helped bring it about that the poet resumed work on abandoned projects like that of *Faust*. Thus Eckermann exercised in a lesser degree the promotional function whereby Schiller had proven so helpful in Goethe's middle period.

That despite his great age Goethe continued to be so enormously productive, and was even able to do justice to the new demands which every day thrust upon him, was surely first and foremost the result of the inexhaustible energy of his nature. But even this energy could not have produced so colossal a yield if Goethe had not schooled himself to wisdom and the discipline of gearing his daily life entirely to its achievement. "It is now my highest duty to circumscribe my activity more and more." Often enough he spoke of the solitude of old age.

An aged man is always like King Lear!
Who shared your doings, hand in hand,
Long since went down the highway;
Who loved and grieved at your command
Is courting in another byway.
Just for its own sake youth is with us here;
It would be folly to demand:
Come, age with me, my dear.[1]

But Goethe never became unsocial. There has scarcely ever been a great poet who like him remained in his old age in contact with his contemporaries, young and old. After the beginning of the twenties, he ceased visiting the homes of his Weimar friends; after 1823, he also gave up his customary trip to the baths and his habitual sojourn in

[1] Ein alter Mann ist stets ein König Lear!— / Was Hand in Hand mitwirkte, stritt, / Ist längst vorbeigegangen; / Was mit und an dir liebte, litt, / Hat sich wo anders angehangen. / Die Jugend ist um ihretwillen hier; / Es wäre töricht, zu verlangen: / Komm, ältele du mit mir. (*Zahme Xenien*, translated by B. Q. Morgan.)

Jena. But people came to him: his house never grew empty of visitors, and there were always guests at his table. Without being a glutton, Goethe liked the pleasures of eating. Friends sent him the delicacies of their region: young turnips from Berlin, artichokes and good wines from the Rhineland. To share enjoyments with others always afforded his hospitable nature the highest satisfaction. The number of visitors who came to Weimar from all countries in order to see Goethe was constantly on the increase. And they were welcome. For they served the old man as a substitute for the journeys which were no longer possible. And if they took from him many an hour, if they sometimes disturbed and bored him, nevertheless on the total reckoning he found that he profited much. It was entertaining for him to have "physiognomies, speech, behavior of the most diverse sorts" march past. Often enough he received important people, from whom his eternally inquisitive mind could learn something new. Indeed, he was of the opinion that one could learn more from good conversations than from books. Only people with eyeglasses had trouble with him. More than others they gave him the impression that people wanted to spy on him or gape at him as at some big animal. This was the hardest thing for him to bear.

To intelligent visitors he liked to show the art treasures which he had collected with great care and expertness. His greatest fondness was for etchings. He owned about four thousand originals, among them a large number of beautiful works by such great masters as Dürer, Rembrandt, and Schongauer. Even more precious and choice was his collection of drawings (about two thousand). He loved to spend quiet evenings studying these works "in which at least the spirit of the artist always shines forth, even though his other achievements were much greater." He also collected bronzes and majolica vessels, and above all portrait medallions. In his will of 1831 he explains the significance which this hobby had for his spiritual existence: "I have not collected for the sake of whim and caprice but always with a plan and a purpose for my consistent education, and I have learned something from every piece I own." Here, too, there is probable evidence of the effect of his profound need of learning wherever possible not by report and book but by the immediate scrutiny of things themselves.

The impression which Goethe made in conversation has been described by many visitors. Those he did not know he met at first with a rather stiff dignity. The same sort of conventional politeness, congealed into a set of impersonal formulas, is also to be found in the letters of his later period. He comported himself in about the same manner when he gave an evening party for important guests in his house. Such was the experience of Grillparzer on his visit to Weimar in 1826. "Finally a side door opened and he himself entered. Dressed in black, the star of his order upon his breast, erect and almost stiff of posture; he came among us like a monarch giving audience." It is obvious that this was a mask by which the famous man sought to protect himself from importunate curiosity. If the visitor did not succeed in penetrating this reserve and arousing the interest of the great man, the mask was not laid aside. But if Goethe sensed that the embarrassed visitor who sat beside him on the sofa in the reception room was in earnest and himself a person of worth, there soon developed a conversation which the visitor never forgot his life long. Such is the report of many visitors. Even with important people Goethe did not enter easily into a natural conversation. But if one managed to find the right approach, then (as Mme de Staël says) his moods, indecision, and stiffness were only like clouds which float along the foot of the mountain upon which a genius dwells. Many have praised the agreeable sound of his voice, as well as his manner of speaking. "He spoke slowly and comfortably, somewhat as one thinks of the speech of an aged monarch. One could tell that he is self-assured and above praise and blame" (Eckermann, June 10, 1823). Goethe liked to have fun with his intimates and friends, and would indulge in intentional or hypochondriac paradoxes, defending sophistically and ironically the most contrary views. If the others showed themselves unskilled or inadequate in the understanding of his writings, he would tease and twit them. Then he might deride them, saying, "You poor things, if you were only not so stupid!"

Even greater than the quantity of visitors was the number of those in all the countries of Europe with whom Goethe exchanged letters. A special group comprised the scientific correspondents, both professionals and amateurs, with whom he exchanged information or who sent him rare pieces, above all minerals and stones, for his collections. He maintained a regular and intimate correspondence with the bosom friend of his old age, the Berlin musician, Karl Friedrich Zelter, who also came to Weimar frequently to visit him. Because of his vigorous, cultivated good sense, Zelter enjoyed Goethe's high esteem as conversational partner. When he traveled Zelter would send detailed and vivid reports, which Goethe enjoyed particularly. But the bulk of the letters from Goethe's last two decades show him as the great man who was forced by the excessive amount of such obligations, as well as by the decline of mental suppleness, to restrict himself to the forms of well-bred politeness. His letters in this style are models of discretion (as touching both Goethe himself and his fellow men). He permits himself no sharp or vehement word; anything that might offend or lead to disputes is carefully avoided. From long experience he had ceased to expect others to think as he thought, since he himself had grown too old to adopt the views of others. For him it was enough to find out how people thought and what they did in the world about him. He now thought that it was folly to expect people to agree with us; an irreconcilable antagonism between ways of thinking was something one must reckon with. He had learned long ago that one's knowledge and understanding is in the first instance only a personal acquisition, and that one involves himself immediately in contradiction and quarreling when he gives it expression. Concerning many things, he once remarked to Boisserée (August 2, 1815), one can never make himself completely understood; hence he frequently told himself that concerning this or that matter he could only speak with God and that it was none of the world's business. "Either the world grasps my way of thinking or it does not, and in the latter case all of humanity will avail me nothing."

This conciliatory spirit embraced, to be sure, a large measure of skepticism and of bitterly acquired resignation. It also reduced his inclination to personal confession and his desire to win others over to his own views. If he found it necessary to express a dissenting opinion, he did so in a manner which eluded all discussion. Even to his friends Goethe persisted generally in the somewhat mannered epistolary style which he had developed. Then, so that a familiar, cordial element should not be wholly lacking, at the close of the letter a phrase is added which is indeed stereotyped but still like a handshake. Such closing formulas are: "Ever yours," "With constant interest," "Faithfully yours," "Unalterably yours." Or he writes with solemn cordiality, "Peace and joy to all well-wishers, especially those near and allied."

Letter writing was not for Goethe (as, for example, for Rilke) a part of his literary production. Here, as in his intercourse with friends and visitors, he even decided how much time he was willing to give to it. If one were to answer every letter and read every book sent him, he said, one would go bankrupt. He set an ever higher estimation upon the value of time. "In the end our life is like the Sibylline books; the less of it there is left, the more precious it becomes" (to C. L. F. Schultz, June 29, 1829). To be active as long as the day lasted: this he regarded as the governing precept of his life. The course of his day was determined by that. On New Year's Eve in 1829, the year in which Goethe had come to be eighty, he wrote in his diary: "Continued with my occupation and so completed the year." And two years later, not long before his death, the tireless old man remarked: "I keep learning; only thus do I notice that I grow older" (to Zelter, September 17, 1831). And so it remained to the end: he had to be active in order to live. His diaries show how lively his interests remained, how fresh his receptivity. On the average he read a book a day. In a letter written in 1826 to his friend Sulpiz Boisserée, who was his junior by a generation, this undiminished pleasure in learning and creating, thinking and doing, and the principle involved therein is given magnificent expression:

Since God and his nature have left me to myself through so many years, I know nothing better to do than to express my grateful acknowledgment by youthful activity. I wish, as long as it may be granted me, to show myself worthy of the good fortune which has been vouchsafed me, and I devote day and night to thinking and doing, to the extent that it is possible and so that it may be possible. Day and night is no mere phrase, for a good many night hours which I spend sleeplessly, in keeping with the vicissitudes of my age, I devote not to vague and unspecific thoughts but to precise consideration of what is to be done on the morrow, which I then begin faithfully in the morning and execute as far as possible. And so, perhaps, I accomplish more and, by planning, complete in the days allotted to me what one fails to do at a period when one has the right to believe or to fancy that there is still a tomorrow and always a tomorrow.[2]

[2] Da mich Gott und seine Natur so viele Jahre mir selbst gelassen haben, so weiss ich nichts Besseres zu tun, als meine dankbare Anerkennung durch jugendliche Tätigkeit auszudrücken. Ich will des mir gegönnten Glücks, so lange es mir auch gewährt sein mag, mich würdig erzeigen und ich verwende Tag und Nacht auf Denken und Tun, wie und damit es möglich sei. Tag und Nacht ist keine Phrase, denn gar manche nächtliche Stunden, die dem Schicksale meines Alters gemäss ich schlaflos zubringe, widme ich nicht vagen und allgemeinen Gedanken, sondern ich betrachte genau, was den nächsten Tag zu tun? das ich denn auch

In what way could he be more useful to the world than by keeping himself productive? It was for the sake of this supremely important occupation that he shut himself off from his world as often as it was necessary. For its sake he endeavored to avoid experiences which would disturb the tranquillity of his mind and mood.

Even Goethe's contemporaries found it difficult to accept his very human behavior in the face of suffering and death, and posterity has never ceased to sit in judgment upon it. On the death of Goethe's mother, Bettina writes: "People say that you like to turn away from what is sad, from what cannot be changed . . ." That was indeed his nature and had always been. "I was reluctant to see her, the sight of suffering pains me," we read in *Hermann und Dorothea.* The passage goes on to say that it is better to avoid sad pictures, lest fear and care ("which are more hateful to me than the evil itself") should coerce the heart and cripple the spirit. Just as there are men whose moral feeling is so highly developed that the slightest deviation from the true and the good causes them severe torment, so Goethe's feeling for the beauty of the human form was developed to the most refined sensitivity. In that form he revered the highest achievement of the creative God-Nature. Disfigurations such as those caused by suffering and death made the strongest impression upon him, which then would paralyze him for a long time. "Distaste for everything pathological seems to increase more and more with the years" (to Karl August, February 25, 1821). When Ottilie took a fall and her face was disfigured by her injuries, Goethe was unwilling to see her in that state. He apologized for his behavior by saying that he could never get rid of such impressions. "In regard to my sensory perceptivity the character of my make-up is so singular that I retain all outlines and forms most sharply and definitely in my memory, but at the same time find myself affected most violently by deformities and defects" (Conversation with F. von Müller, May 17, 1826). Similarly, he did not like to look at caricatures, nor at faces twisted into grimaces. At his age, he thought, the disposition could not recover easily; hence he must surround himself with impressions of serenity. He avoided looking at the dead, if it were at all possible to do so.

---

redlich am Morgen beginne und so weit es möglich durchführe. Und so tu ich vielleicht mehr und vollende sinnig in zugemessenen Tagen, was man zu einer Zeit versäumt, wo man das Recht hat, zu glauben oder zu wähnen, es gebe noch Wiedermorgen und Immermorgen.

> Who'll take this picture from my seeing eyes?
> I have beheld thee dead! 'Tis thus thou wilt
> Appear to me in many a day and night.[3]

It was from visual experience that faith, courage, and creative energy flowed to the "Augen-Mensch." That all being existed in some form or shape, and only so, was for him the basic phenomenon of life, which he never tired of admiring. In form he saw, as H. Wölfflin puts it, nothing less than "the guaranty of life." Strong, healthy life could exist only where the form in which it had attained independent existence was pure and beautiful. The ugly, the formless, the caricature denoted anti-nature. The distortions of suffering pointed to sick life.

Well as his body withstood the afflictions characteristic of the raw climate of his homeland and the many serious illnesses by which he was visited in his old age, his constitution was nevertheless delicate and sensitive. He had learned to live in a manner which sought to compensate as much as possible for his innate sensitivity. He was living on a strict "diet" and keeping himself calm, he once said in a letter from Rome, in order that the effect of things upon him might be pure. What he means is a spiritual diet, and it was a part of this diet that he consistently avoided all impressions which disturbed his inner composure. To refrain from such impressions, to guard against paralyzing shocks, seemed to him permissible and even necessary, if he was to keep emotion and imagination, all the powers of poetic creativity, in a pure and vigorous state. If one chooses to regard this as a kind of egotism, it was only of that sort which all great creators, each after his own fashion, have displayed. The conditions under which the artist, the poet, can be productive are of a very special character. If the creative man himself did not do everything possible to make and maintain these conditions, many works would have to remain unborn. One who is made for extraordinary achievements cannot live in ordinary fashion, nor can he rely upon the favor of fortune. The habits which appear eccentric and the actions which seem strange to those for whom the poet creates find their explanation in the extraordinary works which grow out of such necessary, though always problematical, conditions.

But we may not think that Goethe was saved from taking upon

[3] Wer nimmt das Bild von meinen Augen weg! / Dich hab' ich tot gesehn! So wirst du mir / An manchem Tag, in mancher Nacht erscheinen. (*Die natürliche Tochter*, Act I, scene 6, translated by B. Q. Morgan.)

himself the measure of suffering which life metes out to everyone. In extreme old age, when it fell to him to comfort a father whose daughter had met with a grave misfortune, he said: "There are moments so cruel that they might cause one to regard the brevity of life as the greatest blessing, so as not to have to feel an intolerable torment for an excessive length of time.—Many sufferers have departed before me, but upon me was imposed the duty of holding out and of bearing a succession of joys and pains, of which a single one might well have been fatal."[4] But he adds that in such cases he had endeavored to parry the thrust of fate by increased activity.

It was the eighty-year-old Goethe whom sorrow was to strike most heavily. On a journey to Rome which had been intended as a cure for spiritual suffering, his son was unexpectedly taken from him by a physical ailment. When the shocking news was communicated to the father, he only remarked, using a Latin expression, "I knew that I had begotten a mortal." But in a letter to Zelter, his confidant, he gives vent to his sorrow, saying that in truth no one can be considered happy before his death. "Expect trials to the last." Fate, he wrote, treats man as if he were woven out of wire; in such a situation "the great concept of duty" must sustain us. "The body must, the spirit will." But his agitation led to collapse. Goethe suffered a serious hemorrhage. Two months later he was again master of his powers: "Over graves and forward!" Life tried him, as it does every other man. Once, he relates, an experienced judge of men, on seeing him for the first time, said of him: "Voilà un homme qui a eu de grands chagrins." Goethe translated this in his way: "There's another who has taken life hard."

If Goethe withdrew more and more into the realm of the arts and sciences and participated as little as possible in the political life of his day, this, too, was one of the ways in which this all too sensitive man sought to secure his inner equilibrium. For him politics was a sphere of lesser value, in which he had increasingly less desire to play an active part as the years passed. The first stirrings of the liberal movement he viewed with decided distaste. His reaction referred entirely to the moral aspect of the events. To him presumption and recalci-

[4] Es gibt so grausame Augenblicke, in welchen man die Kürze des Lebens für die höchste Wohltat halten möchte, um eine unerträgliche Qual nicht übermässig lange zu empfinden.—Viele Leidende sind vor mir hingegangen, mir aber war die Pflicht auferlegt, auszudauern und eine Folge von Freude und Schmerz zu ertragen, wovon das Einzelne wohl schon hätte tödlich sein können. (To C. D. Rauch, October 21, 1827.)

trance seemed to be the principal causes of the excitement which prevailed among academic youth after the period of the Wars of Liberation. He could see in these phenomena only degenerate forms of an individualism based upon the idea of personal freedom, and an excess of abstract idealism characteristic of the German intelligentsia. The English pleased him better, because of their great practical sense and their energy; so did the cosmopolitan sociability and the moderate progressiveness of contemporary French youth. He approved of a clear, energetic "spirit of the age," such as was expressed in the liberal periodical, *Le Globe,* which he valued highly. By contrast with the ripe culture of a thoroughly civilized nation, the Germans seemed to him a people only "of yesterday." But then in 1830 the July Revolution broke out, and Goethe saw in it only a great new calamity. Now he gave up even this last attempt on his part to take a positive view of the political ferments of the age. On the day the news of the events at Paris reached Weimar, Soret visited the old man, and Goethe spoke of the volcano which had finally erupted. It turned out that he meant the scientific dispute between Cuvier and Geoffroy Saint-Hilaire. That other event, he said, did not concern him. His strenuous effort to limit himself to spiritual matters, as having the only real importance, and not to let himself be kept from that even by a revolution, led to still another eccentricity. In that same year Goethe ceased to read newspapers. To Zelter he wrote (April 29, 1830) that it was "only Philistinism to devote too much attention to what does not concern us"; he had saved many hours for his own labors by this abstinence; new ideas of great significance had dawned upon him which must still be put into words. "And so, as long as there is time, let us not occupy ourselves with trivialities."

It was inevitable that this attitude should give the greatest offense to the German liberals. Goethe lived long enough to find himself publicly accused and condemned. The political writers who came to the front around 1830—a new type in Germany—spoke in tones of moral reproof of the old gentleman's disinterest in political movements and social conditions. Ludwig Börne, the most radical moralist among them, turned Goethe's own verses from the Prometheus ode against him: he had not endeavored to allay the pain of the afflicted, to still the tears of the suffering. He ought to have been, like Jean Paul, "the poet of the lowly, the singer of the poor," and to have cast his great prestige into the scales in the struggle against the reactionary policy of Metternich and the German princes. Instead, "Privy Councilor von Goethe" was playing the cold aristocrat and the lackey of the princes. "You were given a lofty mind: have you ever put baseness to shame? Heaven gave you a tongue of fire: have you ever defended the right?" But Börne, in his zeal, says nothing of the fact that by means of his works Goethe, more than any other poet, had mitigated Philistine stupidity, fought the cultural narrow-mindedness of the German middle class, and in general had made the feeling of the intelligentsia elevated and free, their aspirations pure and noble. For Börne, Goethe's "aristocratism" was the greatest obstacle on the road to freedom.

The nationalist enthusiasts were of a similar opinion. They did not understand that through him (as Ludwig Tieck put it) "everything German had been transfigured, that through him the fatherland had, so to speak, come into existence and been discovered in the consciousness of men." They did not see that it was Goethe who first attained world-wide esteem and influence for the German spirit, and that he was able to fulfill his cosmopolitan mission only because he had outgrown the national sphere and its goals. His fatherland was "the good, the noble, the beautiful, which is tied to no special province and to no special country" (to Eckermann, March 1832). Then there was also a party of pious bigots, whose protagonist was the Pastor Pustkuchen, the author of the spurious *Wanderjahre*. He called Goethe a skillful virtuoso and a licentious corrupter of youth. An ephemerally successful scribbler of his day and a Teutonic reactionary, Wolfgang Menzel, even had the insolence to call Goethe an unmanly, materialistic epicure, and to deny him any true genius—talent, but no character. Heine, too, had all sorts of things to say against Goethe. He found his attitude too "objective" and thought that an age of enthusiasm and action could make no use of him. But to the insignificant people who denied Goethe's genius, Heine replied sarcastically that one must at all events admit that Goethe now and again had had the talent to be a genius. Goethe made no direct and special response to these demonstrations of hostility. "What would become of the beautiful days of life still vouchsafed me if I should take notice of everything which is directed against me and mine in my dear homeland?" (to F. von Müller, May 21, 1830). Only in the verses of the *Zahme Xenien* did he strike back, with conscious superiority. But he was wounded by the misunderstanding and the ill will. "A German writer, a German martyr!" He took solace in the fact that after all other writers fared similarly among their own countrymen—Molière, Rousseau, Voltaire, even Byron, whom the hatred of the Philistines had driven out of England (to Eckermann, March 14, 1830).

He had too often been made aware of how difficult it was for him to reach the German public with his works to have any illusions concerning the extent of his influence. He knew that he could never become popular in his own country, above all when he was urging something new upon his readers. As an author, he said, he had always found himself isolated, because only those of his works which were already familiar were effective, and he had been able to find no sympathy for his new works. *Tasso,* for example, was played in Berlin only after twenty years, whereas dramatic rubbish such as Kotzebue's pieces were given performances year in and year out. Since neither "commonplace feeling" nor commonplace morals were to be found in his writings, the Philistines ("and their name is legion") did not know what to make of them. "The Germans always found him offensive" (Nietzsche). Nor did the moralizing censure of his works die out after his death. "Men do not know how to receive gratefully, either from God or from nature or from their fellow man, that which is inestimable" (to Zelter, March 9, 1831). With all this, Goethe was as free from the professional jealousy as from the professional vanity of the author. Whereas others liked to regard his life as all of one piece, to himself it seemed more fragmentary the older he grew—so he wrote a half year before his death. He had early accustomed himself to a "disdain of success" (as Mme de Staël puts it); but this applied only to the success of the moment. To true success, as he himself said, he was by no means indifferent; on the contrary, faith in it had been the guiding star in all his labors. "I should wish never to have written a single verse if thousands and thousands of people reading my works did not think something in connection with them, in addition to them, out of them, or into them" (to Zelter, April 14, 1816). Nor did he lack cultivated readers. For the small community of the finest spirits in all Europe he was—and the tendency to this view became increasingly wide-spread in the last years of his life—the incomparable, the greatest poet and sage of the Western world. Schelling thought that Goethe alone among the poets of his age had rediscovered the way to "the primal founts of poesy." At Goethe's death, Carlyle, speaking for Europe, said that this man had been a poet in a sense true of no other poet in centuries. "That melody of life, with its cunning tones, which took captive ear and heart, has gone silent."

Faust

IN THE COUNTRIES OF THE EUROPEAN CONTINENT THERE ARE BUILDINGS, SUCH AS CHURCHES, OF SPECIAL TYPE. CENTURIES HAVE BUILT AT THEM, AND TO THE expert they show the entire historical sequence of the great periods of architecture. The age when men built in the Romanesque style began them; they were then continued in the Gothic or in the Renaissance style, and completed according to the taste of the Baroque. Such edifices yield no uniform impression; they are hardly to be grasped as a whole. Though individual parts may show one of the styles in pronounced purity, the motley variety of the whole seems to lack an organizing principle. But there the buildings stand, great and enduring, requiring no justification by strict artistic taste. And so, paradoxical as is their existence to the spectator who demands unity and integrity, and baffling as are the problems which such curiosities present, nevertheless the structures may for that very reason possess a charm which a work created in a single unified style does not have.

Somewhat similar is the impression which *Faust* has made in the century which has elapsed since Goethe gave to the world this most problematical of his works. Again and again there have been readers who believed that the multiplicity could eventually be comprehended as a single whole; and there have been others who, despite the efforts which they have devoted to the understanding of individual details, have in the end despaired of passing successfully from the confusing details to the presupposed center. Equally immoderate admiration and rejection have been the lot of *Faust*. For some have exalted this play of God, man, and the devil not only above Goethe's other works, but even above everything that Western literature has produced since

Shakespeare; whereas others have questioned its merit as they have no other poetic work of equal rank. Since Dante's epic poems and Shakespeare's dramas no work has been discussed so frequently and with such ardor. But neither in detail nor in their conception of the meaning of the whole have the commentators reached sufficient agreement to enable us to speak of an assured interpretation. Understanding and misunderstanding appear to cancel each other, and it looks as if no interpretation will ever be reached with which all commentators and critics will be satisfied.

But is this not true of all works of literature, from the most complex to the smallest poem? Words are images, symbols; they are not the thoughts and emotions which they represent. Their meaning, their significance, must be apprehended by the reader; but such apprehending is itself a productive and hence a personal act. Even the divine spirit must speak through the medium of the Word. But the word, *any* word, may have many meanings. From divergent interpretations of Holy Writ, cleavages, sects, even church schisms have developed; and yet all invoke the one "Word of God." A special art and science of interpretation, theology, has taken as its task the correct understanding of the basic writings, and still it seems not to be able to come to a definite end of the matter. Infinite as is the problem in itself, it is further complicated by human inadequacies. In the realm of literature no amount of diligence or of knowledge will avail if the interpreter does not possess sufficient sensitivity to comprehend a work of imagination, if his spirit is not strong enough to hear the voice of the spirit which speaks through the poet. The great work of art opens only to him who possesses the gift and the art of unlocking it. But of *Faust* Goethe himself said that it was "enigmatic enough." Many interpretations are inadequate simply because they have been attempted by people incapable of rising to the region to which this great poem belongs. But who is equal to this task? Our experience is like that of scientists with the enigmas of nature: despite all defeats we cannot cease in our attempts to scale the gigantic mountain. And indeed not all attempts have been fruitless. The toil of a century has laid roads upon which we may now advance with assurance and comfort for a goodly stretch. It has also become clear what ways lead us astray. But the final path, the one to the pinnacle, each man must seek out for himself. Who is to decide whether the ring that has been found is the true ring? Who knows whether anyone will ever find it?

Goethe was about twenty years old when the figure of Faust first began to stir his imagination. Among his earliest dramatic plans was one for a Faust tragedy. But in the end he had to give a whole life to the accomplishment of the task. Goethe was eighty-two when he resolved to regard the gigantic work as completed, in order that he might bring it to an end at last. Among the great works of modern literature there is no other whose growth extended over such a long period of time. The poet himself regarded its genesis as remarkable and unique. A year before the termination of *Faust* he said it would be droll enough if he should live to see it completed. He almost failed to do so, for not many months after its completion he died.

Such a work cannot be all of one piece, either artistically or spiritually; both in details and as a whole it must show traces of the development through which the author himself passed in the course of his long life. The first part appeared in 1808, the second not until twenty-four years later. The work which the youthful titanic "genius" had begun, which the master of the classical school had continued, was completed by an aged man who had grown beyond the bounds of his age. No wonder that even in style this drama shows the most variegated diversity imaginable! Most of Part I is written in verse, although there is also a scene in realistic prose. The verses themselves derive in part from the old German tradition (*Knittelverse*). But in addition there are also some passages in blank verse and in free rhythms, such as Goethe employed in the hymns of his youth, as well as stanzas in the manner of the folk song. Even more variegated is the rhythmical picture of the second part. Here one finds blank verse, alexandrines, the *terza rima* of Dante, Greek meters, arias and choruses in operatic style, and again the doggerel of *Knittelverse*. Equally colorful is the variety of language in Part II. Between opposite poles of blunt realism and the most artistic stylization, all forms of expression are represented which the age of classicism and romanticism had renewed or created. The poet moves with equal mastery on all linguistic levels. A parade of forms passes before us; none richer can be imagined, but also none more confusing. One must imagine the impression which would be produced by a piece of music in which all styles of operatic composition might be found, from Gluck and Mozart to Richard Wagner's early works. And yet this diversity has sufficient formal coherence to enable it to maintain itself as one whole.

The inner form, the compositional scheme of the drama, which is a coalescence of widely disparate portions, consists in its representation of the life-course of a total personality in its principal stages—the totality of life which is as broad as the world itself. In this respect *Faust* is eminently modern, and not to be compared with any of the great dramas of ancient or modern times. It is the phenomena of becoming, of development, which have attracted the chief interest of European thinkers in their study of nature as well as history since the eighteenth century. The emergence of this interest is no less marked in literature. Poems are now written which reflect symbolically the processes of the soul. A new genre, the novel of development, describes the process of individual maturation and the ripening of personality. The nature of life is to be understood from its processes. It is thought that life can be better grasped in the process of gradual, constant becoming, in the succession of germinating, maturing, and dying, than in its results. This mode of thought is directed (as Fichte says) to the "viewing of the genesis." Now men begin to consider both the course of human history and the development of personality according to the analogy of biological processes of growth. It was only in connection with this new evolutionary thought that such works as *Wilhelm Meister* and *Faust* could be planned and created.

But Goethe's drama is a drama of development in a twofold sense. It sets forth the development of the hero and at the same time reflects the author's own development. The stages of Faust's life correspond to those of Goethe's inner being, his growth as a poet, as a thinker, as a personality. Every phase of this process contributed to the structure of the work. The conflict of the hero, in which the action originates, had been the conflict of Goethe's own youth: Faust's striving for the Absolute, his voluntary submergence into the stream of life, his falling into guilt; then subjugation and intensification of his strength by the encounter with the beautiful; and finally the highest satisfaction in the sphere of action—all of these things were experiences by which Goethe's personality was formed, insights to which he had attained as his spirit matured.

(As he introduces himself to us at the beginning of the play,[1] Faust is tortured by his dangerously increasing opposition to a civilization in which heart and senses have become subjected to the dictatorship of practical reason and the mind to a rational conception of the world and life.) What Faust expresses here is the problem of Goethe's generation: the weakening of vital energies by excessive intellectualization, despair of the value of science and of methodical thought in general. As a reaction there develops a passionate longing for the simple vigor of nature, for warm sensual experience. To this time dates Herder's remark that he did not exist in order to think, but "to be, to feel, to live, to rejoice!" It is of such disillusionments and yearnings that the figure of Faust is compounded, as he stands before us at the beginning of the play. Goethe gave him the vehemence, the unrestraint which shook at the bounds of humanity, things which he himself felt at the time. What the rational age called life could not really be life.

But what then was life? Where was there an enjoyment of existence that was more than illusion, a road to living nature which led farther than professional learning? Faust has had enough of the pedantry of the university faculties. He does not want the abstract concept, nor the laborious agencies of analytical research. His spirit struggles, as Schelling says, "for a view of primal nature and of the eternal inwardness of its manifestations." The practices of unorthodox science, of white magic, are to bring his spirit into direct contact with the spirit world, which operates invisibly in nature. This is the secret way to the mysteries of life, which the Magi-legends of the Christian centuries still looked upon as forbidden and called black magic. But even these legends show admiration for the intrepidity of a spirit that is great enough to try to wrest nature's secret from her, mingled with pious horror at the sinner who wishes to reveal what God has hidden from men.

Faust, who knows the magic practices, summons the Earth Spirit, the personification of creative forces in the earthly sphere. But this "superman" cannot endure the monstrous phenomenon, cannot grasp the essence of the spirit. Again he finds himself thrown back upon himself. But he is not made for resignation, not made to be merely

[1] The oldest version of the first part, the *Urfaust,* is dealt with in the chapter on German drama, pages 20–23 above.

a worm crawling in the dust. Better to have no life at all than a petty one. The false enthusiasm of a despair which turns into a lust for death is banished by the Easter message of the risen Christ, who has overcome suffering and death. The problematical unbeliever recalls how as a child he trusted the loving Father who holds the world in his hand. But if this is enough to recall the desperate man to life, it does not heal his wounds nor quiet his longing for a spirit which should have wings to raise itself aloft out of the prison of a physically and spiritually limited world, to see the God who moves the world from within. Again, and still more violently, Faust is prostrated by the realization of how illusory is his longing for happiness, for true knowledge, for communion with the All-God. Deeply disillusioned as he now is, he loses all desire for this existence which seems too wretched to fulfill the highest wishes of ideal aspiration. In vague foreknowledge, he translates for himself the opening of the Gospel according to St. John with the words "In the beginning was the deed." But he himself has not yet learned what a vigorous action can wrest from life. He has now sunk into the deepest despair. In a highly emotional scene he curses the feeling which prevented him from seeking death, curses every sensation and sentiment which bind him to life: the faith of the spirit in itself, the seductive beauty of the world, the striving for fame and permanence, for possession and enjoyment, and finally even the feelings and forces which are most positive in the eyes of Christianity: love and hope, faith and enduring patience. But this extreme despair is not the end of his existence. The will to live is indestructible, and the hope which he has abjured is abiding. It appears that even now he is ready to attempt, for one last time, to find out whether despite everything some meaning that is worthwhile may be extracted from life.

After this return to life there follows the pact which Faust concludes with Mephisto. However, his old despair still asserts itself, but the fact that this will cause the despondent man to sacrifice his soul does not trouble him. The earth and its pleasure are to him the greatest good. Should man for the sake of eternity throw away the world whose child he is? Even if he has stood powerless before the genius of creating Nature, he feels himself infinitely superior to the spirit of annihilation because of his world-worship and his urge for life. What does Mephisto know about that which gives a man his worth but which is at the same time the source of his sufferings? And so Faust does not let the conditions of the pact be prescribed for him; rather he determines them for himself. According to the legend, Faust's soul was to belong to the Devil after the expiration of a specific period. But in Goethe's work a condition is set which gives the transaction an altogether different and higher meaning. If Faust's diabolical companion succeeds in lulling to sleep the hero's "ideal striving" by means of the pleasures which he is able to offer, then the rest shall belong to him. Furthermore, and with a new implication: if skepticism is wrong and life can indeed grant a moment which would make all succeeding moments insipid and empty, a moment into which the fullness of existence appears to have been compressed, so incomparable that one would wish it to endure forever—for such a moment Faust will gladly surrender eternity. But this is not meant as positively as it sounds. For Faust adds that if the urge to life in him should ever be stilled, if his will should, in eternal dissatisfaction, no longer strive for something higher and highest, then he would no longer be himself. How is it possible for him to imagine that it would ever come to that? Must he not always and unalterably be the man he is? The prospect of consummation contains as much enticement as terror. Faust fears it as much as he yearns for it, for he could only attain it by losing that which gives him the sense of his own worth. Yet so contradictory is the nature of this despairing titan, so paradoxical his inner mood, that he makes just this impossibility the condition of his agreement with Mephisto. It is not a question of definite willing or of clear consciousness. He is dominated by the necessity of yearning for that which, according to the judgment of reason, is neither attainable nor desirable.

Such an ideal of life places enjoyment and profit of existence not in the results but in the process of life's activity itself. The goal is not important, but the striving for that goal, the energy for tireless movement, the courage for ever new beginnings. What does it matter whether a man ever arrives or not? Always to be on the way—that is the thing. It might perhaps be said that this is a dynamic ideal; in any case it is modern and Western, as alien to the ancient world as to the Christian Middle Ages and the civilizations of the Orient. Consummation and tranquillity, contemplation and harmony, are values which are not of supreme importance for this view of life.

From his intellectual collapse Faust does not turn to resignation or to flight from life. Again he seeks a path away from reflection into the sphere of actual existence. What faith and thought were not able to offer is now to be supplied by immediate experience, by sensual enjoyment, be it even "the most painful enjoyment." He is ready to accept the pain along with the joy. For he wishes to possess the whole; he desires to enjoy the abundance of life in his personal existence, to feel and recognize the highest as well as the deepest, and thus to expand his ego so as to make himself the representative of all humanity. In *Wilhelm Meister* it is said that such a demand is presumptuous and can only lead to eternal dissatisfaction. Faust himself speaks of the possibility of failure. Even Mephisto warns that the so-called Whole can be comprehended only by a god, and that man is made for the intermediate spheres. His place is between day and night, between above and below. With such an insatiable seeker after the unattainable the Devil thinks he will have an easy game. Faust will surely founder, he believes, upon the problematical character of his own nature.

These scenes, in which the character of the hero is defined and fully developed, are of decisive importance for the idea of the whole work. Most of them belong to that part of the drama which Goethe did not write until after his Italian journey (from 1797 on). They are not in the *Urfaust*. "In sweet darkness of the senses I was able to begin this dream but not complete it." [2] The scene of the witches' kitchen was written in Rome. It prepares the way for the descent to the "depths of sensuality" reached in the Walpurgisnacht scene (written after 1800), but only after Faust had fallen into a new crisis. Love, too, has deceived him; submergence in the dark lusts of the body and the glow of passion have not succeeded in satisfying his thirst for the abundance of existence. Now his unfettered urge seeks intoxication in an orgy with the demons of unchastity. Here Faust's moral existence sinks to its lowest point. He is a beast among beasts. But even in his abasement the voice of his better self makes itself heard, for in the midst of delirium his conscience calls up the image of the beloved whom he has destroyed. The eyes of a dead girl look upon him in mournful accusation, about her neck a bloody stripe, "no broader than the back of a knife." The titan, who had made innocence

[2] In holder Dunkelheit der Sinnen / Konnt' ich wohl diesen Traum beginnen, / Vollenden nicht. (*Faust*, "Paralipomena.")

and beauty serve to quench his thirst for the sweetness of life, now discovers that even he does not exist outside the realm of morality. He must pay a price for his aspiration to the unattainable, the price of guilt. Does it not seem as if every new step on the road to the highest potentialities of existence degrades him morally? The sinister light of an insoluble contradiction appears upon the horizon of the action. Faust's tragedy begins.

The Devil of the Faust legend and of the old plays appears in Goethe's drama as a fellow of more subtle wickedness. Only incidentally, so to speak, is Mephisto still the black seducer to palpable sin, the tempter and corrupter of the soul. If life is assigned a supremely positive value, as it is here, if man's highest test is found both in his faith in the value of existence and in his tireless activity, the spirit of contradiction, too, must have a different character. This Devil is diabolic by being an enemy to life, a denier of all the forces and aspirations which would create new life and higher existence, a demon of negation. The keen, sarcastic mind, the witty cynicism, which even in the legend gave him a grim humor, he retains here also. But Goethe's Mephisto is at the same time a cultivated man of the world, a skillful advocate of philosophical materialism and nihilism. Everything that comes into being is worthy of being destroyed, and hence it were better if nothing at all ever came into being.

But if Goethe certainly saw in this view the height of impiety and atheism, at the same time he gives this representative of No and Nothing something paradoxically positive. The scene in which Faust asks the strange fellow who he is and in which Mephisto lets himself be interrogated concerning his own nature is among the most ingenious bits that Goethe ever wrote. He is a part, Mephisto says, of the force "which ever wills the evil and ever creates the good." Destruction in every sense, everything that works against the creative forces—that is his proper element. He makes this clearer in a brief cosmogonic explanation. He belongs to that part "which at first was all"—that is to say, to primal night, which ruled when there was as yet only chaos. At that time the positive counterforce, light, did not yet exist. It is from the primal conflict of bright and dark, of gloom and light, that the world of forms and colors, and with it space, came into existence. In the schematic summary of his theory of colors written in 1806 Goethe expresses the same idea: "Darkness and light. Two monstrous opposites. Darkness as the abyss and primal source of being . . . Visible world. To be built up out of light and darkness." Later, in the *Farbenlehre* itself, there is again mention of the "primal, monstrous opposition of light and darkness." As in the world of the eye, so it is everywhere. All events of life issue from this primal polarity, which appears as a constant attraction and repulsion, as a pulsating back-and-forth. Once this polarity has linked all forces and connected them with one another, transforming chaos into cosmos, they must seek each other.

The poem *Wiederfinden* in the *Divan* glorifies the primal phenomenon of productive opposition in the form of a creation myth. One may assume that Goethe as a young man had already formed just this conception of the role which the representative of evil was to play in his *Faust*. For in his Shakespeare discourse (1771) he says, citing "noble philosophers" like Mandeville and Shaftesbury, that what we call evil is only "the obverse of the good," necessary for its existence and hence belonging to the entirety of the world. Without the opposition between good and evil there would be no struggle for the realization of the good, no moral decision, hence no moral activity. Thus, along with everything in the world which we are pleased to call negative, the morally negative is likewise justified. "If there were not this contrariety, there would be no life and there would be no good, also no evil . . . for if there were no violence there would be no motion" (Jakob Böhme). This is also the meaning of Goethe's profound saying—he himself calls it a "monstrous" one—that no one can oppose God but God himself: *Nemo contra deum nisi deus ipse*. "God always confronts himself": He confronts himself also in the soul of man.

To be sure, the Devil can "make" nothing, but he is involuntarily effective in another way: he calls creative forces into life. This is what the Lord means when he says in the Prologue in Heaven that man's nature is such that his activity easily slackens; hence He has given man as associate the demon of nothingness, who should act as a goad. Thus even the Devil must serve the eternal Becoming, unwillingly and eternally cheated out of his destructive intentions. The first positive experience which Faust owes to Mephisto is (as Goethe says in the *Maskenzug* of 1818) the realization that life was "given him for the sake of life" and not so that he should take refuge in "vagaries, fantasies and hair-splitting." But in Faust, to be sure, there lives and grows a conception of true life such as Mephisto is incapable of comprehending. Every enjoyment which Faust's materialistic companion offers him evokes in his incessantly growing soul a desire for higher goals. On each occasion Mephisto lags behind Faust's visions and ideas, both in his understanding and in his proposals. If it were only a matter of the Devil helping Faust to seduce "a little seamstress," then Stendhal would be quite justified in the sarcastic remark that any young man is capable of such heroic deeds without the aid of spirits.

In the structure of the action Mephisto exercises the function assigned to Fate in Greek tragedy. By his constant opposition he keeps the play of forces in action. But what thus confronts the hero as an independent figure is essentially a part of his own self. Only in this way could there be a dramatic representation of the conflict which is staged in Faust's soul and which must be fought out from there. At the same time, Mephisto serves as mouthpiece for the poet's own skepticism. He is the antagonist of everything that Faust feels, thinks, and wills. When he criticizes the titan's lack of moderation, it is Goethe, the worldly-wise realist, who is speaking. Over the fire of passion the cold water of his irony is poured; to good will he opposes his cynicism, to idealistic visions his nihilism. He knows everything that can be said against life. Still he wins the interest of the spectator by his clever wit, which occasionally shifts over into the warmer atmosphere of humor. God himself finds so amusing an opponent not altogether repulsive. To be sure, the "poor devil" has as little notion of God's wisdom and power as he has of that which unites man with the Divine. Against his will he serves an aspiration whose only result can be the conquest of the forces of destruction.

I shall not enter into a detailed history of the genesis of Part I. Nor shall I join in the debate as to how Goethe had conceived of the end when he wrote the *Urfaust*—whether Faust would founder, tragically crushed, or be granted in some way or other a brighter fate. There seem to be sufficient grounds for the assumption that the last scene of the first version, Gretchen imprisoned, which was omitted in the first printing (the *Fragment* of 1790), was to have brought the love story but not the drama to a close. Goethe said later that a meeting of the hero with Helena had been planned from the beginning. In 1827 he called Helena a "fifty-year-old ghost." In the *Urfaust,* of course, the Greek heroine would not have appeared as a figure of Euripidean tragedy, but rather (as in the *Faustbuch* and in the puppet play) as a strumpet-devil, as an evil she-demon from the realm of Christian mythology. From Goethe's notes we know that Faust was to enter upon a journey through the world. As a matter of fact, there is not a word in the *Urfaust* that points specifically beyond the scenes actually composed. But we may well assert that Faust's "ideal striving" can be cast down, but not destroyed, by the unhappy outcome of his love affair. A man so forceful is not so quickly broken. As yet he has not tested himself in the sphere of action, not exhausted the possibilities of inner growth.

Part II was written between 1796 and 1831, most of it after 1825. The Helena act belongs, in its conception, to the year 1800, and at that time some portions of it were written down. The poet of classicism felt impelled to forsake at last the "path of mist and clouds," the sphere of "northern phantoms," and to plunge into the clear atmosphere of Greek forms. The structure of this part is even looser than that of the first; certain sections, like the "Classical Walpurgisnacht" or the first half of the Helena act, go so far away from the continuity of the action as to acquire a kind of dramatic independence. The situation is like that of the *Wanderjahre:* the poet desires to give expression to a multiple world and employs his plot as a thread upon which to string whatever suits him. If this makes the whole formally "incommensurable," as Goethe himself remarked, it also involves a certain advantage. The meaning of the whole is thus presented as a sort of unsolved problem, tempting the reader to provide a solution for what the poet has left open.

The beginning of Part II presents us with a transformed Faust. In the face of the "exciting beauty of the morning," the terrifying visions of the night vanish in his soul. In new strength he is restored to the world of light. His inner transformation is set forth in compact symbolism. When the sun rises, Faust, blinded by the sea of flame, must turn aside as he had once been forced to turn aside before the apparition of the Earth Spirit. But he is now sufficiently matured to accept without bitterness the realization that man is capable of grasping life only "in its colorful reflection." That is to say, man is made to behold that which the light illumines, not light itself; the works of God-Nature, not God himself. "Truth, identical with the divine, can never be known by us directly: we see it only in the reflection, in the example, the symbol, in single and related phenomena" (*Versuch einer Witterungslehre*). And so Faust turns away from the sphere of transcendentalism which his soul has attempted to penetrate. He knows that his longing for abundance of existence can only be satiated by reality itself. He turns to the visible world, the world of phenomena and deeds, in order to bind himself to it by activity and creativity. His transformed will addresses itself to the great deed.

But where was the possibility for this in the world of his day and age? The political condition which confronts Faust bears all the earmarks of a corrupt feudalism. The situation at the court of the Emperor is driving toward catastrophe, but there is no question of Faust's offering anything like a program of reform. He seems to be concerned only with exploiting the possibilities offered to resolute energy by such a situation. In order to ingratiate himself with the pleasure-hungry parasite of power, but at the same time to give a picture of true sovereignty, Faust organizes an allegorical pageant. In it Goethe is visualizing the *Trionfi* which Florence had known at the time of the Medici. Mantegna depicted such a masquerade in his "Triumphal Procession of Caesar." Allegorical representatives of the powers which dominate social and political life pass in procession. Faust appears in the guise of Plutus, as god of a wealth which is not synonymous with criminal exploitation but which uplifts and benefits the life of the masses. Hence the genius of poesy, as a kindred genius, may sit beside him, as driver of his chariot—kindred because he, too, distributes his treasures beneficially and unselfishly. But where, in this rotten world, is there a people which would be capable of receiving such treasures in the spirit in which they are given? It appears that the mob possesses no more moderation and reason than the holders of power, for enjoyment and amusement are what they all want, rich and poor alike. Is it possible for a great will to find scope for its deeds in this world of extravagance and irresponsible luxury? When Faust seeks to provide the bankrupt ruler with new resources by advising him to substitute paper money for the old, sound currency, he is himself on the point of falling victim to the sickness of the collapsing state.

From this danger he is saved by a whim of the Emperor. The ruler wishes to celebrate his new wealth by a rare spectacle. He demands to see Helena and Paris, the loveliest woman and the handsomest man, upon the stage. But here the northern Devil can be of no assistance. Faust himself must seek out the shades of the ideal pair who live in a strange Hades, in the Realm of the Mothers, beyond space and time. In this "void," as Plutarch tells, are preserved the forms and primal images of all things which have ever existed or will ever exist. The entire scene deals symbolically with the mysteries of creative nature. Forms of life are brought forward by nature according to models which Goethe calls "protophenomena" and types, ideal primal images which have the function of regulative form-principles. Paracelsus in his day had spoken of *matrices rerum*. In the process of never-ceasing formation and transformation, the pattern is nevertheless retained in every new creature. From this realm of primal patterns Faust leads forth the pattern of the highest form which nature has produced in the domain of organic being: the form of man. One must remember that since his studies in Italy Goethe was convinced that in shaping their works the Greek artists followed the very laws by which nature creates. So Faust calls to life the figure of Helena. Spiritual contemplation of the primal provides the creative force in him with the model after which it is able to produce the individual figure of the loveliest of women. But what Faust causes to appear is actually only a product of his own seeing and fashioning spirit. How presumptuous the delusion which causes him to grasp at the phantom as if it had reality! How presumptuous that he wishes to seize and possess what belongs to the realm of idea and can only be contemplatively apprehended! An explosion hurls him to the ground. Again his demand for the Absolute is rejected.

Two motifs provide the impulse for the action which follows. Faust wishes to convert the idea of the perfect form into reality, because only thus can he possess it in human fashion: "Who once has seen her cannot rest without her" (verse 6559). When he revives from insensibility his first word is: "Where is she?" He seeks to find this model of the perfect form in the "Classical Walpurgisnacht." The other motif is not directly connected with the action proper. It is like a secondary melody which accompanies the principal theme, with which it is finally merged. Goethe takes the liberty of setting forth in mythological symbols his views as to the origin of life and its beings. Homunculus, whom Wagner's expert alchemy is incapable of creating and whom even Mephisto is able only to call up, is a still unembodied entelechy (as Aristotle would say), a human nucleus, a potential individuality. The most definite tendency of this substance is the urge to activity ("Since I am, I must be active": verse 6888). But appreciation of the beautiful is also present. Hence Homunculus is able to understand the dream of the sleeping Faust, through which move images of the myth of Leda, the mother of Helena, with whom Zeus sought union in the guise of a swan. Homunculus also knows that Faust can find fulfillment only in the realm of classical figures, "in the land of beauty"; he himself—in the Orphic night where the cosmic elements and forces are extolled—hopes to commence existence by gaining embodiment.

The "Classical Walpurgisnacht" assembles the lower spirits and demigods of Greek mythology, from the ugly, primitive earth-deities and elemental beings to the water spirits which are already beautiful in form. Even in its ugly elements this world is clearer and brighter than that northern "witch and devil stuff, which could only be developed in gloomy, anxious eras by bewildered minds, finding its nourishment in the dregs of human nature." The cosmic festival ends with the triumph of Galatea, the most beautiful of the goddesses of the waves (Raphael's magnificent painting in the Villa Farnesina provided Goethe with the motif). The process of gradually ascending nature culminates in the creation of man. "The ultimate product of nature, in her constant self-intensification, is the beautiful human being." In the perfect figure the great mother seems to have attained her goal. That organic life first arose in the sea was Goethe's belief; he found it confirmed by contemporary science, as, for example, in the theory of Lorenz Oken. At that time it had also been discovered that ocean phosphorescence was caused by marine creatures of microscopic size. And so Homunculus pours himself into the "life-moisture" of the ocean, in order to begin his existence at the lowest stage, according to the order of the evolutionary process. Beginning and end of the vast, never-ceasing metamorphosis appear side by side in these symbols. In praise of Eros, the all-begetting force, the act comes to a melodious close.

Faust had left the scene before the gay sea festival began. He had descended to the lower regions with the Sibyl Manto in order to get Helena. This scene, "Faust in Hades," was never written. Helena's appearance is not dramatically motivated, but only introduced in a higher, ideal sense. Her worth and her essence, the tremendous effect which issues from the beautiful form as the highest revelation of creative divinity—this is what is to be demonstrated. We are now prepared for the classical mystery play which takes place in the next act.

Helena is Faust's second beloved. Her relationship to Gretchen is that of contrasting complement. By uniting with the child of nature Faust had sought to become one with animal existence, with warm life. But the urge of the senses and of the heart had remained unstilled. It had driven the restless man from desire to enjoyment, and from enjoyment to desire. Helena's effect on him is quite different. She embodies the power and the force which gives form and order to the material of the world. In her, infinite Becoming seems subdued into constant Being, and yet it is present in graceful vivacity.

> For beauty in herself is blest:
> And grace makes irresistible.[3]

Thus she abides in her sphere, self-sufficient, requiring no practical test by which the true and the good, recognition and action, must legitimize themselves; but at the same time she arouses the desire to share in her perfection.

In language, in the rhythm of the verses, in structure, the Helena scenes are fashioned in the spirit of Greek tragedy. When Faust appears the scene changes: a medieval castle forms the background for the meeting of the northern hero and his "romantic" world with the representative of classical antiquity. The unprecedented occasion demands a different Faust. He appears as a Renaissance prince, speaking with dignity and nobility, as is appropriate in addressing the great lady. The sight of her beauty transforms him; his spirit is driven to rise to the loftiness of the idea which stands embodied before him. A new sphere takes shape, the tone changes, and in place of the ancient rhythms and locutions we have the style of grand opera, which seems to be the modern European counterpart of Greek drama. In the beautifully eloquent dialogue which begins, the dissimilar partners move toward one another; the northern prince becomes a Greek hero, while

[3] Die Schöne bleibt sich selber selig; / Die Anmut macht unwiderstehlich. (*Faust*, v. 7403, translated by B. Q. Morgan.)

Helena reveals the richer inwardness which finds expression in the sentimental poetry and music of the West. The programmatic significance of the union is unmistakable. Time and place become unessential; the feeling of fulfilled existence appears to bring on the moment which deserves to be held fast as eternal Present. In glorious verses the enraptured Faust evokes the ideal landscape of the Mediterranean. The mythical picture of Arcady is the symbolic reflection of his new condition. Insatiable will lays itself at the feet of beauty, the problematical activist of the West finds rest in the perfected form of antiquity, as the boundlessly active spirit does in the organic figure. But only for an instant. There is no tarrying in any condition, as little for the spirit of man as for form-creating nature. "Only in seeming does it stand at moments still." Faust's feeling of finally attained perfection in the world of the beautiful is an illusion. Indeed, it is by the fruit of this very union that his spiritual equipoise is banished.

The son Euphorion combines the father's titanic will with Helena's ideal grandeur. A heroism that is completely absolute is raised in him to such excess that he must destroy himself. Because the earth cannot suffice him, he flings himself boldly into the air as if he were a winged creature. We know that in these scenes Goethe had Lord Byron's person and fate in mind. To the heroic poet who had died in Greece in 1824 the chorus of Hellenic maidens sings a magnificent lament. In no other of his contemporaries did Goethe find so grandiose a manifestation of the productive energy which makes the great poet as well as the great hero; but also, nowhere else did he find so titanic a presumptuousness, through which the individualistic idealism of the age brought about its own end. Helena speaks of how questionable and equivocal is the happiness which beauty gives. The most beautiful of women, the daughter of Zeus, is at the same time also the most fateful female figure in Greek legend, bringing doom like Pandora. In the *Iliad* she is called "a beautiful evil"; in Euripides, beautiful and baneful. For her sake peoples were forced to war with one another and the noblest heroes had to die. Just as the perfected form cannot last, so, too, the magic of beauty is incapable of permanently annulling the flow of life and the power of destiny.

Faust's love for Gretchen had ended tragically. Now he seeks the fulfillment to which his will impels him in a passion of a higher, sublimer sort. "To live in the idea means to treat the impossible as if it were possible." Euphorion's death is an example, an allegory of the way in which the absolute must end. But something of inestimable value is left to Faust from this experience. The garment which Helena leaves behind is its symbol. Henceforward Faust's spirit, whatever his thoughts may be, rises above the ordinary, and his projects have a new grandeur. In the monologue which opens the fourth act (it is a counterpart to the monologue with which the first act begins), Faust himself says that the "great meaning" which the meeting with Helena has communicated to him is as little lost as the recollection of Gretchen's "beauty of soul." The image of his first love ascends clearly to the ether above him and draws away with it the best elements of his soul. The role which Gretchen will yet play for him at the end of the drama is lightly foreshadowed here.

Mephisto recalls the dreamer back to the world. The struggle with the Tempter begins anew. Has Faust picked out anything which he would like? Again the offer of the negative demon lags behind the vision of the creative urge which dwells in the great man. Faust does desire dominion, a possession which is worth while. But he does not wish to inherit what others have created; he wishes to create his possession himself, so that his sway may be free of others' claims. To measure his strength against the destructive powers, the elemental forces of nature, to oppose to unbridled force the will of an independent spirit, to ally himself with that "which Nature bears in herself as law and rule" against the lawlessness of chaos—this now seems to Faust a truly worthy deed. There is the sea; ever and again it attempts to drag the earth into its depths and to extend unfruitfulness. Faust wishes to force it back, to gain new land for new life. Can there be a more positive vision, a project by which life would be more glorified than by this? The divine legacy of man, his creative spirit, responds to the demon of nothingness with the vision of a will which is directed toward procuring richer potentialities for existence, new space for the inhabited earth.

What follows now shows Faust at the height of his public activity. He helps the Emperor, who is on the point of losing his realm to a rival, to win a decisive battle. One cannot say that this adventure possesses in itself greatness and splendor. Faust himself has no desire for war. Again Mephisto must act for him. The "three mighty men" who appear as the quintessence of an army are less distinguished than David's heroes, to whom Goethe refers; they are unscrupulous brawlers. In the end, magic must also be employed to secure the victory. Everything proceeds according to the evil rule that he who has power and makes brutal use of it remains right. As a reward for his dubious assistance, Faust is invested by the Emperor with rule over the seashore, where he intends to establish his realm. These somewhat labored scenes Goethe wrote last, only in 1831. They reveal clearly enough the old poet's skepticism toward political life. It was evidently his opinion that power is in itself evil and makes men evil. Faust's plan is great and noble; but the means required to attain success in this sphere are tarnished. Yet success is the god of the politician. At every step Faust's willing is entangled in new fatefulness.

> The noblest things our spirit hath attained
> Are marred by alien matter's base intrusion.[4]

Even Faust's last, highest deed stands before us in the gloomy light of tragic contradiction.

The fifth act seems at first to show the titanic hero at the height of his success. He has won his kingdom; fertile fields round about are green, and heavily laden ships bring rich treasures from the interior and from foreign shores. But not everything is peaceful and righteous gain. Here too Mephisto and his crew have a part to play. Faust himself has grown old, but not contented, rich, but not wise, powerful, but not good. Even now there is something left to wish for. Always there is a lack of something to quiet his restless will. This time it is the little property of the aged couple, Philemon and Baucis. That he cannot have it spoils his enjoyment of his entire gain. What cannot be obtained legally he is about to appropriate in the manner of the colonizer—by force, even though not without compensation. Mephisto takes care of this inglorious affair, too. What happens is like the Biblical story of Naboth's vineyard. The two old people, who are unwilling to give up their property, are killed, and with them a stranger who is their guest. What good is it for Faust to give assurance that his intention was not robbery but peaceful exchange, and what good is it

[4] Dem Herrlichsten, was auch der Geist empfangen, / Drängt immer fremd und fremder Stoff sich an. (*Faust,* v. 634, translated by W. H. Van der Smissen, London: Dent, 1926.)

for him to lament "quickly ordered, too quickly carried out"? He permitted the violence, spoke the fateful words, "Dispose of them for me." Only a moment before, in the quiet of the night, the lookout in the tower has sung his eulogy of the beauty of the world and the happiness of existence (the magnificent verses, written in the last summer of his life, are Goethe's last expression of thanks to life).

But now Faust stands there in the starless darkness as a lonely man, crushed to earth by the feeling of heavy guilt and of the doom which attaches to all his deeds. This is the blackest hour of his life. And now approaches the last, the severest trial which his creative will, his faith in life, has to meet. Care comes to him, the skulking specter which paralyzes men's souls with anxiety and hopelessness. Before she clutches at him, the tortured soul is visited by a cheerful and welcome vision. In this gloomy moment a last transformation begins to shape itself, a last attempt finally to become a human being according to the natural measure of mortals, to shake off the fateful help of magic which had served his will in its superhuman striving and had been the symbol of wicked presumptuousness.

> Stood I, oh Nature, man alone 'fore thee,
> Then were it worth the trouble man to be! [5]

To rely on his own strength alone in confronting the god who is the force in nature would be true freedom, true human dignity. What he desires comes about, but in a different way. Without Mephisto's help, "a man alone," he has to undergo the difficult hour. Now must appear what his worth is.

One of the most magnificent dialogues in the poetry of all time sets in now in the debate between Faust and the phantom of the night. The phantom asks whether he has ever known care. Faust answers with a description of the restless activity which has been his life. He has stormed through life, desiring, completing, and desiring again. This he approves of even now. A capable man should leave the "beyond," the object of faith and hope, alone; for "such incomprehensible things are too remote to be an object of daily contemplation and thought-destroying speculation" (to Eckermann, February 25, 1824). The capable man should stand firmly upon this earth, upon which there is

[5] Stünd' ich, Natur! vor dir ein Mann allein, / Da wär's der Mühe wert, ein Mensch zu sein. (*Faust*, v. 11406, translated by A. Swanwick, London: Bell, 1879.)

enough to do. His field is time; it extends as far as the realm of the knowable and of deeds, as far as clear sight extends. To advance tirelessly, to will and complete, to pick oneself up after every fall, to hope, venture, go forward, impelled by the longing for ever higher achievement, higher happiness, never finding sufficiency within oneself, always en route on the rising and falling road of life—so Faust himself understands life as he has lived it, and that alone, as he believes, can mean a life fulfilled. This is Goethe's ideal, the guiding image of his own life, the spirit in which he himself acted, the maxim which he wished to transmit to future generations. In *Faust,* Care seeks to destroy the power of this belief that it is possible, by capable activity, to wrest a worthy meaning from life, even though life may be limited to this "globe of earth" and must always remain morally problematic:

> Whoso in my toils is caught
> Finds the world is good for nought.[6]

Vitiosa cura! The vehemence with which Faust resists the insidious power of fear and doubt is a clear indication of the great importance which attaches to this discussion. The point is to ward off the paralyzing breath of transitoriness and futility, of all-devouring death. Temptation itself man cannot avoid; everyone is subject to it. But Faust will allow the demon who paralyzes the will-to-live no power over his soul. What cannot be disposed of by thinking and feeling will be taken care of by resolute impulse of practical reason. The power of the man who keeps faith with life is inexhaustible. Faust's "I will not" removes the deadly danger. It is a faith of "Nevertheless and Notwithstanding," darkly tinted by knowledge of the profound problems of human existence, but ready to accept life as it is—*amor fati.* This modern Odysseus, who has roved through the spheres of life, great and small, in many directions, and in so doing has learned that no condition can suffice a will striving for greatness, must make even limitations and defeats serve to increase his readiness for life.

Since Care is unable to break the will of this indefatigable soul, she thrusts a final trial upon him. She takes from him the light of his eyes. Separated from the world which breathes in the midst of light, he is now wholly dependent upon his inner being. Can we call the

[6] Wen ich einmal mir besitze, / Dem ist alle Welt nichts nütze. (*Faust,* v. 11453, translated by W. H. Van der Smissen.)

way in which he parries this thrust anything but great? The centenarian Faust, smitten with blindness, rises only now to his highest vision. The inner light now emerges in sovereign power, the force of his creative spirit, which is projecting a gigantic plan. The will to titanic self-enjoyment transforms itself into a new, social ethos. The man once obsessed with himself now longs to work with and for others. The anticipation of a work planned and directed by his mind, carried out by thousands of hands, swells into the dream of a new, happy commonwealth. This vision, which the course of the action reveals as a symbol of Faust's purified aspirations, derives in its substance from the spirit of the age upon which Goethe gazes from the summit of his life. It is a vision of the century of active men, of busily trafficking peoples, of the "communal urge."

The mind of man cannot cease to demonstrate in ever loftier designs the inexhaustibility of its creative power. But it is always confined within the bounds of the actual. Even the greatest, the most indefatigable will finally comes to the end which is prescribed for all earthly being. What tragic irony that, at the very hour when Faust has fought his way "into the open" and his will has lifted itself up to the greatness of a truly positive purpose, the sand in the hourglass runs out. While he thinks he hears the workmen carrying out his project, in reality he hears the servants of death preparing his grave. In a last monologue, Faust, already half withdrawn from life, gives utterance to what he has recognized as the highest truth and longs to carry out as the highest deed. New land for millions, not created by slaves and for slaves but wrested from the destructive elements by a free people for a life of voluntary effort and toil—this seems to him in the hour of death to be the ultimate to which a man of action can attain. Life, he now realizes, is a never-ending task. Over and over again it must be earned; and each day life's most precious good, an independent existence, must be conquered anew. To live with the valiant and capable would be a goal to make being and working worth while. In the foretasting of this consummation Faust thinks himself experiencing the supreme moment.

The formula of the pact is uttered, and Mephisto is at hand to collect his payment. To him Faust's vision is only a "last, poor, empty moment." But what belongs to Mephisto literally, according to the terms of the pact, transcends in essence and value the sphere in which his contradictory spirit has power. If man were to be lost because he has won through to the belief that a truly positive meaning can be given to life, then existence would be nothing more than a cruel game which an evil demon plays with helpless puppets. The angels, as they snatch Faust's corpse from the Devil, celebrate a different order of the world. They speak of the love which permeates the universe, of universal harmony and unity, into which the force which had organized and governed the personality now returns. Nothing but this force and its willing seems to be great and valuable. It is not a matter of results. What is achieved in detail is always problematical, and so is a man's entire existence if scrutinized for its achievements. For just as no individual being in nature corresponds wholly to the idea which seeks realization in it, so the will, upon whose uniqueness and constancy the personality is based, is not perfected in any one definite act.

Even as Faust dies he experiences an incomparable moment. He is raised above and beyond himself by a feeling of happiness which emanates from the vision of a work that would be more glorious than anything hitherto fulfilled or conceived. But this, too, is only another happy vision born of the endless striving which has impelled him through life. Not in repentance or reversal, not in a "conversion" does Faust's life culminate, but in a supreme expansion of the incessant creative urge which has been the substance of his entire existence. He believes that he has now reached the pinnacle of the existence vouchsafed him and that he can rest and look back, as if his life were concluded. But we know that he is duped by a new illusion. Great and good, to be sure, is the way in which, with this resolute Yea, he obliterates the curse which he had once flung against life in the despair of his collapse. But even if this dream were actualized, would his soul be really calm and ripe for death? Mephisto is right when he says that no pleasure satiates the eternally unsatisfied, no happiness suffices him. Even what Faust now regards as the "highest attainment" would again be insufficient. The law of endless development which prevails in nature is also effective in men. There is no pause, no end.

I must still be mounting higher,
Wider vision must I win.[7]

[7] Immer höher muss ich steigen, / Immer weiter muss ich schaun. (*Faust,* v. 9821, translated by W. H. Van der Smissen.)

Faust had sensed, had known, when he entered into the pact with Mephisto, that it was so and could not be otherwise as long as he was alive. Life vindicated *him*, not the Devil who had believed that by furnishing enjoyment he could bring Faust's active, creative force to a standstill. But in another respect both partners are confuted by this outcome: in the end life teaches both man and the Devil that it is possible to give human existence a meaning capable of meeting the claims of a highly intense spirit, even of the world-spirit itself.

God alone remains in the right—the God who speaks in the Prologue in Heaven. In order to state the principal theme before the play begins, Goethe prefixed the "Prologue in Heaven." In it human life, which is now to be unfolded before us, is seen from the viewpoint of the eternal. What is meant is not merely the Christian conception of an all-directing providence. Yet in this way everything which subsequently happens, the good as well as the evil, turns into a play which is permitted, even willed, by God. In the being and working of man, eternal wisdom seems to enjoy itself, the creator taking pleasure in his creation. As in the Biblical story of Job, God converses with the Devil, who is present among the heavenly spirits as if he too belonged there. And does not the spirit of contradiction indeed belong in the play in which God and man are the partners? Mention is made of Faust. Yes, indeed, Mephisto knows him. To his sarcastic description the Lord responds with the decision which reassures the spectator as to the outcome. It is true that this servant serves his master in a peculiar fashion. But he serves Him even in this way, and hence he deserves to attain in the end to the clarity which God will not deny him. God accepts unconcernedly the wager which the skeptical Mephisto offers. He knows that truth and error are inextricably interwoven in the thought and action of men. "As long as he strives, man errs" (verse 317). If this is so, if error and striving are so interwoven that the one is always present along with the other, error must be accepted as unalterable. But the worth which man can assign to himself must lie beyond the unavoidable frailty whereby error clings to the heels of the doer at every forward step he takes into life. When the stout-hearted man accepted this condition and acted nevertheless, Goethe always valued such resoluteness more highly than a diffidence of conscience which paralyzes the will to activity. After all, error ceases to be a negative element when it transforms itself into a means of productive development. "Every return from error develops a man mightily in particular and in general, so that one can well understand how a repentant sinner can be dearer to the searcher of hearts than ninety-and-nine righteous men." [8] This comforting paradox is manifested clearly enough in the life of Wilhelm Meister.

But God utters still another truth. A "good man," that is, a man whose soul lives in its natural correctness, He says, will in the end always be led to the right way by an innate compulsion. Goethe calls this urge "dark." What is meant is a force which resides in the sphere below conscious willing—an instinctive urge which operates quietly and constantly like a necessity of nature, analogous to the great law of upward development which Goethe had discovered in the morphological processes. This unconscious urge, we read in a paradoxical formulation, represents the consciousness of the right way which lies in man. But what is meant is evidently the instinctive certainty with which he finds his way back again and again from all aberration to that feeling and willing which is in harmony with "the coming into being, which is always vital and effective" (verse 346). So God may safely leave man to the Tempter. Mephisto too in the end must serve eternal becoming. As antagonist of the creative he evokes the most positive of all things, the will to activity. "It is contradiction which makes us productive" (to Eckermann). What the Lord said in the "Prologue" is repeated by the angels in the last scene, as they bear aloft the imperishable part of Faust, his "entelechy":

> Whoso with fervent will strives on,
> We angels can deliver.[9]

To strive with fervent will—we may perhaps phrase it thus: to obey the forward-impelling urge, the will to productive existence, to never-ceasing growth, and at the same time to follow that other impulse, the will to augmentation (of self), which seeks to lift itself up step by step to ever higher deeds and visions of deeds, to the ideal goal of self-perfection. He who has lived so has truly lived, and it is this

[8] Jede Rückkehr vom Irrtum bildet mächtig den Menschen im Einzelnen und Ganzen aus, so dass man wohl begreifen kann, wie dem Herzensforscher ein reuiger Sünder lieber sein kann, als neunundneunzig Gerechte. (Letter to H. C. A. Eichstädt, September 15, 1804.)

[9] Wer immer strebend sich bemüht, / Den können wir erlösen. (*Faust*, v. 11936, translated by W. H. Van der Smissen.)

that God desires of his creatures and for which he will forgive them the earthly frailty which attaches to all human being and doing. Upon the ladder of deeds with which he fills the space of life man ascends to the divine. Error, guilt, and even sin will be forgiven him who strives unweariedly. Only he who keeps marching will reach the house of the Father. The most active citizen of earth will be the best-loved son of heaven.

Faust, the drama of the insatiable life-urge, ends in religious mysteries. Goethe remarked that we all become mystics in old age. The idea of perfection, which is the lodestar of ceaseless striving, transcends the sphere of the actual. What was unfulfilled quest and aspiration on earth becomes "event" only over there. But only the power of divine grace can loose the imperishable core of the personality from its material embodiment. More than forty years before he wrote this final scene, Goethe had seen the basic religious situation which he now attempts to set forth. In Rome he had stood before Raphael's painting of the Transfiguration, which depicts Christ soaring aloft in glory. Of this picture Goethe said: "How can one separate the higher and the lower? Both are one: below is the suffering and the needful, above the effective and the helpful, both connected with one another, affecting one another." [10] Transcendence and reality, man striving upward toward perfection and divine perfection responding from above, needfulness and love: these are essences which relate to one another and affect one another. One is always present along with the other. So human existence presents itself as an interplay of ultimate opposites. In death they part from one another; the confining form is cast off, and the imperishable appears in its purity.

In this scene Goethe employs conceptions and figures from the Catholic world, because it is only here that Christianity has fashioned mythological forms. But this Heaven has little in common with Christian pictures of the beyond and just as little with those of ancient religions. It is not sacred tranquillity, not the peace of the blessed, that prevails here. The movement of life appears to continue beyond the great divide. Death itself is only a stage in the eternal metamorphosis, and the soul does not cease to develop further. Henceforth Faust him-

[10] Wie will man nun das Obere und Untere trennen? Beides ist eins: unten das Leidende, Bedürftige, oben das Wirksame, Hilfreiche, beides auf einander sich beziehend, in einander wirkend (*Italienische Reise, Rom.* December 1787).

self speaks no more. Angels and spirits tell how his entelechy presses aloft in ever purer transformations toward the divine center which he senses and seeks. Even to the last, transcendent stage he is lifted by the ceaseless longing for expansion which had given his existence meaning and direction. But this can only come about because that which is effective and helpful draws him upward to itself. It appears embodied in the supreme female figure of Christianity, the Queen of Heaven. What Goethe calls the "eternal feminine" is the quintessence of all helpful and unifying forces. It is love, which Dante says moves sun and stars. As it is the most positive of all forces in the existence of man, so it also effects the harmony of the cosmos. It binds and it loosens, without violence and without judgment. And so, at the end of a life which was unable to consummate itself, a power which brings all things into balance makes its appearance. It separates the positive elements of Faust's existence from the dross of his inadequacies and restores the imperishable element of his ego to the place whence it derives.

The last word belongs, appropriately, to the Highest Judge. But if his sentence is definitive as fact, his justice is problematic enough. Many readers of *Faust* have found it so and frequently just the most thoughtful ones. How can our moral feeling be expected, so the party of critics has argued, to accept such a solution? It is not enough that it is vouchsafed Faust to be borne into the gloomy realm of death upon the wings of a glorious vision. Even beyond the threshold no Day of Judgment awaits him; his soul, which in the view of stricter ages should justly belong to hell, is redeemed by an act of divine grace as sudden as it is undeserved. This is more than the pious sentiment or the sense of justice of many readers has been able to tolerate. Goethe himself said of the ending that its character resembled the history of mankind: the last-solved problem transforms itself into a new one which requires a new solution.

Goethe was fond of gentle endings. *Götz* and *Tasso,* even *Elective Affinities,* end in a fashion which permits our emotions to recover. An irreconcilably tragic case did not interest him, and in general (he says) the irreconcilable seemed to him "quite absurd." He thought Aristotle was right in demanding that the tragic hero must be neither wholly guilty nor wholly free from guilt, for every drama required a "conciliatory finish." This view derives from his unwillingness to accept insoluble contradictions as the quintessence of human existence; but it corresponds also to Goethe's specific view concerning the spiritual and moral function of poetry. But this does not answer the question whether so conciliatory a conclusion is tolerable in this particular drama. What merits entitle Faust to such gracious treatment? May we believe that God himself does not judge, indeed, that a man who was surely no great lover of men should be pardoned by all-forgiving love? The mother of God seems too much inclined to admit the returning prodigal to the place of transfiguration without any further procedure. How may a man of so many sins be redeemed by a kind of "helpful machinery" without having first purified himself by repentance and atonement? To the Christian reader the erring course of this life, which seeks to free itself of its evil demon only at its close when it is too late, presents itself as something strange and incomprehensible. Until his last breath, as a moral personality Faust remains problematical. There is no basic conversion here, no renewal. All the more questionable, therefore, that Faust is pardoned.

There can be no doubt, however, that this conclusion is not a tacked-on makeshift but is integral to the life here presented. Even if it were true that Faust's end contrasts with his life, by that very contrast his life would be rounded out according to the law of polarity which is for Goethe a basic phenomenon of life. But for this to be realized, Faust must have come close enough to grace to draw its powers to himself. Redemption can only issue from the partnership of God and man. It is of this that the angels speak as they bear aloft the imperishable part of Faust; and it is this that Goethe means when he finds the thought which carries the drama in the thesis "that a man who through grave errors constantly strives for the better can be redeemed." Then is Faust's ascent after all based on the fact that he purifies himself morally? The expression just cited is transmitted by Eckermann; one may therefore doubt, if one will, whether the words "for the better" are authentic. But surely Goethe intended to set forth an existence which leads upward. Yet it is anything but obvious that this ascent is of moral character.

If we examine the stages which mark Faust's development we find that after the collapse of his efforts to perceive the essence of the universe he turns to the natural, to the life of the Great Mother, in which all creatures have their assigned portion. But it appears that for the happiness of natural existence man must pay with the anguish of a wounded conscience. Faust acquires new and higher experience in the sphere which Goethe calls the "higher sensuality," the sphere of forms and figures. By means of this "aesthetic education" Faust is lifted up to a freedom in whose domain desire itself acquires a brighter, more purified character. He attains the highest stage when he is capable of great action. As a whole this is a process of natural growth, whose stages follow upon one another like the successive ages in the life of the individual. At the first stage, life is experienced and enjoyed as an unlimited becoming. From this inception the mature man lifts himself to the contemplation of the creating deity which is (as he now understands) at once endless motion and limiting law. Helena is the symbolic embodiment of everything which is norm, law, and permanence in the organization of the world. A mind elevated to wisdom becomes aware in her of the great order and harmony of which his own boundless aspiration is a part. Only now has Faust reached the point where his action draws upon the entirety of his personality, where he can achieve something which has objective validity and permanence. The growth of the hero is to be understood in some such way.

But what has this process to do with moral purification? What increases in Faust is the force and definiteness of will, and the capacity for seizing upon the potentialities of existence. Faust becomes more powerful, also wiser, but above all more capable of grappling successfully with life and wresting its gifts from it. Who knows whether his new capacity and knowledge will benefit him, whether he will finally liberate himself from the coercion of evil? Though the vision to which his spirit lifts itself in the hour of death is grander and nobler than anything he had previously been able to plan and to do, we foresee that even this "supreme thing" will again not suffice him, and that in his disappointment, if he were permitted to live, he would again be ready to pay the price of guilt when a new illusion should dupe him. No, clearly this play has not the character of the Christian "morality plays." It does not run its course between the poles of guilt and expiation, crime and punishment. Faust has no talent for the Holy, and the world here set forth is not to be comprehended according to the scheme of the moral order which is set forth in the religious plays of the Middle Ages and the Baroque. Nor is Faust of the breed of Shakespeare's heroes, in whose character Would and Should, the moral force within and necessity without, encounter and counterbalance one another. Goethe's hero is one of the modern titans of the will who recognize only one necessity, one law: their own imperious ego.

> For fate and faith take no decisive part:
> Salvation lies within the sinless heart.[11]

For a man of this kind it is surely correct to say that his will is his kingdom of heaven. He would fain be everything by virtue of himself and by means of himself, and achieve everything for the sake of himself. When Mephisto bids him consider that man is made for "day and night" and not for the sake of enjoying in himself the absolute, the undiminished entirety of existence, Faust replies, "But I will."

For his interpretation of man Goethe seeks a standpoint above the plane of moral values. In this view the moral is neither the absolute nor the most important gauge; the worth of an individual is not equated with his virtue. The fact that man is a moral being does distinguish him from other beings (as is stated with a certain bias in the poem *Das Göttliche*). But even if man is set apart by this fact and lifted out of the order of vegetative life, for him, too, nature still remains the maternal soil. From this twofold citizenship there arise mutually contradictory obligations, and from these again special problems, of which the ethical ones are only a part, coördinated (as G. Simmel says) with the others. It was among Goethe's earliest convictions that a person takes a false view of man if he assigns man's essence and worth exclusively to his fitness to be a moral being. Goethe's original nature worship made him do full justice to the other, the animal side of life, and to see man as a sensual-hypersensual whole. Goethe went further yet and saw even moral action itself in its intimate connection with the natural. Here, too, the actual acts issue from the polarity which is everywhere the source of life processes. Thomas Mann says: "The realm of the moral is broad, it embraces the immoral too . . . Only the narrow-minded believe that sin and morality are opposing concepts; they are one." This thought and its utterance are in the spirit of Goethe. To one who holds this view all ethical dogmatism is untenable. In a review written in 1772, Goethe remarks

[11] Schicksal und Glaube finden keinen Teil, / In reiner Brust allein ruht alles Heil. (*Prolog*, 1821, translated by B. Q. Morgan.)

that no one knows whether that which we look upon as good and evil is also good and evil in the sight of God, "or whether that which is refracted into two colors before our eyes may not be able to fuse into a single ray before him." In the Shakespeare discourse of 1771 there is the famous assertion that evil is only the obverse of good, necessary to the entirety of moral life. To the theologian Lavater, Goethe wrote in 1781 that man was surely "God and Satan, heaven and earth, all in one": but that these were only concepts with which we try to make our own nature comprehensible to ourselves. The soul of man was a purgatory in which the forces of hell and of heaven collaborate. Nature itself was good *and* evil, moved by creative and by destructive forces, "an organ upon which our Lord God plays while the Devil treads the bellows" (to Boisserée, 1815). Later, he once said that F. H. Jacobi, the friend of his youth, lacked the natural sciences and that merely "with our insignificant morality alone" the world could not properly be understood. The same judgment might be applied to *Faust:* that complex work is not to be measured by the moral gauge alone.

But if the moral purification of the hero is not the "theme" of the drama, what is? Again and again readers have sought for a sustaining idea which might be understood as the *basso ostinato* of the involved action. The poet himself has given warning that such a search is a futile undertaking. A totality of life so rich and colorful does not suffer itself "to be strung upon the meager thread of a single continuous idea" (to Eckermann, May 6, 1827). And so it is: a rich, abundant existence is set forth, which defies all formulas. We are presented with a picture, the picture of a human existence conceived as a phenomenon of nature, that is, as a multiple unity. Faust is not the ideal representative of a single sphere of values; he is no great researcher and no saint. His personality, like everything living, is a conglomerate whole and as such cannot be conceptually comprehended but only grasped by the eye of the mind. His life is held together and impelled upward from stage to stage by a will which is not concerned with attaining a practical goal, such as ideal humanity. Faust's urge seeks again and again to approach the core of existence, that which gives it its basic value. To possess life, to seize upon life in emotion and thought, even to create life: that is what he wills with all the force that is in him. Mephisto endeavors to teach him that life is not given man for a purpose which lies beyond life's sphere but for him to live. It belongs only to the living.

> Life is the guarantor of life; it rests
> Upon itself, must answer for itself.[12]

Is it not the desire of God, the God of this drama, that man play the game of life with devotion, without allowing himself to be estranged from this most important task by ideals, which alienate him from this existence, however pure and lofty they may appear to the spirit? What Goethe thought of ideals which demand the renunciation of life for the sake of inner purity he put into words in the *Bekenntnisse einer schönen Seele.* That despite all defeats Faust does not turn away from life, but ever and again gives himself up to it, whatever it be, is what really makes him great. What else, says Goethe, is the heart of our individuality "save energy, force, will"? In this view there is only one thing that may be validly regarded as man's proper destiny: to be productive. All forces must serve this supreme goal. "For in a continuing process of doing and acting it is of course not a question of what is individually worthy of praise or blame, significant or insignificant; but of what sort of direction was taken as a whole and whether at last there is any result for the individual himself, or his immediate contemporaries, and hence of what may be hoped for the future." [13]

The critics have said that Faust undergoes no basic change. That is correct. But just in that fact it is evident, according to the poet's intention, that Faust has character. For what else can character mean, says Goethe, than decisiveness and force of will? Upon this the personality is based, in this determined willing alone consists the element of greatness, and moreover "without regard for right and wrong, for good and evil, for truth and error." There can be no question of moral qualities here because the act of willing, as Goethe expressly states, belongs not to the realm of freedom but to that of nature. It "relates to the outer world, to the deed."

[12] Das Leben ist des Lebens Pfand; es ruht / Nur auf sich selbst und muss sich selbst verbürgen. (*Die natürliche Tochter*, Act I, scene 6, translated by B. Q. Morgan.)

[13] Denn es ist ja, bei einem fortschreitenden Tun und Handeln nicht die Frage, was einzeln lobens- oder tadelnswert, bedeutend oder unbedeutend sei; sondern was im Ganzen für eine Richtung genommen worden und was daraus zuletzt für das Individuum selbst, für seine nächsten Zeitgenossen, irgend für ein Resultat sich ergeben, und was daher für die Zukunft zu hoffen sei. (To H. G. Hotho, April 19, 1830.)

But this is only half the truth. For the natural necessity of a determined will, which comprises the heart of personality, meets another force which exists in indissoluble tension: the will to moral autonomy, "that good will which by its nature can only be directed to the right." It too is innate; it too belongs to the nature of man. Can one deny Faust this good will? What else is the eternal feeling of insufficiency, which can be satisfied by no success, but the incessant endeavor to bring Would and Should into harmony? Faust's love for Gretchen is neither weak nor frivolous. To be sure, it does not last. But what does have permanence in the frail existence of man? In the glowing readiness of the beginning, emotion desires "no end"; and that is what Faust wills too. He knows that the end would be despair. But as Rilke says, "Permanence is nowhere." Who may speak of guilt here? There are also Faust's attempts to act. Here again his will, while growing ever more powerful, encounters constantly recurring defeats. Even that last, highest moment, which Mephisto sarcastically calls a "bad, empty moment," cannot be held fast. There is no question of triumph, nor of the simple, sublime grandeur to which Schiller's moral heroes elevate themselves.

At no moment does Faust outgrow the realm of the problematical, which is the distinguishing mark of human existence.

> On runs the man, pursuing
> Forever a changeable goal.[14]

It is in vain that he tugs at the curtain which hides from him the mystery of life. And so Faust stands before us in unadorned truth, great by virtue of the power of his willing, through his capacities and his visions, but at the same time held fast in the frailty of creatures who strive

> To reach the heights of god-head,
> Yet are damned to likeness of themselves alone![15]

Even if Faust is an individual in whom the typically human in character and destiny appears so strong and clear that he becomes a kind of representative of the creature which Goethe calls "the most

[14] Es rennt der Mensch, es fliehet / Vor ihm das bewegliche Ziel. (*Der Zauberflöte zweiter Teil,* translated by B. Q. Morgan.)

[15] Götter zu erreichen, / Und doch verdammt, sich immer selbst zu gleichen. (*Faust,* v. 8096, translated by W. H. Van der Smissen.)

perfect and the most imperfect, the happiest and the unhappiest," yet he does not have the abstract quality of a timeless type. He embodies not a concept but a historic species, the modern variant as developed in Europe after the Renaissance and raised to completest specialization in the age of middle-class civilization, the autonomous personality. *Ecce homo occidentalis!* In him the activism characteristic of the West, the will to the mastery of nature and the conquest of the world, reaches its pinnacle. The civilizations of the East do not know the *Übermensch,* nor did antiquity know him. Of the heroes of Greek poetry Goethe says that they desire only what is possible to men. But modern man attempts to expand his individuality to the titanic; everywhere he wishes to extend the natural boundaries, to transform the moderate into the immoderate. What the Greeks regarded as cardinal sin and called *hybris,* extreme presumption, the striving to equal the gods, is to the modern European the only real possibility of fulfilling oneself and at the same time advancing humanity. Both the greatness of such a willing and the fearful sacrifices its realization demands are represented with unvarnished truth in the figure of Faust and in his life.

Goethe had no intention of writing a didactic piece. The nineteenth-century public has been pleased to see in *Faust* something like a mythical idol of the modern European—as if the last great poet of the humanist tradition had intended to glorify the arrogant individualism and activism of the nineteenth century. The Germans more than others have understood this work as a poetical apotheosis of the spirit which at last made the nation powerful and rich. Whatever seemed in *Faust* to endorse the national character and confirm the belief in a millennium of progress was taken out of its context and misinterpreted. When the understanding of the complex totality of the work was lost, its meaning was lost too. Men forgot that Goethe himself had called *Faust* a tragedy. When he set about working out the second part he remarked that there were still a number of "magnificent, real, and imaginary errors" in which the poor human being might lose himself more nobly, worthily, and sublimely than in the instances of the first, common part. "Magnificent errors"—the paradoxical contrast of this formulation points to the problematic humanity which is embodied in Faust's figure and is made evident in the symbol of his life's course. How can there be any thought of glorification here? It is not a model which is presented but a portrait, the portrait of modern man and his existence, and this portrait is just as problematical as is the latest variety of *homo occidentalis.* Upon this type of man Goethe looks, desirous of comprehending him in his unfalsified reality, and not without sympathy even for his questionable traits. For the pathological elements, the morbid outgrowths of imperiousness, are no less a part of nature. The will which created this great, problematical portrait is the will to achieve and to endure that which is most difficult for man: pure truth, which is at the same time the highest justice.

One who rejects *Faust* because it does not fit into the scheme of guilt and atonement, or does not satisfy our demand for moral idols, fails to do justice to the profound realism of the drama. If the hero is great and extraordinary, and hence worthy of our interest, he is not so because of his morality. Holiness is to be won only at the price of overcoming the world. But this man is wholly a child of the world, a son of the earth, inextricably bound to existence, obedient to no one and no thing but the urge which drives him through life and at the same time ever closer to that which is above life. He is ruled by the spirit which has created the modern world. In his great as in his evil qualities, in achieving and in failing, he is a genius representative of the present. And as for his guilt, is it not true that even the attainments of which Western man is most proud are bound up with endless guilt? One thinks of the colonizing achievements of the European nations, even the greatest of them, the settlement of the New World. What the colonizer Faust does to the patriarchal couple, Philemon and Baucis, has happened always and everywhere, each time the "pioneer spirit" of the Europeans has come into conflict with the so-called primitive peoples. When Goethe wrote these scenes he was full of the great impression made on him by the latest phase of the conquest of the North American continent by the white races. He admired it as a gigantic achievement, but he also knew the bloodguilt it involved. Mephisto says to the hesitant Faust:

> Why entertain such scruples here?
> Is colonizing not thy sphere? [16]

The will to conquest follows its own brutal law, and yet its unscrupulous, unreflecting power can produce most positive achievements.

[16] Was willst du dich denn hier genieren? / Musst du nicht längst kolonisieren? (*Faust,* v. 11273, translated by W. H. Van der Smissen.)

Goethe knows that, while acting, man is basically without conscience. How many of the deeds which history regards as truly great can stand up under moral judgment? One who does not wish to incur guilt may not act. Only the contemplative man can keep his soul pure. This is the inescapable contradiction imposed upon human existence, and most of all upon the activistic man of the present. For by throwing all of his strength into plans and actions he simultaneously withdraws farther and farther from the other sphere to which he belongs. What passes here for achievement and success is rated over there, before the tribunal of morality, as betrayal and guilt. This is Faust's tragedy too.

There can be no question of prototype or of emulation where, as in this case, the irreconcilable contradiction in human existence is disclosed. One might rather say that Goethe intended a warning and endeavored to counteract the dangers of a tendency which was already making itself felt. "Never, perhaps, have individuals isolated themselves and separated from one another more than at present. Each would like to personate the universe and to represent it from within himself." [17] Goethe knew that it is in human nature "to advance ever farther, even beyond its goal." But modern daring, the Euphorion spirit, seemed to him a fateful aberration. "There is nothing sadder to behold than the sudden striving for the unconditional in this thoroughly conditioned world; in the year 1830 it seems perhaps more improper than ever." With no little concern Goethe saw the emergence of another type of humanity, the exclusively practical activist, whose eruptive energies are no longer restrained by any cultural conscience, and who takes no further interest in values.

Faust is not Goethe's last word, not his final message to contemporaries and posterity. The whole of his wisdom is contained only in the whole of his mature works and must be apprehended in them. By the side of the heroic presumptuousness of Faust stands the organic cultural ideal expressed in the *Lehrjahre,* the attitude of reverence and the social activism of the *Wanderjahre,* and the cheerful composure and love of life of the *Divan.* Whoso wishes may regard the tragedy of the magnificently erring titan as Goethe's highest poetic achievement; he may prefer this work to all others for its spiritual riches and

[17] Niemals haben sich die Individuen vielleicht mehr vereinzelt und von einander abgesondert als gegenwärtig. Jeder möchte das Universum vorstellen und aus sich darstellen. (*Geschichte der Farbenlehre.*)

its beauty. But the sum of Goethe's wisdom is not contained in it, the totality of his artistic capacity is not realized in it. The other works of Goethe's middle and late period are related to *Faust* as complementary opposites. Only when we see the tragedy in this context, and grasp it on that basis, shall we be able to understand what it shows as a picture, what it expresses as a symbol.

But it would be erroneous to designate as pessimistic the view of man which is set forth here. Goethe rejects neither man nor life. He is convinced that an inclination to evil—what Christianity means by "original sin"—is as much inborn in man as "original virtue," the inclination to goodness, to righteousness and reverence. This faith Goethe retained to the end as firmly as his faith in the basically good nature of life. The "Prologue in Heaven" gives clear expression to this faith, which is a synthesis of Yea and Nay. Faust's nature, his hunger for the higher and highest, makes him at once great and small. Only if we grasp this in its contradictory unity can we understand the "lesson" correctly. And it is in just this respect that *Faust* is a tragedy; not, however, after the manner of the Greeks, but after that of the West, which has developed its own more liberal idea of man. Goethe did not attempt to solve the moral problem, because he did not believe that it is soluble.

> So wondrously this human race is formed,
> So diversely connected, intertwined,
> That no man in himself, nor with the others,
> Can keep his soul untangled, undefiled.[18]

As moral beings, so this drama declares, we shall never be able to fulfill ourselves, unless it be at the cost of renouncing the world and all action. But this cannot be the will of God, in Goethe's view, for God has placed us between the above and the below. The grace of the superior powers, so we must, so we dare hope, will balance what we ourselves are not capable of achieving. It is not by individual achievements, individual results, that we can merit the pardoning love of the Eternal. Even the best of men will time and again err and stray. "That general direction which has been taken"—"that inwardness which in

[18] So wunderbar ist dies Geschlecht gebildet, / So vielfach ist's verschlungen und verknüpft, / Dass keiner in sich selbst, noch mit den andern / Sich rein und unverworren halten kann. (*Iphigenie*, Act IV, scene 4, translated by B. Q. Morgan.)

us lived, strove, sought, frequently without consciousness"—this is the only thing that can matter. But this "direction" can only be taken by a man who goes forward indefatigably and who cultivates with his deeds the acre of time which is our possession. Could any other goal be great enough to induce us to neglect this mission? Only in and through life does the way lead to God. But no one yet has walked this way to the end without guilt.

CHRONOLOGY

Johann Wolfgang von Goethe

I. YOUTH

1749 Aug. 28	Birth at Frankfort on the Main	
1765–68	University of Leipzig	"Leipzig Songbook" (1770), * *The Lover's Mood* (1806)
1768–70	Frankfort. Pietist conventicle, Susanna von Klettenberg	
1770–71	University of Strasbourg. Herder; Friederike Brion, daughter of the Vicar of Sesenheim	Sesenheim poems (to Friederike Brion); Collection of folk songs
1771–72	Frankfort. Becomes lawyer	"On Shakespeare's Day"; "Wanderer's Storm Song" (1810); *The Story of Gottfried von Berlichingen, Dramatized* (1832); "On German Architecture"; *Faust* begun—"Urfaust" (1887)
1772 May–Sept.	Wetzlar. Charlotte Buff, J. C. Kestner	Hymns
1772–75	Frankfort. J. K. Lavater; F. G. Jacobi; F. G. Klopstock	*Götz von Berlichingen* (1773); "Mahomet"; "Prometheus"; "Satyrus" *Clavigo; The Sorrows of Young Werther* (1774);
1775	Engagement to Lili Schönemann	Songs to Lili; *Stella* (1776)
1775 May–July	First Swiss journey: Zurich (with Lavater), Lake Lucerne, St. Gotthard	

* Dates in parentheses indicate earliest printing.

II. MATURITY

1775 Nov. 7	Arrival in Weimar, capital of the Duchy of Saxe-Weimar-Eisenach. Duke Karl August of Saxe-Weimar; K. L. Knebel; C. M. Wieland; J. G. Herder	
1776	Friendship with Charlotte von Stein (to 1788)	Poems to Lida (Charlotte von Stein); Hymns
1776	Privy Councilor	"Wilhelm Meister's Theatrical Mission" (first version of *Wilhelm Meister*), 1777–85 (1911)
1778	Visit to Potsdam and Berlin	Lyric: "To the Moon"
1779		"Iphigenie" (first version)
1779 Sept.– 1780 Jan.	Second Swiss journey. Visit in Sesenheim and Strasbourg. Thun, Lauterbrunnen, Bern, Lausanne, Geneva, Chamonix, St. Gotthard, Lucerne, Zurich, Schaffhausen, Stuttgart, Karlsruhe, Darmstadt, Frankfort	
1782	Ennobled by Emperor: von Goethe	
1784–85		*The Secrets* (1789)
1786 Sept.– 1788 June	Italian Journey: Karlsbad, Munich, Brenner Pass, Trient, Verona, Vicenza, Padua, Venice, Ferrara, Bologna, Florence, Perugia	
1786 Oct. 29	Arrival in Rome. J. H. W. Tischbein; Angelika Kauffmann; J. H. Meyer; K. P. Moritz	
1787 Feb.	Naples	*Iphigenie*
Mar.	Vesuvius, Pompeii, Sicily	
April	Palermo, Agrigentum	
May	Catania, Taormina, Messina, Naples	
June	Rome	

1788	Apr. 25	Departure from Rome: Florence, Milan, Lake Como	*Egmont*
1788 1792	June– July	Weimar. Christiane Vulpius	
1790	Mar.–June July–Sept.	Journey to Venice. Journey to Silesia, Dresden, Breslau, Tarnów, Cracow	*Roman Elegies* (1795); *Venetian Epigrams* (1796); *Attempt to Interpret the Metamorphosis of Plants; Tasso* (1790); *Faust, A Fragment* (1790)
1791		Direction of Weimar theater (to 1817)	*Contributions to Optics* (1791–92)
1792		Campaign in France: Frankfort, Mainz, Verdun; cannon attack at Valmy; Luxembourg, Düsseldorf, Münster	*The Grand Cophta*
1793		Siege of Mainz	*The Citizen-General*
1794		Friendship with Schiller (to 1805)	*Reineke Fuchs*
1795	 August	Weimar and Jena. Alexander von Humboldt; F. A. Wolf Trip to Karlsbad	*Recreations of German Emigrants; Wilhelm Meister's Apprenticeship* (1795–96)
1796		F. and W. von Schlegel	*Xenien* (with Schiller) (1797); *Hermann and Dorothea* (1798)
1797	Aug.–Nov.	Third Swiss journey: Frankfort, Stuttgart, Schaffhausen, Stäfa, Zurich, Tübingen, Nürnberg	"Amyntas"
1798		Schelling	Ballads; *The Propyläen* (1798–1800)
1799		C. F. Zelter	*The Natural Daughter* (1804)
1804			*Winckelmann and His Century*
1805		Death of Schiller	

1806	Battle of Jena; Napoleon in Weimar; marriage to Christiane	
1807	Bettina Brentano; Minna Herzlieb	Sonnets (1815)

III. OLD AGE

1808	Interview with Napoleon at Erfurt	*Faust I; Pandora* (1810)
1809		*Elective Affinities*
1810	Sulpiz Boisserée	*On the Theory of Colors*
1811		*Poetry and Truth* (4 parts: 1811–33)
1812	Meeting with Beethoven	
1814 July–Oct.	First journey on the Rhine and Main: Frankfort, Wiesbaden, Bingen, Heidelberg. Meeting with Marianne Willemer	*Epimenides' Awakening* (1815)
1815 May–Oct.	Second journey on the Rhine and Main: Frankfort, Wiesbaden, Mainz, Nassau, Cologne, Heidelberg, Karlsruhe	*On Art and Antiquity* (1816–32); *Tame Xenia*
1816	Christiane dies	*Italian Journey* (1816–17); *On Morphology* (1817–23); *West-Eastern Divan* (1819), *Wilhelm Meister's Travels* (1821; second version, 1829)
1821	Ulrike von Levetzow;	*Campaign in France* (1822); *Siege of Mainz*
1823–32	J. P. Eckermann, Goethe's collaborator	"Marienbad Elegy" (1827)
1828	Death of Grand Duke Karl August of Saxe-Weimar-Eisenach	*Novelle* (1828); "Correspondence between Schiller and Goethe" (1828–29); Annals—*Tag- und Jahreshefte* (1830); *Faust II* (finished, summer 1831)
1832 Mar. 22	Goethe's Death	

INDEX

INDEX

NAMES AND PLACES

GOETHE'S WORKS

AUTOBIOGRAPHICAL

DRAMATIC

SCIENTIFIC

MISCELLANEOUS